HISTORY
OF
GREENVILLE COUNTY
SOUTH CAROLINA

NARRATIVE AND BIOGRAPHICAL

By
JAMES M. RICHARDSON

With a New Index

This volume was reproduced from
An 1930 edition located in the
The Greenville County Library,
Greenville, South Carolina

All rights reserved. No part of this publication may be reproduced,
stored in a retrieval system, transmitted in any form,
posted on to the web in any form or by any means
without the prior written permission of the publisher.

Please direct all correspondence and orders to:

www.southernhistoricalpress.com
or
SOUTHERN HISTORICAL PRESS, Inc.
PO BOX 1267
375 West Broad Street
Greenville, SC   29601
southernhistoricalpress@gmail.com

Originally published: Greenville, SC   1930
Reprinted with New Material by:
Southern Historical Press, Inc.
New Material Copyright 1993 by
Southern Historical Press, Inc.
Greenville, SC
ISBN #0-89308-504-9
All rights Reserved.
Printed in the United States of America

History
of
GREENVILLE COUNTY
SOUTH CAROLINA

NARRATIVE AND BIOGRAPHICAL

By
JAMES M. RICHARDSON

A. H. CAWSTON—PUBLISHER
ATLANTA, GEORGIA
1930

This Reprinted Edition is
Dedicated to the Memory

of

the Great, great, great grandparents
of
Mrs. Nina Hasell Hanahan Lucas

Joseph Percival LaBruce
1792-1827
of Oak Hill, Waccamaw

a Founder, Vestryman and Member of the
original Building Committee
of Christ Church, Greenville
1825-1826

and his wife

Mrs. Catherine Jones Ward LaBruce
1799-1866
daughter of Major Josuha Ward
of Brookgreen, Waccamaw

Whose summer home was on
what is now Augusta Road

History of
Greenville County, South Carolina

ADVISORY BOARD
B. H. Peace

Charlotte Templeton	Robert Quillen
R. M. Hughes	W. P. Conyers
Prof. H. T. Cox	D. L. Bramlett
Dr. J. L. Mann	L. M. Glenn

Contents

		PAGE
FOREWORD		11
INTRODUCTION		13

PART I.

CHAPTER	I.	Before The White Man	17
CHAPTER	II.	Traders, Hunters and Cattle Men	21
CHAPTER	III.	Fort Prince George Built	25
CHAPTER	IV.	The First Cherokee War	28
CHAPTER	V.	Pre-Revolutionary Settlers on Greenville County Lands	32
CHAPTER	VI.	The Revolution Begins—Battle of Great Cane Brake	37
CHAPTER	VII.	Indian Massacre of 1776	43
CHAPTER	VIII.	The Years of Banditry	49
CHAPTER	IX.	Formation of the County and Early Land Owners	53
CHAPTER	X.	Pleasantburg—Early Town of Greenville	60
CHAPTER	XI.	Early Political Life	66
CHAPTER	XII.	From 1830 to 1860	71
CHAPTER	XIII.	Nullification and Secession	78
CHAPTER	XIV.	War and Reconstruction	85
CHAPTER	XV.	Marking Time—1876 to 1895	91
CHAPTER	XVI.	The Growth of Manufacturing	97
CHAPTER	XVII.	The Transportation Facilities	103
CHAPTER	XVIII.	Educational Facilities	108
CHAPTER	XIX.	Cities and Towns	116
CHAPTER	XX.	Political Subdivisions and Government	125
CONCLUSION			130
PRINCIPAL REFERENCES USED			133

PART II.

STATEMENT	136
BIOGRAPHICAL SKETCHES	139
BIOGRAPHICAL INDEX	339

History of Greenville County, South Carolina

FOREWORD

It was with much trepidation that I set myself to this task, but as the work has progressed the hearty cooperation given me by such a large number of people has made the undertaking less arduous than I at first thought it would be. In compiling the pages to follow it has been my principal endeavor to present facts rather than interesting reading matter. However, one who has never attempted such a work as this has no conception of the difficulties confronting a person who undertakes to sift the true from the false. Until the days of the Revolution Greenville County remained a part of the Cherokee Nation. Following its acquisition by South Carolina, in rapid succession, it was a part of the Ninety-Six District, a separate county, a part of Washington District, and then Greenville District. In these numerous changes public records were lost to such an extent that practically nothing of an official nature, dating prior to 1800, can be found. After this, for many years, very few and incomplete records were preserved. As a consequence of this lack of records, and my inexperience as a historian, many errors have no doubt crept in. For this I hasten to apologize, since my sole desire has been to present a true chronicle of the events which seem to have contributed most toward the growth of the county.

But my principal difficulty has been selecting material rather than in finding it. Greenville is so rich in historical lore that two or three large volumes would be required to contain it. Taking from this that of most importance has been no easy task.

Little has been said regarding the noble part played by Greenville citizens in the various wars. That field is too large for intelligent discussion in a volume limited in size as this. But after all, it is the cause and effect of war and not the conduct thereof which makes history.

So many have assisted in this work that it is impossible for me to thank each individual, hence I here extend my thanks to all such. However, I desire to specially mention and thank, the Advisory Board, the *Greenville News* and its owner, Mr. B. H. Peace, and all of those who have subscribed for the publication.

Jas. M. Richardson.

Greenville, S. C., July 1, 1930.

INTRODUCTION.

SITUATED in the apex of triangular-shaped South Carolina, Greenville County has an area of 790 square miles, or 505,600 acres. The county is wedge-shaped, having a length of about 48 miles and a width varying from 17 to 33 miles. Stretching from the Blue Ridge mountains at the North Carolina border to the Piedmont plains eastward, the county has a wide range of elevation. The mountainous area on the west is a beautiful and attractive pleasure resort, with Caesar's Head reaching a height of 3,218 feet and Hogback mountain a few feet higher. Five miles northeast of the city of Greenville is Paris mountain, an isolated group of peaks rising to 2,054 feet above sea level.

With a population of 88,498 in 1920, and estimated for 1930 at more than 115,000, of which at least half is engaged in or dependent upon manufacturing, Greenville County presents a condition of balance between agriculture and industry not frequently found in the South. Annually the manufactured products of the county aggregate near $50,000,000 in value, while more than $10,000,000 is paid in wages to the railroad and industrial employees of the county. The soil is adapted to a wide variety of crops, and farming is successfully conducted in all parts of the county, except the most rugged of the mountain section. Cotton is the principal crop, the normal production of which is from 40,000 to 50,000 bales annually; but dairying, poultry raising, and trucking are developing on a profitable scale, and orcharding, begun a few years ago, has reached extensive proportions. Ready markets are found for all food crops among the large urban and industrial populations, which constitutes about two-thirds of the county's total. The annual value of the farm products of the county is in excess of $7,000,000.

Prior to 1776 the present territory of Greenville County was a portion of the Cherokee Nation, but in July of that year the Indians were driven out, and during the following year they signed a treaty ceding the Greenville County lands to South Carolina. The Revolutionary War was then in progress and no steps were taken to "open up" the newly acquired Indian land till after its close. In 1786 the county of Greenville was created by an act of the General Assembly and by 1790 it had acquired a population of more than 5,000. The settlers came principally from North Carolina and Virginia, and were of Scotch-Irish stock. The rich land lying along the streams was first cleared for cultivation, but as the population increased rapidly during the first 15 years of its life, the beginning of the last century found people residing in every section of the county.

Controversy has arisen as to the origin of the name "Greenville." Some years ago A. S. Salley, Secretary of the Historical Commission of South Carolina, wrote an article for a Greenville newspaper in which he stated that the name comes from Isaac Green, an early settler who owned a mill located on Reedy river. Since then the Isaac Green origin has been much used. Before this it was generally thought that the county was named in honor of General Nathaniel Greene of Revolutionary fame. At a still earlier date the name was attributed to the verdant appearance of the country. In 1824 Mills, in his "Statistics", said the county took its name from the luxuriant vegetation which covered the whole country at the time of its acquisition from the Indians. However, while speaking in Greenville during October, 1826, John C. Calhoun said: "The village of Greenville—picturesque and lovely in its situation, may it so prosper as to be worthy of the memory of him whose illustrious name it wears." No other conclusion could be drawn from this expression than that Mr. Calhoun was under the impression that the name came from General Greene. A few years later Governor Perry wrote an article attributing the name to General Greene.

In advancing the Isaac Green derivation, Mr. Salley very successfully explodes the Nathaniel Greene theory by showing that General Greene was exceedingly unpopular in the up-country and the people there would never have permitted his name to be perpetuated by giving it to one of their counties. Another significant fact, which tends to discredit the General Greene origin, is that his name was spelled "Greene", while that of the county never, even in the beginning, carried the final "e". Against the Isaac Green origin the evidence seems even stronger than that against Nathaniel Greene. The public records show that Isaac Green secured his first land grant in the new Indian acquisition during the fall of 1785, and the legislative act naming the county was passed March 22, 1786, less than six months after Isaac Green came into the county, and long before he built a mill on Reedy river. At the time the county secured its name there were many famous men residing within its boundaries, and it is unreasonable to think that the legislators would have overlooked these to bestow the name of a stranger, unknown to the up-country (Isaac Green came from lower South Carolina), upon their new county. Mrs. M. P. Landrum, granddaughter of Vardry McBee, who became a large landowner of the county in 1815, distinctly recalls hearing her grandmother often remark that the name of the county had its origin in the verdant appearance of the country.

HISTORY OF GREENVILLE COUNTY
SOUTH CAROLINA

PART I

NARRATIVE

History of Greenville County, South Carolina

Chapter I.

BEFORE THE WHITE MAN

TRADITION says that Ferdinand DeSoto was the first white man to set foot upon the soil of the great South Carolina Piedmont. Here he reports finding precious metals. But if his heart was attuned to appreciate the grandeur of nature he discovered other things than gold; for many of those who followed speak in glowing terms regarding the beauty of the Appalachian foot-hills during that early period.

James Adair, an Indian trader, who had traveled much for his day, says of the Carolina mountains and the great expanse lying at their feet: "From the historical description of the Alps and a personal view of the Cherokee mountains, I conclude the Alps are much inferior to several of those mountains in height and rockiness. The upper part of South Carolina, we repeat, is full of interesting scenery; her mountains present every variety of the wild, abrupt, sublime, beautiful, grand, and awful. Her rivers offer numerous cascades, placid surfaces, foaming torrents, and deep waters; the climate is the most delightful in the world, the Montpelier of the United States (as the amiable Abbi Corri, Ambassador of the King of Portugal, observed when he visited the State), the seat of Hygeia herself."

Of a period somewhat earlier than that in which Adair wrote, Landrum, in his Colonial and Revolutionary History of Upper South Carolina, relying upon other writers, says: "The face of our country (referring to Piedmont, South Carolina, at the time white men discovered it) was a region of romance, interspersed here and there with forests, prairies, and great canebrakes which lined not only the valleys and streams, but stretched over the evergreen surface of the country for miles. The woodlands were carpeted with grass, and the wild pea vine grew, it is said, as high as a horse's back, while flowers of every description were seen growing all around. The forests were imposing, the trees were large and stood so wide apart that deer and buffalo could be seen at a long distance."

Later, but while the up-country of South Carolina still retained its primeval beauty, Governor James Glen wrote of it, "I should be afraid to indulge the liberty of copying (referring to the Indian descriptions) lest I should be thought drawing a picture or painting a landscape."

And through the towering forests, and across the great open plains of the up-country of this early day, there roamed great herds of buffaloes, elk, and deer; while back in the recesses of the mountains and among the great canebrakes of the larger streams were to be found the bear, wolf, wildcat, and panther in great numbers. Everywhere the fleet-footed fox, both red and grey, was in evidence; and about the streams were innumerable beavers, otters, and muskrats. Wild turkeys, often weighing as much as fifty pounds each, it is said, were too numerous even for them to be made objects of pursuit.

Into this country of transcendent beauty, where luxuriant grasses and flowers grew everywhere, abounding in game of every kind, the first settlers came to find the land in undisputed possession of the Cherokee Indians. Long before Carolina was known to history, her great piedmont and mountain section was occupied by the Creek Indian. Living beyond the Ohio were the Cherokees, a nation of hardy warriors of the Iroquoian stock, who came down from the Great Lakes region. Growing in numbers, the Cherokees began to look with envious eyes toward the marvelous hunting grounds of the Creeks stretching below them, and becoming strong, they moved over the mountains and pushed the weaker Creeks before them till they were soon in undisputed possession of all the mountains and foot-hills of the present States of Tennessee, North Carolina, South Carolina and Georgia.

The Catawbas emigrated South about the year 1582, supposedly from Canada, and established themselves in the north central part of South Carolina, upon the territory of the Old Cheraws. Both the Cherokees and the Catawbas were powerful nations, and conflict between them was inevitable. They met upon the east bank of the Broad river, and there ensued one of the most terrible battles ever fought upon the soil of South Carolina. Neither gained a victory, but each, realizing the strength of the other, after fighting from sun to sun, with a loss of 1,600 warriors on both sides, decided there were lands enough for both. So a treaty of peace was entered into, by the terms of which (and they were faithfully kept) the Catawbas were to remain on the east side of the Catawba, and the Cherokees were to confine themselves to the west of the Broad, while the territory between these two rivers was to become a common hunting ground for the two peoples. And as a consequence of this treaty, that portion of South Carolina now forming the counties of York, Chester, Fairfield and Richland thereafter contained no permanent Indian settlements.

The Cherokees, who inhabited the up-country when the Carolinians first knew it, did not differ greatly in appearance and habits from the other Indians of the colony. However, dwelling in a colder climate, they lived more generally in huts than did those nearer the coast, and confined themselves to hunting rather than fishing. Being hut dwellers and having few navigable rivers on which they could easily move from place to place, the Cherokees were less nomadic than most Indians, and as a consequence they had a deeper love for their homelands than did the others. This attachment for the hill country of their ancestors caused them to become formidable foes when the whites sought to drive them out in later years. It is said by some of the early writers that the Cherokees were the most intelligent, as well as the most numerous of any Indian tribe in South Carolina. They were never defeated by another Indian people.

The Cherokee Nation was divided into three distinct settlements, known as the upper, middle and lower. That portion of the tribe in South Carolina was of the lower settlement, and lived principally in towns located along the Savannah, Tugaloo, Seneca and Keowee rivers. There is positive evidence, however, of their having lived in very nearly all sections of the piedmont region. But when the white man first knew them, their principal towns were all located in what are now Oconee and

PART I — NARRATIVE

Pickens Counties, while the balance of their land was used as hunting grounds. Of their towns, Keowee is the best known. It was located some 12 miles west of the present town of Pickens. Other towns were Estatoe, Quacoretchie, Toxawaw, Aconnee, Sugar Town, Toogoola, Tussee, Old Estatohe, and Tururaw.

But regardless of the fact that the Cherokees were a numerous and warlike people, residing in a country easily defended, the early settlers found them to be kind-hearted and friendly toward the whites. In fact these Indians never gave a moment's concern to the traders and cattlemen, who came and went at will in their country, till near the middle of the eighteenth century when they were being grossly deceived, and defrauded of their lands by the Carolina government.

Around the Cherokees and their early contact with the whites many beautiful romances have been woven. Chief among these is that beautiful little story of Cateechee and Allen Francis. Who, hearing the story, has not felt his heart thrill in admiration for this brave little Indian girl, who with no thought for her own life, raced from Keowee to Ninety-Six, across trackless forests to warn her lover of an intended attack by the Indians? Many versions have appeared in print, but that from the pen of Mrs. Louise A. Vandiver, in her recent History of Anderson County, is very striking. In part it is:

"It is said that long ago a young Englishman named Allen Francis taught an Indian School at Keowee. Among his pupils was Cateechee, a Choctaw maid, captive of Kuruga, a Cherokee Chief. In her own tongue her name was Issaqueena. Both words mean deer's head. The two fell in love with each other, and when Allen left the Indian settlement it was with a promise to return for his dusky sweetheart at some future day. He went to Fort Cambridge and established himself there in a trading business with his father and brother.

"One night Cateechee overheard Kuruga and his warriors planning an attack on Fort Cambridge, intending to massacre all the white people living there.

"The girl determined to save her lover. After the Indians were asleep she stole away to go to the fort, 96 miles from Keowee, and warn the white people of their danger. When morning came she was missed, and the Cherokees, suspecting her errand, started in pursuit.

"As she ran, a succession of mountain streams crossed her path, and she named them as she sped on, comforting herself with the sound of the number of miles she had thrown behind her. At nightfall, footsore and exhausted, she told her tale. When, a little later the Indians reached the place, the fort was garrisoned, and the attack repulsed.

"Naturally Cateechee remained among the people whom she had saved, and she and Francis were married. For several years they lived among the people of the little town, then called Ninety-Six in memory of her race with death over ninety-six miles of forest."

From this point the story continues, telling how the lovers were later captured by the infuriated Kuruga and carried back to Keowee, where after being held for a time, they made their escape and hid in a stump from which comes the name "Stump-House Mountain" in present Oconee County.

A beautiful little story it is, but nothing more, as the facts clearly show. Till 1759 the Cherokees were friends of the whites and committed no massacres. Yet long before this Ninety-Six and all the creeks and rivers between Keowee and that settlement had been named. In 1730 George Hunter made a map of the Cherokee country on which appears the name of Ninety-Six and all of the numerically named creeks between there and Keowee. He says these names were given by early Indian traders. There were no settlers in that part of the country till after 1738, when the site of Ninety-Six was granted to Thomas Brown, and no fort was built there till the time of the Revolution.

But as Mrs. Vandiver says: "At any rate it is a pretty legend, and if the annals of a people or a land be shorn of legend and tradition, none but the Gradgrind family will ever read its history." This is true. We want our facts embellished with somewhat of fiction, and to meet this desire the historian often forgets to say what is fact and what legend, with the result that in future years we find ourselves trying to disprove such stories as Washington and the cherry tree, which was so beautifully told by Parson Weems.

CHAPTER II.

TRADERS, HUNTERS AND CATTLE MEN

RECORDED history tells us of no one who resided in the Piedmont, even temporarily, before the establishment of the first permanent settlement at Charles Town in 1670. However, there is little doubt that it was only a few years after the settlement in Charles Town when white men began to push back from the coast into the up-country and on into the mountainous sections, where they established themselves as traders among the Cherokee Indians. In 1707 John Archdale, in his publication "A Fertile and Pleasant Province of Carolina", tells us that Charles Town then traded "near one thousand miles into the Continent." Anthony Park, one of the early settlers of what is now Newberry County, traveled several hundred miles into the Indian country, going west of the Alleghany mountains. In 1758 he recounted that in his journeyings he encountered a number of white men, chiefly Scotch and Irish, who told him that they had lived among the Indians as traders for more than 20 years, a few for 40 and 50 years, and one whose abode there had been for 60 years.

In advance of the regular settlers of the up-country two classes of whites were to be found. One was the Indian trader and the other "the cow drivers" or cattle men. The traders built posts at strategic points in the Indian nation and engaged in the exchange of guns, ammunition, rum and trinkets for the valuable furs and skins gathered by the savages. This was a profitable business for the traders because the Indians had no idea of the value of either his goods or those of the white man, and was easily cheated. The cow drivers selected desirable grazing lands and there herded cattle and horses in great numbers. They built "cowpens" where they collected and domesticated their cattle and horses for market. It being necessary for the cattle and horse men to have great open spaces for their ranges, this class of settlers was consequently found in more remote sections than was the trader. But in later days it was about these early "cowpens" that many of the towns and cities grew.

Having decided upon a suitable location, the trader or cattle man went to work, with the assistance of the Indians, and soon built for himself a dwelling house. Next was constructed a store house for the trader and "cowpens" for the cattle men. And after thus having established himself, the next act of the white man was to take an Indian maid for his wife, selecting, if possible, a daughter of some local chief. Of the primitive life of these pioneer settlers Logan, in his History of Upper South Carolina, says: "And it must not be taken for granted that because the bold adventurer, thus associated himself with the barbarian, that he was therefore cut off from any of the necessaries of life, or even from many of its luxuries. Under the care of his thrifty wife, his crib was usually well stored with corn, the yard swarmed with poultry and the common pastures with his swine, horses and cattle. Cherokee women of intelligence made the best housekeepers on the continent; in their habits and persons, they were as cleanly as purity itself. The everyday life of the trader in the Nation was one of primitive and most delightful freedom and simplicity. No hollow-hearted etiquette, no grinding social customs, trammeled or annoyed him; he dressed as best suited him, and conformed to nothing except as his own taste dictated."

So profitable was the Indian trade that before the close of the eighteenth century it had become the most lucrative business in all Carolina. About every Cherokee town was to be found one or more trading posts, each doing an enormous annual business. The Indians, being naturally great hunters, were organized by these traders into efficient hunting units and periodically sent out into the game retreats, during the hunting season, well mounted, and fully supplied with rifles and ammunition. And from these hunting expeditions they usually returned bearing great quantities of deer, buffalo and bear skins, taken from their kill. These skins were readily exchanged for the goods of the traders, but upon a basis far below their value. And to add to the profits of the trader and stimulate hunting among the Indians, during the summer, when hunting could not be engaged in, the trading posts made advances to the red men to be liquidated during the following season. The savages being like children—always looking at the present with no thought for the future—were soon in a state of virtual slavery; but little did the trader care for the condition of his Indian neighbor so long as his profits continued to climb.

During the fall and winter, when hunting was in progress, the trader gathered his skins, cured them after the Indian fashion, and then packed them ready for transport to Charles Town when late spring and summer were at hand. Of course there were then no highways, as we know such, leading from these northern wildernesses to the coast; but the "pack-horse trains" furnished a satisfactory means of transportation for these primitive people. These "trains" consisted of from 10 to 50 or 100 horses moving in a body along one of the Indian trails or paths, guarded against attack from robbers or hostile Indians. On its return journey, the "train" bore goods to stock the trading posts, so there was always the much desired "two-way haul." And in the early fall these "pack-horse train" routes were used by the "cowpen men" to drive their horses and cattle to market; hence there was almost continuous communication between the back country and the coast settlements. The route used by these "trains" was almost exclusively the romantic "Keowee Trail" which comes down to us in song and story.

Till 1716 trade with the Cherokee Nation was conducted solely under the auspices of individual enterprise: but now, partly for the sake of its enormous profits, and partly for the purpose of having better control of the Indians, in view of the public safety, the provincial government assumed the direction of all its affairs, and conducted them ever after, as a great public monopoly. But almost from the beginning there existed great abuses in the trade, since the rapid profits from it had drawn into the Indian nation many irresponsible men of the most despicable character. Even as early as 1707 so great had grown these abuses that the assembly, for the protection of the Indians and the honest traders, enacted a law providing for a board of commissioners to manage and direct everything relating to the Indian traffic. By this board, all traders were compelled to take out licenses, and post heavy bonds guaranteeing their compliance with such regulations as might be prescribed. For a time the board sent responsible agents into the nation to watch over the trade, but after a few years these became corrupt, and the law was permitted to fall into disuse. With its nullification, conditions in the Indian country fast passed from bad to worse, and, sad to relate, one of the most serious evils with which the trade had to contend at this period, was the settling on the border of ignorant, dissolute clergymen, who came pretending to be missionaries of the Cross, but who in reality proved to be grafting parasites, highly skilled in the art of appealing to the baser passions by arraying race against race.

Although trade relations had existed between the Carolinians and Cherokees for many years, and hundreds of traders and cattle men had established themselves throughout the Indian country, no actual treaty, or formal understanding, was entered into prior to 1730. Then Sir Alexander Cummings was sent out from England for the purpose of visiting the Cherokees in an effort to bring about a closer trade relation with that people. Sir Alexander landed in Charles Town, and accompanied by interpreters, he and his party set out for the Cherokee country on March 11, 1730, and following closely the "Keowee Trail", arrived at the Indian town of Keowee on March 25th. The Indians were called into conference and after much "speech-making" on both sides the savages promised everlasting friendship and allegiance to King George and his colony. Cummings, thinking to make the bond of friendship more lasting, invited the Indians to delegate some of their chiefs to accompany him back to England, where they might see and talk to the King, and personally secure from him expressions of his gratitude in knowing that the Cherokees were to remain the firm friends of his people in America. The invitation was accepted and six chieftains, including Atta Kulla Kulla, made the voyage to London, where they were showered with attentions and loaded with gifts. Here a formidable written instrument, full of high-sounding words, was prepared and signed by the Secretary for the Lords Commissioners of Trade and Plantations for the King, and by the marks of the Indian chiefs in behalf of the Cherokees. But regardless of the formalities attending the signing of this instrument, it was nothing more than a written expression of "friendship and good wishes" from each people to the other. It settled no differences, for none existed; and the Indians gave to the whites no greater rights in their country than they had freely exercised for many years.

The interval between 1721 and 1743 was no doubt the most prosperous period of the peltry trade, and the most peaceful in the relations of Carolina and the Cherokee nation. As late as 1731, when the trade had fallen off somewhat, there were collected from all quarters in Charles Town, as many as 225,000 deer skins alone. It is not known how many of these came from the Cherokee nation, but authorities hold that Piedmont Carolina at her best, furnished more deer skins than all other sources combined. And even as late as 1755, when the woods of upper Carolina had been well-nigh depleted of their game supply, it is known that there still came down to Charles Town, from the Cherokee country, in the neighborhood of 25,000 skins annually. From this it can be readily seen that the early traders of upper Carolina played a prominent part in the life of the colony.

But as the years went by and the trade fell off, the better class of traders gradually moved westward, leaving only the scum of a people who were not overly righteous at best. And these unprincipled men were at the bottom of most of the difficulties, which began to disrupt the Cherokee nation about 1743. Formerly each trader had a license for two towns, but about this time two, and even three, Arab-like peddlers began to skulk about a single town, exchanging spirituous liquors and cheating trifles for such skins as the Indian still might gather. From this sad state the transition to out-and-out lawlessness was easy; so by 1750 the entire Piedmont was dominated by outlaws who traveled about the country stealing horses from the cattle men and robbing pack-horse trains. As all officers of the law and courts of justice were located at Charles Town, more than 200 miles away, little could be done to relieve this deplorable condition. But in 1753, the first formal treaty with the Cherokees was signed, and thereafter the Carolinians were in a better position to cope with the situation, as they were given permission, by its terms, to build forts in the Indian nation. Fort Prince George was finished in 1755, and with its garrison to assist legitimate industry, conditions began to improve, and the opening of a new era for upper South Carolina was at hand.

In 1754 trouble arose in Europe between the French and English and this soon spread to America, involving all the colonies in the French and Indian war. General Braddock, having suffered defeat at the hands of the French and their Indian allies early in the conflict, the settlements of western Pennsylvania and Virginia were left fully exposed from the French fort Duquesne. This condition was alarming to many of those living there, and they began to look toward the south for new homes. The war had not yet been felt in the Carolinas, and with comparative quiet now prevailing there, great numbers of these frontiermen from Virginia and Pennsylvania decided to leave all and start their lives anew in the foot-hills of the two Carolinas. And before these newcomers, the last of the old traders and cattle men fled toward the west, for they saw in these sturdy Scotch-Irish immigrants the makings of a new order, and they had no desire to become a part of it.

Prior to the coming of the Virginia and Pennsylvania pioneers, practically all of the whites in upper South Carolina were of the adventurer type, who came with no thought of becoming permanent settlers, or of founding a new civilization. The black sheep of a noble family, the worthless son of a statesman, the religious fanatic, the moral or financial bankrupt, the rejected lover—all of these, and worse—became traders and cattle drivers in the Indian country, where they lived and reared families of half-breeds. If upon these the civilization of the up-country had been built, never would the state have produced the like of her Pickens, her Hamptons and her Calhoun. To the trader and early cattle men, we are deeply indebted, it is true, for they opened the way for the civilization to come, but luckily they were no part of that civilization.

CHAPTER III.

FORT PRINCE GEORGE BUILT

ABOUT the year 1750, the piedmont section of South Carolina began to receive its first permanent settlers. These did not come from the coast, however, but principally from Virginia, Pennsylvania and western New York, moving down the valleys of the Alleghanies, bringing their families and all their portable property with them. They were of the crude pioneer type, having little wealth and education, and living in close touch with nature. Every family supplied itself as best it could from the soil and forests. For the most part, these new settlers were Scotch-Irish, and adhered to the Presbyterian faith in religion. Some, however, were of the sturdy Quaker stock. But in contrast to these simple hard-working frontiersmen were the dwellers of the low country, who, by this time, had a well-formed social system, and established religion (Episcopal) and a great deal of accumulated wealth, with many families of culture and refinement. And in order to understand the sectional differences which have played such a prominent part in the social, political, and economic life of South Carolina, one must bear in mind the different types of people making up the citizenship of the up-state and the coastal section.

With the coming of the French and Indian war in 1754, both the French and the English were anxious to secure the aid of the various Indian tribes. The Cherokees had always been friends and allies of the English, but the French had never lost an opportunity to court their favor, so they now sent emissaries among them, with costly presents, who spoke in glowing terms of the advantages to be obtained by a French alliance. But the Cherokees were satisfied with existing conditions and hastened to assure the Carolinians that they would remain true to their pledge of friendship with the English. They expressed fears, however, of the French making an attack upon the colony by marching through their country. Such a move on the part of the French, they did not feel themselves strong enough to check, and an attack upon the Carolina frontier from their nation, they realized, might cause the English to question their sincerity. For years the government in Charles Town had realized that it was unprepared to withstand an attack upon its frontiers made from the Cherokee country, whether coming from the French or the Indians themselves. Now seemed an opportune time to gain the consent of the Cherokees to build a few forts at strategic points in their nation, so Governor Glen went out from Charles Town in 1755 to enter negotiations with the Cherokees, relative to securing sufficient lands in their territory upon which to build these fortifications.

The Governor and his party were met in one of the lower Indian towns by Atta Kulla Kulla, who, it will be remembered, had gone to England in the Cummings party, and about 500 warriors. Out of this conference came a formal treaty (the first between the Cherokees and Carolinians), by which the colony was given permission to build forts in the Indian country, and in addition it was granted a vast territory of Indian lands of uncertain boundary. This treaty was reduced to writing and formally signed by Governor Glen for the colony, and Atta Kulla Kulla and other Indian chiefs for the Cherokees. The original is on file in the office of the Historical Commission at Columbia, and should prove interesting to those who delight in using high-sounding words and well-turned phrases to obscure their real meaning. Reading that document now, in the light of later events, one can but think it was the studied purpose of the Carolinians when preparing the instrument, to acquire color of title to a major portion of the Cherokee holdings while leading the trusting savages to think that only fort sites were being granted. If not, why the vagueness of wording? One taking title to land does not trust to such hidden meanings and vague descriptions as are found in this treaty. But regardless of the intention of the Cherokees, and in the face of vigorous protests from their chief, Atta Kulla Kulla, the Carolinians took possession of the major portion of the Indians' rich grazing and hunting lands in South Carolina, claiming it under the treaty. Roughly, this new acquisition comprised the territory now constituting the counties of Edgefield, McCormick, Greenwood, Abbeville, Laurens, Newberry, Union, Spartanburg, York, Cherokee, Chester, Fairfield, Richland, and a portion of Lexington. The Cherokees retained only that portion of the colony embraced within the present counties of Anderson, Greenville, Pickens, and Oconee. After the treaty was entered into, England made haste to erect a fort across the river from the Cherokee town of Keowee, and called it Fort Prince George. Another fortress was built on the Tennessee river and named Fort Loudon.

During the year of the Cherokee compact, General Braddock was defeated and for a time thereafter the French arms were in the ascendency, thus leaving the frontiers of Pennsylvania, Maryland, and Virginia exposed to French and Indian attacks from Fort Duquesne on the Ohio. Faced with this danger, great numbers of the settlers there turned southward to join their neighbors and friends who had already moved into upper South Carolina. Colonel Clarke had come from Virginia and settled on Pacolet river, in what is now Spartanburg County in 1750. Here he was now joined by eight or ten families from Pennsylvania, who established themselves on the three forks of Tyger river. They were Scotch-Irish Presbyterians, and within a few years established Nazareth church, out of which grew Fairview of present Greenville County. The names of some of these were Barry, Moore, Anderson, Collins, Thompson, Vernon, Pearson, Jamison, Dodd, Ray and Nichols, all names still common in Greenville and Spartanburg Counties. Patrick Calhoun (ancestor of John C.) settled on Long Cane in present Abbeville County in 1756, finding there two families who had preceded him, one of whom was named Gowdy, and the other Edwards. By 1760 this settlement had grown to a population of near 200. From 1751 to 1754, eight or ten families emigrated from Pennsylvania and settled on Fair Forest creek, in what is now Union County. First among these to come were George Story, James McIlwaine and a Mr. Dugan. Another settlement near the present town of Union was made from Pennsylvania about 1754. Among those constituting this community appear the well-known names of Brandon, Brogan, Jolly, Kennedy, and McJunkin. Settlements were made in present Newberry and Laurens Counties on waters of Enoree river, Kings creek, Gilders creek, Indian creek, Duncan creek and Tyger river as early as 1749. Others are known to have taken up lands in all other of what are today referred to as Piedmont Counties, except such as were undeniably Cherokee territory. In fact, such a steady stream of immigration flowed in, that by 1759 there were several thousand inhabitants in the up-country.

How these new settlers came, and the manner in which they set about the task of making a home for themselves in this new country, is well described by Dr. William A. Schaper in his valuable work, "Sectionalism in South Carolina" in the following words: "The people came in groups, many driving their stock before them, from the frontiers of Pennsylvania, Virginia and North Carolina. They followed the great valleys and adjoining plateaus that run in a general southwesterly direction, from western Pennsylvania to northern Georgia. These natural highways afforded an easy approach to the uplands of South Carolina, where lands were fertile and far removed from the Indian disturbances of that time. They located first in Waxhaws, in what later became Lancaster District, and on the Cane Lands of Abbeville. From these points, settlement gradually spread over the more accessible tracts toward the mountains. These frontiersmen were mostly Scotch-Irish, a hardy band of frontiersmen who stood guard over the advancing civilization from the Carolinas to Western New York. Only the hunter and trapper, and the Indian trader had preceded them into the wilderness. But unlike their predecessors, they came to stay, at least long enough to see a more settled community arise. . . . The Carolina pioneers brought their families, their rude and scanty store of household goods, their crude implements, seed, and domestic animals, ready for the work of frontier farming. The first task was the building of the log cabin. This was the work of a day or two. With a jug of cider or whiskey to make merry, the pioneer invited his neighbor to lend a helping hand. . . . The furniture was scarce, but the faithful rifle always hung in the chimney corner within easy reach. . . . The great task of the pioneer was the work of clearing and breaking up the land. Each family owned from 50 to 200 or 300 acres. . . . They were almost completely shut in from the outside world. There were no navigable streams to join them with the civilized world or the older settlements. Below them was the middle country—a sandy tract, covered with dense pine forests. . . . In a region where every man must rely on his own strong arm and his rifle for the support and protection of his family, there are no distinctions. It was a strongly democratic society, then, that grew up here, typical of the West. Wealth accumulated very slowly and there were very few slaves until the close of the century. The people enjoyed their rude but wholesome life spent in close touch with nature."

And now had begun the actual settlement of the "back country", as it was then termed. For more than a half century, this great section had been the source of one of the colony's richest natural resources in its peltry trade; but that asset was about to give way for another—its sturdy Scotch-Irish men and women, who were to furnish the future state with some of her most conspicuous leaders in every activity of life.

CHAPTER IV.

THE FIRST CHEROKEE WAR

THE effect of the Cherokee treaty of 1755, followed by the defeat of General Braddock in Virginia, was to bring an influx of new settlers upon the frontiers of South Carolina, as has been previously discussed. But unfortunately, due to the blundering tactics of Governor Lyttleton of South Carolina, these newcomers were soon faced with the same dangers from which they had fled—hostile Indians upon their frontiers. Early in the conflict, the Cherokees joined forces with Great Britain and her American colonies, against the French and their Indian allies. And after the British reverses in Virginia, the Cherokees dispatched a number of warriors there to reinforce their hard-pressed allies. In 1758, Fort Duquesne fell before a combined attack of the English, Virginians and Indians, the Indians being led, it is said, by Captain Richard Pearis, afterward a resident of present day Greenville County; and with the removal of this great French stronghold, the southern colonies began to breathe freely again. The Cherokees, seeing that they were no longer needed, set out upon their return to Carolina, but on their homeward journey they incurred the wrath of a few Virginia settlers who fired upon them. Being greatly enraged, the warriors hurried to their Carolina homes and reported the ill treatment which had been accorded them. The young men of the Nation were for immediate and indiscriminate war upon the whites, but the leaders endeavored to restrain them from committing any overt acts till a conference with the governor at Charles Town could be arranged. However, a number of the young Indians, without the sanction of their head-men, raided the frontier settlements of present Spartanburg, Laurens and Abbeville Counties, killing a number of the inhabitants.

When it became known in the Cherokee nation that the wishes of the head-men had been disregarded, there was great alarm among the Indian people, and a deputation of 32 of the leading chiefs, led by Occonostota, was immediately started to Charles Town, where it was hoped a settlement of the difficulties could be effected. The Cherokees had always been on terms of the closest friendship with the Carolinians, and they greatly desired that this friendly relationship continue. But unfortunately, James Glen, who fully understood the Indians, was no longer governor; instead William Henry Lyttleton, a hot-head, who had his own ideas of how to handle the situation, now held that position. So after traveling for more than 200 miles upon their mission of peace, the Indian envoys were not even permitted to lay their petition before the governor. Instead, they were bluntly told that the governor did not care to hear them, and that he was even then about to march upon their people with an army. The Indians were assured, however, that they would be permitted to return to their own country since they had come on a friendly mission; but they were advised that the safest way for the return would be with the troops.

Within a few days after the coming of the chieftains, fully confident that the governor would receive them in the same spirit of friendship which had prompted their mission, these chosen leaders of a proud people, found themselves in the humiliating position of returning to their country, virtual prisoners in the hands of avowed enemies. Till the Congarees (Columbia) was reached they were permitted to march with the army, but upon leaving this encampment they were all made prisoners, and carried back to Keowee under heavy guard. Such treatment was inconceivable to the Indian mind, except it come at the hand of an enemy. In friendship, and on a mission of peace, their chiefs had journeyed to the seat of the white man's government, and they were brought back in chains and lodged in prison. Could such conduct be condoned? Never in the eyes of the proud Cherokee race! An unpardonable injury had been done them, and nothing short of bloodshed could propitiate that wrong.

Governor Lyttleton was as ignorant of the methods of Indian warfare as he was of the savage's ethics of life. The expedition had been hurriedly undertaken, and his troops were ill supplied with food, clothing and ammunition to withstand an Indian attack in that remote region. Many of the soldiers, realizing the incompetency of their leadership, soon began to show their discontent, and the governor, fearing mutiny, hurried messengers to Atta Kulla Kulla, the leading chief of all the Cherokees, requesting his immediate presence at Fort Prince George. Upon the arrival of this old chief, Governor Lyttleton, making as great a show of strength as possible, told him that he had brought his army into the Indian country to make war upon the red men if 24 of their number (this being the number of whites killed in the recent raid) were not immediately delivered up to be dealt with as might seem best. Atta Kulla Kulla proposed that three of the imprisoned chiefs, including Occonostota, be liberated to assist him in finding 24 of the young men who had taken part in the massacre. The suggestion was taken, and three of the Indian prisoners were released. But on the following day, after two of the guilty young men had been brought in, Atta Kulla Kulla set out upon his journey home. He had not proceeded far, however, when he was overtaken by a messenger from the governor requesting his return. Accordingly, the old warrior retraced his steps and again presented himself at the camp of Governor Lyttleton, where he frankly stated that additional time must be given if any more of the raiders were to be captured. The governor having already realized his mistake, and knowing that his army could not be held together longer, proposed a treaty by which 22 of the chiefs, then held prisoners, should be retained as hostages till an equal number of Indians were delivered in compliance with the original demand. This was acceded to by Atta Kulla Kulla, and such an agreement was reduced to writing and formally signed by Governor Lyttleton for the colony, and six Indian chiefs in behalf of the Cherokees. This done, the army was withdrawn.

Although the treaty was signed by the Cherokees, they never seemed to hold themselves bound by its terms, and no effort was made to deliver up any portion of the 22 Indians demanded. Occonostota continued to smart because of the treatment accorded him and his friends who had gone to Charles Town, and set himself to the task of releasing the hostages still confined in Fort Prince George. After gathering his warriors, he delivered an assault upon the fort, but little impression could be made. Seeing that he could not hope to accomplish his purposes in this manner, he used deception to draw Captain Cotymore from the fort, and no sooner was he outside its protecting walls than he was shot down by Indians previously placed in ambush for that purpose. As a consequence of this Indian treachery, orders were given in the fort to put the hostages in irons, but they resisted, and the garrison fell upon them and butchered them all in a most horrible manner.

The Cherokee issue had been unwisely handled from its inception, and this last act was a fatal blunder. There was hardly an Indian in the Nation who had not lost a relative in the massacre of the hostages, and now a cry for the blood of their enemies "to propitiate the spirits of their dead brothers" went up over the entire Cherokee country. With the hatchet, scalping knife and torch in hand, the savages rushed down upon the frontier settlements, leaving death and destruction in their wake. Men, women and children fell innocent sacrifices everywhere to the inefficient rule of Governor Lyttleton. Some escaped the tomahawk by fleeing to the woods only to die there of hunger, while others were taken prisoners to be subjected to inexpressible hardships and tortures. The frontiersmen, being unable to defend themselves, hurried messenger after messenger to Charles Town imploring aid, while the savages each day added new victims to their harvest of blood. But an epidemic of smallpox was sweeping over the coast country and no help could be furnished, and these unhappy people were left to contend with the savage scourge as best they could. Small forts and block-houses were hastily constructed along the entire Cherokee frontier, and into these crude fortifications the sorely beset settlers crowded with their movable property, where they remained in a state of defense, till the fury of their enemies exhausted itself in the systematic destruction of their unprotected homes, provisions and fields. At this time, the present Greenville County, still being Indian territory, bristled with these places of defense all along her eastern and southern boundaries, where are now found Spartanburg and Laurens Counties.

After a time, Virginia and North Carolina came to the rescue of the South Carolinians by sending down seven troops of rangers which were joined in a short time by Colonel Montgomery with a small force of British regulars. Montgomery, assuming command, marched into the Cherokee country where he inflicted heavy losses on the Indians. But he was recalled to the northern provinces within a short time, and again the Carolina frontier was left exposed to the savage attacks. A provincial regiment was then raised and put under command of Colonel Middleton. Among the officers of this regiment, who later gained prominence in South Carolina military and political history, were Henry Laurens, William Moultrie, Francis Marion, Isaac Huger and Andrew Pickens. This force united with a regiment of British regulars under Colonel Grant, who had been sent to Carolina when it seemed that the Indian trouble there was becoming so serious as to endanger the British cause in America. The command of the united forces was entrusted to Colonel

Grant, who, now at the head of 2,600 men, pushed rapidly into the wilderness of the Cherokee country, utterly destroying the homes, granaries and growing crops of the Indians, who fled before the approaching army into the mountains, where they often attacked from ambush, but without inflicting sufficient losses upon the advancing forces to seriously impede their progress. This expedition was known as the Grant Indian war; and it brought the Cherokees into complete submission, thus ending the first conflict of arms between the Cherokees and South Carolina.

Note.—The agreement between Governor Lyttleton and the Cherokees with reference to holding the hostage chiefs, and the treaty which terminated the Grant campaign were both reduced to writing, and are on file in the office of the Historical Commission at Columbia. It is with regret that copies are not incorporated here, but space will not permit.

CHAPTER V.

PRE-REVOLUTIONARY SETTLERS ON GREENVILLE COUNTY LANDS

THE Cherokee Indian trouble having already been satisfactorily settled, the treaty of Paris, concluded in 1763, left the South Carolina frontier free to pursue a life of industry for the first time since it began to receive the Virginia, Pennsylvania, and New York settlers. Long years of war and pillage had greatly retarded its development, but a new life was now opening for the up-country. A vast extent of virgin territory, claimed by Carolina under the treaty of Governor Glen, and confirmed in her by the Cherokees after Grant's Indian war, offered many advantages to those people residing further north. Here, where ideal weather conditions prevailed the whole year through, and rich lands could be purchased for a song, the residents of western Virginia, Pennsylvania and New York saw opportunities innumerable, and soon started a steady stream of emigration into Piedmont South Carolina.

It was not till 1777 that present-day Greenville County was acquired from the Indians, but it is evident that a number of white people took up their abode here during the period after the French and Indian war, when so many pioneers were establishing themselves upon adjoining lands. Never had Greenville County as of today, been used by the Indians for the location of their permanent towns, practically all of these being in present Pickens and Oconee Counties, hence there seemed to be little objection to white men living there. Under treaties with Great Britain, the Cherokees were not permitted to sell their lands to individuals, but there is evidence that they disregarded this provision of their agreement and sold extensively to at least one man (Richard Pearis) and perhaps others, while they permitted many to become "squatters" in their country.

The best known of all pre-Revolutionary settlers in Greenville County was, of course, Richard Pearis (Paris), who took up his residence on the site of present Greenville City, between the years 1766 and 1768. Pearis was an Irishman of some education and pronounced ability, who settled in Frederick County, Virginia, prior to 1750. He later established himself on Long Island of the Holston river as an Indian trader, and was at one time associated with Nathaniel (afterward General) Gist. Governor Dinwiddie of Virginia, recognizing his ability, commissioned him a lieutenant of Virginia Provincials in 1755 and soon afterward he became a captain in command of a company of Cherokees and Catawbas in an expedition under Major Lewis against the Shawnee towns west of the Ohio. He served gallantly throughout the French and Indian war and is said to have been the first man to enter Fort Duquesne, being captain of a band of Cherokee warriors (probably from South Carolina). In commendation of his services in the war, he was publicly thanked and given the post of agent for Southern Indians with headquarters at Fort Pitt. But after filling this position for a short time, he decided to move to South Carolina and take up his residence among the Cherokees, since his wife was a Cherokee woman. Some authorities, however, say that he was ordered south where he might be "more centrically located to gather the Cherokees in the event of an Indian outbreak." But later events in his life tend to show that his real motive in going into the Indian country was to gain their confidence through his wife and then rob them of their lands.

Pearis established his trading post and erected a corn mill near the present location of Camperdown mill, at what was then called "Great Plains", and was soon engaged in a lucrative business with the Indians. His holdings of land were extended year by year in every direction, till at the outbreak of the Revolutionary war, he is said to have claimed title to ten miles square. But he never, at any time, held legal title to any lands, for as has already been said, the Indians by their treaties had agreed to sell no lands to individuals, and he could therefore have acquired only a sort of permissive use of his holdings. Just how he probably acquired these broad acres is revealed in a letter written to the Cherokee people by John Stuart, superintendent of Indian affairs, in 1775, which reads in part: "I am very sorry of the little regard paid to my advice, and your own interest, respecting your land which you compliment away to every white man who asks for it. You have been constantly told and admonished by me, not to treat or bargain for your land with any person but me. . . . You are constantly listening to Richard Pearis, who cheats you of your lands." From Pearis comes the name of "Paris Mountain", which beautiful and pleasant summer resort of Greenvillians today was included within his holdings. Later, in the days of the Revolution, Richard Pearis was a prominent Tory, and his activities as such will be discussed later.

About the time Richard Pearis took up his residence at Great Plains, a Colonel Hite, with his family, moved down from Virginia and established himself on the Enoree river near where that stream is now crossed by the old Spartanburg road. There are records extant showing that he was in possession of at least 1,300 acres. Tradition says that Captain Pearis and Colonel Hite were friends while still in Virginia, and that this friendship continued for many years after the two had settled in South Carolina. A son of Colonel Hite, it is said, was engaged to be married to Pearis' daughter, which romance was ended by the death of young Hite at the hands of the Indians during the early days of the Revolution. The Hite family adhered to the cause of the Whigs in the war of the Revolution, and the Colonel, his wife and at least one of his sons (the one engaged to the daughter of Pearis) were killed in a bloody Indian raid during the summer of 1776.

Among the very early settlers in what is now Greenville County, was Nathaniel Austin, who came down from Virginia about 1761 or 1762 and settled on Gilders creek, a few miles northeast of the town of Simpsonville. He was an Englishman, having emigrated from that country to Virginia only a few years before coming to South Carolina. It is said that he held a commission from King George III as high constable. J. Thomas Austin, a great-grandson of the original settler, it will be recalled by the older residents, was prominent in public affairs of the county for many years during the latter part of the last century, being a member of the celebrated "Wallace House." Family tradition has it that a daughter of Nathaniel

Austin was killed by Indians some years prior to the Revolution, and that several years later a brother of the murdered girl succeeded in slaying one of the Indians who had been concerned in her death. However, the killing of this young lady probably took place in 1776, during the raid in which several members of the Hite family lost their lives, as there is no record of any Indian massacres in this section between the time the Austin family came to South Carolina and that date. Nathaniel Austin and all of his children were ardent supporters of the Patriot cause in the Revolution.

There is evidence that a family by the name of Gilder resided near the home of the Austins; and it is said that one of the Gilder girls was a witness to the slaying of Miss Austin, a friend and neighbor, with whom she was out walking when the Indians swept down upon the little settlement. It is no doubt from this family that Gilder creek derives its name.

In the northeastern part of the county several families are thought to have resided prior to the Revolution. Among these were the Gowen, Howard, Fisher and Dill families. Major Buck Gowen and Captain Howard, members of two of these families, won distinction during the Revolution as daring leaders of small forces operating in semi-guerilla style against the Tories of upper Spartanburg and Greenville Counties. Near the present Gowensville settlement (named in honor of Major Buck Gowen) Gowen's fort was located in Greenville County. Further south and not far from Greer, was Wood's fort, which was also in Greenville County. Both of these fortifications are known to have existed during the Revolution, and some authorities fix their construction date as of the Indian massacres during the French and Indian war. If these forts existed at that early date, no doubt there were several families residing near them.

Near Piedmont, on Grove creek, it is thought that Alexander Cameron, Indian agent, and much despised Tory of later days, maintained "cowpens", although he did not live there. The Cameron place was granted to Henry Pendleton, a Carolinian of prominence, from whom Pendleton District and the town of Pendleton derived their names, in 1784, following the acquisition of the county from the Cherokees. And in this immediate vicinity, there were doubtless a number of settlers, for the "Golden Grove" seems to have been a choice location when the county was later opened to regular settlements.

At this late day, in the absence of any records, it is impossible to ascertain the names of many of the pre-Revolutionary settlers, but evidence which comes down through descriptions and plats from early land grants warrants the statement that some white men were to be found in practically every section of the county. Roads led in almost every direction, and some of these were evidently of the "public" variety. There was one leading from Pearis' plantation to Ninety-Six and Augusta, and another along the approximate route of the present Old Spartanburg road through Colonel Hite's plantation "to the Settlements" in present Spartanburg County.

Living near these early Greenville County settlers, in what is now Spartanburg County, were a number of people whose later lives were so closely identified with Greenville County and its development that brief reference to them here would not be out of place. Residing two or three miles northeast of the town of Greer was a family whose name in after years became famous the South over. This was none other than Anthony Hampton, great-grandfather of Governor Wade Hampton of "red shirt" days. Anthony Hampton and several members of his family were killed in the Indian massacre of 1776. Another was Judge Baylis Earle of the Landrum section of Spartanburg. The descendants of Judge Baylis Earle and his brother, Colonel John Earle, who resided near him, but just over the state line in North Carolina, have been prominent in the political, social, business and professional life of Greenville County from its organization down to the present. Another resident of Spartanburg County of this period, was Colonel John Thomas, who later led the expedition against the Cherokees which terminated in a treaty under which Greenville County was ceded to Carolina. Just north of Duncan, in the Nazareth church settlement, lived a considerable community of Scotch-Irish people who had come down from Pennsylvania some time before the French and Indian war. Among these were the Pedens, Alexanders, Mortons, Morrows and Nesbitts, who, after the Revolution, moved to lower Greenville County and established Fairview Presbyterian church in 1786.

As the country grew in population, it became evident to the frontiersmen that a stable government must be established if prosperity and happiness were to be enjoyed by the people. The war just concluded had thrown upon these regions a host of idlers, who sought to live by their wits. No courts had yet been established in the back country, and no law enforcement officers were stationed nearer than Charles Town, with which communication was anything but rapid. Because of this state, these idle people, seeing that it would be an easy matter to live upon the industry of their neighbors, soon banded themselves together to prey upon the community. Horse stealing and cattle "rustling" became fine arts; and murder and rapine were daily occurrences. But petition after petition directed to the Governor and Assembly by the law-abiding people were ignored till, by the year 1767, that portion of the colony lying between the Saluda and Broad found itself in a deplorable state.

The law-abiding people of the up-country, knowing that something must be done to curb such outlawry if they were to continue living there, decided to take the law into their own hands. A semi-military organization was formed, and it set about ridding the country of the marauding bands infesting it. This self-constituted "law and order league" was known as the Regulators. But however commendable might have been the purpose of the Regulators, many inexcusable acts of rowdyism and oppression were committed in the name of the organization; and opposition to its activities soon began to be heard from many who had no more sympathy for lawlessness than did the most rabid Regulator. Feeling ran high and the entire back country soon found itself divided into two armed camps. The authorities in Charles Town became alarmed and sought to quell the disturbance by proceeding against the Regulators. In pursuance of this policy, one Scoville (or Scofield) was sent into the district lying between the Saluda and Broad with instructions to break up that organization. But he proved to be a man of low character, and in executing his commission, he adopted very harsh and extreme measures with numbers of the better classes among the people, involving multitudes in great distress. Those who opposed the Regulators were soon termed Schophalites, and so intense was the feeling engendered between the two followings that every resident of the frontiers eventually found himself classed as a member of one or the other faction. Richard Pearis was an outspoken adherent of the Schophalite cause, whether from honest convictions that the Regulators were too freely resorting to "Lynch law", or because he secretly sympathized with and supported the lawless element is not known; but his conduct during the Revolution leads one to suspect the latter as his real motive.

Scoville was soon withdrawn, but the bitterness engendered among the people by his activities lingered for many years, and became a strong contributing factor in the internecine warfare which was so savagely prosecuted in upper South Carolina during all the years of the Revolution. But the determined attitude of the Regulators seems to have impressed the authorities with the justice of their cause, for no sooner was Scoville out of the country than remedial legislation was undertaken. The machinery of government moved slowly, but in 1769 a bill was passed establishing courts at six locations outside Charles Town. One of these was at Ninety-Six. These new courts were given very limited jurisdiction, but the up-country felt that it was now being recognized by the government and this had a pacific influence on the inhabitants there. Conditions immediately began to improve, and by 1770 comparative quiet had been restored.

CHAPTER VI.

THE REVOLUTION BEGINS—BATTLE OF GREAT CANE BRAKE

JUST as the frontiersmen were beginning to compose themselves in the thought that they could now settle back into a life of reasonable tranquility, the bitterness engendered by the issue between the Regulators and Scophelites having somewhat abated, a new cause of disturbance began to loom large upon the horizon. For many months occasional visitors to Charles Town had returned to the up country with news of conflicts between the mother country and various ones of the American colonies over the right of Great Britain to tax them, but little was thought of the matter here on the frontiers. These hard working people had never taken an interest in politics—in fact, the coast country had not permitted them to exercise any of the privileges of citizenship—and they reasoned now that this was no concern of theirs. This state of apathy on the part of such a large proportion of its people was viewed with alarm by the Council of Public Safety, which had now taken the reins of government from the hands of the British governor, and it was decided to dispatch a commission from the seat of government at Charles Town, "to go into the interior parts of this colony at the public expense, there to explain to the people at large, the nature of the unhappy public dispute between Great Britain and the American colonies to quiet their minds, and to enforce the necessity of a general union in order to preserve themselves and their children from slavery."

The commission sent out consisted of William H. Drayton, formerly a Judge of the King's Court, and the Rev. William Tennant, a Presbyterian minister, both of whom were noted for their diplomacy and persuasive manner. These gentlemen left Charles Town early in June, 1775, and proceeded immediately to the Congarees (now Columbia), where they stopped for a few days to confer with representative men from the up country, who had come down at their request. After these informal conferences they moved northward, holding public meetings wherever the people could be assembled together. But the inhabitants were found to be, not only indifferent to the cause of the colony against Great Britain, but in great fear of trouble with the Indians. Already Alexander Cameron was in the Cherokee country inciting the savages to hostilities against the frontiers, and a sharp conflict had actually taken place between a small detachment of Patriots under Colonel William Thomson and a larger number of Indians led by Cameron.

The commissioners now saw that if any cooperation at all was to be had from the frontiersmen, the ever-present menace of an Indian attack must be removed. So negotiations were undertaken with Richard Pearis in an effort to have him bring down some of the Indian head-men for a conference. It was with some trepidition, and contrary to instruction from Charles Town, that Pearis was chosen for this purpose, as his loyalty to the Patriot cause was even then doubted. But he was a man of great influence among the Indians, and having demonstrated his value as a friend to Virginia in the late war with France, Mr. Drayton decided that no effort should be spared to secure his aid. He thought this show of confidence might be the means of linking him firmly with the friends of Independence.

As a consequence of these negotiations, Pearis appeared at the Congarees on September 25th, 1775, with several chiefs from the Indian Nation. Here they were met by Mr. Drayton. The Indians expressed considerable indignation, and seemed greatly concerned that the colonists had stopped all movements of ammunition to the traders in their country. They had long since put aside the bow and arrow for the use of firearms, and now, not being able to secure ammunition, they had no means of obtaining food, since they still depended upon the fruits of the chase for a livelihood. But Mr. Drayton explained to them, in a talk suited to the occasion, the nature of the dispute between Great Britain and America, and why it had become necessary to discontinue the trade in ammunition. His explanation was satisfactory, and the Indians promised "to hold fast to the chain of peace." Believing that the purpose of the meeting had been accomplished, and that no further danger of an Indian attack existed, Mr. Drayton assured the chiefs of his government's friendship and promised that powder and lead would be sent them at once.

The pacific attitude of the Indians, when made known to the frontiersmen, caused a number of the up country leaders to align themselves with the colonists. Soon it began to appear that the old Scophalite faction was friendly to the King, and this had much weight in carrying the Regulator adherents to the other side. However, Colonel Thomas Fletchall, commander of a regimental district in the up country, announced that he would remain loyal to Britain, and this action left the Patriots between the Saluda and Broad without organization or leadership. But they set to work as best they could to perfect an organization, and in a short time had chosen leaders and were rapidly enrolling the anti-British inhabitants. John Thomas, later a resident of Greenville County, was chosen colonel of the Spartan regiment, an organization which did valiant service in the war to follow. However, a communication from him to Mr. Drayton about this time clearly shows conditions on the frontier still were in a bad state of disorganization.

A portion of the letter from Colonal Thomas is as follows:

Spartan Regiment,
Sept. 11, 1775.

"To the Honorable W. H. Drayton, Esq.:

"*May It Please Your Honor:*—I this moment received your Honor's favor of the 10th instant, and very fortunately the command of this district was just assembled at my house in order to address the Council of Safety almost on the very purport of your Honor's letter, as we had all the reason in the world (and still have), to believe from good information, that the malignants are forming the most hellish schemes to frustrate the measures of the Continental Congress, and to use all those who are willing to stand by those measures in the most cruel manner. Your Honor will be fully convinced of the truth of this by perusing the papers transmitted herewith, to which I refer your Honor.   JOHN THOMAS."

Pursuant to the promise made by Mr. Drayton, the Council of Safety, on October 4th, 1775, voted a supply of ammunition for the Cherokee Nation, and immediately dispatched one thousand pounds of powder and two thousand pounds of lead by ammunition train into the up country. A few days before this, Major Williamson had secured the arrest of Robert Cunningham, of present Laurens County, because of purported "seditious statements" and sent him under arrest to Charles Town. Patrick Cunningham, hoping to effect the release of his brother, Robert, organized a body of his friends and started in pursuit of those conveying him to prison, but was unable to overtake them. However, he met the ammunition train coming up from Charles Town, and feeling much aggrieved because of the manner in which his brother had been treated, he took possession of the ammunition and conveyed it back to the vicinity of Ninety-Six. When this information reached the Council of Safety there was great alarm, for the Indians had been promised the ammunition, and their disappointment in its failure to be delivered, might cause them to fall upon the frontier settlements; so steps were immediately taken to forestall such an event. Mr. Drayton, thinking Pearis still loyal to the province, wrote him a letter requesting him to inform the Indians of what had occurred, and to assure them that the ammunition would soon be recovered and forwarded to them. Colonel Richard Richardson was ordered to proceed with his army from the Congarees, where it was encamped, into the up-country, not only to recapture the ammunition, but to arrest those who had taken part in its seizure.

Major Andrew Williamson, then in command of the few up-country settlers bold enough to take up arms for the Patriot cause, realizing the serious nature of the Cunningham incident, without awaiting orders from headquarters, sent out a detachment of militia from his camp at Hard Labor creek (in what is now Laurens County) in an effort to cut off and capture the Cunningham band as it returned. Cunningham eluded his pursuers, however, and returned safely to his home. But while the Council of Safety at Charles Town and Major Williamson in the up-country were putting forth every possible effort to allay the insurgency and pacify the Indians by recovering and delivering to them the powder and lead taken by Cunningham, Richard Pearis was exerting himself to poison the minds of the frontiersmen against the Patriot cause. Up to this time he seems to have been assuring each side of his friendship, only for the purpose of gaining time to learn which was the stronger and more likely to succeed in the coming conflict. Now it seemed to him that he was safe in choosing. Great Britain must win, and casting his lot with her would mean much to Pearis. As was well known to those who had dealt with him, he had no regard for the truth when its perversion would serve his purpose, so he now resorted to the most infamous lies conceivable to inflame the minds of the people. He even went so far as to sign and circulate an affidavit to the effect that the ammunition being sent to the Indians was intended to be used by them to kill all those of the border settlers who were friendly to the Crown. And since Pearis had been with the Indian chiefs upon the occasion of their visit to the Congarees, his affidavit carried all the earmarks of truth.

Urged on by the malicious treachery of Pearis, the Tories, now greatly augmented by those who believed his assertions to be true, acted quickly. Before Colonel Richardson could reach the frontier, they marched upon Ninety-Six, where Major Williamson and Major Mayson had stationed their small forces. On the 21st of

November, 1775, the Whig and Tory forces came in contact with each other in an open field a few miles north of Ninety-Six. The combat was short, with small damage to either side, but here was shed the first blood of the Revolution on South Carolina soil. Neither side seemed anxious to force the issue, so on November 22nd a mutually satisfactory pact was signed. But of more than passing interest here is the fact that the witnesses to this agreement were Richard Pearis and Andrew Pickens. These two were to meet five years later, perhaps in Greenville County but more likely in Anderson, when Pickens, then a general in command of all the upper divisions of the state, surrendered to Pearis, and then again near the close of the war when the life of Pearis was saved by Pickens at Augusta.

But Colonel Richardson, marching rapidly towards Ninety-Six, gathering reinforcements as he moved, was in no frame of mind to deal leniently with the enemy, so after conferring with Colonel William Thomson, who joined him on November 28th, he decided that he would not respect the terms of the Ninety-Six agreement, but on the other hand would take Pearis and other leading Tories into custody. And it was only a few days till Pearis, "the first citizen of Greenville", found himself a prisoner of war, for on December 16th Colonel Richardson wrote Henry Laurens, President of the Council of Safety, as follows: "I herewith send you the persons of Colonel Thomas Fletchall, Captain Richard Pearis, Jacob Fry, and Captain George Shuburg—these being all adjudged by the officers and people here to be offenders of such a nature that from the active part they have taken, it would be dangerous for me to let either of them go."

With the capture of their principal leaders, most of those remaining hostile to the Patriot cause quietly disbanded and returned to their homes; but there still remained a band of the leading aggressors encamped on Reedy river, four miles within the Indian Nation at "Great Cane Brake," under the leadership of Colonel Patrick Cunningham. It was reported to Colonel Richardson that young Pearis, son of Captain Pearis, and a member of Cunningham's band, had gone to the Indian towns in an effort to secure re-inforcements, so he concluded that "this last hot-bed of Toryism in the district" should be broken up before the recently disbanded Tories thereabouts should have an opportunity to reorganize. He therefore moved his forces up to Hollingsworth's mill, about 25 miles south of "Great Cane Brake", and ordered Colonel Thomson to march against the enemy. Colonel Thomson called for volunteers to join him in this undertaking, which promised to furnish the first real fighting of the entire campaign. Colonels Polk and Lyles and Major Williamson offered their services, and these officers, with 1,300 men composing both infantry and cavalry companies, were chosen.

The detachment under Colonel Thomson set out from Hollingsworth's mill during the early evening of December 21st, and after marching all night came upon the camp of the enemy near daylight of December 22nd. The Tories were taken completely by surprise, as the force of Colonel Thomson had succeeded in almost surrounding their camp before being detected. Seeing that resistance would be useless, they took to flight in a most precipitate manner, abandoning baggage, arms, and ammunition as they fled. Five or six of the Tories were killed, and 125 or 130 captured. Colonel Cunningham escaped, it is said, by mounting the first available horse and riding away bare-back during the confusion. None of Thomson's men were killed, and only one was wounded, this being a young son of Colonel Polk, who was shot through the shoulder. Among those of the Tories captured was the son of Captain Richard Pearis, who a few days before had been reported as being among the Indians seeking aid. However, if he had been to the Indian towns on such a mission he probably did not meet with success, for no Indians were among those captured.

The campaign of Colonel Richardson, known to history as the Snow Campaign on account of a heavy fall of snow which began in the up-country on December 25th and contined for several days, was brought to a successful conclusion with the battle of "Great Cane Brake." And on January 2nd, 1776, after he had returned to his base at the Congarees, Colonel Richardson wrote the Council of Public Safety: "The people are now more convinced than ever of their being wrong. The lenient measures have had a good effect, the spirit and power is gone from them. And I am sure (if not interrupted by designing men) that the country which I had the power to lay waste (and which the people expected) will be happy, and peace and tranquility take the place of ruin and discord. On the rivers, had I burnt, plundered, and destroyed, ten thousand women and children must have been left to perish, a thought shocking to humanity."

The historians disagree as to the location of this concluding battle of the Snow Campaign. Some place it far down Reedy river near the point where it empties into the Saluda, while McCrady shows it on his Revolutionary map as being only three or four miles below the present city of Greenville. But Dr. H. T. Cook, in his *Rambles in the Pee Dee Basin,* places it about 16 miles southeast of Greenville City. A careful consideration of the known facts, gathered from various sources, leads to the conclusion that Dr. Cook is correct, and that the battle of "Great Cane Brake" was fought on what is now Greenville County soil. The early accounts locate it on Reedy river, four miles within the Indian country, and it is known that the Indian boundary line crossed Reedy river near Fork Shoals. At page 1, in Location book "A" in the office of the R.M.C. for Greenville County, appears the record of a grant to General Richard Winn of a tract of land on Reedy river, containing 640 acres and known as "the Great Cane Brake." General Winn acquired the lands in 1784, and he conveyed them to James Harrison by a deed which refers to the plantation as "Great Cane Brake." It will be noted that these descriptions are specific and not general; hence the property conveyed and the description given of it in the deeds must have had some signification to the grantors and grantees. At that time, of course, the site of the battle ground was well known. The Winn lands are located on Reedy river about 15 miles south of the city of Greenville, and some four miles north of Fork Shoals, and consist of lands yet belonging to descendants of James Harrison, being at this time a part of the estate of the late S. E. Harrison.

General Richard Winn, who was a man of prominence in South Carolina, took part in the battle of "Great Cane Brake" as a lieutenant. When the war was over and he held high rank in the military life of the state, perhaps it was the knowledge that at "Great Cane Brake" he fought his first battle which impelled him to become the owner of the battle-field. But his attachment for the site of his boyhood prowess could not have been overly strong, for in just two years after becoming its owner, he sold it to James Harrison "for one black horse." Tradition has it in the community where this engagement took place that after the battle, a number of Tories were hanged; and some of the older residents, whose ancestors have lived there for a century and a half, will today point out one of the trees which family tradition says was used as a scaffold.

Note.—Historians are not agreed as to the date of the conflict between Colonel Thomson and the Indians near Keowee. Some put it as late as the summer of 1776, but Colonel Thomson, writing from his camp "Two miles below Keowee" on August 4, 1775, gives an account of the engagement. However, the Cherokees seem not to have taken offence because of this difficulty, as they continued to negotiate with Mr. Drayton. If this be considered a military engagement, it was here, and not at Ninety-Six, that the first blood of the war was shed. (See page 125 of Gibbs' "Documentary History of the American Revolution from 1764 to 1776.")

Chapter VII.

INDIAN MASSACRE OF 1776

After the flare-up of 1775 had subsided, a majority of the frontier settlers were doubtless friendly to the Patriot cause, but their proximity to the Indian country kept them from taking an active part in the war. They knew that Alexander Cameron, deputy superintendent of Indian affairs under the Crown, had taken up his residence among the Cherokees and was exerting every effort to secure the assistance of the Indians in behalf of the British. And they also knew that the success of his plans would bring the Indians down upon them in all the fury of a savage massacre; and should this happen, they desired to be free from military obligations which might call them away from their frontier homes.

During the early summer of 1776, the frontiersmen began to feel that all was not well in the Cherokee country. Rumors to the effect that the Indians had chosen the side of the King and were making preparations for a raid upon the settlements drifted in. And knowing that something must be done at once if the Indians were to be induced to remain neutral, the settlers in present Greenville and Spartanburg Counties thought it well to send emissaries into the towns of the Cherokee country to urge those deluded people to continue the friendship which had existed between them and the whites since the close of the French and Indian war. Among those to go were Captain Edward Hampton and his brother, Preston, who resided a few miles east of the Indian boundary, four or five miles northeast of the present town of Greer. These two young men had often been into the Indian country on trading and hunting expeditions, and had many friends there, so it was thought that they might be able to win back the savages. Another to go into the Cherokee country was a son of Colonel Hite, who lived within present Greenville County near where the Old Spartanburg road crosses Enoree river. By some chroniclers, this young gentleman is referred to as Jacob O'Bannon Hite, but he could not have been Jacob O'Bannon, as will be shown later. But regardless of name, this noble Patriot was a young man of character and culture. At the time, he was a student of the law, about to apply for admission to the bar in Charles Town. It is also said that he was engaged to be married to a daughter of Richard Pearis.

When the two Hampton brothers arrived among the Cherokees, they found that they were too late. Cameron and other British sympathizers had thoroughly poisoned the minds of the red men against their former friends, and now they were in an ugly mood. Everywhere the war dance was in progress and hurried preparations were being made for a raid upon the frontiers. The Hamptons were made prisoners and their horses, guns, and other supplies seized; but by some means (possibly with the assistance of friendly Indians) they made their escape, and hurrying back to their homes on foot, reporting their sad experiences to the people there. Young Hite, traveling into the Cherokee country a few days later than did the Hampton brothers, met a large band of warriors headed toward the white settlements. By these he was killed and scalped, thus becoming the first victim of the most bloody massacre ever suffered by the Carolinians at the hands of the Cherokees. The place of his death was on the Estotoe river in present Pickens County, in a narrow pass between two mountains. After killing the young man, the Indians proceeded to the residence of Richard Pearis, where the daughter of Pearis, recognizing "the raven locks of her lover" in the bloody scalp displayed by the savages, knew only too well what were their intentions. In an effort to save the family of her lover from the sad fate which had already befallen him, she set out on foot to warn the Hite family of its impending danger. But whether this dusky maid of the forests reached her destination and had her warning disregarded, or was overtaken by the Indians and brought back before she had delivered her message, is unknown. At any rate, the Hite family was visited by the Indians and paid a fearful toll.

When information reached the frontier that the Indians had taken up the tomahawk, there was great alarm among those adhering to the Patriot cause. Quickly they set about strengthening the crude forts and block houses which had been constructed along the Indian boundary during the troublous days of the French and Indian war, and into these rough fortifications many of them fled, taking as much as possible of their portable property with them. Still there were others who remained at their homes—some because no fort was within reach, and others because they thought the Indians would pass them by on account of past friendships. But it was only among those who had espoused the cause of the province that a feeling of impending danger existed, for secret messengers had previously advised the Tories that they would be safe from attack, if their loyalty to the King were shown by the erection of peeled poles, wrapped around with white cloth, before their homes. This emblem, or badge of loyalty to the King, was referred to as "the passover" and was to be a sign to the Indians to leave that household undisturbed. Sad to relate, many were the passovers erected among the frontiersmen.

Since the commencement of the war, Cameron and his Tory friends had neglected no opportunity to poison the minds of the Indians against the Whigs, and in July, 1776, the savages marched to the attack. After killing young Hite, they proceeded to the Pearis plantation where they were joined by a number of Tories. Then they moved on to the home of the sorely distressed Hite family, where Colonel Hite and a number of his children were killed, and his wife taken captive. From here a number of the savages moved southward, into what is now Laurens County, killing Miss Austin of the Gilder creek section on their way; but the major portion of the red invaders turned toward the north and into the territory which is now Spartanburg County. The Indians going toward the south probably joined a larger body which had gone out from the Indian towns down through present Anderson, Abbeville, and Greenwood Counties. Having effected a union, these Indians joined forces with a body of Tories which was moving to the attack of Lindley's fort, located near the mouth of Rabun creek in the present county of Laurens. Here a large number of the residents of that section had taken refuge, hoping the better to defend themselves against the enemy. Upon reaching the fort, however, the savages and their Tory allies, painted as Indians, were repulsed, since a portion of the regiment of Colonel Williams had moved there and was awaiting their coming.

PART I — NARRATIVE

The body of Indians turning northward from the Hite home next visited the Hampton plantation. Here Mr. Hampton, his wife, his son, Preston, who had recently returned from his mission to the Cherokee country, and a grandson (infant child of James Harrison), were killed and their home burned. Another grandson, John Bynum, was captured and carried away into the Indian country, where he was held prisoner for several months. The Hampton family here suffering so heavily at the hands of the savages, was the same which produced the immortal Wade. His grandfather, also named Wade, was at the time with the army of North Carolina. James Harrison, father of the slain child, later moved to the "Great Cane Brake" in Greenville County and became the head of that large and illustrious family, living today throughout all the upper counties of the state. In later years, B. F. Perry of Greenville was to engage in a duel with a descendant of the captured grandson, John Bynum.

Now the savages, having taken up the tomahawk in earnest, were not to be stayed in their bloody course. Wherever the whites could be found they were murdered in cold blood, the "passover" itself being small protection. Captain Ford, a well-known Tory, was killed as he sat in his yard under the peeled pole which he had raised for the protection of himself and family, and two of his daughters were taken captive. Among others killed were Mr. John Miller and a Mr. Orr. These two, together with a Mr. Leach, were returning from Poole's Iron Works (near the present city of Spartanburg) to their homes in the Gowensville section of today, when, as they crossed a crude bridge over Middle Tyger river, several Indians sprang from their place of hiding under the bridge and struck them down. Mr. Leach escaped with his life by feigning death. The Hannon family, residing near the present town of Landrum, was visited, and Mr. Hannon, several of his older children, and a baby were killed. Another victim was a Mr. Bishop then residing near present Shiloh church in Spartanburg County. He was killed and three of his children carried away. Later these children were recovered by a brother-in-law, Mr. Davy Lewis, ancestor of the Wingo families of the Gowensville section of Greenville County. In fact, so many were the atrocities committed and so savage was the Indian in his attack as he swept from one to another of the frontier settlements, that abject terror seized the inhabitants. Those who had not been killed or captured fled the country or found protection in the border forts, leaving their homes to be plundered and burned, and their growing crops destroyed.

And while matters were in this sad state, a Captain Howard, who resided within the Indian country, a few miles northwest of the present Gowensville settlement, was able to organize a small company of men from among the number, who like himself, had taken refuge in the old Block House. This old fort is still standing, having been converted into a residence, and may be seen in traveling north from Landrum to Tryon along the old road connecting these two towns. It is said that the Greenville-Spartanburg County line, as well as the North Carolina-South Carolina line, pass through it. Among those taking part in this expedition was Captain (later Colonel) John Earle, the illustrious ancestor of so many present-day Greenville County citizens. Equipping themselves as best they could from the meager resources at hand, this little band of resolute men, led by a sturdy mountaineer whose descendants still reside in upper Greenville County in great numbers, marched out from the Block House against the Indians then encamped in a mountain gap four or five miles away in North Carolina, under Chief Big Warrior. In their march, they were guided by a friendly Indian, Schuyuka, who led them through a hitherto unknown gap, which enabled them to approach the enemy from the rear. Big Warrior and his men had noticed the activity of the whites and were expecting an attack, but they thought it would come directly up the pass in which they were located—hence the assault from the rear took them completely by surprise.

Captain Howard and his men attacked the Indians fiercely, killing and wounding many of them, but they were greatly outnumbered, and might have been defeated except for the suddenness of the onslaught and the rapidity of their withdrawal. The Indians, however, were in no mood to withstand an organized attack after their orgy of bloodshed and pillage. They had brought their women and children with them and knew that their march back must be slow; and the spirit shown by Captain Howard and his men did not bode well for them, should any great number of Whigs assemble before they were safely on their way home. So they buried their dead there on the mountain side and began a hasty march back toward Pearis' plantation, where they no doubt expected to receive ammunition and Tory reinforcements. This skirmish, unknown to history, but well authenticated in tradition as "the Battle of Round Mountain", gave the frontier settlers their first respite from the most savage Indian massacre they had ever experienced.

The Battle of Round Mountain was fought a short distance east of the present town of Tryon, North Carolina. One of the mountain peaks guarding the pass in which the Indians were encamped is known as "Big Warrior" in honor of their chief. The pass through which Schuyuka led the Patriot soldiers is now "Howard's Gap", named for the brave Captain Howard. The present Spartanburg-Hendersonville highway leads through this gap, and for many years has been known as the Howard Gap road. Tradition says the friendly Indian was later captured by his red brothers and made to suffer a horrible death. It was sought by many to name the county seat of Polk County, North Carolina, Schuyuka, in his honor, but for some reason this was not done. Yet today, beautiful Schuyuka mountain stretches along the border of North Carolina, looking down upon the scene of battle.

At this time Colonel Andrew Williamson was in command of all organized Patriot forces between the Saluda and Broad, and when it became known to him that the Indians were raiding the frontiers, he ordered Colonel Thomas to move against them. However, there was some delay in getting the troops in motion, probably occasioned by the action of the Charles Town authorities in releasing certain up-country prisoners. After the British attack on Charles Town during the latter part of June had been repulsed, the Government thought that generosity on its part would have a good effect, so Richard Pearis, Robert Cunningham and "the rest of the back country prisoners who were in confinement" were released. But the troops of Colonel Williamson were greatly incensed at this action and for several days could not be prevailed upon to enter the conflict. However, as the savages were beginning to retreat after the Battle of Round Mountain, Colonel Thomas appeared with a small force and gave chase. The Indians moved from the North Carolina border across the northwestern portion of Spartanburg County toward the plantation of Richard Pearis. They were overtaken near Paris mountain by a small detachment from Colonel Thomas' force, and a skirmish took place. The Indians continued their retreat, but being hard pressed, killed a number of their prisoners, who were hampering their progress. Among these was Mrs. Hite. But other prisoners were either released or permitted to escape. Of this number were the two daughters of Captain Ford, the Tory who had been killed during the raid.

When the Pearis plantation was reached, the Indians did not find the expected reinforcements, and continued their retreat. But for several days prior thereto, the Pearis home had been closely watched by spies sent out by Colonel Williamson, and these emissaries having reported unusual activity about the place, Colonel Williamson concluded that Pearis was up to his old tricks again and sent couriers to Thomas, ordering him to give the Pearis home a call as he passed it. So on July 16th Colonel Thomas took possession of the property of Richard Pearis, burned his home, mill, and trading station, confiscated all his cattle and horses for the use of his army, and carried away his wife, two daughters and one son. Captain Pearis was away at the time and thereby saved himself a second imprisonment. It is said that the family of Pearis was subjected to much abuse and punishment by their captors. According to some accounts, they were marched on foot 25 miles a day with little food and no covering for their heads against the heat of a summer sun, and were then confined for three days with practically no food, and afterwards sent off in an open wagon to a point near Augusta, 100 miles away, where they were left among strangers to shift for themselves, without money or provisions.

After a few days' delay, awaiting reinforcements and supplies, Colonel Thomas set out for the Cherokee country with a fixed determination to revenge the bloody desolation which the savages had left behind them. Among his troops were many of the frontiersmen who had suffered sorely at the hands of the Indian, and who were in a mood to fight as they had never done before. Everywhere the Indians fled before them, leaving their homes and growing crops to be destroyed. By August 13th, the destruction of all the lower settlements was complete. The Patriot army was now reinforced, and on September 13th a force of 2,000 men started its march over the mountains toward the middle settlement towns, which were reached on September 23rd. Here, as in the lower settlements, the destruction was soon complete, and early in October, the army, having fully performed its mission, was disbanded.

The successful termination of the Cherokee war of 1776 ended forever the danger of Indian massacres in the Carolina up-country. For perhaps 100 years, white men had resided there, but not until after 1755 had there existed any ill feeling between the two races. Although the Cherokees were a strong and warlike people, who dealt ruthlessly with their red neighbors, Carolina had always had in them friends of great value both in war and peace. But with the treaty of Governor Glen in 1755, by which the Indians were swindled out of the major portion of their lands in South Carolina, were sown the seeds of discord, which grew into open conflict under the blundering actions of Governor Lyttleton in 1759. And thereafter there was never the same trusting friendliness between the two peoples. The

Indians felt that the Carolinians had defrauded them of their lands, and then without cause made war upon them to gain an acknowledgment that the lands had been voluntarily ceded. By the treaty of 1763, outward peace was restored, but always there rankled in the savage breast the thought that his honor had been outraged; and seeing that the Indians were forever restive, the frontiersmen lived in daily fear of an outbreak. And in the midst of bitter civil conflict, when brother fought against brother, there came the bloody denouement in which these sturdy pioneers repaid a hundred fold for the wrongs which had been inflicted upon the Cherokees by a government in which they had never been given a voice. But having fully paid, they were now free.

CHAPTER VIII.

THE YEARS OF BANDITRY

Following the defeat of the Cherokees in 1776, that people and the Carolinians entered into a treaty of peace, which was formally signed on May 20, 1777. By the terms of this treaty all the remaining Indian lands in South Carolina, except a small portion of what is now the northwestern part of Oconee County, were ceded to South Carolina. The preamble to this interesting and valuable document, taken from the original itself, which is on file in the office of the Historical Commission at Columbia, reads:

"The King of Great Britain in the prosecution of his unjust design to enslave America, regardless of the means, through his ministers, officers and superintendents, by false representations has deceived the Cherokee Nation and persuaded them to massacre indiscriminately, according to their custom in war, the men, women and children inhabitants on the Western frontier of South Carolina and other states at the time last summer when his forces invaded that state from the sea, and then having abandoned his Cherokee allies whom he had deceived, urged and persuaded into the war to just resentment of the people, thus at the same time unexpectedly attacked on the sea coast and opposite frontier. It has pleased the Master of Breath so to direct the progress of the war and the (word illegible) of the contracting parties, that at the conclusion of last summer they were disposed to extend mercy and do justice, and the Cherokee Nation having during the course of last winter, sent Deputies to Charles Town to implore pardon and thereupon it being determined to bury the hatchet and re-establish peace, the contracting parties", etc.

This instrument was signed at Due West, then called Devits, or DeWitts Corner, which was then the site of a well-known trading post, located on the south line of the Indian boundary where crossed by the Cherokee path leading to fort Charlotte.

For a number of years after the Cherokee peace, South Carolina was too busy prosecuting the war against her British and Tory enemies to take any action toward opening up the new acquisition for settlement. A few families took up residence there, but this was without warrant of law, and upon conclusion of the Revolution they were dispossessed. From 1777 till 1784, when legislative action to open up the new acquisition for settlers was taken, it was recognized as being a portion of the Ninety-Six District, and that political subdivision exercised a theoretical jurisdiction over it. Actually, however, there was no law here, but "the law of might." Roving thieves and cut-throats made it their favorite haunt, from which they sallied forth at pleasure to rob and plunder, under the guise of either Whig or Tory, as the occasion warranted.

With the seizing of his property by Colonel Thomas, Richard Pearis never again was a resident of Greenville County. Whatever might have been his intentions when he was set at liberty following the British failure at Charles Town, the treatment accorded his family made him an active supporter of the King's cause for the remainder of the war. In company with David Fanning and other Tories, he secretly raised a troop of 400 men, recruited largely from the old Cherokee country and its adjoining frontiers, but before he could join the British in Florida, as he had intended, his plans became known and he fled on foot to the west coast of Florida. From that time till the fall of Charles Town in 1780, Pearis was extremely active in behalf of the British, but remained away from his old home, and for the most of the time outside the boundaries of South Carolina. The year 1778 found him captain of the Light Horse Troop in Colonel Stuart's Corps of West Florida Loyal Refugees. For several months thereafter he operated about the mouth of the Mississippi and around Mobile, capturing Maushac on the Mississippi during the time. Later he helped reinforce St. Augustine against Howe's expedition, and was with Prevost in his invasion of Georgia. When Savannah was besieged by French and Americans, Pearis was among those defending it. He was also present at the siege and capture of Charles Town.

With the fall of Charles Town, the entire province of South Carolina was overrun by the British and their Tory allies. Sir Henry Clinton offered favorable terms of surrender and many of the leading Whigs, thinking that further resistance was useless, accepted them and laid down their arms. At this juncture, Pearis returned to the up-country with a commission as lieutenant colonel of South Carolina Provincials, with authority to go into the Ninety-Six District "to raise and embody the friends of Great Britain, disarm all rebels between the Savannah and Broad rivers, and destroy their forts." During this period, General Andrew Pickens, then in command of the Patriot troops of the entire up-country, surrendered to Pearis. With this undertaking completed, however, Richard Pearis, the first white man of historical note to reside for any length of time in present-day Greenville County, quitted the South Carolina frontiers forever. He joined his family, then residing at Augusta, where he remained till his capture in the fall of that place before the onslaught of General Pickens, near the close of the war. When taken, Pearis was set upon by a number of enraged Whigs from his old back-country home, who would no doubt have killed him except for the timely intervention of General Pickens himself. With the close of the war, Pearis, with his family, moved to Abaca in the Bahamas, where, it is said, he died in the year 1804 in great poverty. One of his daughters married a son of Colonel Robert Cunningham.

While Pearis was in the up-country "disarming all rebels" Colonel Clarke of Georgia, who had been operating extensively in the piedmont section of the two Carolinas in the cause of Liberty, decided to return home and disband his army. But after reaching Georgia, Colonel Jones, who held joint command with Colonel Clarke, opposed withdrawing from the conflict and proposed that if the men would follow him he would lead them through the mountains of upper South Carolina and into North Carolina where the Patriots were rallying. Thirty-five men volunteered to go with him, and this little band set out through the woods toward their destination, gathering recruits wherever they could be found. Their journey led them across the upper part of what is now Greenville County, and as they were emerging from the mountains to the northwest of present Gowensville, they learned that a body of Tories were encamped a few miles away. Pretending to be friends of Britain, they secured the services of a Tory to lead them to the enemy. Arriving there about

11 o'clock in the night, they opened fire upon the unsuspecting Tories and after killing one and wounding three they accepted the willing surrender of all those who had not been able to break through the lines and escape. This conflict is thought to have taken place at Gowen's fort, located a mile or two northeast of Gowensville.

During the months of suspense and bitter travail following the fall of Charles Town, and preceding the Battle of Kings Mountain, which is recognized as the turning point of the Revolution, the Whigs of upper Carolina were continually harassed by those two arch fiends, "Bloody Bill" Cunningham and "Bloody Bill" Bates. Cunningham was a resident of what is now Greenwood County, and Bates lived in the upper part of present Greenville County. Among the frontiersmen Bates was referred to as "the Plundering Scout" because of his thieving proclivities, while Cunningham was known as "the Bloody Scout" on account of his brutal murders. But Bates did not hesitate to kill when that would assist in his robberies, nor did Cunningham leave anything of value behind him. Both, soon after their activities began, acquired the name of "Bloody Bill."

At the outbreak of the war, William L. Cunningham, unlike his cousins, Robert and Patrick, chose the Patriot cause. He enlisted in Captain John Caldwell's company, which was composed of the most respectable young men of the upper country. But after taking part in numerous engagements, including the expedition against the Cherokees in 1776, he became offended for causes now unknown, left his company, then stationed on James's or John's Island, and returned home to become one of the most despised Tories known to South Carolina. Often during these latter years many of his atrocities are attributed to either Robert or Patrick, but to do so is to vilely defame the characters of these men, who, although opposing the province in the war, were sincere in their convictions and honorable in their conduct.

After "breaking" with the Whigs, Cunningham gathered to his side a small band of marauding cut-throats, who swept through the back country of South Carolina, leaving death and destruction in their wake. The present county of Spartanburg was visited, where it is thought he was joined by "the Plundering Scout" (Bates) with his band of outlaws from the Glassy and Hogback mountains. In the Nazareth Church section Captain Steadman, who lay sick at the home of Charles Moore, two young men stopping at the Moore home, and young John Caldwell were killed. On Lawson's Fork, Colonel John Wood and his brother James were dispatched in cold blood. Colonel Edward Hampton, who it will be recalled, had gone to the Cherokee nation as a good-will emissary in 1776, while passing through the section on his way to the home of his father-in-law, Baylis Earle, was called from his bed at the home of a friend and shot down. Another victim of the bloody pair was Major John Caldwell, the old commander of Cunningham, who was slain in his own yard while standing unarmed by the side of his wife. William Anderson, ancestor of Dr. J. L. Anderson of Greenville City, was another killed.

The widow of Colonel John Wood, killed by Cunningham, later married Colonel John Earle, whose descendants by his first wife reside in Greenville County in great numbers, and became the ancestress of the Prince and Bomar families so widely known in Spartanburg County. Colonel Edward Hampton was a son of Anthony Hampton, killed by the Indians in 1776 at his home near Greer, and brother of

General Wade Hampton, who was the great grandfather of Governor Wade Hampton. Major John Caldwell was an uncle of John C. Calhoun. Of James Wood, killed along with his brother John, Landrum says: "Some fifty years after the burial of James Wood, his nephew, Dr. John Young of Spartanburg, caused his remains to be disinterred and carried to Greenville, South Carolina, for burial."

On one occasion Bates led a party of his followers against Wood's fort, located in what is now Greenville County, between Greer and Gowensville, where a number of the settlers of that section had gathered. Being poorly armed and ill supplied with ammunition, the occupants of the fort soon concluded that they could not successfully withstand the opposing forces, and opened negotiations for a surrender. Bates readily promised them protection, but no sooner had they marched out of the fort then they were set upon and brutally massacred. None escaped except Mrs. Thompson, wife of Abner Thompson, who, although seriously wounded and scalped, recovered and lived in Greenville County for more than fifty years after her harrowing experience.

After the fall of Wood's fort, Major Buck Gowen, from whom Gowensville derives its name, gathered a small force and gave chase to Bates as he fled back to his mountain stronghold. Beyond the head waters of the Tyger, supposedly in what is now Greenville County, he was overtaken and suffered the loss of practically all of his followers, but Bates himself escaped. After this defeat, however, he seems not to have been able to raise sufficient men to seriously molest the settlements.

During the activities of Bates he killed old Mr. Motley on Motlow's creek in Spartanburg County. At the same time he captured a son of Mr. Motley, but the young man succeeded in making his escape. After the war Bates was arrested for horse-stealing and confined in the Greenville jail to await trial. Young Motley, then living in upper Greenville County, learning that the murderer of his father was within his reach, gathered a few of his friends and led them to the Greenville jail where they seized Bates and with little ceremony shot him to death. His burial place is thought to be upon the lot where is now located the Post Office Building.

With the Whig successes at Kings Mountain and Cowpens, the up-country people took new heart. After all, there still might be a chance to win out in the struggle. And with the coming of new hope, a determined effort to drive out Cunningham and Bates was put forth, with the result that Cunningham was soon forced into the British lines about Charles Town, and Bates was driven into the deep recesses of the mountains. At last the Carolina frontiers were able to breathe freely; and with the coming of this feeling of semi-security, the inhabitants threw themselves wholeheartedly into the conflict, and the whole of South Carolina was soon free of enemy forces.

Note.—In this chapter, as well as all those preceding it, the principal city of the province has been referred to as "Charles Town", but hereafter the name "Charleston" will be used. Till about 1719 it was always "Charles Town", but from then till 1783 or 1784 it was officially "Charlestown", but still more often called by the older name. After the Revolution it became Charleston, and has so remained ever since.

CHAPTER IX.

FORMATION OF THE COUNTY AND EARLY LAND OWNERS

WITH the successful termination of the Revolution in 1783, immediate steps were taken to incorporate the "Cherokee acquisition of 1777" into the new State of South Carolina. For the time being it was all placed under the jurisdiction of Ninety-Six District; but realizing that the districts of the state were much too large to give a stable government, the General Assembly on March 16, 1783, passed: *"An Ordinance for Appointing Commissioners in Each of the Circuit Court Districts, for Dividing the Same into Counties.* On March 12, 1785, the General Assembly ratified an Act which directed the laying off of "Six counties for the district now called Ninety-Six". While on March 22, 1786, was enacted the law establishing Greenville County proper. It reads:

An Ordinance for Establishing a County and County Courts in the New Ceded Lands on the North Side of Saluda River:

WHEREAS, the inhabitants of the new ceded lands on the north side of Saluda river below the Indian line, have experienced many inconveniences by being annexed to some of the counties heretofore established;

BE IT ORDAINED by the Honorable, the Senate and House of Representatives, now met and sitting in General Assembly, and by the authority of the same, That a county shall be established in the new ceded lands, by the name of Greenville, and shall be bounded by Saluda river and the South fork thereof, the old Indian boundary, and the North Carolina line, and shall be entitled to County Courts, to be held on the third Monday in February, May, August and November; which courts shall hold, exercise and enjoy the several powers and jurisdictions which are by law vested in the said county courts heretofore established.

South Carolina had no money with which to pay her soldiers during the Revolution, and promised many of them payment in slaves, which were to be confiscated from the Tories. But upon the conclusion of the war, the redemption of these pledges, in this manner, was found to be impracticable, and in lieu thereof, lands in the new acquisition were offered at ten dollars per hundred acres, payable in debts due from the state. On May 21, 1784, what became Greenville County by act of the General Assembly in 1786 was officially opened for settlers, with a Land Office at Pendleton in charge of Colonel John Thomas as Commissioner of Location, and within two years practically all of the desirable lands in the county had been taken up, largely by Revolutionary heroes.

The first tract of land "set off" in Greenville County was unto James Hamilton, a record of which may be found in Location book "A" at page 5, in the office of the Register of Mesne Conveyance for Greenville County. A description of these lands is as follows: "A tract of land containing 640 acres, situate, lying and being above the Old Indian Boundary on Reedy river and known by the name of Pearis' Shoals." Attached to the record of this "Location" is an interesting statement which reads,

"the survey being made between the hours of nine and twelve o'clock in the forenoon after opening the Location Office and previous to any other survey made thereon." This first location in Greenville, except for the fact that on the same day a tract of 640 acres was surveyed off to Colonel Thomas Brandon which is clearly traceable to the present "Textile Center of the South", might be thought to include the present city of Greenville. Why should James Hamilton have had first choice of all lands in Greenville County, and just what acreage did he select? These questions start a train of interesting thoughts, but the public records do not show any disposition of these lands and they cannot therefore be traced down to their present owners.

On the day Greenville County was opened for settlement (May 21, 1784) Colonel Thomas Brandon of Union County became the owner of the site of Greenville City; his acquisition consisted of "four hundred acres on both sides of Reedy river of Saluda, including Richard Pearis' plantation." Colonel Brandon was an active supporter of the Patriot cause during the Revolution, taking part in many of the up-country battles. He was a resident of Union County, and so far as is known, never lived in Greenville County. In 1788 he sold his Greenville lands to Lemuel J. Alston.

Another man of unusual prominence in the Revolution to acquire lands in Greenville County was General Richard Winn, who obtained "640 acres on Reedy river and known by the name of the 'Great Cane Brake'." At the conclusion of the war, Richard Winn was a colonel, but the General Assembly, recognizing his great services for the cause of his state, bestowed upon him the title of Brigadier-General. He resided in Fairfield County and filled a number of civil offices in the state, and was a member of Congress for several terms. In 1786 he sold his Greenville County land to James Harrison for "one black horse", never having resided here.

Henry Pendleton, a noted jurist of the state, and for whom Pendleton District was named, on May 21, 1784, acquired "640 acres on the Golden Grove and known by the name of Cameron's Cowpens." Judge O'Neall, in his *Bench and Bar,* says that Judge Pendleton resided in Greenville County "on or near Golden Grove creek", while Dr. H. T. Cook in his *Rambles in the Pee Dee Basin,* makes the statement that he died here. But the court records in Charleston show that Judge Henry Pendleton died there in 1788, where his estate was later administered. It is likely that the Judge owned a summer home in Greenville County, and resided here during a portion of each year as did so many of the Charleston people during that period.

Another Jurist of note to own lands in Greenville County was Aedanus Burke, who on May 25, 1784, acquired "640 acres on a small branch of Golden Grove creek, waters of Saluda river, bounded by lands laid out to Henry Pendleton, William Wood and others." Judge Burke was an Irishman, educated at St. Omer's for a priest, but he came to America at the outbreak of the Revolution from the West Indies, where he had previously gone, and volunteered to fight for liberty. During the war he attained the rank of major, but it was as a lawyer and judge that he became prominent in the affairs of South Carolina. Judge Burke, however, was not content to administer the laws, but would also have a hand in framing them. Prior to 1790 he was several times a member of Congress while still retaining the office of Judge. He could not be persuaded to forego this multiple office-holding, and in 1789 a law was enacted which prohibited a judge, on pain of the forfeiture of his office, from leaving the state without the consent of the governor. At one time Judge Burke acted as second for Aaron Burr in a duel. Judge Burke bitterly opposed the Society of the Cincinnati, an organization of Revolutionary soldiers, which for a time threatened to destroy a republican form of government in America, and furnished the material for the celebrated pamphlet prepared by Mirabeau, the Frenchman, in collaboration with Franklin, attacking that Society. He opposed the ratification of the Federal Constitution; nevertheless he was elected the first United States Senator from South Carolina. So far as is known, he never resided in Greenville County.

James Harrison acquired "600 acres on both sides of Reedy river of Saluda about two miles above the old Indian boundary" on June 15, 1784. It was he whose child was murdered by the Indians at the time of the "Hampton massacre." He had married a daughter of Anthony Hampton, sister of the elder General Wade, and with his brothers-in-law took a very prominent part in the Revolution. It is said that a child was born to his wife while the family traveled in a covered wagon from the old home in Spartanburg County to this new one on Reedy river. This land adjoined the "Great Cane Brake" which he purchased from General Winn in 1786.

On May 25, 1784, Isaac Morgan received a grant for "a tract of land containing 640 acres situate, lying, and being above the old Indian boundary on Enoree river and known by the name of Hite's old vacant land on every side." And on the same day Henry Benson had set off to him "a tract of land containing 640 acres situate and being above the old Indian boundary on both sides of Enoree river and known by the name of Hite's Canebrake." Attached to the Morgan record is a plat of the land showing a road extending across it from east to west. The road crosses Enoree river and its eastern end carries the notation, "to the settlement", while on the western portion of the road appear the words, "To Parris's." These conveyances cover the plantation where Colonel Hite resided before the Revolution and up to 1776, when he was killed by the Indians.

John Conner obtained title to 400 acres on Shoaly creek, a branch of Pacolet river "including John Armstrong's improvements and Boiling Springs Meeting House." Of interest here is the fact that "a meeting house" was upon the land when granted. This is evidence that there were many people living in the territory of Greenville County long before it was officially opened for settlement. Further proof is found in the fact that this, and many other grants convey lands "including improvements."

Controversy has arisen among those seeking to establish the location of the old forts along the old Indian boundary as to whether Wood's fort was east or west of this line. Some claim it was to the east and therefore in Spartanburg County, while others locate it in Greenville County. A few even deny that there was a fort of that name. But reference to the record of a grant unto Elisha Thompson shows that he acquired "100 acres on both sides of the Indian boundary on a branch of Tyger river, including 'Wood's Old Fort'." The plat accompanying the record shows the fort to be in Greenville County. One often finds reference to a "Thompson's fort", but this is no doubt "Wood's fort", which after its acquisition by Thompson was so called.

Among those receiving early grants from the state were George Hite and Jacob O'Bannon Hite, who together acquired 3,000 acres located on Grove creek. To no other persons was so large an acreage conveyed; and the liberality of the state to these two was no doubt occasioned by the grievous losses which they had sustained in the death of their father, mother, brother and sisters at the hands of the savages. And it was probably in this manner, too, that they were compensated for the lands occupied by their father on Enoree river. In 1799 all of these lands were sold to Alexander Pitt Buchanan. The grantors at that time resided in Berkley County, Virginia. Tradition has it that all of the Hite family, remaining after the Indian massacre, returned to their home in Virginia. Very likely this is true.

To James Bradley went "a tract of land on the Bounty of the State, containing 200 acres on Golden Grove, a branch of Saluda river." Doctor William Smith Stevens was granted "a tract of land on the Bounty of the State, containing 300 acres on Saluda river." Another tract of land "on the Bounty of the State" went to Thomas Prince, Gentleman, being mentioned as "200 acres of land allowed by law to a Lieutenant in the independent service of the Palmetto State, on waters of Enoree river." A grant of "500 acres on Reedy river about two miles above Rich'd Paris's old place on said river" goes to Baylis Earle. Incorporated in the instrument of conveyance is a recital reading, "Pursuant to a warrant from John Thomas, Esq., Commissioner of Location, and agreeable to a Resolution and Ordinance which passed both Branches of the Legislature of this State." All of the plats attached to the Location Certificates for these lands are marked "Bounty Lands."

Among others receiving grants of land in Greenville County during the year 1784, were John Earle, John Winn, Sr., John Milling, Joseph Hughs, Henry Woolf, Thomas Farrow, William Giles, William Goodlet, Captain William Smith, James McElheney, John Gowin, George Martin, James Winn, John Winn, David Milling, Robert Gilliland, Alexander Johnson, Michal Persal, Alexander McElheney, Thomas Jenkins, John Goodwin, John Clark, Kilpatrick, John Henderson, Joseph Atkinson, Samuel Earle, William Davis, Alexander Ray, Thomas Rowland, Henry Metcher, William Brandon, Joseph Whitner, John Timmons, John Davis, John Langston, Joseph Reynolds, Abraham Case, Ferdin'd Hopkins, Rachel Gaugh, John Lindsey, Joseph McLaughlen, Henry Wells, Robert Goodlett, John McQueen, Uriah Conner, Joseph McJunkin, William Anderson, John Davis and James Jorden.

During this period of rapid growth, Greenville County did not differ greatly from all other "boom" communities in respect to law observance and law enforcement. From the time of its acquisition from the Cherokees in 1777 till 1786, when it was formally organized into a county, the territory now composing Greenville was theoretically under the civil jurisdiction of the Ninety-Six District. But at its best, the up-country had never been given its due in respect to law enforcement and the protection usually afforded by the courts. It will be remembered that for some years prior to the Revolutionary war, the back country settlers had clamored for courts and law enforcement officers so vigorously as to precipitate the conflict between the Regulators and the Scophelites, which terminated in the establishment of courts of inferior jurisdiction in the up-country. One of these was at Ninety-Six, but its lack of power and the general inefficiency of its officials rendered it absolutely unable to cope with conditions which now existed in Greenville County. Feeling between Whigs and Tories was still bitter; grievances from the war were yet to be settled, and often this culminated in personal conflicts. Sneak thieves and highwaymen roved at will about the country-side, preying upon honest citizens. But conditions were alleviated to some extent by the actions of self-chosen and generally recognized leaders (usually ex-army officers) who took unto themselves the authority of meting out justice unto the most flagrant law-breakers. The manner in which this was done is well illustrated by the methods of Colonel Benjamin Cleveland, the Kings Mountain hero, as told by Johnson in his *Traditions*. Says Johnson:

> "This gentleman (Colonel Cleveland) at the termination of hostilities, retired with his family to this frontier settlement in Greenville, and being accompanied by a number of hardy camp associates, established among them a patriarchal government, until the courts of justice could be extended over that part of the State. Colonel Cleveland was, of course, at the head of the government, and executed the duties of his office with much judgment and discretion. On one occasion, when he was absent from home, some of his neighbors brought a horse-thief to his residence for adjudication. They waited awhile for his return, but as the day advanced they began to apprehend that their prisoner might escape, or they have much more trouble with him. Mrs. Cleveland was at home, occupied in her domestic vocations, and at the time smoking her pipe. The men asked her for instructions what they should do with their prisoner. She inquired in turn the particulars of the offense, and of the evidence against him, and on being assured that it was a clear unquestionable case of horse-stealing, she asked what the colonel would order to be done? They as promptly answered he should be hanged'. 'Well then', said the old lady, 'you must hang him', and he was accordingly hung at the gate."

Johnson is incorrect in saying that Colonel Cleveland resided in Greenville and that this act of summary justice transpired there (he lived in present Oconee), but it fairly illustrates the condition of affairs in all the newly settled country till near the end of the century.

Although great numbers of the early settlers of Greenville County were devout Christians, several months seems to have elapsed before any churches were organized in the county. This delay was no doubt occasioned by the unsettled condition of the country. But during the years 1785 and 1786 a number of families from the Nazareth Church section of Spartanburg County moved in and settled a few miles above the Laurens County line. These people were Scotch-Irish, who had come over from County Antrim, Ireland, just before the Revolution, and settled among friends and relatives about Nazareth. Being devout people and having left Ireland principally on account of religious persecutions, these additions to the new county, almost immediately upon their arrival, set about organizing a church; and in 1786, their efforts succeeded in gaining admission into Presbytery for their church—Fairview Presbyterian Church. Of those constituting the membership of this first church organization in Greenville County, much can be learned by reading the account given by Howe in his *History of the Presbyterian Church in South Carolina*. In part he says:

> "Fairview Church is situated in the district of Greenville, on waters of Reedy river, which is a branch of the Saluda. It is two hundred miles from

Charleston, nineteen miles from Greenville court-house, and three miles east from Fork Shoals. It was formed in the year 1786. Five families—those namely, of John Peden, James Alexander, Samuel Peden, David Peden, and James Nesbit—migrated from the bounds of Nazareth and settled in this neighborhood. In that year they formed their first association, and on April 10th, 1787, were taken under the care of presbytery. One of their earliest acts had been to erect a house for divine worship. This year 1787, their numbers were increased by the addition of three other families—those of John Alexander, David Morton and James Alexander, Senior, the father of John and James Alexander, all of Nazareth. . . . The Pedens above named were the offspring of John Peden and Peggy McDill, who emigrated from the county of Antrim, in Ireland, in 1773. They had seven sons and three daughters. These last intermarried, one with an Alexander, another with William Gaston; the third was twice married, first to a Morton, and upon his death, to one of the name of Morrow. . . . In the course of a few years, all their children (that is, John and Peggy Peden) gathered around Fairview Church, where they settled, with the exception of Thomas, who lived and died in the bounds of Nazareth. Their large families composed no small portion of the church and congregation."

No history of Greenville County would be complete without mention being made of Colonel John Thomas and his wife, who were among the early residents. Colonel Thomas was born in Wales, but early in life emigrated to Pennsylvania, where he resided till 1755, when he moved to South Carolina and settled in what is now Chester County. In 1740 he married Miss Jane Black, sister of the Reverend John Black. The outbreak of the Revolution found him in Spartanburg County, residing on Fair Forest creek.

Early in the struggle for Independence, Colonel Thomas resigned his positions as a Militia Captain and Magistrate under the Crown, and alligned himself with the Patriot forces. He was elected colonel of the Spartan regiment, and rendered valiant service till the fall of Charleston, taking a prominent part in the Cherokee campaign of 1776. Soon after the fall of Charleston, he was taken prisoner and remained in confinement at Ninety-Six and Charleston till the close of the war. His son, John Thomas, Jr., succeeded him as colonel of the Spartan regiment.

While Colonel Thomas was confined at Ninety-Six, his wife visited him, and while there overheard one of two women in conversation say: "On tomorrow night the Loyalists intend to surprise the Rebels at Cedar Springs." Cedar Springs was near her home and a number of her children were posted there, so Mrs. Thomas was greatly disturbed by that chance information. It was more than 50 miles to the scene of the proposed attack, and the intervening country, then over-run by Tories, presented many difficulties; but Mrs. Thomas was not to be deterred in the face of obstacles. She set out to warn the Whigs at Cedar Springs, and after undergoing many hardships reached the camp-site in advance of the enemy. Preparations for defense were made, and when the Tories swept down upon the encampment, expecting to find all there asleep, they were met by such spirited opposition as to suffer defeat with heavy losses. An interesting sketch of Mrs. Thomas is carried by Mrs. Ellet in her "Women of the Revolution."

After peace had been restored Colonel Thomas secured a grant of several hundred acres of land in the Locus section of Greenville County, where he moved with his family to remain a valuable and respected citizen till his death in 1805. He was the first person to hold the office of Commissioner of Location with jurisdiction over Greenville County.

Another of the women mentioned by Mrs. Ellet in her great work is Dicey Langston. This brave woman lived in upper Greenville County for a number of years following the Revolution, and now lies buried near Locus. Recently her grave was located by the late Adam C. Welborn, and suitably marked by the Daughters of the American Revolution.

CHAPTER X.

PLEASANTBURG — EARLY TOWN OF GREENVILLE

Several years before the village of Pleasantburg came into existence, and no doubt before there was a single house upon its future location, there existed somewhat of a community about the present Tanglewood school section. There, near the present intersection of the White Horse road and state highway No. 2 (newly paved road to Easley), was the general store of A. McBeth & Company, which is known to have been doing a flourishing business as early as 1794. Near the McBeth establishment lived a number of planters and summer residents who had early selected that vicinity because it commanded such an excellent view of the mountains to the north, and was at the same time considered more healthful than other nearby locations on account of its elevation.

In 1788 Thomas Brandon conveyed the 400 acres granted to him in 1784 unto Lemuel J. Alston, who already resided in the county, and was the owner of much land adjoining and near that purchased from Brandon. It will be recalled that this property included the "Richard Pearis mill site" which was later to become the village of Pleasantburg, now Greenville. Alston was a man of wealth and great political influence, and no doubt for this reason the commissioners who had been appointed to select a site for the location of a court house in Greenville County chose the eastern side of Reedy river near the Pearis mill site. And here started the first "real estate development project" in the county, when in 1797 was laid out the town of Pleasantburg by Alston, upon the lands which he had purchased from Colonel Brandon.

The first plat of Pleasantburg included roughly, all that portion of the present city of Greenville to the east of the river, two city blocks wide, and extending to what is now Washington Street. Through the center of this plot ran a wide street at very nearly the present location of Main Street, with three other streets (present Broad Street, Court Street and McBee Avenue) crossing it at right angles. Lots were cut to the number of 50, with 20 of them facing the principal street. The present Blue Building and Dean Building cover the greater portion of lot No. 1; lot No. 15 is almost entirely taken up by the post office property; the Masonic Temple is on a part of lot No. 12; lot No. 7 is covered by the Poinsett Hotel Building and one or two other structures north of it; the Palmetto Building and Carpenter Bros. drug store are upon lot No. 6; the City Hall stands on number 44; No. 47 supports the seventeen-story Woodside Building. Where the court house and Chamber of Commerce Building now stand were parts of a square made up of the open courts in front of the Blue Building, Palmetto Building, Poinsett Hotel Building and old Law Range, together with the portions of the street now covered by these two buildings. The court house, which was of log construction, was placed in the middle of the square, while the goal (jail), also of logs, was located a block to the south of the court house in the middle of the street near the present intersection of Court and Fall Streets.

The sale of lots in the new village of Pleasantburg was slow. Although the county had filled up rapidly and now had many thousands of inhabitants, there was little demand for "town property." The inhabitants were primarily an agricultural people who "lived at home", therefore there was little business to be had for merchants and artisans, so few had need of lands not suitable for farming.

The first sale in the village seems to have been made on April 22, 1797, when one acre, consisting of lots Nos. 11 and 12, was conveyed to Isaac Wickliff for $100.00. These two lots now comprise the Masonic Temple property, the Donaldson property on which is the row of old wood buildings known formerly as the "Law Range", and the vacant lots on Court Street to the rear of the Masonic Temple and the Donaldson property.

Next comes a sale of "6 lots at Greenville C. H. Village of Pleasantburg, one-half acre each, Nos. 1, 2, 3, 16, 17 and 18", on September 5, 1798, unto John McBeth for $600.00. This conveyance comprises the entire block now bounded by Main Street on the north, Court Street on the east, Fall Street on the south and Broad Street on the west.

During the year 1799 lot No. 36 was conveyed to Thomas Alexander; and lots Nos. 37, 39, 40, 47, 48 and 22 were sold to John W. Wood.

In 1800 Francis Wickliff acquired lots Nos. 14 and 15; John B. Blackman was conveyed lots 13, 5, and 10; and John McBeth became the owner of almost half the block on which now stands the First National Bank Building, by purchase of lots Nos. 33, 34, and 35 for $187.00.

Elias Earle purchased lot No. 6 for $500.00 in 1801.

In 1804 John Taylor became the owner of lot No. 4 for $40.00.

John Archer purchased "lot No. 46 in Greenville village, where my blacksmith shop now stands," in 1807.

The little village was now 10 years old but there seems to have developed no real estate activity, as just half the 50 lots into which it had been divided were sold, and of this number four had been resold by the Sheriff under execution against their owners. Values had not enhanced, and there had been few re-sales except under the "forced" method. Shops were few and of inferior construction, while only four or five residences had been erected in the entire village, and these were of logs. But near the present High School Building, which was then outside the village, stood the beautiful home of Lemuel J. Alston, which was said to be the most elaborate residence in the entire up-country, and leading from it to the village was a wide avenue (now West McBee) lined on either side by trees. Alston was the owner of more than 10,000 acres of land which he very successfully cultivated with slaves. About him and his magnificent home, where well-stocked cellars could always be found, revolved the social life of early Greenville and its surrounding plantations.

A very good picture of the impression made upon a stranger by the village during its babyhood may be had by reading an extract from the diary of Edward Hooker, a native of Connecticut, who paid Greenville a visit in 1806. He says:

"Approaching the village of Greenville, we pass in view of Chancellor Thomson's (Thompson) seat—quite retired in the woods, about two miles from the Court House. Arrived at Col. Alston's about 12. His seat is without exception the most beautiful that I have seen in South Carolina. The mansion is on a commanding eminence which he calls *Prospect Hill*. Fronts the village of Greenville from which it is distant just six hundred yards; and to which there is a spacious and beautiful avenue leading, formed by two rows of handsome sycamore trees planted twenty four feet apart—the avenue being 15 rods wide. In like manner another handsome avenue formed by cutting a passage through the woods leads from the north front of the house to the mountain road, about a quarter of a mile in length. The cultivated grounds lie partly on the borders of the great avenue leading to the village and partly on the borders of Reedy river, south and west of the house. . . . The Court House is a decent two story building. The jail is three stories, large and handsome. The situation and aspect of the village is quite pretty and rural; the streets covered with green grass and handsome trees growing here and there . . . but there is a want of good houses—the buildings being mostly of logs. About six dwelling houses, two or three shops and some other little buildings. The place is thought by many to be as healthy as any part of the United States. Not a seat of much business. The courts sit but twice a year and often finish this session in two or three days. Only one attorney, and law business dull. One or two physicians in or near the village; but their practice is mainly at the Golden Grove, a fertile but unhealthy settlement ten miles below. One Clergyman within six or seven miles who preaches at the Court House once in three or four weeks."

The year 1805 marked the entry of Captain Jeremiah Cleveland into the business life of the little town, where he and his descendants were to play such a prominent part even down to the present time. He then purchased lot No. 36, under execution, from the Sheriff for $50.00, and soon thereafter erected upon it a small shop in which the firm of Erwin, Patton & Cleveland launched itself into the general mercantile business. From this modest beginning Captain Cleveland expanded his businesses till they were to amass him a fortune of several hundred thousand dollars, while Greenville was still a village.

All who know anything at all of the early history of Greenville have heard the name of Vardry McBee, ancestor of so many, who with himself, have contributed greatly to the upbuilding of Greenville, both city and county. In 1815 he purchased the entire holdings of Lemuel J. Alston, consisting of 11,028 acres in and around the village of Greenville. Mr. McBee then resided at Lincolnton, North Carolina, and did not move to Greenville till 1835, but almost immediately after his Greenville purchase he set on foot many enterprises which were soon to give a zest of life to the languishing community. In fact, the advent of Vardry McBee into Greenville marked its real beginning.

From the beginning of permanent settlements in 1784, Greenville County had been recognized as a desirable summer resort, and many residents of Charleston were soon spending a few months of each year here. Some of these purchased plantations, while others became "paying guests" with their friends. But there seems to have been no effort put forward to commercialize the health-giving quality of the climate till 1815, when Edmund Waddell rented the Alston residence from Vardry McBee, and opened it into a hotel, or summer resort. Waddell was of the type who make ideal hosts, and this quality, combined with the excellent accommodations which the Alston mansion afforded, soon filled Greenville with the aristocracy of the coast. To care for the increasing numbers, two or three other hotels, and a number of boarding houses, were opened. Prior to 1824, when the Mansion House was built, Captain David Long operated a resort hotel on the corner of Main and Washington Streets, where Gapens Cigar store is now located, while diagonally across Main Street, where stands the Beattie Building, Blackman Ligon was proprietor of another.

But it was not till the year 1824 that Greenville began in earnest to entertain these summer visitors, who by this time had become one of the principal sources of income for the village. Colonel William Toney, probably the wealthiest citizen of the village, purchased lots Nos. 7 and 8 from Thomas Crayton in 1822 at the unprecedented price of $5,000.00 with the expressed purpose of building thereon a hotel which would "excel any house in the upper part of the state in appearance and accommodation for the traveling public"; and in 1824 the Mansion House was completed. Immediately it became popular and was soon famous, not only for its commodious and artistic design and appointments, and the excellent quality of the food and drink served from its tables, but more especially for the aristocracy and wealth of the guests who frequented it. And for 30 years or more the Mansion House was the axis around which revolved the gay, but cultured, society which thronged the streets of this little piedmont village nestling under the shadow of Paris mountain.

Very little was done toward educating the youth of Greenville for many years after it became a village. In the homes of the more wealthy, private tutors were employed to instill the rudiments, and an occasional young man was sent away to one of the northern colleges, but no effort seems to have been made till 1817 or 1818 to establish anything in the nature of a public school. But so much association with the culture and refinement which poured into the community during the summer turned the thoughts of the villagers to education; and about 1818 a few of the leaders among them undertook to secure, by private subscription, enough money to build two academies, one for the boys and another for the girls. After much difficulty, enough money was in hand to insure the ultimate success of the undertaking, and in 1819 there were established the Greenville Male and Female Academies, which flourished for many years. In 1820 the trustees of the schools acquired a tract of land containing 30 acres "adjoining the village, for the purpose of establishing the Greenville Male and Female Academies." This property included the present grounds of the Greenville Woman's College on College Street. Soon after, securing these lands the erection of suitable buildings was commenced, and in 1821 these were occupied by the academies.

Undoubtedly of interest to many now living in the city of Greenville is the old subscription list on which were recorded the names and amounts of many subscribers. Among the names appearing there are many still familiar to Greenvillians; and should it be necessary to circulate such a subscription list in Greenville today, it would very likely carry many of the names appearing on that of more than a century ago. The list in part is as follows: William Toney, $500.00; Jeremiah

Cleveland, $500.00; Thomas G. Walker, $500.00; Francis H. McLeod, $500.00; A. R. Parkins, $250.00; John H. Harrison, $100.00; A. Carruth, $100.00; Samuel Townes, $150.00; B. J. Earle, $100.00; B. Dunham, $100.00; John Blassingame, $200.00; A. Sloan for the estate of J. Mauldin, $100.00; Thomas Ballonby, $100.00; John McClanahan, $100.00; Richard Thurston, $25.00; Robert A. Maxwell, $50.00; Tandy Walker, $50.00; A. Vickers, $10.00; John H. Joyce, $50.00; Robert D. Moon, $20.00; William Hubbard, $25.00; Street Thurston, $20.00; Zion Goodlett, $10.00; John H. Goodlett, $10.00; Josiah Kilgore, $50.00; David Westfield, $25.00; Philip C. Lester, $10.00; Elijah Pike, $3.00; Richard Harrison, $50.00; John Brown, $20.00; John T. Ligon, $10.00; Peter Cauble, $5.00; Richard Williams, Sr., $100.00; James McDaniel, $100.00; Garland Walker, $30.00; William Young, $100.00; John Stokes, $50.00; Tully Bolling, $100.00; John Gowen, $100.00; Micajah Berry, $50.00; George Seaborn, $50.00; Jeremiah Stokes, $50.00; Levi Stokes, $25.00; George W. Earle, $200.00; Warren R. Davis, $30.00; Thomas B. Williams, $50.00; Bannister Stone, $10.00; William Crynes, $50.00.

The first church of which any record can be found to be established in Greenville was an Episcopal mission, known as St. James Mission. This was in 1821, but no House of Worship was constructed till some years later, the congregation in the meantime holding its meetings in private homes. This organization was brought about "by a few zealous Episcopalians whose families were spending their summers in the upper country". Out of this mission grew present Christ Church. The "Greenville Baptist Church" was organized about the year 1821 with a membership of one male and nine females. From this modest beginning has grown the "First Baptist" which is by far the largest church in Greenville County today. The Greenville Baptist was at first a sort of mission established by the Brushy Creek Church, which was perhaps the oldest Baptist church in the county.

In 1823 the old wood structure used since 1797 as a court house gave way for a brick building, erected on the lot now occupied by the Chamber of Commerce Building. This new court house was designed by Joel R. Poinsett, then living in the present Tanglewood section. He was a man of great refinement and culture, who had traveled extensively in Europe, South America, and Central America, and after returning to his home in Charleston paid Greenville a summer visit and found here "as fine a climate as can be found in the old world." Under President Fillmore, Poinsett was Secretary of War, and at another time he was Minister to Mexico. The beautiful Poinsettia was introduced into this state from Mexico by him. Poinsett Bridge in the Callaham mountain section was designed and built by him. Greenville's court house, designed by him, was marvelously beautiful, not alone at the time of its completion, but till its destruction exactly a hundred years later. To those now living in Greenville, this old structure was known as the "Record Building."

Robert S. Mills, designer of the Washington monument, in his *Statistics of South Carolina,* published in 1824, says of the village:

"The village is regularly laid out in squares, and rapidly improving. It is the resort of much company in the summer, and several respectable and wealthy families have located themselves here on account of the salubrity of the climate. These have induced a degree of improvement, which promises to make Greenville one of the most considerable villages in the state. It has been preferred as a residence to Pendleton, perhaps on account of its not being affected so immediately by the cold damps of the mountains. . . . The public buildings are: a handsome brick court house (lately erected), a jail, a Baptist meeting house, an Episcopal church, and two neat buildings for the Male and Female Academy. . . . The private homes are neat; some large and handsome. Two of the former governors of the state have summer retreats here—Governors Alston and Middleton. . . . The number of houses is about seventy, the population is about five hundred. The returns of the commissioners of free schools for the last year show $1,039.00 expended, and 166 children educated."

From time to time in the past, controversy has arisen as to when the name of Greenville was changed from that of Pleasantburg. Some have fixed it as late as 1831, when the village was incorporated as the town of Greenville, while others contend for a date as early as 1815, when Vardry McBee became owner of the major portion of the village. However, a study of the public records, combined with the historical data available, leads to the belief that the name "Greenville" was used from the very beginning, and that a very few years only, had elapsed before "Pleasantburg" was dropped entirely. In 1798, when the second conveyance in the village was made, the location of the property was fixed as being "at Greenville, C. H., Village of Pleasantburg", and thereafter very few, if any, conveyances refer to Pleasantburg. Edward Hooker in the account of his visit in 1806 uses the name "Greenville", and never once refers to a Pleasantburg; and the "Statistics" of Mills published in 1824 uses only the name "Greenville." Very likely Alston called his subdivision "Pleasantburg", but since it was the site of the Greenville County Court House, the residents referred to it as "Greenville Court House" instead, and quite soon the original name was entirely gone.

CHAPTER XI.

EARLY POLITICAL LIFE

For the first 25 or 30 years of the county's life the names of three men stand out more conspicuously than any others in her political affairs. These are Samuel Earle, Elias Earle, and Lemuel J. Alston.

Samuel Earle was one of the first settlers in the new county, having secured a grant of "400 acres on both sides of Reedy river, northwest of the ancient boundary, including the improvements formerly claimed by Robert Paris". Whether or not these were lands formerly held by Richard Pearis, and the description in the Earle deed erroneously referred to him as "Robert", is unknown. There is no record of any Robert Paris ever having resided in Greenville, but the spelling of the name is here "Paris" while Richard always used the spelling "Pearis". Could it be possible that there was a Robert Paris, and that Paris mountain derives its name from him and not Richard Pearis, as is so generally thought? Possibly, but not at all probable. Samuel Earle was the son of Judge Baylis Earle, who settled in the northern part of Spartanburg County in 1773, having emigrated from either Westmoreland or Frederick County, Virginia, where Samuel was born to himself and his wife, Mary Prince, daughter of John Prince of Prince's fort fame, on November 28, 1760.

Although under 17 years of age at the time, Samuel Earle entered the forces of the Patriots on May 20, 1777, under the direct command of General (then Major) Andrew Pickens, and continued active till the close of the war, at which time he held a commission as captain. After the war, as Deputy Provost Marshal, he is said to have served the first writ ever made returnable to old Cambridge, or Ninety-Six. He was elected from Greenville County to the State Convention which framed the first State Constitution, and was also a member of the State Convention which adopted the Constitution of the United States. In 1795 he became a member of Congress from the Congressional District of which Greenville was a part, being the first Congressman from that district after the adoption of the Federal Constitution, and succeeding General Andrew Pickens, who up to that time had been the representative under the old "Articles of Confederation."

Of him Governor B. F. Perry writes:

"Mr. Earle was a man of high and pure character, and I don't think his honor and integrity were ever questioned throughout his long life. . . . No one in the upper country knew so well as he did the Revolutionary history of the state, and the early settlement of the back country, as it was termed. . . . He knew all the prominent men of those times, and did not hesitate to sketch their characters as they appeared to him. . . . He spoke well of General Robert Cunningham. . . . He said, though Tories, Cunningham and his two brothers, John and Patrick, were gentlemen of honor and integrity. They had unfortunately taken the wrong side, as so many honest and intelligent men did."

PART I — NARRATIVE 67

Speaking further of Mr. Earle and his political career, Governor Perry says:
"He was once a candidate for the State Senate in Greenville before he moved to Pendleton, and was beaten by his kinsman, Colonel Elias Earle, who afterwards represented the District in Congress for a great number of years. Colonel Elias Earle was a great and most successful electioneer. He treated bountifully, which Mr. Samuel Earle refused to do. There was but one place of voting then in the whole district (county), and that was at the Court House. Colonel Elias Earle came riding into the village, with several hundred of his voters, on horseback. When Mr. Samuel Earle saw this strong array of partisans, and heard them huzzaing for the Colonel, he cried, 'Huzza, for the half-pint tickets'."

Colonel Elias Earle, half brother of Judge Baylis Earle, and therefore half uncle of the Honorable Samuel Earle, was born in Virginia in 1762 and moved to Greenville County, South Carolina, in 1787 where he settled on the Rutherford road, about two miles from the village of Greenville, at "the Poplars". He early identified himself with the political affairs of the new county, and for 25 years or more was a "power". His nephew, Samuel Earle, he defeated for the State Senate from Greenville County early in his career by "the too free use of liquor", it was charged, and then after a four-year term became a candidate for Congress from the district then composed of Greenville, Pendleton (Anderson, Pickens and Oconee), Laurens, Abbeville, and Spartanburg. He was successful in his Congressional venture and thereafter held that position—first from 1805 to 1807, then from 1811 to 1815, and later from 1817 to 1821. In his 1806 race to succeed himself, he was opposed by Lemuel J. Alston, who defeated him, but four years later he defeated Mr. Alston and returned to Washington.

While still in Virginia, Colonel Earle married Frances Wilton Robinson. They became the parents of seven children, one of whom, Elizabeth, married George W. Earle, a nephew of Colonel Elias, and son of Colonel John Earle, on whose property near the Spartanburg County line, but in North Carolina, was located Earle's fort during the Revolution. This son-in-law was for many years Clerk of Court of Greenville County and was the grandfather of United States Senator Joseph H. Earle and Dr. T. T. Earle. Dr. T. T. Earle was the father of State Senator Wilton H. Earle and Dr. C. B. Earle, both present-day Greenville citizens of prominence. A son, Dr. Robinson Earle, became the grandfather of United States Senator John L. M. Irby of Laurens County. Dr. Robinson Earle was killed in an encounter with his nephew-by-marriage, William L. Yancy, afterward a Confederate States Senator from Alabama, and often called "the Father of Secession".

Already something has been said of Colonel Lemuel J. Alston, the other member of the trio. He came to Greenville early in its history, and soon became a man of influence. It was he, as has been stated, who founded the present city of Greenville, and from his magnificent home overlooking the tiny village, he presided over its destinies in lordly fashion for the first 18 years of its life. In 1806 he was a successful candidate for Congress against Colonel Elias Earle, who then held that office, but four years later he was defeated by Colonel Earle, which is said to have proved such a humiliation that he immediately offered his Greenville lands for sale. Four years later he found a purchaser in Vardry McBee, and soon thereafter left the state.

During the contest between Alston and Elias Earle in 1806, Edward Hooker of Connecticut paid Greenville a visit, and for several days was a guest at the home of Colonel Alston. He noted his observations in a diary which furnishes present-day readers with a very good insight into the political methods and social customs of that early day in Greenville. Extracts taken from this journal read:

"*Thursday, Sept. 18th.* This part of the state is just now in a state of some agitation on account of the approaching elections. It is curious to see how high is the popular tone in all such subjects. A stranger would be led to think the fate of the United States depended on the choice of which these people are about to make of Capt. Earle (should be Colonel) or Col. Alston, or Dr. Hunter for Congressman, neither of whom, nor the people who vote for them, are probably valued a straw at the seat of government. We met with one of them this forenoon, at a spring where we stopped to drink, and suspecting from his looks and demeanor that he was some candidate for public favor on an electioneering campaign, soon discovered that his name is Earle."

On September 21st Mr. Hooker and his companion (a Mr. Lilly) attended a church service in present upper Pickens County. Here they met Colonel Alston "on an electioneering trip", as Mr. Hooker states, who invited them to visit him at Greenville. The invitation was accepted, and of his experiences and observations as a guest of Colonel Alston, Mr. Hooker writes:

"Col. A. is as liberal in treating with liquor as anybody, perhaps, yet not extravagant. Not aiming to show his liberality by having wine and brandy cover the table and floor in slops, not leaving it standing about open, but on leaving the drinking room to go to dinner or elsewhere, he carefully corks and sets up the decanters and bottles in the sideboard, himself. . . . After dinner I took a pleasant walk to the village with Mr. Henderson, a young lawyer who is half-brother to Col. Alston. Introduced to G. W. Earle, Esq., the Clerk of Court, and Capt. Cleveland, a merchant. . . . On our return, at tea time, we found a young Mr. Cleveland from Tuguloo settlement in Pendleton, and several others who had met Col. Alston to consult about the electioneering matters. A social company spent the evening here. It was somewhat amusing to hear the various conversations on such topics. From what I heard, I learned that the great objections relied on in the electioneering war are that Hunter is so good a physician that he can't be spared long enough to go to Congress—that Earle does not respect religion, for when he is on his electioneering campaigns, instead of going into the church he stays out in the shade with such as choose to stay and drink with him, and that Alston is a Federalist and in favor of a stamp act and too rich a man."

The Clerk of Court, G. W. Earle, mentioned by Mr. Hooker, was the son-in-law of Colonel Elias Earle, one of the contestants in this race. Mr. Cleveland referred to by Hooker as a merchant was, no doubt, Captain Jeremiah who had purchased a lot in the village the preceding year, and was for a long time afterward, one of the leading business men of the county. And the young man, Cleveland, from Tuguloo, was probably a son of Colonel Benjamin Cleveland of Kings Mountain fame.

On September 24th Mr. Hooker and his friend were away from Greenville, probably in Pendleton, but he could not forget his experiences while visiting at the home of Colonel Alston, and we find him still commenting in his diary. Here is what he says:

"Henderson, in the course of his pleasant chat, related several anecdotes about his brother Alston's art in electioneering. Among other things he told me that the large family Bible which lies on the table in the keeping room was not bought till since he became a candidate for Congress, and was then got for the purpose of making a good impression on such as might call."

On September 27th the party returned to Greenville and in company with Colonel Alston rode to Pickensville (near the present town of Easley, and seat of government for Washington District, of which Greenville County was then a part), to take part in a political meet. Mr. Hooker's account of the happenings on that day gives a vivid picture of politics as played in that early time. He says:

"We arrived at Greenville about 9, and after breakfast rode to Pickensville, 13 miles, in company with Col. Alston and a young Mr. Lester. Forded the river Saluda on our way, become by this time a wide, but shallow, stream interrupted by rocks and considerably rapid. Arrived about noon. Quite a public day there. A regiment of cavalry paraded in the woods, made a martial appearance, but there was a coarseness and rusticity about them, characteristic of the country they inhabit. It is said the troops were called out in subserviency to electioneering purposes. Several hundred people came together; the houses and streets were thronged. The three candidates for Congress, Alston, Hunter, and Earle, were present electioneering with all their might—distributing whiskey, giving dinners, talking and haranguing, their friends at the same time making similar exertions for them. Besides these, there were a number of candidates for the Assembly. It was a singular scene of noise, blab and confusion. I placed myself on a flight of stairs where I could have a good view of the multitude, and there stood for some time, an astonished spectator of a scene, the resemblance of which I have never before witnessed; a scene ludicrous indeed when viewed by one who considers at the same time what inroads are made upon the sacred right of suffrage. Hand-bills containing accusations of federalism against one, of abuse of public trust against another—of fraudulent speculation against a third—and numerous reports of a slanderous and scurrilous nature were freely circulated. Much drinking, swearing, cursing and threatening—but I saw no fighting. The minds of uninformed people were much agitated—and many well-meaning people were made to believe the national welfare was at stake and would be determined by the issue of this backwoods election. Dr. Hunter conducted with most dignity, or rather with least indignity on this disgraceful occasion—confining himself to a room in the tavern, and not mixing with the multitude in the street— Alston fought for proselites and adherents in the street; but took them into the barroom to treat them, but Earle, who loved the people more than any of them, had his grog bench in the middle of the street and presided over the whiskey jugs himself. Standing behind it like a shop boy behind his counter, and dealing out to anyone who would honor him so much as to come up and partake of his liberality. . . . Earle is the present member. . . . I was introduced to a number of strangers on this occasion—among the rest to Chancellor Thompson and Mr. Andrew Pickens. The Chancellor is a sleek, beauish young man of about 30—whose dress and general appearance as illy accorded with my notions of a Judge's gravity as the active part which he was taking in this electioneering squabble accorded with my notions of a Judge's impartiality. He treated me very politely and invited me to visit him at his home. Mr. Pickens is a worthy young gentleman of about 26, son of old General Pickens, who figured in the Revolution. . . . Toward night I left this scene of confusion and disgrace, which seemed likely to continue through the night, and rode nine or ten miles on my way to Pendleton."

Knowing of the demagogy and chicanery which permeate the political structure of Greenville County and the state of South Carolina today, and seeing how, regardless of the "Religious Freedom" clause of our Federal Constitution, the Protestant churches are endeavoring to dictate national politics and candidates, one can but conclude that we have fallen upon evil days. But in the light of Mr. Hooker's recital we do not fare so badly, after all, in this day removed a century and a quarter from "the good old times when the foundations of civil liberty and personal righteousness were being laid" as is so freely prated about; and we are reminded that mankind in the aggregate does not differ greatly in one age from that of another.

CHAPTER XII.

FROM 1830 TO 1860

THE early settlers of Greenville County, as previously stated, came principally from the more northern states. Many of them before locating in South Carolina, had already moved several times, as was the wont of our pioneers, ever in search of cheaper and more fertile lands. From afar the new Cherokee acquisition offered everything they might desire, and here they came in an ever-increasing stream for the first fifteen years following the Revolution. In 1790, just six years after it had been opened to settlers, Greenville County had a population of 6,500, all of which but 600 was white. By 1800 there were 11,500 people in the new county, of which 10,025 were white. But about this time there set in a heavy migration to the more westward states, and the white population of the county remained very nearly stationary till the days of the War Between the States.

For many years after 1800 Greenville drew heavily upon the populations of Virginia, North Carolina and the coastal section of South Carolina, but in the face of this constant immigration she hardly held to a normal birth increase. Modern methods of cultivating the soil were unknown, and only a few years served to "wear out" the hill plantations which had been so eagerly sought. The older residents, who had witnessed this deterioration in the productivity of their lands, sold out to the newcomers at any price obtainable and moved on in search of something better. Being of the typical pioneer stock (always in search of new fields to conquer) they no doubt welcomed this opportunity to escape the few bonds of civilization which were beginning to tie them about.

The first settlers engaged in the culture of tobacco, corn, and wheat as their principal agricultural pursuits. Wheat and corn mills were built at the falls of water courses where the grain was converted into flour and meal. Much of the flour went to Charleston and Augusta, along with the tobacco. These two (wheat and tobacco) constituted the "money crop." But there was need for little money. Cattle, hogs, and poultry were grown for meat; sheep were kept for wool, and flax grown for linen, from which the thrifty housewife manufactured cloth for the family clothing; tools, farm implements, and wagons were made at the plantation forge; horses for plantation use, and some for sale, were raised; whiskey and brandy for home consumption were made, the first from corn and rye, and the latter from peaches picked in the extensive orchards everywhere in evidence. Only such things as sugar, coffee and spices, was it necessary to buy. Standards of living were not complex, and wants were few. Living meant hard work, but these people had been accustomed to that for several generations back, and did not complain.

Near the close of the eighteenth century the cotton gin was invented, and within a few years the cultivation of cotton became the principal industry of the state; but the first quarter of the nineteenth century had passed before Greenville

County was growing the staple to any considerable extent. Its successful cultivation at that time depended primarily upon an abundance of slave labor, and this was lacking in Greenville. The early settlers, for the most part, were poor and owned no slaves; but with the passing of years, and the moving away of many of the pioneers, some wealth began to accumulate, and with it came slave ownership. So by 1830 much cotton was being grown in the county, but still not to the neglect of other crops. In fact, Greenville County remained virtually self-supporting till after the war of the sixties.

A digest of the population of the county from 1790 to 1860, as taken from the United States Census reports, should be of interest here, and it is given.

POPULATION, COUNTY OR DISTRICT OF GREENVILLE.

	1790	1800	1810	1820	1830	1840	1850	1860
White	5,888	10,025	10,739	11,017	11,385	12,491	13,370	14,631
Free Negroes	9	36	41	90	32	43	95	212
Slaves	606	1,439	2,353	3,423	5,064	5,305	6,691	7,049
Total	6,503	11,500	13,133	14,530	16,481	17,839	20,156	21,892

With the increase in slave ownership, the more wealthy of the farmers added gradually to their land holdings, and by 1860 there were a number of large plantations in the county. Upon these slaves were employed in the growing of cotton upon a large scale, but never to the extent that the industry reached in some other of the piedmont counties. These large planters lived in comparative luxury, but the great mass of the people remained small land owners, living in primitive style till long after the close of the war of 1860. However, the coming of the first railroad in 1853 seems to have had a stimulating effect upon farm values as revealed by the Census reports. In 1850 the total value of all farm lands, farm implements and live stock was $2,506,891.00; while ten years later their values had jumped to $4,594,700.00.

Although farming was the principal industry during this period, there were a number of small manufacturing plants located at the falls of many of the streams throughout the county. For the most part these were sawmills, grist mills, and wheat mills. At the falls of Reedy river, within the village, was an iron working plant from a very early date, while a large carriage factory, also located in the village, supplied vehicles for hundreds during the first half of the century. Blacksmiths, gunsmiths, and wagon makers were much in demand to supply the needs of the residents, and shops where they plied their trade (most honorable at that time), were located in every community. In 1824 there were two textile manufacturing plants in the county. One of these was near present Cedar Falls (two miles below Fork Shoals), but the location of the other is unknown. A paper mill was built in the county in 1835, and was successfully operated for many years.

Although the town or village of Greenville prior to 1860 was small, it nevertheless exerted a powerful influence upon the affairs of the county. Till 1831 it was a mere village or settlement, but in the latter part of that year it was incorporated as a town, which it remained until 1868, when it became a city.

PART I — NARRATIVE   73

In 1903 Colonel S. S. Crittenden published his *Greenville Century Book,* in which he gives his earliest recollections of Greenville. These reminiscences go as far back as 1835 and are not only interesting and instructive to present-day citizens of Greenville, but worth preserving for future generations. Consequently, free use is made of Colonel Crittenden's writings in the pages of this chapter to follow:

Colonel Crittenden says:

"My memory goes back to about 1835 in the history of our city, and the first thing that strikes me in relation to it is that there were formerly much more up-hill and down-hill than now. There has been a constant leveling or grading going on during the last 60 years.

"The distance 'across the river' in old parlance, is very much shortened by the regular grade of the street, and by the high bridge over Reedy river. The first bridge I can remember was a substantial foot log. But it was in the administration of Mr. Thomas C. Gower, as mayor of the town, that the present bridge was built. It was opposed by many at the time, upon the ground of the expense involved."

The Main Street bridge to which Colonel Crittenden refers gave place to the present structure in 1912, the old bridge being moved up to the River Street crossing, where it remained till 1929. Mr. Thomas C. Gower was mayor of Greenville in 1870-'71. He was the father of A. G. Gower, T. C. Gower and Mrs. W. P. Conyers, all of whom are well-known Greenville citizens of today.

Says Colonel Crittenden further:

"The only houses on Pendleton Street, or the Pendleton road, as we then called it, were perhaps two or three one-story buildings about where the railroad crossing now is, and then the residence of Mrs. Susan B. McCall, afterwards owned by Col. T. Edwin Ware, and now the residence of his son, Mr. Henry Ware. This was then a beautiful place surrounded by broad acres (not less than 30), and spreading oaks overlooking the village. Mrs. McCall, who was the mother of Mrs. Governor Perry, was among the large number of families from Charleston who were early attracted to Greenville. Mr. Whiteford Smith, father of the celebrated Methodist divine, who was once a citizen of Greenville, lived many years just beyond Mrs. McCall's, which he first settled. A little further on was the residence of Mr. Luther M. McBee, father of Mr. Alex and Mr. L. M. McBee of our city. Still further on in the same neighborhood on the valuable farm where Mr. and Mrs. John A. Honor reside, there lived for many years two maiden ladies, Misses Anna and Charlotte Alston, from the low country. They were relatives of Lemuel J. Alston, the founder of Pleasantburg. These were the only houses I remember between the Pendleton road and Reedy river."

The Honor place referred to by Colonel Crittenden lies beyond the present Brandon and Woodside mill villages, yet there were only three or four houses between Reedy river and that point in 1835 or later. At least two and a half miles of solidly built streets cover the route today.

In referring to the two Alston ladies as being relatives of Lemuel J. Alston, Colonel Crittenden is probably in error. The Honor place is the old Joseph Alston plantation, and these two ladies were probably relatives of his—perhaps daughters. Joseph Alston, who maintained a summer home in Greenville, was governor of the state from 1812 to 1814. It is thought that he was unrelated to Lemuel J. Alston.

Following Colonel Crittenden:

"On the Augusta road, now Augusta Street, I remember as standing where it now stands, and did before my recollections, the Doctor Richard Harrison house on the knoll this side of the G. & C. Railroad track. Dr. Harrison was the first physician of Greenville and at one time took care of the whole village. He married a daughter of Chancellor Waddy Thompson and died before my recollection. The beautiful place of Mrs. Mary Cleveland was the residence of Tandy Walker and his accomplished wife. He was one of the very early settlers of Greenville, a gentleman of the highest character, lawyer and member of the Legislature. The adjoining residence of Mr. H. C. Markley was built by Mr. Eben Gower in 1858. A former residence of Chancellor Thompson stood just across the G. & C. Railroad from Mr. Markley's at my earliest recollection. With seven acres of land, it was bought by Mr. Nathan Whitmire some 50 years ago and the cottage of Judge Thompson is now a part of the building he then erected. The brick house just beyond, now the home of Mrs. Annie P. Thurston, was built by Mr. Willis Benson about the same time. These were all the buildings on the Augusta road and near the village at that period, until you reached, at a mile from the court house, the two noted residences of Mrs. Robert Earle, now the Cagle place, and the opposite residence of Capt. J. Westley Brooks, now owned by Capt. O. P. Mills."

The beautiful place of Mrs. Mary Cleveland is now the location of the Mary Cleveland school where there is soon to be built a high school building for the Greenville city system. The Cagle place is easily recognized as "Cagle Park" with its many streets of handsome residences. Across from this, and including the present residence of Mrs. O. P. Mills, is the old Brooks farm. After it was purchased by Captain Mills it became known as "Millwood." Mills Mill occupies a portion of old "Millwood."

Leaving the "West End" and coming up the west side of Main Street from the river, Colonel Crittenden continues:

"The Greenville Coach Factory—Mr. H. C. Markley—has with its progressive improvements stood at this end of the bridge for full fifty years. During all that time it has been a busy hive of industry and an exemplar of the highest methods of doing business. Coming up the west side of Main Street the buildings now standing that I remember sixty-five years ago are, first: The old residence adjoining the Coach Factory, then occupied by Mrs. Cox, the mother of T. M. Cox, formerly one of Greenville's notable citizens. Above on the same block, were no houses until you came to the corner, where was a dark, unpainted old two-story wooden building, occupied by Mr. Ben F. Horton, the principal bricklayer of the village.

"On the corner where the U. S. Court House stands was a wood shop occupied at one time by 'Uncle Abe Willimon', ancestor of all the Willimons still living among us. Colonel David Hoke's residence came next on the same lot, as he owned most of the square. Colonel David Hoke was a busy and stirring figure about the public square for many years. He was Clerk of Court and Sheriff for several years.

"The Mansion House was standing when I was born, having been built in 1824. It has the same front, except the wing next to the court house has been added, and the Carpenter drug store end built.

"McBee's Hall that stood on the corner of Main Street and McBee Avenue was a comparatively recent structure. It was built in 1849 by L. B. Cline and burned down in 1861. The opera house built upon the same site by Capt. J. W. Cagle, was burned in 1878, when just completed and but one performance had been held in it. Two negroes were convicted of burning it and hung in the jail yard for the offense. About where the 'Big Bee Hive' stands was a store seventy years ago that was unique even then. It was built by Mr. McBee and occupied by McBee & Irvine as a general dry goods store. It was brick and two stories. Next door above was the residence of Rev. John M. Roberts, and next to it was the old wooden store of J. M. Roberts & Co., afterwards Roberts & Duncan. Above this and to the corner is the property long owned by Mr. Samuel Mauldin and now by his son, W. L. Mauldin."

Crossing Washington Street and proceeding north, still on Main Street, with Colonel Crittenden:

"My first recollection of the corner now occupied by Smith & Bristow was an old hotel. It belonged to Mrs. Rowland and was kept by Blackman Ligon. There were several stores on this square, all wooden. Turpin & Powers (Major J. M. A. Turpin and Philip Powers) were above the centre. Just above them was the dry goods firm of Greenway & Beattie (a Mr. Greenway and F. F. Beattie, father of Hamlin Beattie, founder of the First National Bank). Above Greenway & Beattie was Cauble's blacksmith shop. Peter Cauble here hammered out a fortune of at least $100,000.00. His son, Henry A. Cauble, was Intendant of the village in 1849. Across Coffee Street from the blacksmith shop there stood the Mrs. Paul house (site later occupied by the opera house). Excepting a cottage, there was nothing above on the west side of Main Street except the old Hollinguist, afterwards the Douglas house. In the early days of which I am writing F. H. McLeod, a wealthy planter from the low country, owned and lived at the Coxe place at the head of Main Street (present Ottaray hotel, Carolina theatre and Mackey's Mortuary). In early days Chancellor Thompson owned this place in connection with a large tract reaching to Richland creek, and including the Boyce Lawn property. On the east side of Main Street there were no houses above North Street. On the block below were the Major William Turpin house, the old Burnham residence, and the two-story building yet on the corner of Coffee Street. On the block below were several wooden stores and shops, mostly one story, until you came to the corner where stood the old 'Kentucky and Tennessee Inn', kept by David Henning, at one time Sheriff of the county."

Crossing Washington Street and continuing south, still in the words of Colonel Crittenden:

"On the next corner stood the hotel of Capt. Davis Long. Below it were the wooden store of Long & Co., the tinshop of B. Dunham and a brick house belonging to Roger Loveland. The Cleveland mansion (now Woolworth, Seybt and others), was built in 1822. On the next square were all wooden buildings, and except at the two corners were but one story. Hastie & Nicol, merchants, were on the upper corner, then the book bindery of E. R. Stokes, the barroom of Larry Saxton, the shoe shop of William John McCluney, and on the corner the store and residence of Dr. John Crittenden. Below the old Court House on the next square were the residences of Mrs. Sloan, grandmother of the late A. Sloan Duncan and Governor Perry, with the law office of Governor Perry next. The Heldman house, of brick, built by V. McBee, was on the next corner. Between that and the river was the residence and blacksmith shop of David Westfield, and on the lower corner lived Mr. George B. Dyer."

With this is concluded the recital of Colonel Crittenden as to the buildings which, in 1836 and several years thereafter, were standing on Main, Pendleton, and Augusta Streets. A few other shops were within the present confines of the city, but none of importance. Greenville was nothing but a rambling village with here a store or shop and there a residence, but largely composed of farm lands.

It will be noted that there were an unusually large number of hotels, inns and other public houses for a village of Greenville's size during those early days. This is, of course, accounted for because of the fact that Greenville was then a popular summer resort. The village was also the terminal of roads leading over the mountains into North Carolina, Tennessee and Kentucky, and because of this furnished accommodation to many travelers.

As has been previously said, the Mansion House was the fashionable stopping place for the low-country visitors. They came into the village in their own carriages or by public stage coach. Of course, the more wealthy usually used their own coaches for this purpose, and a magnificent spectacle it was to view the arrival of one of these wealthy families of summer visitors. Often the carriage was drawn by four horses, and accompanying it were baggage wagons and "outriders", often numbering three or four conveyances, eight or ten horses, and several slaves to each family. Neighbors and friends came together, and with four to six of these families traveling in one company, quite a cavalcade was formed. Reaching their destination, they parted to take up their summer's residence at the Mansion House, some other hotel or public house, or perhaps at the privately owned summer home, of which there were many about the village. There were three lines of stage coaches, each furnishing transportation into the village three times a week. One of these was from Asheville, another from Augusta, and the third from Columbia.

Asheville and Hendersonville were not known in those days as resorts. Chicks Springs was popular, and it, with Greenville and Flat Rock, North Carolina, were the fashionable places during the summer months. Through the influence in the General Assembly of the low-country visitors to Greenville and Flat Rock, the State road was built through Greenville County and across the mountains at Saluda gap. Politics then took the down state tax payer's money to build roads in the up-country, and now descendants of these same politicians are taking money from the up-state to build roads for the low country. But politics must go on, and somehow the state pays the bills and keeps itself a "few jumps" ahead of the creditor's agents.

Colonel Crittenden says:

"Greenville was then not only a place of resort during the summer months, but a thoroughfare of travel from the west during the winter. Droves of horses, mules and hogs from Tennessee and Kentucky poured through the Saluda gap, down the Buncombe road to Greenville, and from that point were distributed through the state. Every four or five miles along the Buncombe road, and also below Greenville were taverns or houses of entertainment, where many fortunes have been made from this year-round travel."

On November 17, 1843, there appeared in *The Greenville Mountaineer*, a weekly newspaper of old Greenville, an advertisement reading:

"WANTING"

A teacher to take charge of the Greenville Male Academy.

The Village of Greenville is situated in the State of South Carolina, near the Blue Ridge, in a high and healthy region, noted as a place of resort during the sickly season, and for health is scarcely equalled by any village in the Union; and there are but few that possess so many local advantages.

It contains a population of eleven hundred persons, has three churches, well attended; has near one dozen stores, and a goodly number of industrious mechanics. Three stages arrive at Greenville three times a week. It is on the highway from the Western States to the cities of Charleston, Columbia and Augusta.

(Signed) T. C. AUSTIN,
Secretary.

Mention is made in the foregoing advertisement of three churches located in the village. Already in these pages the organization of Christ Church and of the Greenville Baptist Church have been mentioned. The churches referred to are these two and the Buncombe Street Methodist Church, the latter being organized in 1834 with six members. Of this church Colonel Crittenden says:

"Methodism flourished in the early days of Greenville. In the boyhood of the writer it was the most popular church in the village, and he remembers well the crowded audiences that were attracted to the old church. Most of the school girls attending the Female Academy and boarding in the village attended that church, and as a natural consequence, the young men did also."

The Presbyterians, next after the Methodists to enter the village with a church, came in 1848, when the First Presbyterian Church was organized with a membership of 18. In 1850 the lot at the corner of Washington and Richardson Streets was deeded to the new church by Vardry McBee, just as he had previously given a lot to the Methodist, and upon it a building was erected.

It was during the days from 1850 to 1860 that the real and lasting foundations of the present-day county were laid. The pioneers had already opened up the new country and a substantial citizenship was fast taking a prominent place in the affairs of the state at the opening of the period. As the years passed, although the population of the county did not materially increase, its people gradually bettered their economic condition, and at the close of the period the county ranked high among those of the up-state.

CHAPTER XIII.

NULLIFICATION AND SECESSION

IN 1822, in 1824 and again in 1828, Congress passed tariff laws which were generally opposed in the South, and especially in South Carolina. It was thought that these measures would be highly prejudicial to agriculture, and since that was the chief industry of the Southern states, the Representatives from that section voiced their disapproval in vigorous style, both in and out of Congress. Leading in this opposition were the members of Congress from South Carolina. When defeated in the tariff fight of 1828 the South Carolinians felt it keenly, and returning home they proceeded to organize the people of their state in opposition to the Union. Since 1822, when the tariff question first began to be agitated, South Carolina had two distinct tariff parties, known locally as the Calhoun and Smith parties. And surprising as it may now seem, the Calhoun adherents were proponents of the tariff, while the Smith advocates opposed it. The first argued that such laws were necessary for the well-being of the Union, while the other contended that the interests of the individual states should be put above those of the Nation. This was the beginning of the "states rights" fight which ultimately led to secession and bloody war.

Although a majority of the citizens of South Carolina are thought to have been opposed to the tariff laws from the beginning, it was not till 1828 that the anti-tariff or "states rights" faction began to dominate every phase of the political life of the state. In 1822 Judge Smith, leader of the "state righters", was defeated in consequence of his position on that question, and from time to time thereafter anti-tariff men were unable to gain election over their tariff supporting opponents. John C. Calhoun was then, as later, political dictator for the state, and so long as he favored the tariff the proponents of the states rights and anti-tariff school had difficulties. No doubt Calhoun had the power to effect the defeat of all those opposing the tariff, but he seemed content to adopt a "watchful, waiting policy" till such time as he might be able to definitely determine his future actions. But after the law of 1828, which was considered the most inimical of all, the people were fully aroused, and it soon became evident that they would have no more of the hated tariff, or its advocates, if it were in their power to avoid it. Now it was that Calhoun let it be known that he would no longer support the tariff act of Congress, and thereafter he became the leader of the states rights faction, and so vigorously and far afield did he lead it that many of the original anti-tariff advocates, including Judge Smith himself, refused to follow him.

Soon after Calhoun became the leader of the states rights faction he advocated his famous Nullification theory. This met with very general approval throughout the lower part of the state, but the piedmont section, with the exception of Pendleton District (the home of Calhoun), did not think well of it. The election of 1830 turned upon that question, with B. F. Perry of Greenville leading the fight for the up-country against Nullification. A large majority of the members of the General

Assembly elected that year were Nullificationists, but Greenville County chose a solid delegation opposed to the principal. However, it was necessary to have a two-thirds vote of the assembly to call a convention to nullify the tariff acts, and this could not be had, so the session was adjourned without any action being taken on that question. But two years before this (1828) Waddy Thompson of Greenville had introduced a resolution in the House of Representatives, of which he was a member from Greenville County, providing that if Congress at its next session did not repeal the tariff laws, then South Carolina should call a convention to nullify them. The resolution failed of passage, however, and Thompson was not returned to the General Assembly as his constituents were opposed to his action.

In 1832 there was another election for assemblymen, and this too turned upon the old question. This time, however, a clear two-thirds majority for nullification was secured, although Greenville County was still found against the principle. Among the first acts of this new Assembly was to pass a resolution calling for the election of members to a convention to consider the situation created by the tariff laws, and take such action thereon as might seem proper. Of course it was the intention of the legislature that the convention should pass an Ordinance of Nullification.

Elections were held in all the counties of the state, with the result that a large majority favoring a nullification resolution were chosen as members of the convention. However, Greenville County sent a solid delegation opposing such action. These delegates were Governor Henry Middleton, B. F. Perry, Colonel Thomas P. Brockman and Silas R. Whitten. The Nullification party offered as candidates Judge B. J. Earle, Doctor William Butler, William Thruston and Colonel Benjamin Arnold, but these gentlemen were defeated by a vote of almost four to one. It was evident from the first that the convention would pass an Ordinance of Nullification, so those opposing such action took no active part in the deliberations of the body, knowing that for them to do so would only add fuel to the raging fires which already threatened to destroy the state. Hence the convention was not long in concluding the business for which it had met. The Ordinance of Nullification, which it adopted, was to take effect in February, 1833, and in the meantime the General Assembly would meet to take such action as it thought best to enforce its provisions.

Immediately upon the passage of the Ordinance of Nullification, President Jackson let it be known that the United States government would enforce the tariff laws in South Carolina, as well as all other states of the Union, regardless of any action already taken or contemplated by that state or any other. If necessary, he stated, the army of the United States would be sent into the state of South Carolina, with full authority to force compliance with the laws. On the other hand, the South Carolina Assembly, when it met in December of 1832, provided for a voluntary army of state troops to resist the threatened coercion. Soon every district of the state had raised companies, and South Carolina became one vast military camp, ready for war, and only awaiting the date for the Nullification Ordinance to take effect. Waddy Thompson of Greenville, a strong advocate of Nullification, was elected Brigadier General in command of the First Brigade of South Carolina Militia.

But as the time for the Ordinance to become effective approached, the ardor of the Nullificationists seemed to cool. The most rabid of these had always known that South Carolina could not hope for success if the Federal authorities offered bona fide opposition, and it now began to seem that President Jackson contemplated doing so. While this state of indecision existed in South Carolina, the day for the operation of the Nullification Ordinance arrived, but nothing happened, as it was decided to delay its effective date till Congress could take action on a compromise measure then pending. Later this act of Congress became law, and although it did not furnish the relief desired by South Carolina, it modified some of the tariff schedules, and South Carolina, now desiring to get herself out of a dangerous situation, called a second convention to reconsider the Nullification Ordinance. This convention met in March, 1833, and promptly repealed the acts of the former convention, and thus officially closed the first of a series of public acts which finally led to secession.

But repealing the Ordinance of Nullification did not restore South Carolina to her former position of internal tranquility. The controversy had left a feeling of intense bitterness between the Unionists and States Rights men, and for many years the progress and well-being of the state were jeopardized by the factional fights between these two political forces. The up-state, and especially Greenville County, very generally supported the Unionists, while the lower state, with the exception of Charleston, which had now joined hands with the Piedmont, advocated the States Rights principles. The recognized leader of the Union forces in the up-country was B. F. Perry of Greenville, while the States Rights people of the whole state were led by John C. Calhoun of Pendleton. Of course the Calhoun party constituted a large majority of the people of the state, but the Unionists were aggressive and often won in county and Congressional elections. During all this period of conflict, which increased in bitterness year by year till 1859, Greenville County and her leading citizens played a conspicuous part.

In 1834 B. F. Perry of Greenville became a candidate for Congress against the incumbent Warren R. Davis of Pendleton. A bitter campaign followed, with the Unionist, Perry, supported by Joel R. Poinsett, then Minister to Mexico and a warm personal friend of President Jackson, and his States Rights opponent, Davis, strongly endorsed by Calhoun. Perry swept Greenville County, but lost the election by 60 votes out of a total of more than 7,000. But soon after the election, Davis died, and again Perry became a candidate. This time his opponent was his fellow townsman, Waddy Thompson. For many years Calhoun and Perry had been bitter political enemies, and the nearness to which Perry came of being elected in his race against Davis alarmed Calhoun, and he now put forth every effort within his power to defeat Perry and elect Thompson. Unfortunately for the Unionists, Perry suffered an injury early in the campaign, and was unable to make any speeches. Thompson was elected, but Greenville County remained Unionist.

The defeat of Perry was keenly felt by the Unionists of Greenville, and soon after the election they met to consider means of overthrowing the Calhoun-Thompson coalition in the Western District. Thompson was Brigadier General in command of the militia of this district, and it was decided to embarrass him by advising all Greenville officers to refuse to attend the next annual brigade encampment. In September, 1835, the encampment was held at Pickensville and no officers from Greenville attended. Their absence created much excitement, but they were subsequently courtmartialed and dismissed from the service.

When, upon his election President Jackson refused to appoint a South Carolinian to membership in his Cabinet, many political leaders of the state resented it, and his popularity rapidly waned. The firm stand taken by him against Nullification only added to the opposition, and Calhoun, feeling personally aggrieved, now announced that he and his followers in South Carolina would leave the Democratic (then Republican) party and join the Whigs. A majority of the Unionists were Whigs, and this action on the part of the State Rights supporters put South Carolina in the position of having one National party and two State factions. But Calhoun's allignment with the Whigs did not last for long. When Van Buren ascended to the Presidency in 1837, Calhoun deserted the Whigs and carried South Carolina back with him into the Democratic ranks. However, Waddy Thompson, still Congressman from Calhoun's home district, refused to be stampeded into such action, contending that he had become a Whig through conviction and saw no reason why he should not remain with that party.

Of Calhoun, his power in South Carolina at this time, and the resentment with which he met opposition, Colonel Henry T. Thompson in writing of Waddy Thompson says:

"For many years, Calhoun had been a veritable dictator in the politics of South Carolina. Such was his hold upon the state that few had the temerity to oppose him, and fewer still did so successfully. It is not surprising, therefore, that he carried South Carolina almost *en masse* with him into affiliation with the Democratic party. . . . Calhoun was no doubt sincere in the belief that the interests of South Carolina and the South lay with the Democratic party; yet his nature was such that he could not understand how any man could have convictions differing from his, and he could not brook opposition patiently, especially in his own state. He deeply resented it that some of the state's delegates in Congress should refuse to follow him in acting with the Democratic party, and particularly was he incensed against Preston and Thompson, the one because he was his colleague in the Senate, and the other because he was the representative of his (Calhoun's) district."

In 1838 Waddy Thompson was a candidate to succeed himself in Congress, and of course he met the determined opposition of Calhoun. Judge Whitner, much against his wishes, was induced to oppose Thompson upon promises being made that he (Calhoun) would take the stump in his behalf. B. F. Perry, with his strong following in Greenville, joined forces with Thompson and there followed one of the bitterest political fights ever known in upper South Carolina. Joint debates were held in all counties of the Congressional District, and at these Calhoun demanded and obtained the opening and closing. But regardless of the fact that Calhoun was a past master of political strategy, who had few equals in debate and no superiors in his grasp of tariff legislation, he was no match for Thompson as a stump speaker; and soon after the campaign started, it began to appear that Calhoun would suffer defeat. But both the newspapers of the district were Calhoun organs, and "in the extravagant language common to political publications of the day, these papers poured forth fulminations against Thompson." To Joel R. Poinsett, personal friend of Jackson and Perry, and a leading Unionist, Calhoun made an appeal for assistance, but Poinsett, although unfriendly to Thompson, refused to join hands with his old foe, Calhoun, to encompass his defeat. And in the words of Henry T. Thompson: "Thompson's personality and his inexhaustible fund of humor appealed more to the voter than Calhoun's logic, with the result that Thompson was re-elected by a very large majority."

From nullification the states rights supporters rapidly became advocates of secession, till by 1850 the secession and disunion feeling had become so high that it was a unit in breaking up the government and forming a new Confederacy. Greenville County of all the state, still led by B. F. Perry, stood alone "proclaiming its opposition to nullification, secession and disunion." Every newspaper in the state had gone over to the Secessionists and loudly they proclaimed their doctrine, with scarcely a voice raised in opposition. But having fought so valiantly for a quarter of a century against what he considered principles "destructive of liberty and every institution of the South", Mr. Perry now suggested the propriety of establishing a Union paper at Greenville. None were willing to join him in the undertaking, although the Union sympathizers thought such a project would do untold good. But the Roman courage which characterized his life would not permit him to let the matter die for want of support. He decided to establish and edit the paper alone. Some of his personal friends told him that if he persevered in establishing his newspaper, neither his life nor his property would be safe. But he replied: "I will go on with the paper if it sinks my fortune and sacrifices my life."

The House of Representatives elected in 1850 was unanimously secession, except for the Greenville members, who stood solidly, but alone, against the calling of a convention instructed to pass a Secession Ordinance. Speaking for himself, and his constituents, before that body on December 11, 1850, Mr. Perry, who, as always, had headed the delegation from Greenville, said:

"I am ready, Sir, and ever have been, to defend, at any and every hazard, the rights of the South. But I am disposed to defend them prudently, wisely and successfully. I am unwilling to see South Carolina pursue a course which must inevitably prove disastrous to her, and ruinous to the cause of the South. . . . While I feel conscious of the sincerity of my own heart, far be it from me to impugn the motives or conduct of others. They are doubtless as honest and as patriotic as myself. We differ as widely as the poles are asunder, but it is a difference of judgment, in pursuit of the same object—the honor, happiness and prosperity of our state. . . . They believe that the honor, happiness and prosperity of the South would be promoted by a dissolution of the Union. I do not. . . . But does anyone suppose that so great a political event as the separation of these states can take place without some bloody war ensuing? . . .

"I have thus spoken, Mr. Chairman, the truth, as I conceive it to be, and as my duty prompted me to speak. I may be mistaken in my views, but they are honest and sincere convictions of my best judgment, the feelings and promptings of my heart, my devotion to the principles of liberty and the stability of government, the rights of the South, the honor, prosperity and happiness of South Carolina."

The General Assembly of 1850 provided for a convention to consider secession, and this convention met in 1852. To it Greenville sent delegates opposed to secession, but there were few others in the body to advocate staying in the Union. However, a wave of conservatism seemed to sweep over the convention, due in large part, it was said, to a reaction which set in after the mighty efforts put forth by the Greenville legislative delegation in the assembly of 1850. A resolution declaring the right of the state to secede was passed, but it also declared that the opportune time for leaving the Union had not yet arrived. So for eight years longer South Carolina remained in the Union.

In 1860 the Democratic convention to nominate a candidate for President met in Charleston; and one of the South Carolina delegates was B. F. Perry of Greenville. Since the Secession Convention of 1852 he had continued to fight for Unionism, and the state had, no doubt, been kept in the Union because of his efforts. But the North was yearly becoming more strongly anti-slavery, and this new issue had now become the predominant one, rather than that of the tariff. The Democratic party, however, was badly split over this question, and it was freely predicted that the Charleston convention would witness an open breach between the northern and southern delegates. William L. Yancy, a former citizen of Greenville, South Carolina, but a delegate to the convention from Alabama, was expected to introduce the much-agitated "Alabama Resolutions" and should they not be adopted then to lead his state's delegation from the convention. Yancy had formerly resided in Greenville, where he studied law in the office of B. F. Perry and edited a Union paper, but for several years past he had been a citizen of Alabama and a powerful force in behalf of states rights. No one in touch with the situation expected the convention to adopt the Yancy resolutions, consequently it was freely predicted that Alabama and many other of the southern states would take no part in nominating a candidate for President on the Democratic ticket.

True to predictions, Yancy introduced his resolutions, they were voted down, and many southern delegates left the convention. All of the South Carolina delegates except B. F. Perry of Greenville and Colonel Boozer of Lexington joined the absentees. Perry arose to address the convention, and secession sympathizers in the gallery hissed him so loudly that the president of the body ordered the galleries cleared, but Mr. Perry begged that this not be done as he desired the spectators to hear what he had to say. The manly bearing of the Greenville man appealed to the sportsmanship of those who would have silenced him, and he was permitted to continue with his address. But to nominate a candidate was out of the question. The northern delegates voted consistently for Douglas, while those from the South remaining in the hall cast their ballots for Hunter of Virginia. A two-thirds vote of the entire delegates was necessary for a choice, and none could secure this number. The convention adjourned to meet later in Baltimore and there continue its balloting for a nominee. But the break had come, and later at Baltimore both Douglas and Breckenridge were nominated, with the inevitable result that Abraham Lincoln, the Republican nominee, was elected President.

With the election of Lincoln as President, South Carolina lost no time in taking the necessary steps to secede from the Union. All portions of the state had now become rabid anti-Unionists, Greenville having for the first time defeated her Union candidates when she sent a solid secession delegation to the convention of 1860. So in December, 1860, South Carolina passed the Secession Ordinance and ceased to recognize the government of the United States. But regardless of the long fight which Greenville County had made against secession, she now became as loyal to the cause of South Carolina as any portion of the state. As one man, it seemed, her citizenry rushed to the defense of their native state. Mr. Perry, in speaking to a group of secessionists after the passage of the Ordinance, said: "You are all going to the devil and I will go with you." This seemed to be the spirit which took possession of the whole county, for before the bloody war which followed had ended, Greenville County furnished more than 2,000 soldiers to the Confederate armies out of a total voting population in 1860 of less than 2,200. Although the county had opposed secession till the last, no portion of the state entered the war with more enthusiasm, or a greater determination to win, than did Greenville. Although firmly believing that the state had committed a fearful blunder in withdrawing from the Union, Greenville never once, throughout the long struggle and the trying years to follow, did other than face the issue in the brave and determined spirit which had characterized her people in their long fight preceding secession.

CHAPTER XIV.

WAR AND RECONSTRUCTION

THE election of Lincoln to the Presidency of the United States, followed quickly by the secession of South Carolina, plunged Greenville County, along with all other portions of the state, into the bloody struggle of the War Between the States. Although the county had put forth almost superhuman efforts to stay the coming of such an event, when it did come her citizens rallied as one man to the defense of the state. The total white population of the county in 1860 was only 14,631, and the voting strength just 2,200, yet before the war closed Greenville had contributed more than 2,000 men to the arms of the Confederacy. The first to go was the Butler Guards, followed closely by a company entirely of students of Furman University. The spirit of the time was everywhere in evidence, and no "slackers" were to be found. Men of fighting age clamored for admission into the army, and the authorities were sorely beset to make room for them fast enough. Even the mountaineers, unlike many of those from North Carolina and Tennessee, rushed to the nearest recruiting stations. They had followed the lead of Perry for many years past and were still with him. By 1862 the need for additional troops became acute, and a call for the men of 45 and above was issued. Greenville responded with the Sixteenth South Carolina regiment, recruited entirely from the county and almost exclusively from men past middle age.

The highest ranking officer to be furnished by Greenville County to the cause of the Confederacy was General M. C. Butler. At the beginning of the war he was a young man, just beginning the practice of law at Edgefield, but he had been reared in Greenville and his mother still lived there (as she did till her death), so it was Greenville he claimed as his home when he entered the services of his state. He served through the whole of the war, entering as a captain and attaining the rank of Major General of Cavalry before its close. At the battle of Brandy Station he lost a leg. After the war he performed valiant service in ousting the carpetbag regime, and later was elected United States Senator from South Carolina. Being of the "old school" in politics, he, along with his lifelong friend, General Wade Hampton, suffered defeat at the hands of the Tillman faction of later years, and retired from public life after a notable service in both war and peace.

During the years of the war the Confederate government maintained an arsenal in Greenville, where rifles for the army were manufactured. A hospital for wounded and sick soldiers was operated by the ladies of the county in a building located about where the Gibson Building, on the corner of Main and Washington Streets, now stands. The Batesville Cotton Factory and three other small textile plants located in the county, manufactured goods exclusively for the army, while a number of wagon makers and gunsmiths of the county furnished such supplies as they were able to turn out. In the town of Greenville the Gower, Cox, & Gower carriage factory furnished its entire output of wagons to the Ordinance and Quartermaster's departments of the army. By 1865 these two departments owed the firm $140,000.00 for supplies furnished. Just before the close of the war the Ordinance department paid it $70,000.00 in Confederate money, which became worthless before it could be utilized in the business. The balance of the account was never paid.

Although Greenville had few men of wealth, she contributed liberally to the Confederacy by the purchase of bonds, which of course were never redeemed. Inspection of the records in the office of the Probate Court will show how many estates of that period were rendered insolvent by the ownership of these bonds.

Being far removed from the battle fields, it was thought that Greenville was a safe hiding place for valuables. Consequently many wealthy coast dwellers sent their valuable furniture and paintings to Greenville for storage. The State bank in Charleston sent $35,000.00 in silver to Mr. Hamlin Beattie, which he secreted in his store, located on the present site of the First National Bank.

After General Lee had surrendered, and President Davis, with his Cabinet, was fleeing toward the south, General Stoneman's cavalry occupied Greenville. A small fort, or earth embankment, was erected just north of the town of Greenville near the present American Spinning Company village, and manned by a few soldiers who were home on leave of absence. But before the troops arrived it was decided that resistance would be futile, and the "fort" was abandoned. During the latter part of April, 1865, Stoneman and his cavalry rode into the town and made camp on the Furman University campus. No resistance was offered from any quarter. Through the town authorities the citizens were ordered to give up all their arms, and to deliver a quantity of horse feed and provisions to the troops. This order was complied with, and the town thus escaped the torch, in the use of which the Federals were so efficient. But all warehouses about the town were visited and the valuables stored there destroyed. The money sent up from Charleston to Mr. Beattie was found and taken. As a rule the people were treated with courtesy, and only one casualty was sustained—Captain Choice of the "old rock house" on the Buncombe road was shot down when he threatened to kill anyone who took his horse. After a few days the soldiers departed and the county was left to enter upon the years of reconstruction.

For many weeks following the war there was chaos in South Carolina. All offices had been declared vacant by the military authorities of the United States, and no one had power to conduct the affairs of the state. Lawlessless reigned supreme. But in Greenville County the situation was not so bad as it was in some other sections of the state, as less than a third of the population was composed of the newly freed slaves. Yet it was in Greenville that the first concerted movement to obtain a provisional government for the state was launched. On July 3, 1865, a mass meeting of citizens was held in the court house to discuss the matter. The principal speaker upon this occasion was B. F. Perry, who said in part:

"This public meeting of the citizens of Greenville is one of deep humiliation and sorrow. A cruel and bloody war has swept over the Southern States. One hundred and fifty thousand of our bravest and most gallant men have fallen on the field of battle. The land is filled with mourning widows and orphans. There is scarcely a house in which there has not been weeping for some lost one. Three thousand millions of dollars have been spent by the Southern States in carrying on the war. And now we are called upon to give up four millions of slaves worth two thousand millions of dollars. Moreover, our country has been ravaged and desolated. Our cities, towns, and villages are smouldering ruins. Armies occupy the country. The Confederacy has fallen, and we have been deprived of all civil government and political rights. We have neither law nor order. There is no protection for life, liberty, or property. Everywhere there is demoralization, rapine, and murder. Hunger and starvation are upon us. And now we meet as a disgraced and subjugated people to petition the conquerors to restore our lost rights. Such are the bitter fruits of secession.

"Mr. Chairman, I will here frankly say, as I have often said during the past four years, that there was not a man in the United States who more deeply regretted the secession of the Southern States than I did at the beginning of the revolution. There is not now in the Southern States any one who feels more bitterly the humiliation and degradation of going back into the Union than I do. Still, I know that I shall be more prosperous and happy in the Union than out of it.

"The resolutions which I have the honor of submitting for the adoption of this meeting simply express our willingness to adopt the terms of the President's proclamation and return to our allegiance. We likewise ask for the appointment of a provisional governor and the restoration of the civil authorities. There is nothing in these resolutions to which the most sensitive can object. If a man is in a loathsome dungeon there is no impropriety in asking to be released, no matter how innocent he may have been. Nor is there anything wrong in his promise to behave himself. The resolutions likewise provide for sending someone to represent the situation of the country to the President."

The resolutions offered by Mr. Perry were adopted, and he was elected chairman of a committee to call upon President Johnson and lay the matter before him. Already provisional governments had been established in all other Southern States except Florida, and the need of some sort of civil authority in South Carolina was seen to be imperative. Meetings to discuss the situation had been held in Abbeville and Columbia, and one attempted in Charleston (that in Charleston was broken up by negroes at the instigation of Federal army officers), but nothing of consequence had been accomplished. Governor Aiken and W. W. Boyce had been to Washington and there called upon the President, and while the Greenville meeting was in session friends of Governor Aiken were in Washington attempting to secure his appointment as provisional governor.

The Greenville delegation left immediately for Washington, but when it had proceeded as far as Ninety-Six met the friends of Governor Aiken, who bore a commission from President Johnson appointing B. F. Perry provisional governor of South Carolina. No effort from any quarter had been made to secure the appointment of Mr. Perry and it came as a surprise, not alone to the people of the state, but to Mr. Perry himself. However, the choice of President Johnson was a happy one, as the appointment met with the approval of every section and faction of the state so long torn by political discord.

After receiving his commission, Governor Perry proceeded to Washington, since he desired to confer with the President and receive first hand instruction as to the duties of a provisional governor. In the words of Governor Perry himself, "I went in company with Judge Orr (James L. Orr of Anderson, who succeeded Perry as governor) and several other gentlemen from South Carolina. We were received graciously by the President. In speaking of the convention (Constitutional) which would have to be assembled in South Carolina, he advised me to make the white population alone the basis of representation. I inquired of him if our new State Constitution, when adopted, would have to be submitted to Congress for their approval? He replied that it would not."

Immediately after his conference with the President, Governor Perry issued his Proclamation establishing civil government in South Carolina. It restored to office all officials who had last held places under authority of the Southern Confederacy. Although Governor Perry had been a staunch Union man up to the very last, he made no effort to put his former political friends in office. Writing of a conversation he had with President Johnson relative to this phase of his Proclamation, Governor Perry says, "I informed him that I had restored to office all the civil officers of the state, except those who were under arrest. I said I thought that I could rely on their loyalty, that they had been elected by the people, were familiar with their official duties, and would give more satisfaction than new appointees. I told him it was impossible to fill the various offices with Union men in South Carolina. The people had all taken sides with the state when she seceded, and that there was no Union party in South Carolina after the Civil War commenced." Speaking years later of this lack of Union sympathizers during the war, Governor Perry said, "This was strictly true, but afterwards, there were a great many political scoundrels who pretended for the sake of office, that they had always been true to their allegiance to the United States."

For 25 years or more preceding secession, Greenville County had been given no voice in the governmental affairs of South Carolina, since she was Union and the state was for nullification and secession; but with the appointment of Mr. Perry to the highest office within the state all this was changed. The eyes of the whole state now turned to Greenville and her leading citizen. But such has ever been the nature of man. When one is without power his opinions are scorned, but let the mantle of authority settle upon him and immediately he becomes the embodiment of wisdom, whose views are sought after and whose utterances are loudly proclaimed to the world.

The state was without laws. even the Constitution itself having been abrogated by the United States authorities, so the first step in reconstruction or reorganization was the calling of a Constitutional Convention by the provisional governor. But there were few people in the state qualified to vote for delegates to such a convention, since all who had taken part in the late war were deprived of citizenship. However, Governor Perry authorized all magistrates recently appointed by him to administer the "oath of allegiance" to any who might desire to take it and thereby regain their citizenship. In this manner many men of the state were soon qualified to vote, and when the Convention assembled Governor Perry was able to telegraph the President "that no political assemblage in South Carolina had ever surpassed it in virtue, intelligence, and patriotism. All the Judges, Chancellors, ex-Governors, United States Senators, and members of Congress, with few exceptions, were members of the Convention." Many of the elected delegates had not yet taken the oath and were therefore disqualified to sit; but without exception, they were pardoned by President Johnson and restored to full citizenship.

The Convention having met, "with a laudable spirit to accept the situation to which the fate of the war had reduced them, and make the most of it", a new constitution was readily adopted. Under its provisions slavery was abolished, but the freedmen were not given the right of suffrage. Following the adoption of a constitution, elections were held for members of the legislature; then came an election for governor. The first legislature under the new constitution numbered among its membership such notable men as General Butler, General Hagood, Governor Bonham, and General Elliot. James L. Orr was elected governor. Formerly he had been Speaker of the United States House of Representatives and a Senator of the Confederate States. South Carolina was again in the Union, with men of character and ability at the helm, and it seemed that she was soon to be on the road to rehabilitation.

The administration of Governor Perry lasted for six months, and during that short time a constitution was adopted, members of a General Assembly were elected, a new governor was chosen, civil officers of every nature and kind, both State and Federal, were appointed and inducted into office. Although it had full authority to do so, the Perry administration neither levied nor collected any taxes. Poverty over the state was so general that the governor thought the people should be given a few months' respite from added burdens. In his own words, "I stated to the Convention in my message on their assembling together, that they would have to provide ways and means to defray their expenses. For six months no money was received or paid out by the state. In every other state there was money raised in some way to maintain the state government. In South Carolina alone, there were no taxes levied, and no money received into the public treasury."

But the period of tranquility existing during the provisional government was soon at an end. Radicals seized the reigns of authority in Washington, and proceeded to reorganize the state government to suit themselves. The state constitution was abrogated and all officials elected under it were removed from office; negroes and carpetbaggers were placed in office and maintained there by the military authorities of the Federal government; a new constitution was adopted by the Radical regime and ten years of horror begun for South Carolina.

Governor Perry would not permit his name to be used as a candidate for governor under this reconstruction government, but the General Assembly elected under the 1865 constitution chose him as one of the two United States Senators from South Carolina. However, he was not permitted to take his seat. Later he was elected to Congress from his home district, but again he was refused a seat in the National body. For 30 or more years this prominent citizen of Greenville had gone unheeded in the state which he had so valiantly fought to save from disunion, but at last his advice was being taken and his leadership acknowledged.

During the long and trying years to follow the administration of Governor Perry, Greenville County suffered, along with all other portions of the state. True, her negro population was comparatively small, and for this reason her degradation and humiliation were not so great as that of some other portions of the state, but here negroes, carpetbaggers, and scalawags were as much in power as elsewhere. The white population was held in subjection by the military authorities, while the thieves and scoundrels held sway. But with the nomination of General Hampton in 1876, Greenville County, being largely white in population, played a prominent role in ridding the state of its shame. Joseph H. Earle, later United States Senator, and father of Dr. Baylis H. Earle, probably did more than any other one citizen of Greenville County to elect the Hampton ticket. He was a candidate for Attorney General on the Democratic ticket and secured election along with all the others whom the Democrats had nominated.

CHAPTER XV.

MARKING TIME—1876 TO 1895

For a quarter of a century following reconstruction, Greenville County moved along the even tenor of her way without contributing much of historical note to the steady progress of the state. But during those years she was growing in population and building the foundation upon which her future development was to stand. About 1900 the textile industry began to play a prominent part in her life, and since then the history of the county has been largely a record of the growth of cotton manufacturing. However, before a discussion of the industrial growth of the county is undertaken, it might give the reader a better understanding of later day development to picture briefly the movements of the county during those years.

The growth of the population over this period as furnished by the United States Census reports for both the county and city of Greenville are interesting in that they show a trend from rural to urban growth as well as a rapid "filling up" of the county. Tables follow.

POPULATION

COUNTY OF GREENVILLE

	1870	1880	1890	1900
White	15,121	22,983	27,516	33,999
Negro	7,141	14,511	16,789	19,488
Total	22,262	37,494	44,305	53,487

CITY OF GREENVILLE

	1870	1880	1890	1900
White	1,382	3,369	4,526	6,443
Negro	1,375	2,791	4,079	5,414
Total	2,757	6,160	8,605	11,857

By referring to the census reports an interesting fact is noted in the rapid growth of the negro population for the first several years of the period and then its gradual decline.

During the last few years our well-beloved townsman, Mr. Charles A. David, has written many articles for the *Greenville News,* in which he deals with "Greenville of Old." In doing this he relies almost wholly upon his memory, but great credence should be put in that which flows from the memory of one so versatile as is Mr. David. Roughly the period covered is that from 1860 to 1900. Dates are seldom used and there does not pretend to be any chronological recital, but the subjects with which he deals do not depend on this for interest.

Thinking that more permanent form should be given to much of the subject matter of these articles than may be had in newspaper files, and believing that there are many who will enjoy reading a digest of them, the author has set himself to the difficult task of collecting what he considers best from the entire series, and gives it here with comments interspersed where the subject matter can be clarified by so doing.

Regarding the Greenville and Columbia railway which made its way into Greenville in 1853, Mr. David writes:

"The old passenger depot (College Place Station) during the Civil War was a place of much interest, for it was on its platform that the bodies of Confederate soldiers were placed while waiting to be claimed by friends; and it was no uncommon sight to see one or more pathetic pine boxes resting there. At that time there was no telegraph office in Greenville, and consequently there was no daily paper, so news from the front was often several days in getting here. Towards the latter part of the war, the beloved Dr. E. T. Buist, pastor of the Presbyterian Church, made it a rule to meet the train from Columbia, get a morning paper, and standing on the platform, read in a loud, clear voice, the casualty list and any other news of importance to the assembled crowd."

Speaking of the town of Greenville prior to the coming of the Richmond & Danville Air Line railway (now main line of the Southern) which entered Greenville in the early seventies, Mr. David says:

"Business began at Coffee street; everything above that was vacant lots where wagons camped. . . . From Coffee street up to about where Armstrong's drug store (Main and North) stands was known as Sandy Flat, and it was given over to swapping horses and getting drunk. . . . Where Bruce & Doster's drug store (Main and Coffee) now stands was an ancient blacksmith shop . . ., and from there south to Washington street was an unbroken line of wooden stores.

"Even the topography of some of the streets has changed; for instance, where Washington crosses Main going west there was a considerable hill; and at the highest point of the rise, about where the Wallace building now is, right in the middle of the street, was a tiny brick building that Greenville folks referred to as 'the market'. . . . Washington street wasn't much of a thoroughfare in those peaceful days, as it only extended to the Presbyterian church, where it butted up against a rail fence that enclosed Mr. McBee's corn field, and right there it stopped.

"On the southeast corner of Main and Washington streets was the old Mauldin home, set well back from the street, with a flower garden in front and a corn patch and vegetable garden in the rear. Then came a store or two, mixed up with other dwellings. The only brick building that I recall was a two-story building on the space now occupied by the modern First National Bank (corner Main and McBee). Below this on the same side of the street were scattered several small brick buildings used as offices. One of these housed the only barber shop in town, and it was run by Henry Gantt, a very much respected negro. . . . And this single shop didn't have much to do, as the adult male population lived, breathed, and ate behind whiskers. Just south of Law Range, as the offices were called, was the Mansion House, built in 1824. It was a hotel of note in its time, but now it has gone the way of the wild pigeon, the hoop-skirt, and the spinning wheel, having been shoved out of the way by the new twelve-story Poinsett. Then came the court house with its brood of dinky little wooden law offices sprawled around. . . . The square now occupied by the post office and the Federal court house was the home of Colonel David Hoke. On the next corner below were two fairly good wooden stores. . . . From this point Main street rambled down a steep hill to the river and a rocky ford. A little way above the ford a narrow foot-bridge connected Greenville and the 'other side of the river.'

"The east side of Main street, beginning about where the Ottaray hotel is located, consisted of occasional dwellings down to Coffee street. The first business house was the drug store of Dr. Earle, which stood on the lower corner of Coffee and Main streets. The front part was used as a drug store, with the dwelling in the rear. . . . Next door was a two-story brick store—the finest in town. . . . On the southeast corner of Main and Washington towered a rambling brick building of three stories that started out as a tavern or hotel; it was then known as the Goodlett House. During the Civil war it was used as a Confederate hospital; in reconstruction days it housed a garrison of negro soldiers, and they stabled their horses in what had been the dining room facing on Washington street. . . . When the troops were withdrawn, the old hotel became the dormitory for students of the Southern Baptist Theological Seminary; and when the school was moved to Louisville, the First National Bank (then National Bank of Greenville) opened up for business in one of the rooms opening on the piazza. . . . There were two other brick buildings in the block, one the millinery shop and home of the McKays; and the other on the corner was the old Cleveland home. As far as my recollection goes, all the buildings on that side of the street (that is below McBee Avenue) down to the old court house, or Record building, as it was afterwards called, were of wood. The next brick building stood on the lower corner of Broad street."

Before the day of paved streets Greenville seems to have acquired somewhat of a reputation for the bottomless condition of the mud which covered them in winter. Of this Mr. David says:

"In those days before paved streets, in the winter particularly, the streets became almost impassable, and if anything, the sidewalks and crossings were even worse. Greenville mud was something out of the ordinary and in places it seemed to be bottomless, and when you put your foot down you had a feeling that it was liable to stick out somewhere in China. . . . I have seen empty wagons stall on Main street and have to be pried out of the sticky mud. Between McBee avenue and Washington street was one of the worst places in town, as the water seemed to gather there and could not run off, and along there was often muddy when the rest of the street was comparatively dry."

And while Greenville floated in this sea of mud the active mind of one of her citizens conceived the idea of bridging the chasm in a manner to furnish reasonably comfortable transportation along the principal streets. Mr. David writes:

"Mr. Thomas C. Gower (father of T. C. Gower and Mrs. W. P. Conyers) was a man with a vision, and while no one else seemed to think the town needed street cars, he tested the question by buying a couple of cars, four mules, and iron for the track, laid it on stringers from one depot to the other, and started a regular street car service that put Greenville ahead of any of her neighbors.

"The line began at the Greenville and Columbia passenger depot (now College Place), ran down Augusta street to Pendleton, and then via Main and West Washington to what was then known as the Air Line depot, now Southern Station. . . . As the patronage of this little friendly car line increased, the owner decided to add a freight car to take care of the hauling, so he bought a flat-car and another pair of mules which were added to the equipment."

This unique transportation system was inaugurated about the year 1890, but as time passed there was an improvement in the condition of the streets, which removed the necessity for "iron runners" and after a successful operation for several years, the first street car system was abandoned.

The Buncombe road, which now stretches its ribbon of new-laid concrete over the mountains to bind Greenville County closely with the many resorts of western North Carolina, has not always been used as a speedway. Back in the days of old, as now, it was the route by which the mountaineers of the two Carolinas and Tennessee transported their corn (in liquid form) to an eager market. But Mr. David, in his characteristic vein, tells of other purposes to which it was put. He says:

"When I was a boy this same old highway (Buncombe road or State Highway No. 21) was literally swarming with hogs, real hogs (not the road-hog variety), and each one carrying to market from 150 to 300 pounds of hams, shoulders and sides, to say nothing of sausages, spare-ribs and chitterlings. The reason for this annual passing of pork was because Greenville happened to be on a direct line between the great stock farms of Tennessee and the nearest seaport, which was Charleston.

"In the autumn when the hogs had put on all the fat the corn could give them, the men who dealt in hogs, thought in hogs, and lived by hogs, sent buyers over the land and bought up whole hog crops. These were brought together in immense droves and driven across the mountains into South Carolina, and down the Buncombe road to Greenville and thence to Charleston. . . . From Charleston they were shipped by water to the eastern distributing points, and eventually found their way to the tables of the nation. . . . Sometimes there was only a short distance between the droves, and at the height of the season the road would be blackened with the slow-moving brutes.

"Besides the endless stream of hogs that poured down the Buncombe road, it was no unusual sight to see big droves of turkeys driven in the same way—and they came from Tennessee, too, but they made much better time than the hogs."

Today there are comfortable motor busses passing almost hourly along that old road, which, in an easy half hour's ride from Greenville City, carry one into the very heart of a section where may be found some of the most beautiful scenery in all the world, but of old there were other means of public conveyance quite different from the "wheeled palaces" of today. Of these Mr. David says:

"Another thing that the old Buncombe road probably misses are the four-horse stages that used to run between Asheville and Greenville. . . . One of my earliest recollections is sitting in my mother's lap late in the evening and listening to the bugle-like notes of the stage driver's horn as he came down the long hill, opposite which is now Poe Mill Village."

PART I — NARRATIVE 95

The winter of 1898-'99 was hardly equaled in severity till those of 1917-'18. During the first, Camp Wetherell was located at Greenville, while the last two came when Greenville was the "Mother City" of Camp Sevier. Of Greenville at the time of Camp Wetherell, Mr. David writes interestingly as follows:

"Greenville mud reached its climax for depth and sloshiness the winter that Camp Wetherell was located here, during the Spanish War. Five regiments of the National Guard from New York, Massachusetts, West Virginia, New Jersey, and Missouri were ordered to Greenville to get in shape before the mix-up. They had all heard of the Sunny South, but mighty few of them had a correct idea just where South Carolina was located. Somehow they had it associated with the states further south, and when they were ordered here they imagined that they were headed for the sub-tropics, where they expected to loll around in the shade of palm trees and gorge on oranges and bananas. So many of the troops flung away their blankets and overcoats, as they thought they would not need them, and that they would just be in the way.

"But the night the first contingent arrived, it began to snow and freeze, and the weather was simply awful the whole time they were here, and it turned out to be the coldest winter Greenville had ever known. The term "Sunny South" got to be a great joke, as the sun seemed to have gone out of business.

"Naturally this kind of weather gave Greenville a black eye with soldiers, and about all that they remember about the town is the weather and the mud. . . . Just after the regiments were mustered out, and had gone home, the weather turned beautifully spring-like, just as our southern winters had always been."

Twenty years later when soldiers of the World War were encamped near Greenville, there was a repetition of the 1898-'99 weather, but this time without the discomforts of mud, since all the principal streets of the city were then paved.

The last time Greenville attempted a County fair was in 1919 or 1920, when a 40-acre tract of land was purchased on the Laurens-Columbia road about four miles from the city; but after three or four years it became evident that the county would not support such an institution, and the property was disposed of. Several years prior to this, a fair was held for a number of years at the present location of Sans Souci, but this too was abandoned. Long before that, however, a county fair was held near the city for many years. Of this Mr. David writes:

"They call it Park Place now, but it used to be the Fair Grounds, and for a number of years that was the only name it had. It included pretty much everything on the left hand side of the Rutherford road, beginning a little above where Mr. J. M. Charlotte now lives, and extending north clear up to the patch of woods that fringes the tracks of the Southern railroad, just before they duck under the overhead bridge. . . . The main building was a very creditable two-story affair, with a wide roomy veranda extending along the west side that overlooked the quarter mile race track. I do not remember the exact date of the fair, but it was in the fall, after the crops had been laid by. . . . Then the farmers began to arrive in buggies, carry-alls, and all kinds of vehicles except wagons; and the town folks drove out in the family carriages, and in hacks, and a lot of them walked. The crowd that gathered in and around the building was a jolly one; everybody was in a good humor, and seemed glad to meet everybody else."

Long before the adoption of the National Prohibition amendment, South Carolina had forbidden the sale of intoxicants, and prior to that Greenville County was "dry" under a local option statute. But there was a time, before the advent of the State Dispensary system, in the early eighteen nineties, when Greenville supported as many as 18 saloons at one time. This period in the growth of the city is discussed by Mr. David in the following manner:

"It is hard to realize that at one time intoxicating drinks of all kinds were sold as openly in Greenville as sugar and coffee, and nobody thought anything about it. I can remember when bar-rooms were as common as Roger's chain grocery stores are now. When the town 'went dry' or in other words, when the state of South Carolina went into the liquor business and undertook to do the poisoning herself, there were exactly eighteen regular licensed establishments where any man, woman, or boy could walk in, plank down a dime, and buy enough trouble to last a month. There was nothing furtive or hidden about it; the doors invitingly open; the steps were easy to climb, and the interior appointments were as fine as money could buy. Everything was open and aboveboard, and the men who owned and ran the bars advertised their different brands of whiskey just as any merchant would advertise his stock of shoes, clothing, or hats.

"Naturally they rented the best locations on the best streets, usually the most prominent corners, making it easy for all to quench their thirst at so much per quench. At that time merchants paid little attention to making their stores attractive, but the owners of bar-rooms vied with each other in having the furnishings and decorations elaborate and costly. . . . The first cut-glass chandelier that was ever brought to Greenville, as far as I know, used to hang in the bar of the old Mansion House. . . . People who didn't even drink lager beer used to go there simply to gaze on the crystal marvel.

"The first saloon on North Main street was in a ramshackle old wooden building on the corner of Coffee, where the Bank of Commerce is now. . . . The Mansion House bar was probably the finest one in town, but the one just across the street, on the corner where Carpenter Bros. drug store now stands was a close second. I do not remember that there was more than one 'over the river', and as there were eighteen all together, that left seventeen to be scattered along Main street. When the Dispensary took over the bar-rooms the town at one fell swoop lost $18,000.00 in revenue, as each bar was paying a license of $1,000.00 a year. Many people thought the town was ruined; but somehow it managed to pull along, and it is a good deal larger now than it was then."

CHAPTER XVI.

THE GROWTH OF MANUFACTURING

IN 1819 William Bates came to Greenville County from Pawtucket, R. I. He had a fair knowledge of cotton mill machinery, having been reared in a community then noted for its cotton manufacturing industries, but he had no money or influential friends. Greenville County had not yet entered upon the manufacture of cotton, but just over the county line in Spartanburg a small plant known as Lester's was being operated with indifferent success. Here Bates found work for a number of years till he and friends, who had acquired confidence in his ability, established "Batesville", a mile or two below Lester's, but on the Greenville side of the Enoree.

Just when Batesville began operations is unknown, but it is thought to have been about 1830. Machinery for the plant was shipped to Charleston and from there conveyed by wagons to the site of the new mill. This is generally thought to have been the first textile plant built in the county, but in 1825 there were already two small cotton factories, one of which was very likely located at Cedar Falls, and prior to 1820 there must have been a small plant in the county, for the United States census report for that year shows that $2,000.00 worth of cotton goods were manufactured during the preceding year. On South Tyger river, two miles from Greer, on the present site of Appalache, the Cedar Hill factory was built in 1820, but this, as well as Lester's, was in Spartanburg County.

Batesville was enlarged as the years passed, and by 1840 the county was producing $72,000.00 worth of cotton goods, principally from that plant. Its product was sold throughout the country, being hauled by wagon. About 1850 H. P. Hammett, a son-in-law of Bates, entered the firm which was then composed of William Bates and Thomas Cox, and known as William Bates & Company. The business was still further enlarged till the mill was operating 3,000 spindles in 1862, when it was sold to Trenholm, Frazier & Company. The year 1860 found the county producing cotton goods valued at $108,070.00, still principally from the Batesville mill.

When the Batesville mill was sold, Mr. Hammett used a portion of his share of the proceeds to buy Garrison Shoals on the Saluda river, with the intention of building a cotton mill there. However, the war was in progress and it was not till 1873 that sufficient capital could be raised to undertake the project. On February 13, 1874, a charter was secured for the Piedmont Manufacturing Company with a capital of $200,000.00, to be erected upon the site of Garrison Shoals. But no sooner was the mill under construction than a financial panic overtook the country, and construction was stopped. However, building was resumed in 1875, and on March 20, 1876, the machinery, consisting of 5,000 spindles and 112 looms, was started. This marks the real beginning of the textile manufacturing business in Greenville County. Colonel H. P. Hammett was the mill's first president, with J. E. Gregg, J. H. Martin, W. C. Norwood, James Birnie, T. C. Gower, Alex McBee, and Hamlin Beattie constituting the board of directors. In 1877 the plant was enlarged by the addition of 7,800 spindles and 112 looms. During the next year a second mill was built and in it were installed 9,860 spindles and 320 looms, and in 1883 the basement was filled with 3,136 spindles, making a total for the two plants of 25,796 spindles and 554 looms. At that time Piedmont was the largest mill in the state. Number 3 mill was begun in 1888 and finished in 1890. It was equipped with 22,848 spindles and 720 looms. In 1895 a fourth plant was constructed, and started operations with 10,000 spindles in 720 looms.

The advent of the Piedmont Manufacturing Company caused a marked increase in the value of manufactured products in the county. The value of all manufactured goods in 1870, according to the United States census reports, was $351,875.00, but by 1880 this amount had grown to $1,413,556.00.

Prior to 1895 the cotton mill industry of the county did not represent a very large invested capital. In addition to Piedmont and Batesville there was a small mill at Reedy river (now Conestee), one at Fork Shoals, the Lanneau Manufacturing company on Reedy river, just below the city of Greenville, one at Pelham organized in 1880, and the Camperdown Cotton Mills and the Huguenot Mills (present Nuckasee), both within the city of Greenville. In 1894 the machinery was taken from the Camperdown mill building and moved outside the city of Greenville to form the nucleus of the American Spinning Company, first known as the Sampson mill. Subscriptions to the capital stock of the F. W. Poe Manufacturing Company were made in 1895, and the company was organized with a capital of $250,000.00 for the purpose of building a 10,000 spindle mill; but within two years 5,000 additional spindles were added. During the same year (1895) the Mills Manufacturing Company, with 5,000 spindles was organized, while at Greer the Victor Manufacturing Company, with a capital of $200,000.00, began operating 5,000 spindles. The growth of the textile industry in the county was now well under way, and during the 35 years since, progress has been steady and consistent, there being hardly a year to pass without additions to the invested capital of some branch of the business.

The Spanish-American War came in 1898, and during the winter of 1898-'99 troops from a number of the northern states were encamped in Greenville (Camp Wetherell), awaiting a formal signing of the peace treaty. The coming of the soldiers stimulated business in Greenville and a number of new citizens of substantial business proportions were added to the permanent population. This new blood, and the broadening vision afforded by the problems of the war, gave to Greenville an optimism which urged her on to progress; and from about 1900 Greenville City began to feel itself a manufacturing centre, rather than the agricultural "shopping town", which it had been for so long. And with this broadening vision, the building of new and larger cotton mills became a passion. Successful business men in various lines disposed of their holdings to risk all in the new venture, and by 1901 a number of additional textile plants were being erected at various locations over the county.

During the years of 1900 and 1901 the Brandon Mill, the Woodside Mill, the Monaghan Mill, the Carolina (now Poinsett), the Franklin Mill of Greer, and the old McGee Mills all came into existence; and in 1902 the Union Finishing and

Bleaching Company was erected. Closely following these, the Dunean and Westervelt (now Judson) were built.

The method pursued in the financing of practically all of the mills built during this period was for some group of local business men to subscribe for a substantial portion of the necessary capital and then offer stock for sale to the public. Public meetings were held to explain the proposition. These were well attended, and an enthusiastic gathering purchased large amounts of the stock. The purchase of this stock by the general public was more in the nature of a civic duty than as a business investment. The people expected to be reimbursed for their holdings in enhanced land values and increased business, rather than directly from the earnings of the new enterprise. After as much stock as possible had been sold locally, the promoters went to the northern and eastern centers to sell the balance. This was usually disposed of to machinery manufacturers and cotton goods selling agents. No doubt such a method of raising capital was the best that could be found at that time, but it certainly served to place a great burden upon the textile industry, not only in Greenville, but over the whole South, where the same methods were used, for many years to come. Machinery paid for in stock was often antequated and always high in price, while the "selling agents" in return for their stock subscriptions exacted contracts for selling the mill's output at exorbitant commissions. Often a majority of the stock was held by these northern and eastern concerns, but the managements were local.

Usually one engaged in the manufacturing business is either "born into the business" or has undergone long years of preparation to fit him for the work. In the South, however, this was not true as regards early textile manufacturers. Those organizing and controlling the Greenville mills were almost entirely native South Carolinians, and for the most part residents of Greenville, with no previous training in their new work. Many of them had never been inside a cotton mill before entering the one they were expected to operate. Naturally the textile business was not remunerative for many years, under such conditions; but on the whole the Greenville mills were fortunate in their first managements. True, these men did not know anything about the manufacture of cotton, but they had been successful in other lines and were willing to learn. The stock in many of the new enterprises declined in value till it had very nearly reached the vanishing point before the mills began to show a profit. In fact a number of them were forced into receiverships and the original stockholders lost all in the reorganizations. But in the aggregate, the Greenville mills were more fortunate than most of the new mills of the South, and many of the original investors held on to their stocks till the years following the World War made them very valuable.

One of the outstanding manufacturers during this early period of the business in Greenville County was Lewis W. Parker. He came to Greenville from Abbeville in 1888 and began the practice of law. In 1897 he was called upon to "straighten out" the financial thangles of an embarrassed cotton mill, and so well did he acquit himself that he was prevailed upon to relinquish his law practice and enter the cotton manufacturing business. His first mill was the Victor Manufacturing Company of Greer. He next became one of the organizers of the Monaghan Mill at

Greenville. Later the so-called "Whaley group" of mills was reorganized and Mr. Parker assumed the management of them, becoming president and treasurer of the Olympia Cotton Mills, the Richland Cotton Mills, the Granby Cotton Mills, and the Capital City Mills, all of Columbia, S. C., and the Appalache Mills of Greer, a combination representing a capital of $5,000,000.00 and 340,000 spindles. Later these mills were merged with others, including the Victor of Greer and the Monaghan of Greenville, into the Parker Cotton Mills Company, with a capital of $15,000,00.00, operating 1,000,000 spindles. This consolidated concern, controlling more spindles than any other in the United States, maintained its offices in Greenville, occupying an entire floor in the Masonic Temple. For ten years or more Mr. Parker steered this huge concern to the satisfaction of his Board of Directors and the profit of his stockholders.

When the textile business had recovered somewhat from the shock of the 1914 depression, the mills of Greenville, almost without exception, entered upon a period of prosperity. Mill stocks were sought as the best investment to be obtained. No longer was it necessary for the managements to hunt a market for their securities; the market was now hunting them. New mills were built and old ones enlarged and improved. Enormous dividends in cash and stock were paid—the mill business of the South was at last firmly upon its feet. The stock of many mills held in the North and East since the construction of the mills now passed into the hands of local people.

Following the World War there was a period of prosperity in the cotton mill business wherever located, but about 1924 competition had become so keen that the northern and eastern mills found themselves unable to compete with the mills of the South, and a movement from the East to the South began. Some of the eastern manufacturers bought southern mills outright, while others came South to build new plants, in many cases bringing with them the machinery from their New England plants. Among the Greenville mills bought by these newcomers were the American Spinning Company, the F. W. Poe Manufacturing Company and Judson Mills; while some of the new ones to come were the Slater at Marietta and the Renfrew at Travelers Rest.

Along with the textile manufacturing plants have come many other closely related and allied manufacturing businesses. Although the county is still largely engaged in agriculture, its principal industry is "textiles." The city of Greenville boasts the name of "Textile Center of the South." The number of textile establishments in the county is 35, and includes not only cotton mills, but dye plants, bleacheries, finishing plants, plush mills, an underwear factory, and a worsted mill. The capital invested in the business is $33,299,603.00; average value of products manufactured annually, $40,000,000.00; number of employees, 12,976; annual payroll to employees, $10,000,000.00; number of spindles operated, 776,360, and number of looms, 20,316.

The employees of the Greenville County textile plants are wholly white, and almost entirely native born. Each mill maintains a community of homes in which the employees and their families reside. These mill communities contain every essential for living a comfortable and pleasant life, and the "mill people" confine themselves largely to these communities, not coming into contact with the citizenship generally. This self-imposed isolation has a tendency to make mill employees "clanish" and does not produce the best type of well-rounded citizen. The mill managements are looked upon somewhat as "overlords" and the system tends to build up a sort of paternal government in the mill communities. This has its advantages as well as its disadvantages. The mill employee is enabled to live much more cheaply than his eastern brothers, due to low rents, free lights, water, and recreation, which in turn permits him to work at a lower wage than eastern employees, and thus put his employer in position to continue operations when other mills are forced to close down. Labor unions have not yet secured a foothold in the Greenville mills and labor troubles are virtually unknown.

Although textiles constitute the principal manufacturing business of the county, still there are numerous diversified industries which contribute largely to the annual manufactured products of the county. Among these lesser manufacturies may be mentioned machine shops and foundries, wood working plants, textile machinery and supplies, cigars, leather belting, furniture, baseball bats, concrete pipe, peanut products, mattresses, food specialties, and a packing plant. The capital invested in these businesses amounts to more than $5,000,000.00; annual products have an average of more than $9,000,000.00; persons employed number about 1,900; and these are paid annually wages aggregating $1,451,215.00.

The manufacturing plants of the county are propelled for the most part by electric power, furnished by the Southern Power Company. Being located in the piedmont section where the falls of many rivers are near, the county was among the first of the state to profit from the development of water power sites. The only development of this class, which ranks as a major project located within the county, is on the Saluda River five miles west of Greenville City, but the power lines of the Southern Power Company traverse the county in every direction, furnishing power where needed.

Others, in addition to those already mentioned, who have taken a prominent part in the industrial development of the county during the last 35 years are: the late J. H. Morgan, founder and for many years President of the American Spinning Company; F. W. Poe, organizer and till his death in 1928, President of the F. W. Poe Manufacturing Company; W. E. Beattie, for many years President of the Piedmont Manufacturing Company, and his son, S. M. Beattie, now President of that company; the late Thomas F. Parker, founder and first President of the Monaghan Mills; B. E. Geer, President of the Judson Mills, and his brother, John M. Geer, deceased; Aug. W. Smith, President of the Brandon Corporation; John T. Woodside, President of the Woodside Cotton Mills Company, and his brothers, J. D. Woodside and E. F. Woodside, who have been closely associated with him; Thomas M. Marchant, President of the Victor-Monaghan Company; R. E. Henry, President of the Dunean Mills; Fred W. Symmes, President of the Nuckasee Manufacturing Company, and the Piedmont Plush Mills; the late C. E. Graham, President of the Huguenot and Camperdown Mills; J. W. Arrington, President of the Union Bleachery; E. A. Smythe, formerly President of the Pelzer Manufacturing Company, and for many years a resident of Greenville and financially interested in a number of her mills; H. J. Haynsworth, prominent attorney of Greenville, and a director in many of the cotton mills of the county; J. E. Sirrine of the firm of J. E. Sirrine & Company, mill architects, who has long been a heavy investor in mill stocks and a director in many of the companies; J. W. Norwood, Chairman of the Board of Directors of the South Carolina National Bank and director in a number of the Greenville mills; the late W. H. Balentine, founder of the Balentine Packing Company; and Captain O. P. Mills, deceased, founder and first President of the Mills Manufacturing Company.

CHAPTER XVII.

TRANSPORTATION FACILITIES

WHEN the piedmont section of South Carolina began to attract settlers from the more northern colonies, one of the principal hardships faced by the pioneers was the state of isolation in which they found themselves. The Indians and white traders, for many years, had used the historic "Keowee trail" in passing back and forth from the Indian country to Charles Town, and this was the only available route over which the early settlers could reach "civilization." Later a trading station was established at the head of navigation on the Savannah river, and to it another path, or trail, was made from the up-country settlements. But these two routes were nothing more than paths to be traversed only on horseback; still they served for many years as the only "outlets" from the back country to the coast.

A few years after the Revolution a State road was built from Greenville to Columbia, where it connected with another leading into Charleston. This was followed by another State road to Ninety-Six and Augusta, and within a short time a third one was constructed to the North Carolina line, where it connected with a road leading to Charlotte. There seems also to have been another road leading into the county from Pendleton at an early date. All of these main highways had their juncture near the present Tanglewood settlement, which was then the site of many summer homes belonging to wealthy families from the coast section. About 1825, during the administration of Joel R. Poinsett as Superintendent of Public Works, wealthy and politically influential citizens of Charleston, who maintained summer homes in Greenville and Flat Rock, North Carolina, were successful in obtaining the construction of a road over the mountains. This became known as the "Saluda Turnpike" and was recognized as an engineering feat of note in that day. Still portions of the old road are used, and in 1925 a public celebration, in which the assistant secretary of war took part, was held at "Poinsett Bridge" to commemorate the hundredth anniversary of the opening of the road.

It was not till the middle of the last century that Greenville was touched by a railroad. From its birth till the coming of the Greenville and Columbia Railroad in 1853, mail and public passenger service into the county was by stage coach from Charleston and Asheville. Freight came in by private conveyance from Charleston and Augusta, and farm products went out in the same manner to Charleston, Augusta and Hamburg. The larger merchants usually owned a "fleet" of wagons which were in continuous use between the home and port markets, while during the fall season the farmers spent much of their time transporting their cotton, grain, hogs and cattle to the markets. But the "live at home" policy, then in vogue among the up-country residents, greatly lessened the amount of goods and products to be moved, as compared to present-day requirements.

But as the population of the piedmont section grew, and manufacturing began to gain the attention of the people, agitation for a railroad into that section began, and grew rapidly, till it crystallized into a determined movement during the forties of the last century. Greenville played a prominent part in all stages of the movement and was from the first considered as the northern terminal of the road, with Columbia as the junctional point for connection with other lines leading to Charleston. Between Greenville and Columbia were many other towns anxious to have the road, and during the time its location was under consideration bitter rivalry arose among many of them. During the early part of the year 1847, Judge J. B. O'Neall of Newberry and Greenville was elected president of the proposed Greenville and Columbia Railroad, toward the construction of which large subscriptions to stock had already been secured; and to his business ability and great personal popularity may be attributed the ultimate success of the project. The distance from Columbia to Greenville via Newberry and Laurens was found to be 110 miles, and this was selected as the most feasible route. But Ninety-Six, Greenwood and Anderson wanted the road, and they came forward with heavy subscriptions in an effort to secure it. However, Laurens had furnished much of the stock already being used, and promises had been made that the road would pass through that district. The matter became involved in politics and much litigation developed. Greenville at one time withdrew from the project and the northern terminus was changed to Anderson. But a number of the leading citizens of Greenville never gave up hope of securing the road and continued to fight till they were finally successful. Credit for getting this first railroad for Greenville should go largely to Joel R. Poinsett, Colonel John T. Coleman, Governor B. F. Perry and Vardry McBee.

In 1853 the Greenville and Columbia Railroad reached Greenville, toward which it had been slowly moving from Columbia for nearly six years. Its cost was more than $2,000,000.00 (a tremendous sum for that day), which had been furnished by sale of stock to private citizens and the State of South Carolina. The coming of this first railroad may be said to mark the end of the pioneer period in the development of Greenville County. From 1800 to 1850 the white population of the district (now county) had increased by little more than 3,000, and the town of Greenville, although more than 50 years old, had less than 700 white inhabitants. But from that day forward, if the fearful war days be excluded, the growth of the county and city of Greenville have been steady.

Shortly after the close of the War Between the States, a movement was set on foot to build a railroad from Charlotte to Atlanta. Greenville set herself to the task of securing the road and was at last successful in her efforts. Many of her leading citizens subscribed heavily to the stock of the company, and none of them spared any effort to acquaint the promoters with the advantages offered by the section. But to General William K. Easley, more than to all others, is probably due credit for securing the road. At the time of its completion the railroad was known as the Richmond and Danville Air Line, but for many years it has been an important link in the main line of the Southern Railway system leading from New York to New Orleans. For fifteen years or more it has been double-tracked.

Greenville secured this second of her railroads in 1872, and since then there has been no slackening in her progress toward becoming one of the leading industrial centers of the great Piedmont Section. Immediately there began an unprecedented increase in the population of both city and county. From 1790 to 1870 the increase in population for the whole county was 15,759, while during the ten year period from 1870 to 1880 it was 15,232. Greenville City in 1870 had 2,757 people, but ten years later she had grown to a population of 6,160. Never before or since has either the city or county grown so rapidly as during this ten-year period.

After the "Air Line", came the Greenville and Laurens Railroad, which entered Greenville in 1882. The Greenville and Columbia had "opened up" the section of the county lying between Greenville and Pelzer and caused the building of large cotton mills at Piedmont and Pelzer, and the "Air Line" had given direct accommodation to the large and fertile section lying between Greenville and Greer; but this new road served a much greater portion of the county than had any other. It extended through one of the best farming sections of the county and added much to property values there.

For many years it had been the dream of residents of upper Greenville County to have a railroad through that section, and during the late nineties it seemed that this dream was to be realized. A road from Greenville over the mountains to Knoxville, Tennessee, was projected, but it failed of completion. Rails were placed as far as River Falls, to which point trains were operated for a number of years with indifferent success. Finally the road fell into possession of the Saluda Land & Lumber Company, which owns extensive timber lands in the mountains of the county, and is now being operated as a sort of semi-private line for the benefit of this company and textile plants located at Travelers Rest and Marietta.

During the early part of the twentieth century came the street railway system which serves to join the city of Greenville with the many industrial communities surrounding it. And then the Piedmont & Northern Railway Company, a concern affiliated with that owning the street system, began the construction of interurban electric lines, and soon these reached out from Greenville to Anderson, Belton, Greenwood and Spartanburg, furnishing rapid and easy freight and passenger service to these points and the intervening territory. Both of these transportation systems are controlled by the Duke Power Company, which is one of the largest owners and distributors of electric power in the South.

Although the population of the county had grown rapidly and the era of manufacturing had set in, the end of the nineteenth century found the highways in very little better condition than they were a hundred years before. More roads traversed the county than in the earlier days, but their condition was deplorable. Even the streets of Greenville City could hardly be traversed in winter. Ten years before, the county had begun the use of convict labor upon her roads, but modern road building machinery did not come into general use till several years after the turn of the century, and "pick and shovel" gangs can do little to keep the roads of a hill and mountain country in repair. But about this time the automobile appeared upon the scene, and with it came a demand for better roads. The stock appeal of every office seeker was for "better roads" regardless of the office for which he aspired. Of course this had the effect of putting the stamp of public approval upon larger appropriations for road building. More and more money was annually provided for the purpose, but much of it was wasted, as no effort to build roads of a permanent nature was made before 1914.

When the General Assembly met in January, 1915, the World War had the whole of the eastern hemisphere in its bloody grasp, and business conditions were in a state of depression. Cotton was selling at around six cents a pound, and the cotton-growing states were facing bankruptcy. In the midst of these adverse conditions the Greenville delegation in the Assembly thought of a way to help its constituency. The people wanted better roads, and now was an opportune time to build them. Labor and material could be had cheaply, and at the same time the sorely distraught farmers could be given work in constructing the roads. South Carolina had no state system of highways or any state-wide legislation pertaining to their construction—the county was the unit. Many of the far-seeing citizens of Greenville were advocating a county bond issue for road building, but no one was optimistic enough to think that the people of the county would vote bonds for such a purpose. They all seemed to want roads, but few were willing to pay for them. But some members of the legislative delegation suggested submitting a half-million-dollar bond issue "just to see what they think about it." At this juncture, however, Mr. T. P. Cothran, a member of the house, proffered the opinion that it was not necessary to submit a county bond issue to a vote. No one, it seemed, had ever before thought of such a proceeding being other than unconstitutional. A majority of the Greenville delegation favored a bond issue, the people had elected them on "good road" platforms, and why not pass a bond issue without a referendum? The novelty of the proceeding appealed to the assemblymen, and having decided to "bond the county" without a vote, they went the whole length of the county's capacity to issue bonds, and fixed the amount at $950,000.00. A wail of protest went out from every section of the county, and legal proceedings were immediately started to stay the issue of bonds. The Courts, however, held the act of the Assembly constitutional and the bonds were sold. The members of the Greenville County delegation responsible for the first county-wide system of improved highways in South Carolina were, Senator Wilton H. Earle, and House members, Thomas P. Cothran, Joseph A. McCullough, H. H. Harris, A. McQ. Martin, R. A. Means and Allen Hawkins.

Under the "million-dollar bond issue", as it was known, Greenville entered upon a road-building program which put her well to the front among the counties of the state in modern highways. The construction went rapidly forward under the supervision of a Highway Commission of which J. W. Norwood of Greenville City was chairman, and soon the county had a system of roads upon which traffic was easy during all seasons of the year. Following the lead of Greenville, other counties of the state (principally in the piedmont section) undertook road improvement by bond issues, and within the short space of three or four years there were many hundreds of miles of improved roads throughout the state. Legislation was enacted creating a state-wide system in 1918, and the whole state has gone steadily forward in the matter of road improvement since that time.

By 1924 the ownership of automobiles in South Carolina had become so general that there was an insistent demand for a state system of paved highways. Already Greenville and other counties of the state had built a few miles of hard surfaced roads, but no attempt had been made to build any state system of connected roads. But the General Assembly of that year (1924) adopted a system of approximately 4,000 miles of roads connecting every portion of the state; and at the same time made provision for the ultimate paving of this mileage under what was known as the "Pay-as-you-go Act." During the next session of the General Assembly the Greenville delegation composed of James M. Richardson, Senator, and A. F. McKissick, J. L. Love, W. H. Keith, J. McH. Mauldin, F. S. Davenport and C. E. Sloan as House members, sponsored legislation permitting Greenville County to issue bonds for the immediate paving of all the State highways in that county, pledging her estimated annual receipts under the "Pay-as-you-go Act" as security for the bonds. Serious question was raised as to the constitutionality of such a proceeding, but the courts ruled in favor of the plan, and Greenville County immediately launched her second road-building program. Many of the other larger counties of the state rapidly "fell in line", and soon much paving was under way.

Two years after Greenville undertook her paving program, her legislative delegation, then composed of Jas. M. Richardson in the Senate and J. L. Love, W. H. Keith, H. B. Black, A. N. Brunson, W. C. Goodwin and L. E. Wood as House members, decided to go a step further than did the law makers of 1925 and provide for a cheap form of paving to be laid on the principal roads of the county, not in the State system. This was done by another issue of bonds, with the result that more than a hundred miles of what are generally known as "cross-country" roads were paved. This gives the county, including the State roads, approximately 225 miles of hard surfaced highways, the major portion of which was completed, and the balance under construction, at the beginning of the year 1930.

In anticipation of the coming of these new highways "bus lines" were promoted throughout the state. Seeing that this new industry would soon be an important factor in the transportation system of the state, Jas. M. Richardson in the Senate and J. L. Love in the House of Representatives, offered bills at the 1926 session of the General Assembly providing for the regulation of these bus companies in a manner similar to that exercised by the state over railroads. The bills were enacted into law, and immediately motor bus transportation became popular; and within a period of two or three years busses were doing practically all of the local passenger transport business and much of the small package freight. Since Greenville now had hard surface roads radiating in all directions from it, and lay in the midst of a section of industrial communities, and was located near the numerous mountain resorts of upper South Carolina and western North Carolina, it became second only to Columbia in the number of bus lines operating from it as a terminal.

Today the transportation problems of the county seem to have been solved. Railroad facilities of the best are furnished by the Southern Railway with its main line over the old "Air Line" route and its branch line to Columbia using the Greenville and Columbia road, the Atlantic Coast Line owning, and operating over, the Greenville and Laurens road, and the Piedmont and Northern. And on all the principal roads of the county may be seen, during every hour of the day and often into the night, large and comfortable motor vehicles filled with passengers.

CHAPTER XVIII.

EDUCATIONAL FACILITIES

GREENVILLE County made little progress in the education of her youth till near the end of the last century. For near a hundred years after the organization of the county no attempt was made to establish a public school system, so the children of the county, during this long period, were dependent upon such advantages as private schools afforded. It is true that these private institutions of learning were often conducted by educators of note, who had attained high standing in their field; but the haphazard methods used in the major portion of them served to leave the "rank and file" of the people with practically no school advantages. The more wealthy families often sent their children to schools outside the county, or employed private tutors, but this was an advantage enjoyed only by the few.

Following the War Between the States there were ten years of chaos, during which no efforts were made to enlarge educational facilities. This, coupled with the five years of war preceding, caused education in the county to reach a low state from which it did not begin to recover till the late eighties or early nineties of the last century. But about this time the people began to awake to the fact that an educated citizenship was essential to the well-being of the state. And with this new outlook there began a slow but steady improvement in the schools of the entire state. Nevertheless, it was many years before the schools of Greenville County began to rank on a parity with those of the more wealthy lower state counties. In fact it is only during the last 15 years that the Greenville schools have taken a prominent place among those of the state.

But regardless of what may have been her situation in the past regarding education, Greenville County now stands at the very top in the state. Greater Greenville (Greenville City and suburbs) has two complete and distinct systems (Greenville City Schools and Parker District Schools) which enroll near half the pupils of the county. Parker District is said to be the wealthiest school district in the state of South Carolina. The Greenville City district ranks closely behind it in this respect. Located at Greer, Fountain Inn, Simpsonville, Taylors, Piedmont and Travelers Rest are also large and financially strong schools.

The schools of the county are all operated under the "6-0-1" state law, which provides that all schools of the state give at least seven months instruction each year. The salaries of the teachers for this period are paid, six months by the state and one month by the individual school districts. However, all of the larger schools, and many of the smaller ones, have terms of nine months. Salaries for these additional months are paid by the district in which the particular school may be located. All school buildings and equipment are provided by the several school districts. The money for this purpose is raised by bond issues of the districts.

The latest available statistics pertaining to the work of the public schools of Greenville County are for the year ending June 30, 1929. A table reflecting that work and showing the tremendous amount of public funds annually expended by the schools of the county follows:

High Schools for whites	18
High Schools for colored	0
Elementary Schools for whites	128
Elementary Schools for colored	65
Number of white teachers employed	806
Colored teachers employed	188
White pupils enrolled	23,743
Colored pupils enrolled	7,922
Annual expenditure for whites	$1,351,579.00
Annual expenditure for colored	$87,015.00

The 18 high schools of the county are so located that one of them may be easily reached from any section of the county. To these, as well as the elementary schools, "busses" run daily from all communities where a sufficient number of children to justify the expenditure are to be found. In fact, there can now be no excuse for any child residing in Greenville not securing an education.

In striking contrast to the county's educational system of today is that of 1903. That year there were 195 public schools in the county, but only 169 teachers were employed. Of the teachers 98 were white and 71 colored. The enrollment of white pupils was 8,761 and of colored 4,420. The total expenditures for the year were $47,131.40. And even as late as ten years ago the schools of the county had only begun their progress, as reference to statistics for the year 1919 shows. During the school year ending July 1st of that year the total expenditures by the schools of the county aggregated $204,687.92, while the enrollments of pupils was 14,889.

Although they form no part of the public school system of Greenville County, Furman University and the Greenville Woman's College have been closely identified with the educational life of the county, and are generally looked upon as local institutions.

Furman University.

Furman University came to Greenville from another part of the state in 1851, but before any buildings were completed, teaching commenced in "McBee Hall", a building located at the corner of Main Street and McBee Avenue. In December, 1850, the reorganized institution was granted a charter by the legislature as "The Furman University" with authority "to hold property not to exceed $300,000.00" and to be located "at or near Greenville Court House." The first faculty was completed in the fall of 1851. It was composed of Professors J. S. Mims, J. C. Furman, P. C. Edwards and Charles H. Judson. Soon thereafter building operations commenced. The first construction was a two-room wooden cottage for classrooms, which building yet stands "as a sacred place to every man who loves Furman." It is now occupied by the Quarternion Club. Next came a professors' home, which, within recent years was used as the president's home, and is now the Administration Building. Work on the Main Building, now called Richard Furman Hall, was begun in 1852 and two years later it was completed.

The first session 68 students were enrolled; the second year the University had 99 students; in 1854 there were 206; and in 1855 the number had reached 228. Responsibility for the management of the institution was placed upon the faculty, which annually elected a chairman to perform important administrative duties. Dr. James C. Furman was chosen by the faculty for this position, and he was re-elected each year till 1859, when he became president. Professor Judson was elected treasurer of the institution in 1856, and for 40 years he held that position, managing its funds with faithfulness and great ability.

From its inception till some years after its location in Greenville, Furman was primarily a theological institution, but its activities were local for the most part. But in 1857 the Southern Baptist Theological Seminary was established and the Theological Department of Furman discontinued. This necessitated the transfer of $26,000.00 of the Furman endowment to the Seminary, and removal of the theological library to the new institution.

Furman had not recovered from the effects of the loss of its theological department when the war broke over the state. Before this, mainly due to radical political agitation, the student body had been declining each year, and now the institution closed its doors. The student body of 155 organized the "University Rifles", and through Dr. Furman, tendered their services to the Confederate cause. Dr. Judson became president of the Greenville Baptist Female College (now G. W. C.) but all other members of the faculty remained on the pay-roll of the University, drawing a small stipend by way of salary, and awaiting the close of the bloody conflict. On February 15, 1866, the institution was reopened with an enrollment of 140, of whom four were from the student body of 1861. Three of these—W. H. Anderson, Duncan Brooks and James L. Brooks—were from Greenville.

But the bright prospects which accompanied the opening of the University in early 1866 did not last for long. Crop failures and "carpet bag" government, combined with the tremendous property losses of the war, soon began to make themselves felt at Furman. Much of the institution's endowment had been lost in the financial cataclysm of the war and little income was being secured from what remained. During the session of 1866-'67 only 45 students enrolled, and about half of these were on free scholarships. Only 27 students were enrolled in February and no commencement was held in June. It seemed that the institution must fail; but Dr. Furman, still president, said "I have been urged to abandon the university and seek a field of labor more certain, but I have resolved, if the university should go down, to sink with it." On July 13th a public meeting was held in the Court House to lay before the citizens of Greenville the distressing situation. The result was the securing of 12 three-year scholarships of $30.00 each, and this is said to have saved the institution.

Although the action of Greenville citizens in providing for scholarships relieved Furman of the financial embarrassment which she then faced, her troubles were not at an end by any means. During the next ten or twelve years dissentions arose within the Baptist denomination and among the Furman professors. The faculty was eventually made the "goat", with the result that all its members resigned in the summer of 1879 and the Board ordered the operations of the University suspended. However, the institution was soon reorganized and in September it was opened for the reception of students, with Dr. Charles Manly as president, Dr. Furman and Dr. Judson as senior professors and Professor H. T. Cook and Professor J. C. Newman as instructors. Fifty-one students enrolled that year. The following year there were 88, and for the next two years the enrollment remained at that number. In 1885 Rev. R. H. Griffith was elected financial agent, and during the next five years considerable progress was made, and by 1890 the institution seemed again on the road to success, with its finances upon a sound basis.

On March 3, 1891, Dr. James C. Furman died. Since 1844 he had been connected with the institution as a member of the faculty, and much of that time as its administrative head. In 1895 Dr. Judson resigned as treasurer and H. J. Haynsworth of the Greenville bar was elected his successor. Dr. Manly resigned as president of the institution in 1897.

Following Dr. Manly to the presidency of Furman came Dr. A. P. Montague, who held that office from 1897 to 1902. And although he was with the institution for a comparatively short time, much progress was made during his administration. He was a layman (the only one to be president of the institution), an educator with experience, acquainted with the technique of college administration, and firmly convinced that the possibilities of Furman were large. In short, he was a man of vision and executive ability. Soon after he came the Alumni Hall was erected from funds furnished largely by old students; next came the old Fitting School Building, now used as a residence by the business manager; then followed the Montague Hall, named in honor of the mother of Dr. Montague. Unfortunately Dr. Gordon B. Moore, professor of Philosophy in the institution, became involved in a bitter controversy over his teachings and Dr. Montague resigned, not because he was a party to the strife, but as many thought, because the situation greatly embarrassed him.

Following the resignation of Dr. Montague the University operated for one year without a president, and then in June, 1903, came Dr. Edwin M. Poteat, who remained till 1918. As justly said by his successor, "His administration was marked by important general progress in the life of the institution, shown by numerous minor improvements and by large increased endowment, decided raise in professor's salaries, the addition of two important buildings (the Library and the Hall of Science), and greatly increased efficiency." For a number of years prior to the coming of Dr. Poteat the enrollment had been declining, and during the fifteen years of his administration he put forth no particular effort to enlarge it. He was thoroughly committed to the advantages of the small college, believing, as he expressed it, in "hand-picked fruit", and only twice during his years at Furman did the student body exceed 200.

In 1907 Dr. Charles H. Judson, closely identified with Furman during the entire time it had been located in Greenville, died. Dr. McGlothlin says of him: "He was a great character, a great teacher and scholar, a humble and devoted Christian. He was probably Furman's greatest educator." During his life he made substantial contributions to the institution, and finally he made the endowment of the Furman Library his residuary legatee.

Dr. W. J. McGlothlin came to Furman in 1918 and under his guiding hand the institution has grown by leaps and bounds. In 1918 the student body numbered 206 and the faculty consisted of ten professors, whereas 35 are now employed in teaching 571 young men. About $700,000.00 has been put into improvements upon the campus. All old buildings have been renovated and improved and five substantial new buildings have been erected. The salaries of the faculty members have been increased about 50 per cent; a summer school with an annual enrollment of near 1,000 has been added; the endowment has been increased about 1,000 per cent; and a School of Education and a School of Law have been established. The institution is a member of the Association of Colleges of the Southern States, the Association of American Colleges, and the Association of American Universities; the Law School has been admitted to membership in the Association of American Law Schools, which permits its graduates to be admitted to the bar of South Carolina without examination.

The University has been greatly assisted in its rapid progress during these last few years by reason of a substantial allotment from the "Seventy-Five-Million-Dollar Campaign" conducted by the Baptists of the South, a gift of $175,000.00 from the General Education Board, a contribution from Alumni and friends of $325,000.00, allotment of 5 per cent of the income from the James B. Duke Foundation, a gift of $80,000.00 by J. W. Norwood, B. E. Geer and other citizens of Greenville for the building of a gymnasium, a pledge of $25,000.00 by C. S. Webb of Greenville for building an infirmary, a gift of $25,000.00 by Mr. and Mrs. W. E. Mason of Greenville as an additional endowment of the library, and many other contributions coupled with much hard work done by friends of the institution in Greenville and elsewhere.

Furman University is an institution of learning belonging to the Baptist denomination of South Carolina, but it has been so closely associated with Greenville for three-quarters of a century that it is usually considered by Greenvillians as a local enterprise. During the trying times which it has faced through the years, Greenville has always been ready and willing to assist, and now in the days of its success the city takes pride in its accomplishments.

* * * * * * * * *

Greenville Woman's College.

In the founding of Greenville Woman's College both Greenville and the Baptist church have had a share. As early as September, 1819, a foundation of $4,500.00 subscribed by Greenville citizens, and later increased to $9,000.00, together with a tract of land donated by Vardry McBee, provided for the establishment of two academies on the site where Greenville Woman's College now stands. The two academies, one for boys and one for girls, were operated for a number of years under a Joint Board of Trustees elected by the subscribers to the fund. In the early fifties, however, the Baptists of South Carolina began to feel that a woman's college should be established. A committee with power to act was appointed by the Convention of the denomination which met in Greenville in 1854. Immediately this committee entered into negotiations with the trustees of the academies, and succeeded in securing a conveyance of the Academy lands to the Baptist State Convention of South Carolina.

With the acquisition of the Academy lands, the Greenville Female College, as it was then called, came into being. The first unit of the Main Building (still standing) was constructed in 1855, and in 1870 another unit was added to the building. Since then the building has been remodeled, the administration offices now occupying the first section to be built. The East Building was erected in 1900 from funds raised by Dr. C. S. Gardener and H. P. McGee. This constituted the plant of the college till it began its marvelous growth soon after Doctor David M. Ramsey assumed the presidency of the institution in 1911.

During the period of the War Between the States, Doctor Charles H. Judson, that grand old man of Furman University, was president of the Woman's College. His sister, Mary C. Judson, was connected with the institution continuously for more than half a century till her death. At the Greenville Woman's College she was as generally loved and respected as was her brother at Furman. The Mary C. Judson Library, named in her honor, is located on lands originally donated to the college and prior to that time occupied by the Male Academy. This portion of the college property was sold to help secure funds for building the first unit of the Main building; but through efforts of the alumnae the property was re-acquired and in 1924 the buildings located on the lot were remodeled and converted into a modern library.

In 1911 Doctor David M. Ramsay, a native son of Greenville County, was called to the presidency of the Greenville Woman's College to succeed Doctor E. C. James, and from that day onward the institution has moved steadily forward. During the very first year of his administration the West Building was erected and the next year saw the completion of the North Building. The David M. Ramsay Fine Arts Building was dedicated in 1922. It has an auditorium with a seating capacity of 1,200, which is the largest in the city of Greenville, with the exception of the Textile Hall.

Since 1911 five of the eight buildings on the college campus have been erected, the enrollment has more than doubled, the faculty has been greatly strengthened and enlarged, and a three-acre lot on which the library now stands has been acquired. And during all this period of progress, the college has run without a deficit, notwithstanding the fact that it has no general endowment for most of the time. And not alone have operating expenses been paid from tuition fees, but thousands of dollars from that source have been used for permanent improvements. These are splendid achievements which are proudly regarded not only by the Baptist denomination in South Carolina, but also by the city of Greenville and the entire state of South Carolina.

An extensive campaign is now under way to raise an endowment of $500,000.00 for the college, with prospects for its success bright. Recently the institution has been admitted to membership in the Association of Colleges and Secondary Schools of the Southern States. It has an enrollment of more than 500 and a faculty numbering 27 full-time professors and instructors.

THE GREENVILLE PUBLIC LIBRARY.
By Charlotte Templeton, Librarian.

The Greenville Public Library was established in the spring of 1921. Largely through the efforts of Thomas F. Parker, a Library Association was formed with the following persons as a board of trustees: Thomas F. Parker, F. W. Symmes, Mrs. Wilton H. Earle, J. W. Norwood, Mrs. H. H. Harris, and Mrs. M. P. Gridley. A small store back of the Bank of Commerce, on East Coffee Street, was rented, and Miss Annie Porter was engaged as librarian.

The library, with pine tables and shelves built by a carpenter, and with 500 books on its shelves, was opened in May. The expenses of rent, salaries, and books for the first year were borne by Mr. Parker. Early in the second year a campaign was conducted to raise funds for an enlarged service. An adjoining room was rented and two assistants to Miss Porter were employed. The use of the library grew by leaps and bounds and in the summer of 1922 the citizens of Greenville voted a two-mill tax for the continued support of the library. After the election, the Library Association turned the library over to the control of a City Board of Trustees appointed by the Mayor and City Council. The first Board consisted of Thomas F. Parker, J. W. Norwood, Mrs. H. H. Harris, Miss Jim Perry and John A. Russell.

Miss Annie Porter resigned in 1923 as head librarian because she found the work overtaxing her strength, but continued on the staff as an assistant. Miss Charlotte Templeton of Atlanta was elected librarian and assumed her duties on Sept. 1, 1923. In October of that year the library entered upon a program of expansion. On funds supplied by Mr. Parker and Mr. Norwood, an auto truck was purchased and equipped for library use, and a schedule of fortnightly visits arranged for the communities in the newly organized Parker School District. This was the first library truck service established in the South.

The plan of the truck service adopted in the beginning is still followed. With adult book shelves on one side of the truck and juvenile books on the other, the truck was driven out to a mill village, where it went first to the school to permit the children to get books, then to the mill where the workers could exchange their books during the lunch hour. This visit was repeated every two weeks, always on the same day. By taking books to the people and lending them without any red tape, a reading public was immediately secured. The truck carried its own publicity and the informality of its approach made it particularly well adapted to a group unaccustomed to libraries.

On February 1, 1924, the library moved into a three-story building erected by Dr. Fletcher Jordan on North Main Street and leased to the library. The furniture and equipment for the new building were the joint gift of Mr. Parker and Mr. Norwood. The more commodious quarters made possible a greatly increased use of the library. The attractive children's room fitted up on the ground floor and in charge of a trained children's librarian was the first special children's library in the state.

In January, 1925, the library took the second step in its expansion program. With funds again supplied by Mr. Parker and Mr. Norwood, a second library truck was purchased, together with a special book collection, and a rural service to the county was begun. Miss Porter was put in charge of this work. Library stations were placed at various points in the county, collections of books were loaned to schools and a direct truck service for the industrial villages was established. It was the desire of Mr. Parker and Mr. Norwood, who were financing the county work, that it should be carried on as a demonstration in order that the people of Greenville County, to whom the idea of such a general library service was new, might have a chance to test its worth before being asked to support it. In the third year of the demonstration the interest of the county people was put to the test at an election called to vote on a one-mill library levy. The tax was voted and a county library board was appointed in accordance with the law. The first county board was composed of Miss Elsie Barton of Tigerville, Dr. P. J. Johnson of Greer, V. M. Babb of Fountain Inn, E. A. Webster of Greenville, and Mrs. E. B. Nash of the Parker District. The County Library Board entered into a contract with the trustees of the Greenville Public Library under which the Greenville Public Library extended its use to the county.

Soon after the city tax was voted, a branch for Negroes was established in the Phyllis Wheatley Community Center with a Negro librarian. When a new building was erected for the Center, the library rented the front room on the first floor and equipped an attractive branch library. The library was opened to all Negroes of Greenville County and has been well used by the county teachers. This was the first public library service for Negroes in the state.

The Greenville Public Library was a pioneer in county service. It was the first library in the South to offer so complete a service to a large area. With its central library, auto trucks, branches, deposit stations, and home libraries, it worked out a variety of methods to reach all the people of Greenville County, and succeeded so well that a total of 361,323 books were loaned in 1929.

No account of the Greenville Public Library can be complete without special tribute to Mr. J. W. Norwood and Mr. Thomas F. Parker. Mr. Norwood always stood ready with financial aid through the early period of the library's experimentation and expansion, while the library owes its very life to Mr. Parker. With great breadth of vision, unfagging effort, and generous gifts of money he labored to bring into reality the library of his dreams, which was one of service for rich and poor, educated and uneducated, urban and rural, white and negro.

CHAPTER XIX.
CITIES AND TOWNS
GREENVILLE.

THE Greenville City of today would hardly be recognized as being the same as that of a quarter of a century ago. Beginning to grow during the nineties of the last century, it has made phenominal strides and now has a diversity of interests which would do credit to a municipality of a hundred thousand people.

Closely surrounding the city proper, which has an incorporated area of only 4.82 square miles, lie a number of thickly settled communities where very nearly all the industrial plants of the county are located. The interests of these communities are so closely allied with each other and those of the city proper that the Census department of the Federal government has recognized the unity of these various subdivisions and classes the whole as the "Greenville Metropolitan Area." Commercially, Greenville City consists not only of its own incorporated limits but of these communities as well. The whole is sewered and watered under the same systems and the schools of the entire territory closely interlock. Many of those doing business in the city reside in these suburbs, while practically all of the executives for the industrial plants live in the city, or one of its residential suburbs.

The names of these various suburbs, or industrial communities, with their population figures as given by the 1930 census reports are as follows:

NAME OF COMMUNITY	POPULATION
City of Greenville, Incorporated	29,081
West Greenville, Incorporated	1,917
Northgate Heights, Residential	446
Park Place, Residential	1,407
Poe Mill, Industrial	2,050
American Spinning Company, Industrial	1,691
Sans Souci, Residential	1,720
Union Bleachery, Industrial	1,064
Riverside, Industrial	1,098
Monaghan Mill, Industrial	2,201
City View, Residential	1,563
Pendleton Heights, Residential	559
Woodside Mills, Industrial	2,459
Brandon Mills, Industrial	2,335
Highland, Residential	1,578
West View, Residential	1,059
Judson Mill, Industrial	2,467
Booth, Residential	1,437
Dunean Mill, Industrial	2,321
Mills Mill, Industrial	1,647
Cherokee Park, Residential	1,206
Kanatenah, Residential	760
Eastover, Residential	794
Overbrook, Residential	807
Total population for Greenville Metropolitan Area	63,668

Greenville City proper and West Greenville, being incorporated, is each governed by its own elected officials. The other districts have no officers, except that the industrial areas employ deputy sheriffs to maintain order.

The Greater Greenville sewerage system, completed in 1928, furnishes "trunk line" facilities to the entire Metropolitan Area. A bond issue of $3,000,000.00 was floated for the purpose of carrying out this project. Greenville City, West Greenville, and many of the suburban sections maintain "lateral line" systems which tie into the larger plant. Water is furnished to the whole area from the system owned by the city of Greenville. This was recently completed at a cost of more than $2,000,000.00 and has a capacity of eleven million gallons daily. The water comes from an impounding basin with a capacity of 9,522,000,000 gallons, located in the midst of an eleven-thousand-acre water-shed in the Blue Ridge Mountains, thirty miles away.

The city of Greenville owns four parks, aggregating 350 acres. Three of these are for white people and the other for colored. In addition to these, parks and public play grounds are to be found at very nearly all the textile plants of the Greenville Area. The major part of the population of the industrial communities comes from the mountain sections of the Southland. Here they were isolated, and living thus they did not have the means of recreational facilities, except such as called for individual prowess. They knew nothing of participation in team play, group activity, group competition, or even community life. When they entered the mills they needed direction in this respect. This was freely provided by the mill owners, so the parks and play grounds of the industrial sections are presided over by full time, paid, instructors and directors.

An air port owned jointly by the city of Greenville and Greenville County is located near the Eastover section. Air mail planes plying between New York and Atlanta stop here daily.

The Greenville Metropolitan Area is served by two excellent public school systems, in the Greenville City Schools and the Parker District Schools. The 1928-'29 enrollment in the City Schools was 7,600, while that of the Parker District was 6,300. In the City School system there are 13 grammar schools for whites and three for negroes, with a separate high school building for each race. The Parker District has 19 grammar schools and one high school, with the largest white enrollment of any school district in the state. The City system employs 265 teachers and expends $417,000.00 annually, while Parker District has 239 teachers and is operated at an annual cost of $373,000.00. Furman University and the Greenville Woman's College, the first named for young men and the other for young ladies, furnish as good higher educational facilities as may be had in the state. Both are located within the incorporated limits of Greenville City.

Practically every religious denomination is represented in the Metropolitan Area of the city, with Baptist, Methodist and Presbyterian leading in the order named. There are 52 churches within the territory.

The leading newspaper of South Carolina—*The Greenville News*—is published every morning in Greenville City. Not only does it lead all other daily newspapers of the state in circulation, but it carries a larger volume of advertising and news matter than any other. The afternoon paper—*The Greenville Piedmont*—is owned and published by the Greenville News Company. Its circulation is the equal of any afternoon paper in the state. The combined circulation of the two papers is 44,500, with more than 30,000 of that credited to the morning paper. *The Observer,* a weekly newspaper with a large circulation, especially in the industrial sections, is also published here. The official publication of the Baptist denomination in South Carolina—*The Baptist Courier,* is likewise published in Greenville.

The value of club life is fully appreciated in Greenville as is attested by the large number of flourishing organizations of that nature to be found in the community. Strong units of the Rotary, Kiwanis, Civitan, Lions and Monarch Clubs are rendering a commendable service. Greenville also has a splendid Elks Club, which maintains an elegant home on East North Street. The Young Men's Christian Association has a five-story building on East Coffee Street, and on West Washington Street the Young Woman's Christian Association owns a five-story building. The Greenville Country Club occupies a beautiful site in the Kanatenah section, where it maintains a modern club house with an 18-hole golf course, a swimming pool, tennis courts and other attractions. Both the Boy Scouts and the Girl Scouts have large memberships in the Greenville Area. The Phyllis Wheatley Center is a social and civic organization for the colored people of the city, which does much to cement the bonds of friendship which exist between the two races to such a marked degree in Greenville. Here a branch of the Greenville Public Library is maintained for the exclusive use of the colored people. The American Legion has a large membership in the city and its environs and does much to assist veterans of the World War. Practically all of the industrial communities of the Metropolitan Area have organizations of the Y. M. C. A., Y. W. C. A., Boy Scouts and Girl Scouts.

In the Carolina, the Rivoli and Egyptian, Greenville has three of the finest amusement palaces to be found in the Southeast. The Carolina, modern theatre and motion picture palace in one, is said to be the most beautiful establishment of its kind in the Carolinas. It has a seating capacity of 1,218, while that of the Rivoli is 746 and of the Egyptian 428. Other picture show houses are The Majestic and Bijou with smaller ones in West Greenville and at the textile plants. The colored people operate the Liberty. And while not classed as a theatre, the Textile Hall, home of the Southern Textile Exposition, is equipped with a stage and all the paraphernalia of a modern theatre, and concerts and conventions are often held here, where 5,000 people can be accommodated.

Much of Greenville's progress during the last few years has been due to an unusually active Chamber of Commerce. This body has the unique distinction of owning its own home—an eleven-story office building—which stands upon the site of the old County Court House.

Greenville has four first-class commercial hotels—the Imperial on West Washington Street with 250 rooms, the Ottaray on North Main Street with 100 rooms, the Poinsett with 200 rooms on South Main Street, where formerly stood the historic Mansion House, and the Virginia with 54 rooms on West Coffee Street, where the Opera House formerly stood. Besides these there are numerous smaller hotels, apartments and public rooming houses, designed to care for a large transient population.

The city has three National and two State banks, which furnish it extraordinarily good banking facilities. Two of these are branches of the strong South Carolina National Bank chain, while another is a branch of the equally strong Peoples State Bank system. Four of these institutions own their banking houses, while the fifth (Peoples State Bank) maintains quarters on the first and second floors of the seventeen-story Woodside Building. The combined resources of these banks amounts to near $75,000,000.00. In the city are six building and loan associations, while many of the large insurance companies have local mortgage loan representatives here. Four home-owned life insurance companies have their headquarters in Greenville.

There are two public hospitals within the city proper, while another is maintained at Chick Springs, eight miles east of Greenville. The Shriners operate one for crippled children four miles east of the city. A modern plant for the treatment of tubercular patients is just being completed in the suburbs. It is owned and operated by the county, and is the only one of its kind in the state. Greenacre, a home for abandoned and ill-supported children, is located just outside the Eastover section. It is supported primarily by appropriation from the city and county.

Greenville claims to be the "Textile Center of the South." Within a radius of one hundred miles of the city there are 467 cotton mills, with 3,176,638 spindles, 162,618 looms, and 9,361 knitting machines. Greenville County itself has 35 textile establishments. Within the Greenville Metropolitan Area are cotton manufacturing plants operating 592,508 spindles and 15,758 looms. Also numerous industries complementary to the spinning and weaving of cotton are to be found in the county. Two of the largest bleaching and finishing plants in the South are located here, as well as one of the largest dye plants of the country. Greenville also has a large worsted mill, one of the very few in the South.

While Greenville is widely known for the extent and variety of her textile industries, manufacturing is not confined to cotton. There are in the city, machine shops and foundries; establishments for the manufacture of loom harness, reeds, shuttles, shuttle blocks, bobbins and other textile equipment; plants for making store fixtures, mantles, leather belting, cigars, athletic underwear, veneer, concrete pipe, mattresses, peanut products, food specialties, baseball bats, furniture, automobile brake-bands and many other products. Greenville also has the only packing house in South Carolina.

Among the cities of South Carolina Greenville ranks third. Should she be credited with the entire population of the Metropolitan Area she would hold second place. The population of the county is 80 per cent white, while the city and suburbs contain a higher percentage of whites. The foreign-born element is negligible. Negro illiteracy is much lower in Greenville than other portions of the state, which no doubt accounts for the high type of colored population which characterizes the city.

GREER.

In 1873 when the Richmond & Danville Air Line Railway (now the Southern) passed through Greenville County, a flag station was established on lands of

Manning Greer, 12 miles east of Greenville City, and from this time dates the history of Greer, the second largest municipality in the county.

In the rear of the building known as Dr. Few's drug store may yet be seen the remains of an old house site. This is the former location of the Blakely residence. About 1866 Mr. Blakely sold his farm consisting of 200 acres to William Thackston, who in turn sold to Manning Greer in 1868. After the location of the railroad had been definitely established and Mr. Greer had given lands for the station, he sold to W. T. Shumate of Greenville, who cut much of the property into lots, which he sold off at small prices.

The town of Greer was incorporated in 1875. Soon Hughes and Bomar opened a general mercantile establishment. One of the members of this firm was the late Simeon Hughes, father of R. M. Hughes, president of the Planters Savings bank. A few years later D. D. Davenport established a large mercantile business here which became a great factor in the growth of the town. Dr. H. V. Westmoreland began the practice of his profession in the Greer community about 1870 and had the field alone till 1883 when Dr. B. F. Few located there.

About the year 1820 Rev. Thomas Hutchings settled in the present Greer section and built Cedar Hill Factory on South Tyger river in Spartanburg County, two miles northeast of the present town of Greer. This manufacturing plant was operated by various owners till 1888 when its name was changed to Arlington. Under this name it continued business till 1903, when it became the Appalache Mills. Later it was made a part of the Victor-Monaghan group, under which management it is now operated. In 1895 the Victor Cotton Mill was given its charter, and during the next year it began operations under the presidency of W. W. Burgiss, now a resident of Greenville. It is now a part of the Victor-Monaghan group. Next came the Franklin Mill which was organized by Mr. Burgiss in 1900. The Greer Mill was organized by John A. Robison, Sr., in 1908 and he became its first president. Later it became a part of the Parker merger, and is now owned by the Victor-Monaghan Company.

Till 1900 Greer had no local banking facilities, but in that year Lewis W. Parker and others organized the Bank of Greer. This institution is now a part of the Peoples State Bank chain. In 1907 the Planters Savings Bank was organized and Howard B. Carlisle of Spartanburg became its president. Next came the Peoples Bank which later secured a National Charter and became the First National Bank. In 1930 it was purchased by the Planters Savings Bank. The combined resources of these two institutions exceeds $2,500,000. Of the Peoples State Bank, E. C. Bailey is vice-president and active head. R. M. Hughes is president of the Planters Savings Bank.

No progressive community could be long without school facilities, so in 1875 Miss Sallie Cannon opened the first school at Greer in a small log cabin furnished by W. A. Hill. From this modest beginning has grown the present splendid school system of Greer, which is second to none in the state, and exceeded in property owned and pupils enrolled in the county only by the Parker and Greenville City Schools. Today the schools own upward of $200,000.00 worth of property and enroll 1,278 pupils. There are 50 teachers employed.

In the town of Greer are Baptist, Methodist, and Presbyterian churches with large memberships. The Baptist predominate, with the Methodists coming next.

For a number of years after its establishment, the progress of the town was slow, but during recent years, and especially the last fifteen or twenty, Greer has become a remarkably progressive and thriving little city, with two strong banks, a thriving Building & Loan Association, a large number of enterprising merchants, both wholesale and retail, four cotton mills and various other industries, with municipally owned lighting and water systems and many paved streets. According to the census of 1930, the town has a population of 2,350.

SIMPSONVILLE.

The town of Simpsonville, with a population of 1,400, is located thirteen miles southeast of the city of Greenville on State Highway No. 2 and the Charleston and Western Carolina Railway.

First to settle on the present site of Simpsonville was Peter Simpson (from whom the town derives its name), who moved there from the Durbin creek section of Laurens County in 1836. He lived there till his death in 1847, being engaged in farming and the operation of a blacksmith shop. His home was located near the present residence of W. F. Gresham. Mrs. Margaret Thackston, a daughter of Peter Simpson, is still living at the age of 86 in the Simpsonville community.

The pioneer merchant of Simpsonville was Silas Gilbert, who operated a store northwest of the present oil mill plant at the fork of the Old Stage and Georgia roads. His home was located where F. D. Hunter now resides. The mother of F. D. Hunter was a sister of Silas Gilbert.

Before the War Between the States Jariot Cook built a home near where the Gilbert store stood. His is the only house constructed prior to the War Between the States now standing in the town of Simpsonville. It is the T. L. Henderson place.

The postoffice, when first established in the Simpsonville community, was known as "Plain." It seems to have been first kept by William A. Austin at his home, where is now located the McAlister residence, a mile south of the town. Later it was moved to the Jesse Stone plantation, three miles south of town, where J. D. Richardson now lives. From the Stone farm it went to the "Boyd Place", two miles north of the town. Next it was moved to the "Old Store Building" within what is now the town. At first mail was received only once each week, then twice a week and later three times weekly till the coming of a railroad in 1886, when a daily service was established. The name of the post office was changed to Simpsonville during the early eighties.

The principal thoroughfare into and out of the community before the coming of the Charleston and Western Carolina Railroad was the "Old Stage Road" over which stage coaches were operated between Greenville and Laurens. The "Stage" made the trip from Greenville down to Laurens one day and back the next, thus furnishing public transportation in each direction on alternate days. The first driver of the Greenville to Laurens stage coach is thought to have been Reuben

Bramlett, grandfather of D. L. Bramlett, now president of the Farmers Bank of Simpsonville.

About 1879 S. J. Wilson moved into the community from North Carolina and established a general mercantile business in the "Old Store Building." In addition to his mercantile business he operated a large farm, having purchased 200 acres from Dr. M. A. Hunter. After the coming of the railroad he cut a portion of his farm into lots and thus became the "promoter" of the present town of Simpsonville. He built the first brick store in the town, this being on the present site of the drug store. For many years he was a leading citizen of the town and did much to promote its growth.

Before the coming of the railroad the only school ever held was a short summer term in a tenant house (still standing west of the oil mill on "Old Stage Road"). It was taught by Miss Matilda Alverson (later Mrs. Mat Bramlett). But with the advent of the railroad several prominent men from other sections came in and built homes. A two-story frame school building was erected and a good school was started, with Professor A. M. Dawson as principal.

The growth of the town was slow till 1907 when the Simpsonville Cotton Mill, with E. F. Woodside as president, was built. Since then substantial progress along all lines has been made. Within a few years after its organization the cotton mill became a part of the Woodside Cotton Mills Company. About 1925 it was enlarged and now employs near 500 people and has a weekly pay roll of about $4,000.00.

The town of Simpsonville is surrounded by one of the most progressive agricultural sections of the county. It furnishes an excellent cotton market, has two large public ginneries, a strong bank owned by local interests, an ice plant, and numerous business houses engaged in all lines of endeavor. Burdett's White Building and the Bramlett-Smith Drug Store Building would be credits to a city of no mean size.

From its modest beginning the Simpsonville school system has grown into large proportions. For white children there is a school plant worth near $100,000.00, where twenty-five teachers are employed and seven hundred pupils taught. The school has won quite a reputation for itself, not alone for the high educational position which it maintains but also for high rank in athletic achievement. The girls' basket-ball team, known as the "Whirlwind", has won numerous inter-sectional contests. During the last few years much attention has been given to Negro education. A substantial colored school building is maintained. There are eight negro teachers and three hundred pupils.

The town is governed by a Mayor and Board of Aldermen elected each two years. It has a municipally owned light plant and water system. A telephone system (privately owned) is also maintained in the town.

The citizenship of the town of Simpsonville is high, and an unusually large number of her people take an active interest in the religious life of the community. The Baptist faith predominates, with two churches of that denomination in the town. For many years there was only one church in the town (Baptist) but about twelve years ago the Methodists organized and built a house of worship, and some six years ago the Presbyterians entered the town. Among the long established country churches near Simpsonville are Standing Springs (Baptist), Clear Springs (Baptist), and Hopewell (Methodist).

* * * * * * * * *

The facts from which the sketch of Simpsonville has been written were furnished by D. L. Bramlett of Simpsonville.

Fountain Inn.

The town of Fountain Inn is located eighteen miles southeast of the city of Greenville on the Charleston and Western Carolina railway, and on State highway No. 2. The historic Fairview community lies five miles to the southwest, and many of its citizens were born and reared in that vicinity. The town has a population of 1285, according to the 1930 census.

For many years prior to the railroad's advent into the lower part of Greenville County, stage coaches making regular trips from Charleston and Columbia to Greenville and over the mountains to Asheville made stops at an inn located near the McGee branch. In the yard of this ancient hostelry was a bold flowing spring which bubbled up in such a manner as to give one the impression of a fountain. From this comes the name "Fountain Inn."

Soon after the War Between the States, Noah Cannon purchased a large plantation, which included the present town of Fountain Inn, and here entered the mercantile business. His was for many years the only store in the community. Later Mr. Cannon took his son, James A. Cannon, into partnership and together they conducted the mercantile business till Noah Cannon moved to Greer, when the son continued it. In 1886 the railroad came, and soon after this James I. West, now a resident of Greenville, purchased a half interest in much of the real estate then owned by James A. Cannon about the newly established railway station. They cut portions of this into lots which they sold off for business and residential purposes. Practically all Fountain Inn real estate of today comes from this old "Cannon and West" subdivision.

The growth of the town was slow till about 1900, when public-spirited citizens of the community built a cotton mill. At first the mill was small, but it stimulated the growth of the town to such an extent that other enterprises located there. Among these was the Fountain Inn Oil Mill, organized by A. S. Peden, W. S. Peden and others. In a few years the cotton mill was enlarged and later sold to C. E. Graham. Afterwards it became a part of the Woodside Cotton Mills Company, which it still remains.

In 1903 the Bank of Fountain Inn was organized and 1907 saw the advent of a new banking institution in the Peoples Bank of Fountain Inn. These two financial institutions operated with unusual success till 1920, when they had combined resources of more than a million and a half dollars. Since Fountain Inn was so largely a farming community the deflation of farm values in 1920 badly crippled these banks, but they continued to serve the community in the face of conditions which had closed more than half the banks of the state, till the fall of 1926 when, after two complete crop failures in the Fountain Inn community, both banks closed. Such a calamity would have completely discouraged most towns, but not so with Fountain Inn. The stock-holders of the closed banks, regardless of their heavy losses, immediately undertook the organization of a new bank, and in less than thirty days the South Carolina Savings Bank was in operation. This institution is now a part of the South Carolina National Bank chain which has resources of more than $40,000,-000.00. In 1925 the Peoples Agricultural Credit Corporation was organized at Fountain Inn for the purpose of making loans in connection with the Federal Intermediate Credit Bank. It is doing much for the agricultural interests of the community. Soon after the establishment of the Federal Land Bank in Columbia, a local Association was formed at Fountain Inn and through it much money has been loaned to the farmers of lower Greenville County.

About 1910 a new spirit seems to have entered Fountain Inn and it has progressed greatly since that time. Formerly there had existed serious factional differences among the citizens of the town, which tended to retard the growth of its institutions, but now the people forgot these old scores and everyone seemed willing to put his shoulder to the wheel and push for the common good. Immediately it was seen that a new life had been entered upon. The town secured a much-needed telephone system, electric lights, paved sidewalks and improved streets. The school and churches began to function properly and Fountain Inn was on its road for better and more substantial things.

Fountain Inn is proud to claim as a citizen the nationally known syndicate writer, Robert Quillen. Mr. Quillen married a Fountain Inn girl and has lived there for many years. He is owner, editor and publisher of the *Fountain Inn Tribune,* a weekly newspaper with less than 1,500 local circulation, which finds it way into the homes of authors, editors and educators throughout the United States, because of its characteristically Quillen editorials.

Other facts of interest pertaining to the Fountain Inn of today may be mentioned the following:

Water and sewer system owned and operated by the town.

Ample electric power for any needs.

School system employing 32 teachers and enrolling 1,086 pupils.

CHAPTER XX.

POLITICAL SUBDIVISIONS AND GOVERNMENT

GREENVILLE, along with all other counties of the state, is a separate and distinct political subdivision, with certain governmental powers and duties conferred upon her by the Constitution. Within the county are other governmental divisions, some under control of county officials, and others independent of all county supervision. Having a large population and being included among the "wealthy counties" of the state, Greenville necessarily employs many officials and contains an unusually large number of subdivisions.

Unofficially, but actually, the County Legislative Delegation has control of all the affairs of the county. Under the law, these officials are state officers and have no connection with the affairs of the county, except in so far as it is a part of the state; but the legislators, because of their power to make appropriations and secure the enactment of any legislation they may desire pertaining to the county, have assumed what amounts to dictatorial powers over all county officials and county affairs. In state matters they are legislators, but in their county they are executives. This is not a healthy state, but without a reformation of county government, it is necessary for this dual authority to be exercised if the county is to have even a semblance of efficiency in the conduct of its affairs. All county officials expect, and readily acquiesce in, the supervisory authority exercised by the Legislative Delegation and there is no friction because of its usurpation. During the last four or five years the Legislative Delegations have been unusually active because of the great amount of permanent road improvement undertaken by the county. Most of this work has been done under the direct supervision of a committee appointed by the delegation from its membership. The Greenville County Legislative Delegation for 1925-'26 was Senator James M. Richardson of Greenville, and House members, A. F. McKissick, W. H. Keith, J. L. Love, John McH. Mauldin and F. Scott Davenport, all of Greenville, and C. E. Sloan of Greer. In 1927-'28 the delegation was James M. Richardson, Senator, and House members, J. L. Love, W. H. Keith, Hoke B. Black, Alex N. Brunson and W. C. Goodwin of Greenville, and L. E. Wood of Greer. The present Delegation, which serves for the year 1929 and 1930, are Joseph R. Bryson of Greenville, Senator, and W. H. Keith, W. Ben Smith, W. P. Conyers and G. D. Oxner of Greenville, J. Harvey Cleveland of Cleveland, and J. H. Drummond of Fountain Inn, members of the House.

Among the subdivisions of the county are sixteen townships. At one time townships had authority to issue bonds and exercise other functions of government, but of late years they have been shorn of all their power and are now political divisions in name only. They have no officials and levy no taxes as such. Formerly much of the authority now given to school districts was held by townships. The county is divided into townships as follows: Cleveland, Glassy Mountain, Highland,

O'Neal, Bates, Saluda, Paris Mountain, Greenville, Chick Springs, Butler, Austin, Fairview, Gantt, Grove, Oaklawn and Dunklin.

Within the county are six municipalities, consisting of Greenville, West Greenville, Greer, Fountain Inn, Simpsonville and Taylors. All of these exercise the usual functions of towns and cities and are governed by a Mayor and Board of Aldermen elected by the local qualified electors.

Besides the incorporated towns and cities of the county there are many thickly settled communities having no political entity and exercising no governmental authority, but at the same time giving their residents many of the advantages enjoyed by the municipalities. These are the mill villages. Most of them have police protection, while many enjoy such conveniences as paved streets and sidewalks, electric lights, running water and sewerage connections. The cotton mill corporations pay for this. The police officers are appointed by the governor upon the recommendation of the mill officials, with the approval of the sheriff of the county.

Within the county are many school districts. Each of these is under control of a local board of trustees which the residents of the district have the right to elect. As a matter of practice, however, school trustees are usually appointed by the County Board of Education, except for the Greenville City district, where the law requires them to be elected. Taxes for the school districts are levied and collected by county officials, but the funds of each school are credited to the district from which collected, and paid out by the County Treasurer upon warrants drawn by the trustees of the district, and approved by the County Superintendent of Education. Bonds for local improvements are authorized by a vote of the district and issued by the trustees.

The Greater Greenville Sewer District roughly comprising the city of Greenville and the Parker School District was created in 1926 and operates under a commission of five. The purpose of this political subdivision is to furnish trunk line sewerage facilities to the territory which it covers.

Greenville County and the city of Greenville jointly own the Greenville Airport. This was constructed by direct appropriation and is controlled by a Commission. These commissioners have no governmental authority but hold title to the property and pass regulations pertaining to its use. No taxes are levied or collected for this semi-county activity.

In 1916 an annual tax upon the county was provided by a vote of the people to furnish library service for all parts of the county. A board of trustees regulates the manner in which this is to be done. At present, these trustees are operating under a contract with the Greenville City Library, by the terms of which branch libraries are maintained at all central locations throughout the county. Specially equipped trucks take the books out from the city library to these branches and return them. Taxes for the maintenance of this work are levied and collected by the county authorities.

A hospital for the treatment of tubercular patients was provided by a bond issue and annual tax levy voted by the county in 1927. This institution is under the control of a board of trustees appointed by the governor upon the recommendation of the county legislative delegation. The trustees are authorized to supervise the operation of the hospital. They have no governmental authority. Taxes for the conduct of the work are collected by the county treasurer.

Greenville and Pickens counties constitute the Thirteenth Judicial Circuit of the state. Honorable Thomas J. Mauldin of Pickens is resident Judge of the Circuit, while J. G. Leatherwood of Greenville is Solicitor. Annually ten weeks of the Court of General Sessions and nineteen weeks of the Court of Common Pleas are held in the county. In addition to the Circuit Courts, Greenville has a County Court with limited jurisdiction. This tribunal is presided over by Judge Martin F. Ansel, a former governor of the state. The Solicitor of the court is D. B. Stover. The court is open for business at all times, with a jury in attendance for eight weeks of criminal business and eight weeks of civil matters. In 1927 a Juvenile Court for the county was authorized by legislative act. It is presided over by Judge E. P. Riley, succeeding George W. Brunson, resigned, and has jurisdiction of all matters pertaining to children and their well-being. Over the county are located a number of Magistrates with the usual limited jurisdiction. And in addition to these state and county courts, the headquarters of the Federal Court for the Western District of South Carolina is in Greenville City. This court holds regular sessions in Greenville twice each year. Honorable H. H. Watkins of Anderson is Judge of the Court, while D. C. Durham of Greenville is Clerk.

One official, with his assistants, acts as clerk of the Circuit Courts and also of the County Court. And in addition to the usual duties of a clerk of court, the Greenville County clerk is official custodian of the court house and grounds, employing all help necessary to care for the seven-story Court House Building in which all court officials are housed. The clerk is elected for a term of four years, and is at present T. E. Christenberry. Mr. Christenberry was elected in 1928 to succeed Harry A. Dargan who died in office after a service of 13 consecutive years. Lucyle A. Dargan, widow of Mr. Dargan, is deputy clerk.

But courts could not function without law enforcement officers. In Greenville County, as in all others of the state, the chief peace officer is the Sheriff. This official is elected each four years. The present sheriff is Cliff Bramlett, who is assisted by nine deputy sheriffs working out of his office. Mr. Bramlett was formerly a deputy under Sheriff Sam D. Willis, who was killed while in the discharge of his official duties in 1927, and succeeds Sheriff C. A. Rector, who was appointed by the governor to fill the unexpired term of Sheriff Willis. Each magistrate in the county has a constable, and in all the mill villages are one or more deputies. These, with the sheriff and his deputies, constitute the law enforcement power of the county.

The Master in Equity for Greenville County is appointed by the governor upon the recommendation of the Senate. He acts for both Circuit and County courts. The office has been filled by E. Inman since 1914. Of recent years he has had no opposition.

Through the Probate Court all estates are administered, and by it marriage licenses are issued. Pensions paid by the state to Confederate veterans and their widows residing in Greenville County pass through this office. The first woman to hold public office in Greenville County was Mrs. Fannie C. Scott, the present Probate Judge. She was elected in 1921 to succeed her husband, Walter M. Scott, who died from injuries received in an automobile accident while serving his second four-year term.

All deeds, mortgages, contracts and other instruments of like nature are recorded in the office of the Register of Mesne Conveyance. Only two other counties of the state have such an official. J. Walter Moon now holds that position by appointment from the governor to fill the unexpired term of an official who was removed from office.

The official head of the business affairs of the county is the Supervisor. He is charged with keeping in repair all public roads of the county and has custody of, and supervision over, the county convicts. The major portion of all road work is done by these convicts. The annual expenditure for this work now averages about $250,000. The supervisor makes all county purchases and issues his warrants for payment of them. Recently a county engineer has been furnished the office. The present supervisor is A. Frank Pridmore, who was recently elected for a term of four years to succeed H. P. Dill, who held the office for twelve years.

Tax returns are filed with the County Auditor, and by him passed on to the Board of Equalization in the township or municipality where the property mentioned therein is located. Each township and incorporated city or town in the county has such a board. Values are fixed by these boards and then the auditor levies such tax upon that value as is provided by law. This official is appointed by the governor with the consent of the senate; and since he acts for the state, as well as for the county, he is paid by both. The present County Auditor is J. Ben Watkins, who in 1926 succeeded M. L. Gullick, the holder of the office for sixteen years.

Taxes after being levied and charged by the auditor are collected by the County Treasurer. This official is appointed by the governor for a term of four years by and with the consent of the senate, and is official custodian of all funds belonging to the county. Payments are made by him only upon warrants of the proper officials, and when approved by the County Comptroller. Since state as well as county taxes are collected by the treasurer, he is paid by both state and county for his services. The present treasurer is Walter L. Miller, who has held the office for eight years, succeeding J. A. Foster, who likewise was in office for eight years.

All delinquent taxes are collected by the delinquent tax collector. Till 1928, when this office was created by legislative act, such taxes were collected by the sheriff. This official is appointed by the governor upon the recommendation of a majority of the county legislative delegation for a term of four years. D. W. Cochrane, Jr., is the only person ever to hold this position.

The coroner is charged with the investigation of all violent and suspicious deaths occurring in the county. By law he assumes the duties of the office of sheriff in case of the death or removal of that official. Joe Wooten at present holds that position, having been elected in 1928 for a term of four years to succeed John W. Parks.

Each four years a Superintendent of Education is elected. It is the duty of this official to supervise all schools of the county and assist the trustees in operating them. He must also approve all school claims, before they are paid by the treasurer. Formerly this office was given little attention, but the phenomenal strides along educational lines which the county has made during the last few years now makes of it one of the most important in the county. Annually the superintendent of education approves for payment near a million and a half dollars in school claims. James F. Whatley now holds the office, having recently been appointed by the governor to fill the unexpired term of an official removed from office.

The Health Department of the county has been in charge of Dr. B. H. Earle, a retired army officer, for a number of years. He has done much to place the county among the leaders in the whole country for "healthfulness." When a health survey of the county was recently made by the United States Public Health Service, Dr. L. L. Lumsden, director of the work, said of Greenville: "The most sanitary city and county in America." This department, in addition to Dr. Earle, employs the services of a sanitary inspector and a nurse. The office is under the direct supervision of the county legislative delegation.

The county has a Charities and Corrections Commission, which exercises control over the county jail, the County Home (for the poor) and hospitalization for the poor. The commissioners are appointed by the county legislative delegation. They select a jailor, a superintendent for the County Home and a county physician.

A County Attorney is elected each two years by the county legislative delegation, whose duty it is to advise all county officials and conduct the civil litigation of the county. James H. Price now holds this position, succeeding O. K. Mauldin, who was county attorney for a number of terms.

Exercising supervision over the books and accounts of all county officials is the County Comptroller chosen by the county legislative delegation for a term of four years. Before payment, all claims must be approved by this official. Only through this office is there any legal contact of the county offices with each other; and it is in this office alone (where duplicate books of all officials are kept) that one can secure an insight into all the financial affairs of the county. The office was created in 1914, and W. N. Cruikshank occupied it continuously till his death on December 31, 1929. During his regime the office was legally known as that of the supervising auditor. In 1930 the title of the office was changed to that of county comptroller and W. H. Willimon selected to fill it.

Formerly many of the Greenville County officials were compensated through the fees collected in their offices, but in 1926 an act of the general assembly, sponsored by the Greenville delegation, provided that all fees should be paid over to the county, and the officials paid a salary. Since then all public officials of the county have been compensated entirely by salaries.

CONCLUSION

No sooner was the existence of another continent brought to the knowledge of Europe by the discovery of Columbus than all the maritime powers of the Old World eagerly rushed forth to seize a portion of it for themselves. Soon that part of North America embracing the present states of North Carolina, South Carolina, Georgia, northern Florida and extending westward to the Pacific ocean was claimed by England, France and Spain. But near two centuries passed before any permanent settlement was made in what is now South Carolina.

In 1670 a few emigrants from England, under the leadership of William Sayle, came over in two small vessels and settled near Port Royal. Soon they became dissatisfied with this location and moved to the western bank of the Ashley river and there laid the foundation of Old Charles Town. However, it was found that this site could not be reached by large vessels, and in 1780 it was abandoned and the settlement was moved again, this time to the present location of Charleston.

Within a few years after this first permanent settlement was made on the coast traders moved back into the hill and mountain country and, living among the Indians, did a thriving business exchanging rum and trinkets for the skins and furs of the red men. The Indians were early furnished with guns and when they had become accustomed to their use the fur trade rapidly became one of the principal industries of Carolina. The traders, living among the Indians, gathered the furs and transported them to Charles Town.

Following the traders into the up-country were cattle men, who used the great prairie lands of the piedmont section of the state to raise cattle and horses. When ready for market these were also transported to Charles Town and became quite an item in the export business of the colony.

But regardless of the fact that traders and cattle men lived in what is now referred to as Piedmont South Carolina there were no settlements of white men there, which could be referred to as permanent, till well after the first quarter of the eighteenth century. The Cherokee Indians occupied all that portion of the state to the west of the Broad river, but being at all times friendly, the Carolina traders and cattle men came and went there as they saw fit. However, if any serious attempts had been made to cultivate the soil or to congregate in extensive settlements the Indians would no doubt have objected, as they did at a later date.

In 1755 a treaty between Carolina and the Cherokees was entered into, and by its terms the Indians ceded to the colony all their lands in South Carolina except present Greenville, Anderson, Pickens and Oconee Counties. Immediately settlers began to enter the new acquisition, principally from the more northern colonies.

Following the French and Indian war, the piedmont section of South Carolina rapidly grew in population. Some trouble was experienced there on account of lawlessness, but on the whole the frontiersmen made rapid progress till the outbreak of the Revolution. Although what is now Greenville County was still a portion of the Cherokee Nation, many settlers moved in. Notable among these was Richard Pearis and Colonel Hite.

With the coming of the Revolution the Cherokees rose up in arms against the frontiersmen and war with them followed. This was concluded by the treaty of 1777 which ceded present Greenville County to South Carolina. But the war with Great Britain then being in progress, no effort was made for some years to "open up" the newly acquired Indian lands. With the Revolution concluded, however, the county of Greenville was formed by legislative enactment, and much of the land there granted to soldiers of the late war in payment of debts due them by the state.

For fifteen or twenty years after its formation, Greenville County grew rapidly, but near the end of the eighteenth century heavy migrations to the west commenced. In the face of this westward movement the white population of the county remained near stationary for fifty years or more. During this period the principal industry of the county was agriculture, with the town of Greenville drawing a substantial income from summer tourists. Few notable public improvements were undertaken before the War Between the States; however, the citizenship of the county took an active part in the bitter factional politics of the day, being strongly opposed to both Nullification and Secession.

The five-year period from 1850 to 1855 brought to the county the Greenville and Columbia Railroad, Furman University and the Greenville Female College. These acquisitions gave new life to the county and its growth would no doubt have been rapid from then onward except for the coming of the War Between the States. Although the county had opposed secession, when that step was taken the citizens of Greenville County were as one man in supporting the state.

With the coming of reconstruction days following the war, Greenville County played a conspicuous part, furnishing the Provisional Governor. Since her population was predominently white, Greenville was able to keep her public affairs out of the hands of negroes and carpet-baggers for the most part, but she suffered greatly during the radical regime nevertheless. But the coming of the Richmond and Danville Air Line Railway (now Southern Main Line) in 1872 stimulated business to such an extent that the ten-year period from 1870 to 1880 saw the most rapid growth in the population of the town of Greenville of any other decade of her life.

About 1895 an era of cotton mill building set in and continued with the passing of years till Greenville County had become a manufacturing county rather than one of agriculture. The advent of manufacturing on a large scale brought with it wealth and population, and soon Greenville took high rank among the counties of the state. The city of Greenville, in and about which the larger of the textile plants are located, by 1920 had become the third largest city in the state, and for ten years or more has been considered the second wealthiest city of the state. The county has for many years paid more taxes in the aggregate, for state purposes, than any other. Its automobile registrations, gasoline tax contributions, and income tax payments, far exceed those of any other county in the state.

During both the Spanish-American war and the World war, Greenville was the home of large training camps for American soldiers. Both encampments contributed greatly to the growth of the county, by reason of increased business and additions to her population drawn from discharged soldiers and their friends. This is especially true as regards the World War camp.

Greenville has not contributed as many notable men to the public life of the state as have other counties, but there is probably no other county of the state which has furnished as many outstanding industrial leaders as she. Many of these are still living and their activities are being constantly felt in the business life of the entire country. Since the War Between the States the county has furnished two Governors (B. F. Perry and Martin F. Ansel), one Lieutenant Governor (W. L. Mauldin), a United States Senator (Joseph H. Earle), a number of Congressmen and high State officials.

Only the passing of time can tell whether Greenville County is to continue her progress. As this is written, the textile industry of the entire United States is passing through a critical period in its life. On account of changing styles in female attire the demand for cotton goods has fallen off to such an extent as to jeopardize the very life of the industry. But strenuous efforts are being put forth by the cotton manufacturers of the entire county to stabilize the business, and if it survive, the South, on account of the more favorable conditions existing there, should continue to lead in textile manufacturing. With that lead in the South, Greenville should have no fear of retaining her place of prominence. However, real and lasting prosperity can come only through a diversification in both manufacturing and agriculture. Steps in this direction are being taken, and the last quarter century of progress will probably continue for many years yet to come.

PART I — NARRATIVE

PRINCIPAL REFERENCES USED

Logan's History of Upper South Carolina.
Landrum's Colonial and Revolutionary History of Upper South Carolina.
Ramsay's History of South Carolina—2 Vols.
Historical Collections of South Carolina by Carroll—2 Vols.
Johnson's Traditions.
Documentary History of South Carolina, 1764-1775—By Gibbs.
Memoirs of William H. Drayton.
History of the Presbyterian Church in South Carolina, by Howe.
Travels of William Bartram.
Rambles in the Pee Dee Basin, by Cook.
George Hunter's Map of the Cherokee County, 1730, edited by A. S. Salley, Jr.
History of the Old Cheraws, by Gregg.
Kings Mountain and Its Heroes, by Draper.
Memoirs of Joseph McJunkin.
Sectionalism in South Carolina, by Schaper.
American Historical Association Reports for 1896.
South Carolina Historical and Genealogical Magazine—Vol. XXVI No. 4.
Reminiscences and Sketches, by B. F. Perry—3 Vols.
Waddy Thompson, Jr., by Henry T. Thompson.
Annals of Newberry County, by O'Neall.
Bench and Bar of South Carolina, by O'Neall.
Landrum's History of Spartanburg County.
Vandiver's History of Anderson County.
Crittenden's Greenville Century Book.
Baptist Beginnings in Education, by McGlothlin.
Handbook of South Carolina—1908.
Handbook of South Carolina—1927.
C. E. David—Numerous Newspaper Articles.
J. Rion McKissick—Manuscript Sketch of Richard Pearis.
Greenville County, Economics and Social—Pamphlet by Guy A. Gullick.
Greenville News and Greenville Piedmont—Newspaper Files.
Official Publications of Greenville Chamber of Commerce.
Public Records of Greenville County.

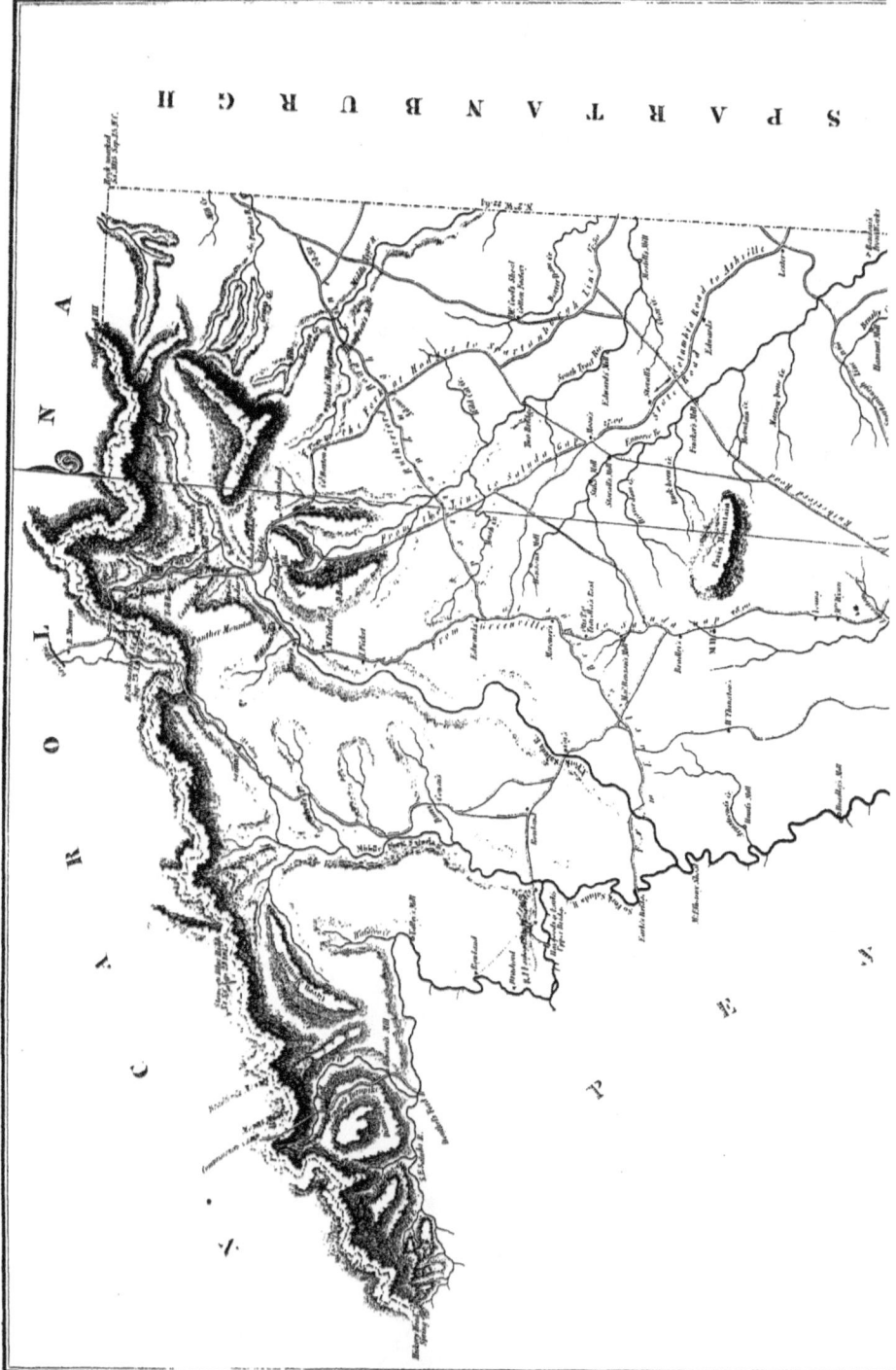

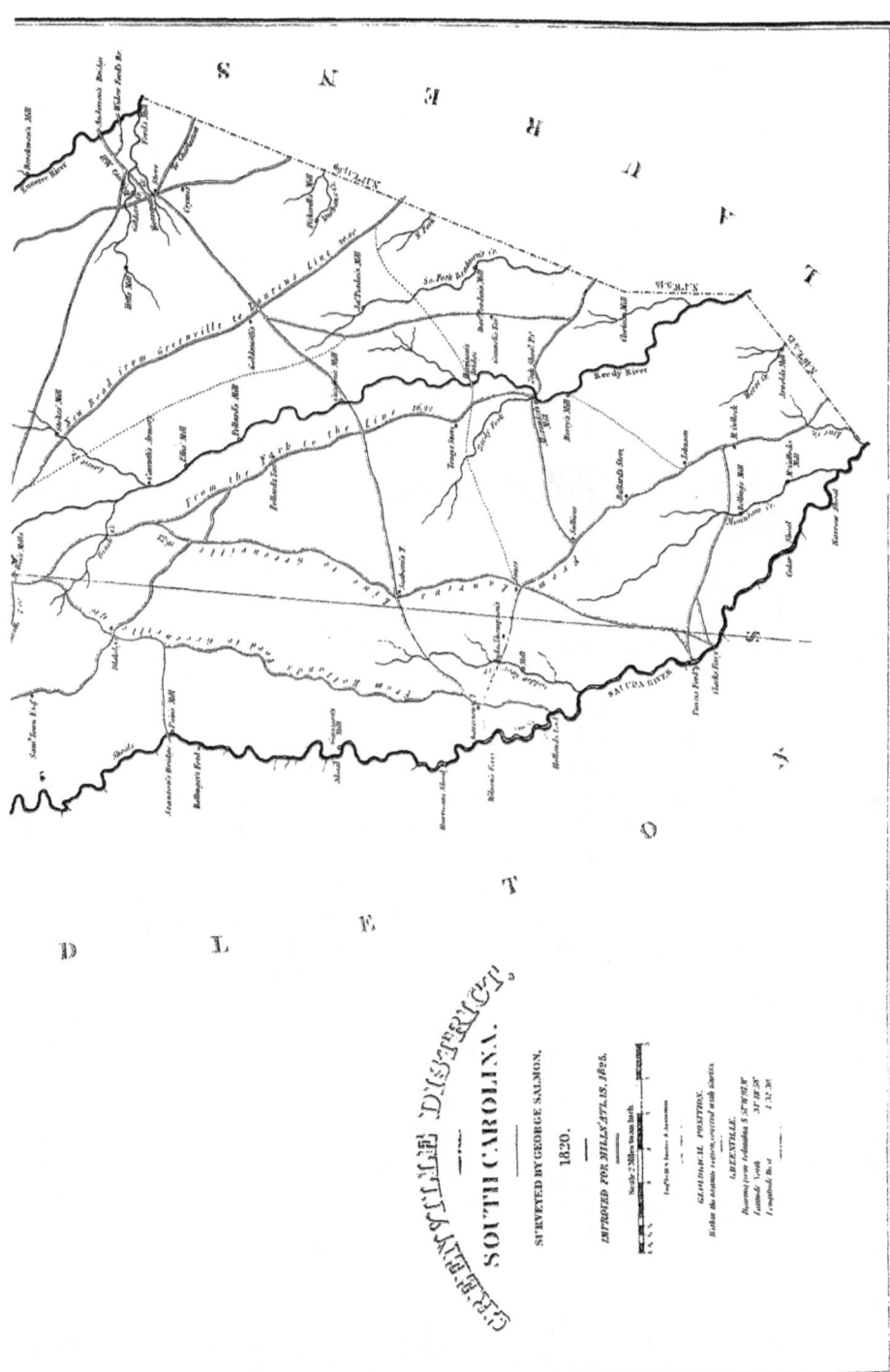

Statement

THE history of a county, state or nation is nothing more than a recital of the activities of its people. Every one of these, no matter how humble his place, contributes something. But he who undertakes to write that history must confine himself to the most conspicuous achievements or his task would never be finished.

The pages which follow carry short biographies of men and women who have had much to do with shaping the history of Greenville County during the last half century. A majority of these have been written by me, and those not so written, I have edited. The facts upon which they are based have been secured from various sources, all of which are thought to be reliable. The order of arrangement, lack of pictures, or type of cut used, have no reference whatever to the prominence of the people.

JAS. M. RICHARDSON.

HISTORY OF GREENVILLE COUNTY
SOUTH CAROLINA

PART II

BIOGRAPHICAL

Biographical Sketches of Leading Citizens of Greenville County, South Carolina

ALVIN HENRY DEAN

Of all the great lawyers who have honored the Greenville bar during the last thirty years, none has been more widely known or generally recognized as a leader in his profession than ALVIN HENRY DEAN. But his reputation as an attorney has never exceeded the regard which has been accorded him as a public-spirited citizen and true representative of the old school of Southern gentlemen. Certainly it may be said that when on the 18th day of August, 1929, he passed away, Greenville lost a citizen whose life has contributed very much indeed to the rapid progress which has marked her history over the last quarter of a century.

Mr. Dean was born in Spartanburg County, near Duncan, within the confines of the historic old Nazareth church community, on March 22, 1863. His parents were Captain A. H. Dean and Eugenia (Miller) Dean, both of Scotch-Irish ancestry. Captain Dean commanded a company of Confederate cavalry in the War Between the States, and represented Spartanburg County in the Lower House during the period from 1898 to 1902, while his son, Mr. Dean, was in the Senate from Greenville County.

As a boy, Mr. Dean worked on his father's farm, and attended the old Reidville Male Academy, then a flourishing school. Later he was a student at the high school of Professor Sams, located at Spartanburg. His college education was secured at Furman University, Greenville, and Vanderbilt University. While at the latter institution, he specialized in law and was admitted to the bar in 1884.

At the age of 21, Mr. Dean began the practice of his profession in the city of Greenville, and because of his sincere interest in the cause of those whom he represented, his natural ability as a lawyer and his polished court-room manner, he very soon had an extensive practice, which continued to expand till the day of his death, 45 years later. For many years he was a member of the firm of Cothran, Dean & Cothran, and upon the elevation of Hon. T. P. Cothran to a seat upon the Supreme bench, Mr. Dean became Senior member, and the firm name was changed to Dean, Cothran & Wyche; Mr. Wyche, a young man then assistant United States District Attorney, having been taken into the partnership. Later Mr. W. C. Cothran withdrew from the firm and it became Dean & Wyche, which it remained till the death of Mr. Dean.

Few lawyers in South Carolina have ever equaled Mr. Dean in their conduct of a case before a jury. His grasp of the law and facts, his grace of manner, and the power of his oratory combined to carry conviction for his cause. And of the great numbers whom he defended on the criminal side of the Court, never was there one to suffer the death penalty. Yet as a practitioner on the civil side of the Court, he was as highly regarded as on the other. His firms were at various times attorneys for the First National Bank of Greenville, the Piedmont Manufacturing Company, the Charleston & Western Carolina Railway Company, the Southern Railway, and many other of the leading corporations.

Through economy and business acumen, Mr. Dean prospered in a material way, as well as in the esteem of his fellow citizens. He invested heavily in real estate and at the time of his death was a large property holder in the city of Greenville. He also engaged extensively in farming, being the owner of plantations in both Greenville and Spartanburg Counties. At one time he was a director in the Norwood National Bank of Greenville and up till the time of his death held that position with the First National Bank.

The first position of a public nature held by Mr. Dean was that of Alderman of the City of Greenville in 1892-1896. Next he was elected State Senator from Greenville County in 1896 and in 1900 was re-elected for another term of four years. Upon the creation of the Greater Greenville Sewer Commission in 1925, he was appointed one of the members of that body, which position he held till 1927, when he resigned to become a candidate for Mayor of the City of Greenville, at the urgent solicitation of many friends. He was elected Mayor over three opponents and filled that office with such satisfaction that he was elected to succeed himself, but died before taking his seat for the second time, and while still serving his first term. For ten years he was a member of the Board of Governors of the Greenville City Hospital.

Mr. Dean was a Presbyterian, being for many years a Deacon in the Second Presbyterian Church, but upon his removal to another section of the city adjacent to the Third Presbyterian Church, he worshipped with that congregation till his death. He was an Elk, a Woodman, a Pythian, an Odd Fellow, and a member of the Sigma Alpha Epsilon College fraternity. He held membership in the American, South Carolina and Greenville Bar Associations, being President of the Greenville Association in 1927. At one time he was Exalted Ruler for the Greenville Elks, and at another, he served as Deputy Grand Exalted Ruler of the Elks for the district of South Carolina.

Mr. Dean's favorite recreation was motoring and horseback riding. On cool mornings and evenings he was often seen either riding or driving about the country roads of Greenville.

In March, 1886, Mr. Dean was married to Miss Lida Byrd, now deceased. Miss Sallie Preston, member of a prominent Virginia family, became his second wife, they having married in 1898. She survives him and resides at the family home on Buncombe Street in the City of Greenville.

JOHN JACKSON McSWAIN

JOHN JACKSON McSWAIN, attorney, soldier and Congressman, was born at Cross Hill, in Laurens County, South Carolina, on May 1, 1875, being the son of Dr. Elridge T. McSwain and Janie (McGowan) McSwain.

The grandfather of Mr. McSwain was the Reverend William A. McSwain (who married Elizabeth Randall), a Methodist minister in South Carolina from 1836 to

PART II — BIOGRAPHICAL 141

1866. The father of William A. was Charles McSwain (who married Susanna Washburn), a farmer of Montgomery County North Carolina. Charles McSwain's father was David McSwain, Jr., a farmer of Cleveland (then Lincoln) County, North Carolina. The father of David McSwain, Jr., was David McSwain, Sr., who came to America from "Island of Lewis", Scotland, in 1734, and shortly after his arrival married Martha Hamrick. Soon after coming to America, David McSwain, Sr., who was the great-great-great grandfather of John J. McSwain, won the friendship of the Indians and settled among them on Sandy Run creek in what was then Lincoln County, North Carolina. The log cabin in which he lived till his death a few years before the Revolution, is (1930) still standing.

The maternal grandfather of Mr. McSwain was John Jackson McGowan, a farmer of Cross Hill, South Carolina, who served in the United States Army during the Seminole War of 1837, and later as a captain in the Confederate Army. Captain McGowan's father was William McGowan, a farmer of Laurens County, South Carolina, who came to America from Ireland at the age of nine. The father of William McGowan was Patrick McGowan, who with his wife, Mary (Thompson) McGowan, four daughters, and the son, William, emigrated from Ulster County, Ireland, in 1798, and landed at Charleston, South Carolina. Shortly after his arrival in America, and while on his way to the up-country settlements of South Carolina, Patrick McGowan died and was buried by the wayside. The father of Patrick McGowan was John McGowan, who was killed in County Antrim, Ireland, during the uprising of "United Irishmen" in 1798.

The early education of John J. McSwain, subject of this sketch, was had in the public schools of his home community and through private tutoring by the Reverend A. M. Hassell. Later he attended the Wofford Fitting School at Spartanburg, South Carolina, to which he had won, by competitive examination, a scholarship. From this institution he went to the South Carolina College (now University of South Carolina), where with the aid of a scholarship and earnings had from tutoring, he was graduated (A. B. *summa cum laude*) in 1897. He then taught school for several years, at the same time devoting himself to the study of law. In 1899 he was admitted to the bar of South Carolina, but did not enter regularly into the practice of his profession till 1901, when he moved to Greenville.

After joining the Greenville bar, Mr. McSwain was not long in acquiring a substantial practice, which he enjoyed with increasing volume till 1917, when he entered the first Officers' Training Camp at Fort Oglethorpe, Georgia. During this period he was Referee in Bankruptcy for five years (1912-'17), Chairman of the Executive Committee of the Democratic party in Greenville County one year (1916), and for a number of years a trustee of the Greenville City Schools.

In January, 1918, Mr. McSwain, who had had no military training before entering the Officers' Training Camp, was commissioned a Captain and ordered to Camp Beauregard (La.) where he was assigned to Company "A" 154th Infantry. On August 1, 1918, he sailed, with his regiment, to France, where he remained till the close of the war. Being mustered out of the service on March 6, 1919, from Camp Lee at Petersburg, Virginia, Captain McSwain returned to Greenville and again entered upon the practice of law. But in 1920 he became a candidate for Congress from the Fourth Congressional District (composed of Greenville, Spartanburg, Union and Laurens Counties) and was elected. Since then he has continuously held that position, devoting to the law only such time as he can spare from his official duties.

In Congress Mr. McSwain has been very active in the service of his constituents, interesting himself especially in improving farm conditions in South Carolina. He spent sixty days in 1929 in Europe, visiting nine countries, investigating farm conditions there. In 1925 he attended as a member of the American Group, the Sessions of the Inter-Parliamentary Union at Geneva. This Union is more than 40 years old, and during all of that time has been a leader in the movement looking to international cooperation and promoting world peace.

Mr. McSwain is deeply interested in the promotion of aviation in the United States. He supported General Mitchell in his efforts to improve conditions in Army aviation. He was a member of the sub-committee which wrote the Act creating the Air Corps for the Army, and which set up a five-year building program. He is also author of the law relating to the purchase of aircraft for the use of the Army and navy, under which planes of a higher quality and safety are being purchased for the government at a saving of many thousands of dollars.

He is a Methodist and holds membership in several fraternal orders, including the Red Men, Elks, J. O. U. A. M., Masons, Odd Fellows and Knights of Pythias.

In 1905 Mr. McSwain was married to Miss Sarah McCullough of Greenville, daughter of John W. and Janie (Sullivan) McCullough, and they have a daughter, Janie McSwain.

ZECHARIAH THORNTON CODY, D.D., LL.D.

It is a characteristic of greatness for one to be able to stand by his convictions in the face of bitter opposition from life-long friends and associates; and in South Carolina it takes real courage for one to oppose the Democratic ticket. But in 1928, DOCTOR ZECHARIAH THORNTON CODY, born and reared a Southerner and for more than 25 years a citizen of South Carolina, opposed the election of Governor Alfred E. Smith, Democratic nominee for President, because he believed his election would be a fatal blow to the cause of National Prohibition. A Democrat by birth and conviction, Doctor Cody, as editor and publisher of *The Baptist Courier*, entered wholeheartedly into the fight against his old party. By many of his closest friends he was plead with to "stay out of the fight", while others resorted to personal abuse, hoping thus to quiet him; but throughout the campaign he did not waver for an instant in the task to which he had set himself.

Doctor Cody was born near Franklin, Henry County, Alabama, on May 21, 1858, being the son of the Reverend Edmund Cody and Sarah (Henderson) Cody. His father was a Baptist minister and planter. The family was established in the United States by James Cody who emigrated from Ireland as early as 1740 and settled in Virginia. Dr. Cody attended the county and village schools of his community and later entered Mercer College where he studied for one year. He then was a student at Carson-Newman for a time but did not graduate for lack of funds. From 1883 to 1887, he attended the Southern Baptist Theological Seminary at Louisville, Kentucky, from which institution he was graduated with the degree of Master of Theology.

For twelve years after leaving the Seminary, Dr. Cody held pastorates in Kentucky, these being at Louisville, Mays Lick and Georgetown. In 1901 he came to Greenville as pastor of the First Baptist Church, and remained in this pastorate till he resigned to become editor and publisher of *The Baptist Courier,* the official publication of the Baptist Churches in South Carolina, which position he continues to hold.

Doctor Cody stands high in the work of his church, not only in South Carolina but throughout the South; and in recognition of his services, Colleges of South Carolina, Georgia and Missouri have conferred upon him the honorary degree of Doctor of Divinity. He has also been honored with the degree of Doctor of Laws by Furman University and Georgetown University. Sketches regarding him and his work appear in Who's Who in America, and in Men of Mark in South Carolina. He is a trustee of Furman University, Greenville, South Carolina, and also a trustee of the Southern Baptist Theological Seminary of Louisville, Kentucky, as well as a member of the Executive Committee of the Baptist World Alliance.

But Dr. Cody is not known alone by his church activities for he takes a prominent part in all civic affairs of his county and state, lending his active support to many of those which he considers for the betterment of the people. He holds membership in the Thirty-Nine Club, an organization in the City of Greenville fostering literary attainment.

In 1887, Dr. Cody was married to Miss Susan Belle Anderson who died August 25, 1927. He has two children, Lois Cody and Edmund Cody, both of whom as well as himself reside in the City of Greenville.

ROBERT QUILLEN

ROBERT QUILLEN lives at Fountain Inn, where he publishes the *Fountain Inn Tribune,* a weekly newspaper with less than 1,500 local circulation. On October 17, 1929, *The Tribune* carried a letter by Mr. Quillen, written in the well-known "Quillen style." In part it reads:

"I am writing this to save work.

"I'll have Mark print a few hundred extra copies of this page and lay them away to serve as letters.

"I was born in a little town called Syracuse—a Kansas prairie town a few miles from the Colorado line.

"I don't remember western Kansas. Some other town got the county seat and dad left Syracuse and went back east—meaning the eastern part of Kansas.

"There, in a fat land where the farmers raised corn and alfalfa to fatten hogs and steers, and made oodles of money, dad published a newspaper and taught his boys to set type and write things.

"I went to school until I was sixteen. That wasn't enough, but I had sold pen and ink drawings and seen them in print; I had written and printed a little monthly magazine; I knew I could make a living anywhere as a printer, and might get by as a cartoonist or reporter; and the course of true love wasn't running smooth, anyway, so I decided to strike out on my own.

"The next few years were full of wanderings and queer adventures. I knew how it felt to go hungry day after day. I worked in a dozen states. I crossed an ocean. I learned to smoke cigarettes and drink liquor. I made some tough acquaintances. And through it all I kept trying to write and draw and kept my reverence for good women and my faith in the Lord.

"At nineteen I came to Fountain Inn. I stayed here that time just long enough—three months, I think—to win the heart of a gentle lady who was my comrade for seventeen years.

"Georgia for a while; then two years on the Pacific Coast; then back to Fountain Inn to establish *The Tribune*.

"Nothing happened for ten years, except that I worked hard and kept bombarding the magazines with stuff they didn't want.

"Then a paper in Greenville asked me to write a daily column of paragraphs and things began to transpire. *The Literary Digest* saw the paragraphs and began to quote them—sometimes 20 at a clip.

"Mr. George Horace Lorimer saw the paragraphs in *The Digest* and wrote to ask if I would like to write something for *The Saturday Evening Post*. I would. In fact, I had done a lot of it, without results. But this time I wrote by invitation, and for a year or two had a weekly page called 'Small Town Stuff.'

"About the time I began doing that, Mr. J. H. Adams, then editor of the *Baltimore Evening Sun*, wrote and asked me to visit him. He had seen my stuff somewhere—not in *The Post* then—and wanted me to do a daily editorial and a little batch of paragraphs. He offered me $85.00 a week, but I countered with the suggestion that he pay me only $50.00 and let me stay at home. I didn't want to give up my paper.

"I kept the *Evening Sun* job for about five years.

"But that's getting ahead of the story. About the time I began writing for *The Post*, the N. E. A. people gave me a job writing a daily batch of paragraphs for the Scripps-Howard papers. That didn't last very long, for the Chicago syndicate that now handles my stuff appeared on the horizon.

"It wanted a man to launch a paragraph service, and the boss went to New York to see Mr. Rodgers, who clipped paragraphs for *The Literary Digest*.

"'Quillen is the man,' said he.

"So the syndicate wrote and offered me a contract and there I was in the syndicate business.

"The paragraphs flourished. I quit the *Saturday Evening Post* job and began two more features called 'Aunt Het' and 'Willie Willis.'

"Then I quit the *Baltimore Sun* job and began to syndicate my daily editorial.

"That was enough for one man, but Jim Derieux of the *American Magazine* came down one day and asked me to write a monthly editorial for him. I did it for a year or so, under the caption 'If You Ask Me', but even that little bit extra was too much and I had to quit.

"Now I do nothing but syndicate work—an editorial, 21 paragraphs, an 'Aunt Het' and a 'Willie Willis' every day, and a longer 'Aunt Het' for Sunday papers.

Greenville Courthouse as renovated (demolished 1924).

"All told the five features are in about four hundred papers, mostly in this country and in Canada, but also in London, Manila and Honolulu. Little Willie is translated into Dutch and appears in several Holland papers under the title of 'Pinnie Pimmel'.

"Of course I run *The Tribune* on the side, but that is fun—not work. It's my hobby—my substitute for golf. I can't get away from the smell of printer's ink.

"For the rest, I was 42 years old on the 25th of last March; my second wife is a Fountain Inn girl; I have an adopted daughter of seventeen to whom I write letters that appear in daily papers each Saturday; and I weigh 140 in the buff and am bald as a cooter.

"That's all. What a long letter! I hope it hasn't bored you."

This is what Mr. Quillan says of himself, and not one word about the big heart which pounds inside that 140 pounds. He is too modest for that sort of thing.

CAPTAIN OTIS PRENTISS MILLS

It is hard for the present generation of Greenville citizens to realize how great a debt of gratitude they owe to the pioneer cotton mill men of the county. Now more than 30 textile plants dot themselves about the county, furnishing employment for near a third of the people who live there, yet it is less than forty years since Greenville County really became interested in the manufacture of cotton. For many years, it is true, a small cotton factory could be found here and there about the county, but no one looked upon that industry as one of major importance till the Nineties, when low cotton prices caused business men of vision to investigate its possibilities as a relief from the starvation which faced so many of the country's people. Among these far-seeing men who saw in the textile manufacturing field relief from this deplorable condition, was CAPTAIN OTIS PRENTISS MILLS.

Captain Mills was born in Henderson County, North Carolina, on the 22nd day of February, 1840, the son of John and Eliza Cathey (Graham) Mills. As a boy he attended such schools as his community then afforded, but while still young, he entered the Confederate army from which he was mustered out at the end of the war as a Captain.

Soon after the war, Captain Mills moved to Greenville and there entered the mercantile business as a member of the firm of Miller, Mills & Patton. The location of this business house was on Augusta Street where the son of Captain Mills conducted an automobile business for a number of years. Later, the firm became Mills & McBrayer. After many years of successful operation, the mercantile business was sold out and Captain Mills then entered the dairy business, establishing the "Millsdale Farm", which he conducted for several years. He brought the first registered Jersey cattle to Greenville. About 1890 he organized the Greenville Fertilizer Company, which he operated for several years and then sold out to the Virginia-Carolina Chemical Company.

In 1895 Captain Mills undertook the organization of a company for the manufacture of cotton. Few South Carolinians had any money and the most of those who did were unwilling to risk it in an industry virtually untried in the South, so Captain Mills had a task before him to induce his business friends to join hands with him in this new undertaking, but realizing that if such a business could be made to pay dividends, Captain Mills was the man to do it, enough of them finally came in to insure the new mill. So in 1895 the Mills Manufacturing Company was organized with Captain Mills as President and Treasurer of the company, and this position he held till his death in 1915. Like all the early textile plants of Greenville County, the Mills Mill, as it is called locally, had its trials, but under the able management of its president and Mr. W. B. Moore, his son-in-law who was manager, it was unusually successful.

Captain Mills was not only a successful business man, but he contributed much to the religious and civic life of his city. He was Elder and Trustee of the Second Presbyterian Church, and was Chairman of the Building Committee when the present beautiful church was erected. Being a man of vision he was found always in the midst of any movement which looked to the betterment of the community. And being especially interested in the educational and religious life of his city, he gave of his money freely to the schools and churches. He was a Trustee of Chicora College from the time it was organized until his death.

Captain Mills was married in 1867 to Miss Susan Cordelia Gower, daughter of Thomas Claghorn Gower and Jane Jones Williams, and they had five children, two of whom are now dead. Those living are Annie (Mrs. W. B.) Moore, Jane (Mrs. C. P.) Hammond, and O. P. Mills, Jr. One son, Arthur Mills, died at the age of thirty-five, being at that time Cashier and Vice-President of the Fourth National Bank of Greenville and Ex-President of the Greenville Chamber of Commerce. A daughter, Cordelia Mills, died at the age of eight. Mrs. Susan Cordelia Mills survives her husband and resides in the city of Greenville at the age of 84. She has ten grandchildren and one great-grandson.

OTIS P. MILLS, JR.

OTIS PRENTISS MILLS, JR., is the son of Captain Otis Prentiss Mills, Sr., and Susan Cordelia (Gower) Mills, and was born in the City of Greenville on March 12, 1882. His early education was obtained in the public schools of Greenville. Later he was a student at Furman University, from which school he went to Clemson College. In 1905 he graduated from the New Bedford Textile School.

Upon leaving school, Mr. Mills entered the employ of the Mills Manufacturing Company with which he remained in various capacities until the interests of the Mills family in the mill were sold, at which time he was Vice-President of the Company. He then undertook the development of "Milldale", valuable real estate located in the vicinity of Augusta Street, which was formerly the dairy farm of his father. How well he succeeded in this may well be seen today by paying a visit to that beautiful residential section including Mills Avenue, Prentiss Avenue, Otis Avenue and others of that neighborhood.

After leaving the Mills Manufacturing Company, Mr. Mills, in addition to his real estate activities, engaged in the automobile business. For many years he sold the Velie, then he held the Packard agency, and finally that of the Wyllis-Overland Company. In 1929 he liquidated his automobile business and is now devoting his time to the many business affairs of his mother and the estate of his father.

Mr. Mills takes an active interest in all public affairs of the city of Greenville. He is a member of the Greenville Country Club, and of the Greenville Chamber of Commerce. He was instrumental in the organization of the Greenville County Fair Association and was the first President of the Association.

In 1921 Mr. Mills was married to Miss Alice LeGrand of Wilmington, North Carolina, and they have three children—Otis Prentiss III, Martha LeGrand and Jane Gower.

ARTHUR L. MILLS

When, on the 9th day of June, 1918, ARTHUR L. MILLS met his death by accidental drowning, Greenville lost a citizen who had already won a place of prominence among his home people; and if he had lived a few years longer, he no doubt would have been one of the outstanding men of his state, for rarely are the qualities of leadership and business sagacity shown by him found in one person.

Arthur L. Mills, son of Otis P. Mills, Sr., and Susan Cordelia (Gower) Mills, was born in Greenville on the 9th day of October, 1883. His early education was obtained in the public schools of Greenville. Later he was a student at Furman University. After attending Furman he entered Davidson College, from which he graduated with the degree of A. B.

Leaving college Mr. Mills entered the banking business in his home city. First he held a position with the Peoples Bank (now Peoples National Bank), and next he was with the Norwood National (now South Carolina National Bank). Later he assisted in the organization of the Fourth National Bank and became its Cashier and Vice-President.

In all public affairs Mr. Mills took a prominent and active part, being for many years one of the leading members of the Greenville Chamber of Commerce, and at the time of his death holding the office of President of that body. In recognition of his great services as a public-spirited citizen, after his untimely death, members of the Chamber of Commerce contributed the funds for a beautiful oil painting of Mr. Mills which was hung upon the walls of the organization, where it remains till this time. One of the outstanding achievements of Mr. Mills' administration was the bringing to Greenville of Camp Sevier. Much credit goes to Mr. Mills personally for this.

Mr. Mills met his death in attempting to rescue another from drowning. For this heroic deed he was awarded a Carnegie Medal, posthumously.

In religious affiliation Mr. Mills was a Presbyterian, being a Deacon of the Second Presbyterian Church at the time of his death. He was also a member of the Rotary Club and active in the work of that organization.

Mr. Mills was married to Miss Mary Ella Moore of Wilmington, North Carolina, and to this union were born three children, Arthur L., Jr., Roger Moore, and Mary Moore. All three children and their mother reside on Mills Avenue in the City of Greenville.

W. PRIESTLY CONYERS

W. PRIESTLY CONYERS was born in Clarendon County, South Carolina, on the 19th day of September, 1871, being the son of Samuel E. and Mary (Oliver) Conyers. He is of English descent and both his parents were members of families long distinguished in the affairs of Clarendon County; his father was a captain in the

War Between the States, while his mother truly represented the culture and refinement so peculiar to the ladies of the Pee Dee and Coastal sections of the State in ante-bellum days. First she was married to John R. Haynsworth, father of Henry J. Haynsworth, distinguished member of the Greenville bar. Her first husband gave his life to the cause of the Confederacy at the battle of First Manassas.

Major James Conyers, distinguished officer in the American army during the Revolutionary War, was the great-great-grandfather of the subject of this sketch. Of Major Conyers a well-known historian writes:

> "Major James Conyers was one of the most dashing officers South Carolina furnished in the Revolution. He was the officer chosen by General Greene to bear his confidential communications to General Marion, evidencing unmistakably the high esteem in which he was held by the Commander-in-Chief of the Revolutionary Armies of South Carolina."

Mr. Conyers secured his early education in private schools of his home community and then at the Sumter High School. Later he was a student at the State Military College of Florida (now University of Florida) from which he was graduated in 1889.

Leaving college, Mr. Conyers taught school for one year and then entered the office of his half-brother, H. J. Haynsworth, where he studied law till his admission to the bar in 1892. He practiced this profession for one year, but then decided to give it up for a business career, for which time has proved him eminently fitted. After a few years he formed a partnership with his brother-in-law, T. C. Gower, and for many years the firm of Conyers & Gower has played a prominent part in the business life of Greenville, dealing extensively in real estate, of which it is a large owner of both city and farm property.

In all matters pertaining to the upbuilding of his community, Mr. Conyers is always found taking an active and leading part. The Greenville Chamber of Commerce owes much to his efforts. For many years he has been one of its directors, and has often served as Chairman of the Agricultural Bureau. During the year 1924, he was President of the body, and under his administration great progress was made. He assisted in the organizaton of the Historical Society of Upper South Carolina, and was its first President.

As a public speaker Mr. Conyers is much in demand throughout the state, and especially so in Greenville County. He has a remarkable grasp of widely divergent subjects, which coupled with his ease of manner and natural ability, serves to place him in the forefront of that rapidly vanishing class—the Southern orator.

Although he has always taken a deep interest in politics, working untiringly for the election of outstanding men and women of ability to fill all public offices, Mr. Conyers had consistently refused to become a candidate himself, for any position of trust, till 1928, when he consented to permit his name to be used as a candidate for the House of Representatives from Greenville County. To membership in that body he was elected by a large majority and now is one of the leading members of the General Assembly. Often he has been urged to offer for the Governorship of the state, but so far without avail. At one time he was Chairman of the State Board of Pardons by appointment from the Governor.

Yours Truly
J. E. Gower

Mr. Conyers is a member of the Kiwanis Club and was formerly president of that body. In religion he is a Presbyterian, being a Deacon in the First Presbyterian Church.

A number of years ago Mr. Conyers was married to Miss Marie Gower, daughter of Thos. C. Gower, for many years one of the leading business men of Greenville, and they have three children, Mrs. Sarah (Conyers) Westervelt, W. P. Conyers, Jr., and Miss Mary Oliver Conyers.

Mrs. Conyers, like her husband, is deeply interested in all things pertaining to the public good. Largely through her efforts "Green Acre", a home for needy children, located at Greenville, was built, and is being operated with phenomenal success.

THOMAS CLAGHORN GOWER

Among those who helped build Greenville from a country village into the commercial and industrial centre which she began to assume in the latter days of the nineteenth century, none played a more prominent part than did THOMAS CLAGHORN GOWER. He was born in the State of Maine on April 23, 1822, being the son of James Gower and Suzana Norton Gower. As a boy he attended the schools of his home community, and then entered Foxcroft Academy where his education was continued. At the age of nineteen, Mr. Gower ran away from home and came to Greenville, traveling by sleigh, buggy, stage and rail, to join his brother, Eben, who had previously come South. After coming to Greenville he was for two years an apprentice in the carriage makers' trade at $50.00 a year and board; then he became an employee of Gower & Cox with whom he had served his apprenticeship. Leaving this concern he established a carriage business for himself in 1845 on a farm fourteen miles below Greenville, which had been given to his wife as a wedding present by Samuel Williams, his wife's grandfather. So successful was he in this new undertaking that he soon had taken so much of the business of his old employers that they offered him a partnership. Thinking to better his business he accepted the offer and moved back to Greenville from which he had gone to his wife's farm upon his marriage. The new firm became Gower, Cox & Gower, with the subject of this sketch as junior partner.

The business of Gower, Cox & Gower prospered greatly till the outbreak of the War Between the States, when Mr. Gower, the Junior partner, enlisted in the Confederate army as a member of Brooks Troop, later mustered into Hampton's Legion, where he served one year as Quartermaster. Then he was sent back to Greenville to purchase and manufacture supplies for the Quartermaster and Ordnance Departments of the Confederate army. By 1865 these two departments owed the firm of Gower, Cox & Gower $140,000.00 for supplies furnished. After Lee's surrender, but before the news reached this section, the Ordnance Department paid them $70,000.00 in Confederate money which became valueless before it could be utilized in the business. The balance of the account was never paid.

The losses of the firm had been tremendous during the war but with the coming of peace, its members set themselves to the task of rehabilitating the business and within the next five years had placed it upon its feet again. But at this time Mr. Thomas C. Gower found himself so badly involved financially on account of security debts, that he withdrew from the firm so as not to involve it in his personal difficulties. And being naturally of a business turn of mind it was only a few years till he had paid all his debts.

In 1872 Mr. Gower built the first street car line in Greenville, which operated with horse-drawn cars from the old College Place station on Augusta Street to the present Southern depot. During this period he operated a tannery and was proprietor of the first builders' supply company as well as the first coal company to be conducted in Greenville. He was also interested in a shoe factory, and bought heavily of real estate, much of which he developed. Till his death on October 23, 1894, he continued actively in business, being unusually successful in all his ventures.

But not only was Mr. Gower a business man of exceptional ability; in the various civic, religious and educational undertakings of his community, he was active. In 1870 he was elected Mayor of the City of Greenville on a platform to bridge Reedy river, which at that time was strongly opposed by many leading citizens. About 1886 he led a movement for the establishment of a public school system in Greenville. Being successful in this undertaking, he became Chairman of the First Board of Trustees of public schools, which position he held for a number of years.

After the organization of a City School system, teaching was begun in a rented frame store building, situated on the east side of Main Street, midway between Coffee and North, for the whites and in the building known as the Allen School, for the negroes. This latter school had been previously given for a negro school by a Mr. James Allen, a northern man, who had resided in Greenville for several years just after the Civil War, holding a political office of some sort.

Looking to the time of future need, there being no public funds available to secure lots and erect suitable buildings, Mr. Gower bought two lots next to the corner of Hyde Street on Westfield, a large lot on the corner of Calhoun and Markley Streets and the land now occupied by Oaklawn School, holding them for two years or more until bonds had been voted, then selling to the schools at cost price.

In 1888 $18,000 in bonds were voted, but only after most strenuous efforts for the defeat of the movement had been overcome, as many of the city's most prominent citizens were working for its defeat. Out of this meagre amount, the three lots were paid for and Central, Union and Oaklawn Schools were built and equipped.

At one time Mr. Gower was President of the Greenville Board of Trade which preceded the present Chamber of Commerce.

In religious affiliation Mr. Gower was a Presbyterian, being a Ruling Elder in the First Presbyterian Church of Greenville for forty-three years.

Mr. Gower was married three times; first to Jane Jones Williams, daughter of West Allen Williams, who died in 1855. His second wife was Bettie S. Rowland, nee Brooks, whom he married in 1867. However, she lived for a short time only, dying in 1872, and in 1873 he married his third wife, Sally A. Martin, daughter of John C. Martin of Abbeville. He had fourteen children, of whom six are by his first wife, of whom Mrs. Susan C. (Gower) Mills and A. H. Gower survive, and Marie (Mrs. W. P.) Conyers and T. C. Gower are children of his last wife. The second wife had three children.

In the passing of Mr. Thomas Claghorn Gower, Greenville lost one who had done more than usually falls to the lot of one man to accomplish for his home city.

DOCTOR DAVID MARSHALL RAMSAY

DAVID MARSHALL RAMSAY, college president, educational and religious leader, was born in Greenville County, S. C., on October 10, 1857, the son of Andrew and Martha (Gaines) Ramsay. His paternal grandparents were Samuel and Jean (Marshall) Ramsay of Scotland and Ireland, who came to America in 1818. After living in Charleston for a few years, they moved to the Fairview neighborhood of Greenville County, and assisted in the building of that historic community. Through his mother he is descended from the well-known Virginia families of Broadus, Pendleton and Gaines.

The early education of Dr. Ramsay was obtained in the schools of his community and at Carswell Institute, a private school in Anderson County. Later he became a student at Richmond College (now the University of Richmond), from which he was graduated in 1884. Afterward he entered the Southern Baptist Theological Seminary at Louisville, Ky., where he obtained the degree of Master of Theology. In 1893 Howard College of Alabama conferred upon him the degree of Doctor of Divinity.

Doctor Ramsay was ordained as a Baptist minister in 1887 and soon thereafter became pastor of the First Baptist Church of Tuscaloosa, Alabama, where he remained till 1892. Resigning that charge he accepted the pastorate of the Citadel Square Baptist Church of Charleston, S. C., to remain till 1907, when he went to the historic Grace Street Baptist Church of Richmond, Virginia. In 1911 he resigned from this last charge to accept the presidency of the Greenville Woman's College.

Though he has lived in Greenville as President of the Greenville Woman's College for only 18 years, Dr. Ramsay has been actively identified with the interests of the college since 1892, hence his period of service to Greenville and Greenville County must be said to date from that time. In 1892, while pastor of the Citadel Square Baptist Church, he was elected a member of the joint board of trustees of Furman University and Greenville Woman's College. In 1898 he became chairman of the joint board and served in this capacity until 1907, at which time he resigned upon leaving the State to accept the pastorate of the Grace Street Baptist Church. In 1911 he was called from this pastorate to the presidency of the Greenville Woman's College. He accepted this position after having refused the presidency of five other colleges. And he brought with him not only his scholarly gifts, but also sound business policies for the attainment of the ideals which led him to the work. It is probably this business ability, not always found in a college president, which has made him an outstanding executive, and which explains the almost inconceivable growth of the college during his administration. For example, since he became President in 1911, five of the eight buildings on the campus have been erected, the enrollment has more than doubled, the faculty has been greatly strengthened and enlarged, a three-acre lot on which a modern standard library and the handsome Fine Arts Building now stand has been acquired, standards of scholarship have been raised, a scholarship and loan fund of over $60,000 has been built up and a system of self-help positions worked out for aiding around seventy girls each session. And during all this period of progress the college has run without a financial deficit, almost wholly from college fees.

On February 9, 1888, Dr. Ramsay was married to Mary Robertson Woolfolk of Versailles, Kentucky. Mrs. Ramsay is a gifted and charming woman who has been a worthy helpmeet for her husband, while making a large place for herself in social, literary and religious circles. They have three children: Mrs. Eudora Ramsay Richardson, author and magazine writer of Richmond, Virginia; Lieutenant David M. Ramsay, Jr., aviator and instructor in aviation at Brooks Field, San Antonio, Texas; and Dr. Allan Brodie Ramsay, recent graduate from the Medical department of Vanderbilt University, Nashville, Tennessee.

Dr. Ramsay is intensely interested in all public questions of a civic, educational, and religious nature, and always when time permits takes a leading part in promoting them. He is a member of "The Presbuteroi" Club of Versailles, Kentucky, "The Club" of Richmond, Virginia, and the Thirty-Nine Club and Rotary Club of Greenville. He is also a member of the Baptist Church.

Doctor and Mrs. David M. Ramsay reside at the Greenville Woman's College, Greenville, South Carolina.

DOCTOR WILLIAM J. McGLOTHLIN

DOCTOR WILLIAM J. McGLOTHLIN, educator, minister, author and university president, was born in Sumner County, Tennessee, on November 29, 1867, being the son of W. J. A. and Eliza (King) McGlothlin. As a boy he attended the public schools of Tennessee and private academies in Simpson County, Kentucky. In 1887 he entered Bethel College (Ky.), from which he was graduated with an A.B. degree two years later. The McGlothlins were poor and it had been necessary for the son to earn his own way through Bethel. Leaving there he desired to continue his studies further, but not having sufficient money to enable him to do so then, he taught for two years at the Bardstown M. and F. Institute (Bardstown, Ky.), after which he enrolled as a student in the Southern Baptist Theological Seminary, Louisville, Ky.

In 1894 Dr. McGlothlin was graduated from the Seminary with the degree of Master in Theology. After his graduation he accepted a professorship in that institution to remain with it for the next 25 years, except for the time when he was doing post-graduate work abroad. The University of Berlin awarded him a Ph.D. degree in 1901.

Doctor McGlothlin accepted the presidency of Furman University in 1919, and has continued to hold that position up to the present time. For more than 80 years this institution has played a prominent part in the social, educational and religious life of Greenville, but never before to the extent it has during the last decade. An institution of higher learning often holds itself apart from the life and activities of the city in which it is located, but such has never been true of Furman, and especially may this be said as to the period during which Dr. McGlothlin has been the directing head of the institution. Immediately upon coming to Greenville he entered wholeheartedly into the life of the city, striving at all times to bring about a stronger union and more sympathetic understanding between city and college. And his efforts in this respect have not been in vain, for today all Greenville claims Furman as its own, and is continuously working for the expansion of the institution.

The growth of Furman under the administration of Dr. McGlothlin has been nothing short of marvelous. When he came to the institution it had an enrollment of 205 and employed 10 professors, while by 1929 the student body had grown to 553 with a faculty of 35. And in addition to this a Summer School has been established at the University where in 1929 upward of 1000 were instructed. In 1922 a Law School, giving three full years of instruction was added, and so rapidly has it expanded and so thorough is its work being done, that it was recently admitted to membership in the American Bar Association. The University has for five or six years held membership in the Association of Colleges for the Southern States, and the Association of American Colleges, and in 1929 it was placed on the approved list of the Association of American Universities. But for a school to expand its scholastic activities it must first secure the money to enlarge its plant and add to its equipment. Dr. McGlothlin is a business man as well as an educator and able administrator, so he has been able to secure large contributions for his institution. To the permanent endowment was added $500,000.00 in 1922-'27, and under the terms of the James B. Duke Foundation Fund Furman receives 5% of the income from an investment of approximately $40,000,000. And during the years Dr. McGlothlin has been at Furman the University plant has been enlarged by the erection of the J. M. Geer dormitory which furnishes accommodation for 164 young men, a modern infirmary from funds contributed by Chas. S. Webb, as a memorial to his parents, a gymnasium from contributions of Greenville citizens, a central heating plant from which all campus buildings are heated, a large dining hall, and two new athletic fields.

But Dr. McGlothlin, in the midst of his many and varied activities, has found time to devote much study to church history and kindred subjects and is the author of a number of books dealing with those matters. Among these may be mentioned: "A Vital Ministry", "Baptist Confessions of Faith", "A Guide to the Study of Church History", "The Course of Christian History", and "A History of Furman University."

In 1897 Dr. McGlothlin was married to May Belle Williams, daughter of a distinguished minister who was editor of *The Central Baptist,* of St. Louis, Mo. To them were born, Bessie May (deceased), Kathryn, Mary Louise, William J., Jr., and James Harrison. His first wife having died in 1925, he was married a second time in 1929, to Mrs. Mary Louise (Brazeale) Bates, a highly cultured and refined lady of Greenville.

The McGlothlin home is on the Furman University Campus.

JOHN T. WOODSIDE

During the early days of the twentieth century the presence of a new type of citizen began to make itself known in the life of Greenville County. Some years prior to this, a spirit of optimism began to diffuse itself among the residents of the entire Piedmont Section, and by the end of the last century it was evident that the up-state was about to enter a period of progress hitherto unknown. But it was feared that the leaders in the movement must come from without. South Carolina had so long been an agriculural state that it was hardly possible for her to have developed men of a calibre suited for industrial leadership, and it was clearly seen that the trend was toward industrialism. Yet almost over-night and as if by magic, there appeared a group of young men filled with the spirit of progress and radiating confidence in their ability to cope with the new situation. Of these none have been more successful or brought to their home city more improvement than "the four Woodside brothers."

The Woodside brothers are sons of Dr. John Laurens Woodside and Ellen Pamelia (Charles) Woodside of Woodville in lower Greenville County. There were nine brothers and four sisters in the family. Of "the four Woodside brothers" JOHN T. WOODSIDE is the eldest, having been born on May 9, 1864. His education was obtained in such schools as his home community afforded, which were not of the best as compared with the schools of today, but its limited nature seems only to have stimulated him to reach out and grasp the opportunities which were not of easy attainment. Early in life he evinced a natural aptitude for that future business career in which he has been so markedly successful, and steadily he has moved forward against all obstacles till today he is recognized as a veritable business genius.

First, Mr. Woodside was connected with the Reedy River Manufacturing Company, now the Conestee Mills; then he entered the mercantile business at Pelzer, where he remained for two years (1892-'93). In 1893 he moved to Greenville where he was a successful merchant till 1902, when he sold out his business and organized the Woodside Cotton Mills (now said to be the largest cotton mill under one roof in America). Of this concern he was elected president, which position he has filled with great proficiency up to this time. In 1911 the Woodside Cotton Mill, the Simpsonville Cotton Mills and the Fountain Inn Manufacturing Company (all large mills) were consolidated under the name of the Woodside Cotton Mills Company, and of this new company Mr. Woodside became President. A few years later the Woodside Cotton Mills Company acquired the Easley Cotton Mills, which operates one mill at Easley and two at Liberty. Of this huge cotton manufacturing concern, consisting of six large mills, Mr. Woodside is the head.

But Mr. Woodside does not confine himself alone to the cotton manufacturing business, large as his interests in that may be. He is Chairman of the Board of Directors of the Pioneer Life Insurance Company, director in several banks, the largest of which is the Peoples State Bank, formerly Woodside National Bank; President of the Poinsett Hotel Company of Greenville in which he is a large stockholder; Vice-President of the Woodside Securities Company which built and owns the 17-story Woodside Building; President of both The Myrtle Beach Estates, Inc., and the Myrtle Beach Investment Company, which two companies are the owners and developers of a mammoth resort on the Atlantic Coast in Horry County.

Mr. Woodside is an active member of the First Presbyterian Church of Greenville, and many other organizations of a social and civic nature. By and large, he is a man distinguished by a strong character, altruistic aims, practical business sense and high ideals of citizenship. Truly he is one of the South's great leaders.

On April 25, 1893, Mr. Woodside was married to Miss Lou A. Carpenter, daughter of Dr. F. G. Carpenter of Anderson County, and much of the success which has come to Mr. Woodside is due to the strong and refined character, kind disposition, and pleasing personality of this highly esteemed woman.

The Woodside home is at 210 Crescent Avenue, Greenville, South Carolina.

ROBERT I. WOODSIDE

ROBERT I. WOODSIDE, bank president, financier, able business organizer, and public-spirited citizen, was born at Woodville, Greenville County, South Carolina, March 30, 1873, the son of Dr. John Laurens Woodside, who served in an important medical post during the War Between the States, and Ellen Permelia (Charles) Woodside, a woman of very unusual character and pleasing personality.

After finishing the public schools of Woodville, Mr. Woodside attended Clemson College, and later completed a course at the Eastman Business College, Poughkeepsie, New York. The splendid training he received in these noted institutions, supplemented by his native intelligence, sound judgment, ready tact, quick comprehension and great executive ability, well prepared him for that future business career which has ever been marked by unusual success, and is an honor to his colleges, his native county, and the entire State of South Carolina.

On April 23, 1902, he was married to Miss Lula B. Woodside of Baton Rouge, La. Mrs. Woodside is very prominent in the social, music and civic affairs of the state, and was for three years President of the South Carolina Federation of Music Clubs, after which she was elected Honorary President of that organization. She is also a life member of the National Federation of Music Clubs.

For many years Mr. Woodside has held numerous positions of trust and honor. In 1891, at the age of 18 years, he was appointed Assistant Postmaster at Pelzer, South Carolina. He began his career in banking by serving as Cashier of the Chicora Savings Bank of Pelzer, and later as Cashier of the American National Bank of Spartanburg, and as Secretary of the Southern Trust Company. He organized the Bank of Woodville and the Citizens Bank of Taylors (both in Greenville County) and was made President of these institutions. Since its organization in 1907, he has been President of the Farmers & Merchants Bank of Greenville, which was established by him. In 1919 he organized and was elected president of the Farmers Loan & Trust Company, the Home Building & Loan Association and The Woodside National Bank, one of the city's largest banking enterprises, having at the beginning a capital stock of $250,000.00. In 1920, Mr. Woodside organized the Woodside Securities Company, which in that year erected the 17-story bank and office building in Greenville known as the Woodside Building, jointly owned by the Woodside brothers. With his brothers, Mr. Woodside is jointly interested in and is a Director of the chain of six large cotton mills of the Woodside Cotton Mills Company, located at Greenville and Easley, South Carolina, and with his brothers is a joint owner and developer of Myrtle Beach, a project of 66,504 acres located on the Atlantic Coast in the State of South Carolina.

In 1913, Mr. Woodside toured Europe as a member of the American Commission, studying European cooperative banking and marketing systems. He was (in

1924-1925) made President of the South Carolina Bankers' Association, and has served on many committees of the American Bankers' Association, which attests his practical business ability.

In 1902-1903, Mr. Woodside served in the South Carolina State Militia as Lieutenant and is at present a Lieutenant-Colonel in the Officers' Reserve Corps. In 1928 the American Arbitration Association appointed him a member of the National Panel of Arbitration Commission. He is also a member of the National Economic League, which has its headquarters at Boston. Mr. Woodside was also a Chairman of the First Liberty Loan Drive.

Mr. Woodside is a deacon of the First Presbyterian Church of Greenville and is affiliated with the following organizations: Chamber of Commerce, Kiwanis Club, Chess Club, Thirty-Nine Club, Poinsett Club and Greenville Country Club. Politically he is a Democrat and loyally supports the platform and principles of that party.

In 1928 Mr. Woodside visited Europe, making a study of the Branch Banking Systems of England and France. In 1929, the Farmers & Merchants Bank and the Woodside National Bank were sold to the Peoples State Bank of South Carolina, a large branch banking system, but Mr. Woodside continues as a director of that bank. Mr. Woodside will now give his entire attention to the other financial institutions under his management.

Horseback riding and swimming are his chief diversional pleasures. He says that he would again choose the business man's career were he beginning life anew.

JOSEPH P. POOLE

JOSEPH P. POOLE was born at Tumbling Shoals in Laurens County, South Carolina, on the first day of January, 1873, being the son of W. H. Poole and Emily (Stacey) Poole. While he was still quite young his parents moved to Greenville, and it was here in the public schools that he received his education.

When only 17 years of age it was necessary for Mr. Poole to leave school and begin work. His first position was as clerk in a Greenville store. Here he remained for one year and then became Constable for Oscar Hodges, then a magistrate. Next he was a deputy under the late Sheriff P. D. Gilreath. Following his work as a law enforcement officer he became a motorman for the Southern Public Utilities Company, being the one to stand at the controls of the first electric car to move through the streets of Greenville. Many of the car motormen who came later were taught by him. After his services with the street car company he entered the mercantile business which he pursued for two years.

The parents of Mr. Poole were farmers and from them he inherited a love for the soil which was to follow him for the whole of his life. After his mercantile experience he moved to Montague, where he purchased a farm. Next he bought a farm on the Buncombe road. Both these plantations he cultivated with unusual success, employing modern and improved methods. For a time following this he engaged in the real estate business in the city of Greenville, being in partnership with W. T. Henderson. But the life of a farmer called again and he moved back to his Buncombe road farm and built a magnificent home, known today as the "John Marshall home." Here he lived for a number of years before selling out and

returning to Greenville City. But until his death on January 24, 1929, he continued to be deeply interested in farming and farm problems.

In the organization of the South Carolina Cotton Growers' Marketing Association, Mr. Poole took a leading and active part. After the organization was perfected he became its field representative in four of the Piedmont counties, including Greenville. This position he held till 1924 when he was forced to retire from business on account of his health. Seeing the need of a Greenville County fair, he, with others, organized the Greenville County Fair Association in 1919 and for a number of years a successful county fair was conducted upon the Association property located on the Laurens road. For three years Mr. Poole was superintendent of the fair.

An outstanding characteristic of Mr. Poole and his life's work was a feeling of kindliness for the other fellow. He was large of body and big of heart, and it may well be said of him that he was "a friend of man."

On April 28, 1902, Mr. Poole was married to Mrs. Helen Curry Bentley of Greenville and she survives him. They have no children.

WALTER P. WHITE

"A friend of children" might very fittingly be used to designate the most outstanding characteristic of WALTER P. WHITE, a prominent business man of the city of Greenville, and subject of this sketch. Mr. White was born in Greenville, South Carolina, on the 27th day of March, 1890, being the son of B. R. and Hattie Lee White. At the age of three he moved with his parents to the Owings community of Laurens County, where he secured his early education. Later he was a student at Clemson College where he pursued an Electrical and Mechanical course until 1910 when he was graduated with a B.S. degree.

Following his graduation, Mr. White accepted a position with the Westinghouse Electric Company of Pittsburgh where he remained for a short time. Giving up his position with this concern he became Registrar at Clemson College, his alma mater. Here he remained one year and then returned to his old home at Gray Court and entered the retail grocery business. In 1913 he sold out his Gray Court business and moved to Greenville where he helped to organize the Acme Feed Company. This concern, from its beginning, has enjoyed a profitable business, and has grown steadily till it is now one of the largest wholesale businesses dealing in flour, feeds, hay and grain in Greenville. Of the company Mr. White is President and Treasurer and the owner of a majority of its stock. Until 1929 the company had its place of business on Piedmont Avenue, but during that year, on account of growing business, a large warehouse containing ample office space was constructed on East McBee Avenue and in this the company now conducts its business.

Mr. White is an active member of the Second Presbyterian Church of Greenville and for the last five years has been Superintendent of its Sabbath School. He is a member of the Rotary Club, of which organization he has been a director and has recently been elected Vice-President. In this organization he is extremely active in the various phases of "Boys' work" sponsored by the organization.

Of Mr. White and his public activities the *Greenville Piedmont,* local afternoon newspaper, recently said:

"Every city has a few individuals who are willing to bear a good part of the work which is to be done in public campaigns. In this city the saying, 'Let George do it', has been amended to 'Let Walter do it', and everybody knows that they mean Walter P. White. Mr. White has been an active member of the Rotary Club for many years and has been instrumental in the boys' work of that organization, and other phases of club work. He has also served as superintendent of the Second Presbyterian Church Sunday School for many years, and is known as one of the most consistent workers in that organization.

"Mr. White is a wholesaler and therefore believes in doing things on a wholesale basis. Those who know him best declare that he is a wholesaler when it comes to dispensing energy in behalf of the civic undertakings of Greenville. He does not believe in doing things in a half-hearted manner, and always puts forth his best efforts in any movement with which he is identified."

In 1913 Mr. White was married to Miss Mabel West of Greenville, and they have five children, viz: Robbie, Mary, Caroline, William P. and James Richard. The family home is on Williams Street in the City of Greenville.

J. E. WAKEFIELD

Hailing from the historic county of Abbeville, and bringing with him the best of the traditions of that section, J. E. WAKEFIELD has taken a position in the life of Greenville County which would naturally fall to his lot.

Mr. Wakefield was born in the county of Abbeville in 1873, and is the son of James E. and Elvira C. Wakefield. His education was had in the public schools of Anderson, South Carolina, and at Furman University. This latter institution he attended two years. As a very young man he accepted a position with the Farmers & Merchants Bank of Anderson, South Carolina, which position he retained for several years. This was an auspicious opening for the embryo banker, as his later life has so clearly shown. Resigning his position in Anderson he came to Piedmont, in Greenville County, and became Cashier of the Bank of Piedmont. His painstaking work and his natural ability could not long escape notice, and in the course of a few years he was elevated to the presidency of that institution. Under his wise supervision the bank has prospered steadily and holds an enviable position among the strong financial organizations of the county. It is an independent bank and the oldest small bank in Greenville County. During the trying period of depression just past, he has skillfully negotiated the rapids and today the Bank of Piedmont is recognized as one of the strongest in the county. It has deposits of about $300,000.

Mr. Wakefield is a member of the Baptist Church of Piedmont and is chairman of the Board of Deacons of that body. He is also a Mason.

In 1907 he was married to Miss Alma Brock and they are the parents of one daughter, Kathleen, who resides in New York City.

DOCTOR JAMES LEWIS MANN

During the last fifteen years the Greenville City Schools have expanded at a rate probably not equaled by any other system of the State. And this growth is largely due to the efficient management of DR. JAMES LEWIS MANN, who became Superintendent in 1916.

Doctor Mann was born in Abbeville County, South Carolina, on the 7th day of November, 1872, being a son of the Reverend Coke D. and Eliza Jane (Milford) Mann. He received his early education in the public schools of the State and later attended Leesville Institute. In 1890 he entered Emory College at Oxford, Georgia, from which he was graduated with an A.B. degree in 1893. Later Emory University conferred upon him a B.A. degree. From 1900 to 1903 he studied at the University of Grenoble, France, and the University of Berlin, Germany, from which he received a Ph.D. degree.

For two years (1896-'98) Doctor Mann was Superintendent of the Lancaster, South Carolina, schools; from 1898 to 1900 and again from 1903 to 1910 he was Superintendent of the schools of Florence, South Carolina. Leaving his native state in 1910 he became Superintendent of the schools of Greensboro, North Carolina, where he remained till 1916, when he came to Greenville, where he has been Superintendent of the Greenville City Schools up to the present time.

In all matters pertaining to the social and economic betterment of his community, Dr. Mann is at all times deeply interested, taking a prominent part in the leading civic movements of the city of Greenville. He has traveled widely, and having always been a close student of human nature, he knows men, women, boys, and girls, and enjoys dealing with them. And the smoothness with which the school system of Greenville moves, with its more than 8,000 pupils and 300 teachers, without friction and with little show of effort, loudly proclaims the fact that Dr. Mann has learned how to deal with his fellowmen.

Dr. Mann is a Methodist. a Mason, a Woodman, and an honorary member of the American Academy of Social Science. He is also a member of the Advisory Board of the History of Greenville County.

In 1905 Dr. Mann married Miss Sarah Amelia Moss of Orangeburg and they have three children—Margaret Eliza, James Moss and Catherine F.

The family home is at 221 East Park Avenue, Greenville, South Carolina.

WILLIAM DOUGLAS WORKMAN

WILLIAM DOUGLAS WORKMAN was born in Charleston, South Carolina, in 1889 and is the son of Charles E. and Rose (Douglas) Workman. The Workman family has lived in Kershaw County for many generations, and the Douglas' are of a prominent Charleston family of the early days. The wife of Governor John G. Richards is a sister of Charles E. Workman and aunt of William Douglas Workman.

As a youth Mr. Workman, now known as Major Workman, attended the public schools of Charleston, and then became a student at the Citadel, from which he was graduated in 1909. Following his graduation he taught school and studied law until 1914, when he was admitted to the bar of South Carolina. Immediately after this he located in Greenville, where he entered actively into the practice of his profession.

Soon after coming to Greenville, Major Workman became a member of the Butler Guards, a unit of the old First South Carolina Regiment of National Guard Troops. On June 15, 1916, the Butler Guards was ordered to the Mexican border with Captain Workman in command. In December of that year the Butler Guards was recalled and mustered out. Mr. Workman then became Superintendent of the Chick Springs Military Academy, located at Chick Springs in Greenville County. Here he remained until the United States entered the World War, when he volunteered for service.

Upon entering the services of his country Major Workman was assigned for duty with the 118th Infantry of the Thirtieth Division (National Guard troops), located at Camp Sevier, Greenville, South Carolina (commanding Co. "A", the Butler Guards). From here he was sent to France in the early spring of 1918, in advance of his regiment. There he was assigned to the Infantry Specialty School, but before his course was completed he was transferred to the School of the Line, from which he graduated. Next he was ordered to the Army General Staff College, the highest school of the American army in France. After five months here he was sent back to the Thirtieth Division as Brigade Adjutant of the 60th Infantry Brigade. On October 23, 1918, he was promoted from captain to major. Brigadier General Faison, in complimenting Major Workman upon his promotion, said, among other things:

"Taking this occasion to bear public testimony to his splendid support, uniform courtesy, marked ability, and efficiency in the performance of all duties while on duty at these headquarters. . . . His future is assured."

Soon after his promotion the Armistice was signed and the war was at an end. Major Workman was offered every possible inducement by his superior officers to remain in the military services, but being firm in his determination to return to Greenville and re-establish his professional and social relations, he declined all offers and early 1919 found him back in Greenville.

Upon his return to Greenville Major Workman entered the real estate business and for several years was very active in that line of work. During the last two or three years, however, he has devoted the principal part of his time to the practice of law.

As a public-spirited citizen, Greenville has known few who have been as active as Major Workman. He is much in demand as a public speaker, especially on patriotic occasions; he assisted in the organization of and was the first President of the Young Men's Business League, now the Junior Chamber of Commerce; he helped organize and was a charter member of the Civitan Club; in the American Legion he is quite active and was the first Post Commander of the Greenville Post; a number of times he has been a delegate to the Greenville County Democratic Convention, twice a delegate to the State Convention, and in 1922 was a delegate to the National Convention of the Democratic party.

In 1913 he was married to Miss Vivian Watkins, daughter of the late J. Newt Watkins and niece of Judge H. H. Watkins of the United States District Court, and they have two children, viz: William Douglas, Jr., and Vivian Virginia.

JAMES OVERTON LEWIS

JAMES OVERTON LEWIS, retired druggist and prominent citizen of Greenville, was born in Oconee County, near Pendleton, in 1861, being a son of Dr. Thomas L. and Eliza (Maxwell) Lewis.

The Lewis family is of Welch descent. Four brothers of this family emigrated from Wales. Two of them, General Robert Lewis and John Lewis, settled in Virginia. General Robert Lewis had a son, John, Sr. John, Sr., had a son, John, Jr., who married Frances Fielding. One of their sons married Bettie Washington, sister of General George Washington. John, the emigrant from Wales, had a number of children, one of whom, David Lewis, is the ancestor of the Lewis family in South Carolina. He married a Miss Terrell and one of their sons, John, married Sarah Taliaferro of Virginia. Just before the Revolution he (John) and his family moved to Rutherford County, North Carolina.

Among the children of John and Sarah (Taliaferro) Lewis was a son, John Lewis, who was the father of John Taliaferro Lewis, who married Eleanor Earle, daughter of General John B. Earle. One of the sons of this union was Colonel Richard Lewis. He was Clerk of the Court of Rutherford County, North Carolina, and a member of the convention for revising the North Carolina Constitution. He married Sarah Miller, daughter of General James Miller of North Carolina, who was an officer in the Revolution. He and his wife emigrated to South Carolina and settled on Seneca river, near Pendleton. Both of them are buried in the Old Stone Church cemetery. One of their sons, James Overton Lewis, married Mary Lorton, and one of the children of this union was Dr. Thomas L. Lewis, father of James Overton Lewis, the subject of this sketch.

Dr. Thomas L. Lewis was a graduate of the South Carolina College and a prominent physician of his day. He married Miss Eliza Maxwell, daughter of Captain John Maxwell.

James Overton Lewis secured his education in the public schools of his home community and at Adjer College, Walhalla, South Carolina. From the latter he was graduated in 1882. A year later he moved to Greenville and became an employee of Thomas Sloan, operating Sloan Brothers Drug Company. Here he remained for five years and then went with the National Bank of Greenville (now First National) for three years. Then he formed a partnership with S. M. Reynolds and entered the drug business. Later he became senior partner of Lewis & Hartzog. This firm operated one of the foremost drug stores of Greenville City for many years. In 1917 this partnership was dissolved and Mr. Lewis retired after having been engaged in the drug business for more than thirty years. Since then he has devoted himself to public and civic matters and the conduct of a small but model farm on the outskirts of Greenville.

During the years of his business activity and since, Mr. Lewis has shown an active interest in the upbuilding of his home community. He is an ex-foreman of the Greenville County Grand Jury and a member of the Woodmen of the World.

Mr. Lewis was married to Miss Mary Scott Birnie, daughter of the late James Birnie, and they have eight children, viz: Mary Birnie (Mrs. P. H. Austin), J.

Maxwell, Annie (Mrs. W. A. Williams), William B., Thomas L., Jeanette (Mrs. Rhodes Perdue), Caroline (Mrs. William Webster), and James O., Jr.

The Lewis home is "Birnie Hill", located just beyond the City of Greenville on the Augusta road. This is a beautiful and valuable estate and is the old home of James Birnie, father of Mrs. Lewis. Mr. Birnie was born in Aberdeen, Scotland, of an old and honorable family. The ancestral estate in Aberdeen was known as "Ash Grove." Mr. Birnie was brought to America as an orphan at the age of 12, was educated at the College of Charleston, and admitted to the South Carolina bar at 21. For many years he practiced law in Greenville, accumulating considerable property and leaving behind, at his death, an enviable reputation.

H. CLYDE HARVLEY

During the trying days of the World War, Greenville elected as Mayor the youngest man ever to hold that office; and at the time of his election this young man held the further distinction of being the youngest Mayor in the State of South Carolina. Camp Sevier was located upon the outskirts of the city, and this, coupled with a multiplicity of other war problems, threw upon the shoulders of this young executive much more than ordinary responsibilities. But the affairs of the city were handled in an unusually efficient manner by its Mayor.

The war executive to whom reference is made was H. CLYDE HARVLEY, son of J. K. and Ida Adkins Harvley, who was born in Edgefield County on December 17, 1886. His family early moved to Greenwood where he attended the city schools for several years. But while still nothing more than a boy, Mr. Harvley left school and entered the services of the Charleston & Western Carolina Railway Co., first as a telegraph operator and later in the capacity of station agent. In 1913, while with the railroad company, he was transferred to Greenville where he became local representative for that road, and this position he still holds.

Just two years after becoming a citizen of Greenville, Mr. Harvley was elected one of the City Aldermen. In this position he was Chairman of the Light Committee, and was largely responsible for Greenville's "white way." Upon the expiration of his term he became a candidate for Mayor and was elected. Twice thereafter, he was re-elected, thus having been chosen for three terms to fill that office. During his first term, while the war was in progress, there arose an acute coal shortage, which threatened to cause suffering among great numbers of the citizens of Greenville. But the Mayor took hold of the situation with a firm hand by establishing a municipal coal and wood yard, and forbidding the sale of wood or coal by anyone except upon an order or permit from the municipal authorities. This action stabilized prices and curbed hoarding. So in a few days fuel could be had by everybody at reasonable prices. When Mr. Harvley assumed office, the water system of the city belonged to private interests, but during his first term he successfully advocated the issuance of a million dollars in bonds with which to purchase the city's water supply.

Since retiring from office in 1925, Mr. Harvley has aspired to no other place of public trust, but he is still deeply interested in the public good and devotes much of his time to questions of civic betterment. He is a member of the Baptist Church,

H. CLYDE HARVLEY

a high ranking Mason, a Shriner, a member of the Improved Order of Red Men, a Moose, and a member of the J. O. U. A. M.

Mr. Harvley was married to Miss Blanche Barber of Fairfax, Barnwell County, in 1906 and they have three children, Mrs. Helen (Harvley) White, Clyde and John. They reside in the city of Greenville on East Washington Street.

ERNEST PATTON

ERNEST PATTON is the son of Walter Lenoir and Lula (Garrison) Patton. His father has played a leading part in the business and civic affairs of Greenville for more than thirty years, being at this time President of Patton, Tilman & Bruce, Inc., which is probably the largest independent shoe establishment in upper South Carolina. Avery Patton, President and owner of the Independent Guano Company, is his uncle. The Pattons came to Greenville from Hendersonville, North Carolina, during the latter part of the nineteenth century, and are members of the prominent family of that name in western North Carolina.

Ernest Patton was born in Greenville on June 10, 1899. His early education was had in the public schools of the city, and then at Furman University. After three years spent in Furman and a short period in the army, he entered Yale University, where, after two years' study, he was graduated with an A.B. degree, being at the time of his graduation 21 years of age.

Upon the completion of his education Mr. Patton returned to Greenville and accepted a position with the First National Bank. Here he remained, giving a close study to the banking business in all its details, until 1924 when he resigned to become connected with the Norwood National Bank of Greenville. Later this institution was merged with the Bank of Charleston and the Carolina National Bank of Columbia to form the South Carolina National Bank, which today, with its many branches and affiliated state banks, is the largest financial institution in South Carolina. Having thoroughly proved his ability in the field of banking, Mr. Patton was elected Assistant Vice-President of the South Carolina National Bank in 1928, becoming the youngest vice-president of a bank in Greenville. This position he still holds.

Mr. Patton spends much of his time outside business hours in reading the better class of literary composition. He is also a student of the history of South Carolina and the lives of her great men. In religious affiliation he is an Episcopalian, being a Vestryman of the St. James Church.

In 1923 Mr. Patton was married to Miss Margaret Mitchell, daughter of Dr. A. R. Mitchell of Greenville, and they have two children: Ernest Gibbes and Walter Lenoir II.

JOHN A. RUSSELL

Over a long period of years, one of the most familiar and best loved figures about the streets of Greenville has been that of JOHN A. RUSSELL. His business ability, his church and social activities, and his genial personality have made him a general favorite.

Mr. Russell, who is the son of Major Thomas H. and Jane (Hamilton) Russell, was born in Anderson County, South Carolina, in 1858. The older male members of the Russell family all saw active service in the War Between the States. His father was a major in the Home Guards and four brothers served their beloved Southland long and well. John Russell's youth came at a very trying period of the state's history, but the perseverance evident in later life evinced itself even then. Attending the public schools, first of Anderson County and later of Pickens, he secured the best education possible in those troublous times.

In 1876, having finished his school days, he became a clerk for T. W. Davis, a leading merchant of Greenville, during the 70s. In this position he remained until 1883, when he, with James W. Lipscomb, who was also an employee of Mr. Davis, organized the Lipscomb-Russell Company and purchased the business of their employer, and for 17 years the Lipscomb-Russell Company conducted a wholesale and retail business on Main Street in the City of Greenville. In 1900 the concern went exclusively into wholesale merchandising. Since then the company has confined itself to the wholesale end of the business. In addition to groceries, the establishment owns and operates a large coffee roasting plant, the only one of its kind in this section of the state. Here is roasted and blended many popular brands of coffee. Dry goods, notions and tobaccos are also important items handled by this concern. All of these articles are sold in immense quantities and to the wholesale trade only. As cigar dealers the concern enjoys the distinction of being the oldest company of its kind in the state. In 1906 the health of Mr. Lipscomb failed, and until his death in 1921 he was an invalid. The business was operated by Mr. Russell, who during all those years and up to the present held the position of President and Treasurer of the company. Now John W. Lipscomb, a son of James W. Lipscomb, is Vice-President of the company and assists in the management and operation of it.

In his younger days Mr. James W. Lipscomb was quite active in the public affairs of his city, having served on the Police Commission and also on the City Council of the City of Greenville before his health failed; and Mr. Russell, in spite of his large business interests, has always found time to serve the city and county when called upon. He is an ex-President of the Greenville Chamber of Commerce and it was during his administration that the plan for the handsome Chamber of Commerce building was conceived and executed. He has long been active in the church life of the community, and is a Ruling Elder in the First Presbyterian Church of Greenville. He is also a member of the local lodge of Knights of Pythias.

In 1887 Mr. Russell was married to Miss Alice Bridges, and they have one daughter, Ruth, who is now Mrs. J. D. Turnbull of Charlotte, North Carolina.

The Russell home is on East Coffee Street in the City of Greenville.

OCTAVUS BOWEN HARTZOG

OCTAVUS BOWEN HARTZOG is a native of Bamberg, South Carolina, having been born there on April 9, 1872. His parents, Samuel J. and Mary (Owens) Hartzog, were planters, both being descended from old families of the Bamberg and Barnwell section of the state. As a boy Mr. Hartzog (subject of this sketch) attended the public schools of his home community and then became a student at Furman University. Leaving here he entered the Atlanta School of Pharmacy from which he received a degree in pharmacy.

Having finished his education, Dr. Hartzog moved to Greenville where he held various positions till 1896, when he became connected with Sloan Brothers Drug Company, one of the oldest drug establishments in the city, to remain there till 1899, when he and J. O. Lewis organized the Lewis & Hartzog Drug Company.

From its organization in 1899 until its dissolution in 1917, the Lewis & Hartzog Drug Company was a factor in the business life of Greenville. Both Mr. Lewis and Dr. Hartzog were extremely active in all public affairs of the city and county and their business reflected the gratitude of their fellow citizens.

Upon the dissolution of the Lewis & Hartzog Drug Company, Dr. Hartzog organized the Hartzog Drug Company which continues to enjoy a profitable business. The concern for a number of years past has occupied the former location of Carpenter Brothers Drug Company, adjoining the historic Mansion House site.

In 1899 Dr. Hartzog was married to Miss Rozelle Waddell, and they have a son, Octavus Bowen, Jr. Mrs. Hartzog is one of the city's most gracious and accomplished musicians. For a number of years she has been organist at the Fourth Presbyterian Church. She devotes much time to the music clubs of the city and often appears as a pianist at public performances throughout the State.

Dr. and Mrs. Hartzog reside in the Davenport Apartments.

WILLIAM B. McDANIEL

Few families have been so prominently identified with the affairs of Greenville County throughout its entire life as the McDaniel. In 1785, just one year after the county was officially opened to settlers, the Widow McDaniel came down from North Carolina and settled eight miles east of the present city of Greenville. She brought with her a young son, James, who during the War of 1812 was to attain the rank of Quartermaster-General in the American army. He married Miss Mary Austin, daughter of Colonel William Austin, another early settler of the county, who also founded an illustrious family. About 1830 General McDaniel was elected Sheriff of Greenville County and for many years he held this office and that of Clerk of Court. When in 1852 he died, Governor Perry wrote of him: "He was the only man I ever knew that overcame his enemies by kindness."

General James McDaniel had two sons, Major W. A. McDaniel and John T. McDaniel. Both of these, like their father, held the offices of Sheriff and Clerk of Court in Greenville County. Major W. A. McDaniel married Miss Francis Loucinda Perrett and they had two sons, James A. and William B., and a daughter, Stella K., who married H. B. Tindall, then of Clarendon County but later a prominent citizen of Greenville.

William B. McDaniel, the younger of the two sons of Major W. A. McDaniel, was born in 1850 on the family plantation near the present town of Mauldin, and at two years of age moved with the family to the vicinity of Greenville City. As a boy he attended the Mary Powell Preparatory School and later was a student at Furman University.

Having completed his education Mr. McDaniel entered the office of his father, who was then Clerk of Court of Greenville County, where he remained for a number of years. In 1889 he became City Clerk and Treasurer of Greenville, which position he held for 20 years. Retiring from this office in 1910 he spent the balance of his life in farming and developing his extensive properties in the vicinity of McDaniel Avenue, which street was named for his father.

The home in which he resided was built by General Waddy Thompson on Paris Mountain for a summer home. During the War Between the States it was torn down and rebuilt at its present site. Shortly afterward it was purchased by Mr. McDaniel's father, Major W. A. McDaniel.

Mr. McDaniel, during the whole of his life, like his father and grandfather, was much interested in the public affairs of Greenville County, working at all times for what he considered the public good. Although never aspiring to a county office, he was widely known over the county and those desiring office were always anxious to secure his support.

In 1872 he married Miss Orgie Aggie Cox of Marietta, South Carolina, who died in 1884. To this union were born two children, Mrs. Mary Austin Daniel, now of Chicago, and William Austin, deceased. In 1891 he married Miss Mary Ella Smith of Spartanburg, by whom he has one child, Annie Lou, who married John Leon Newman of Aberdeen, Mississippi. Mr. and Mrs. Newman have one child, Mary Elizabeth.

After a long and extraordinarily useful life Mr. McDaniel died on the 18th day of February, 1928, which was his 78th birthday. In his death Greenville County lost a highly valuable citizen, who held the esteem of his fellow men in every walk of life. His widow survives him and resides with her daughter, Mrs. Newman, and family on McDaniel Avenue in the City of Greenville.

G. FRANK LEAGUE

One of the outstanding business men of Greenville City is G. FRANK LEAGUE. He was born near Simpsonville, in Greenville County, on August 8, 1883, being the son of George P. and Elizabeth (Moon) League. His ancestry, through both his father and mother, have long been substantial farmers and sawmill operators of the lower part of Greenville County.

Mr. League received his early training in the public schools of Simpsonville, later taking a business course at Spartanburg. Following the completion of his education he kept books for a period of six years for various concerns in Greenville and Spartanburg Counties. In 1911 he became City Clerk and Treasurer for Greenville, and this position he held until 1918, performing its duties with care and efficiency. Following his work with the city he became affiliated with Hudson & Rigby, a wholesale lumber concern. Here Mr. League gained experience which, coupled with earlier training by his father in lumber manufacturing, was to prove invaluable to him in the conduct of his future business. After severing his connection with Hudson & Rigby, May 1, 1919, he organized the G. F. League Lumber Company, which handles all types of lumber, laths, shingles, plywood shipping cases and other building supplies as brokers, jobbers and wholesalers. Signal success has attended him in the operation of this business and he is constantly enlarging the scope of its activities.

For many years Mr. League has been an active member of the First Baptist Church of Greenville; he takes a prominent part in the various civic affairs of the community, and is a member and ex-director of the Civitan Club of Greenville.

Mr. League was married at Beaufort, South Carolina, on June 22, 1909, to Miss Edith Oglethorpe Adams, a daughter of Mr. Benj. C. and Mrs. Julia (Caldwell) Adams, prominent residents of Beaufort. Mrs. League is a direct descendant of James Oglethorpe, founder and first governor of Georgia.

Mr. and Mrs. League are the parents of three children, Julia, Frank, Jr., and William, and they reside on East North Street, in the city of Greenville.

WILLIAM T. JONES

WILLIAM T. JONES, son of Edmund and Cynthia (Brown) Jones, was born in the present Simpsonville section of Greenville County on February 9, 1841. His ancestors were among the very early settlers of the county.

When Mr. Jones was a youth there were few schools in Greenville County and all of these were of the "private" order, and required the payment of tuition. The Jones family was poor and tuition for the education of the children was not to be had, so William T. Jones entered upon his life's work with little of the so-called "book learning", but his mind was active, and during his long life he acquired a large fund of "common sense" which made of him a highly valuable citizen in his community.

With the coming of the War Between the States Mr. Jones volunteered, and throughout the war served with the Confederate army, being twice wounded during the conflict, once in an arm and again in a leg. The war concluded, he returned to his old home community to remain till his death on December 6, 1928. For the greater portion of his life he was engaged in farming and with marked success. During his later years, however, he sold the greater portion of his farm holdings and moved to the town of Simpsonville, where he died.

Mr. Jones was twice married. First to Miss Mary Richardson, who died in 1868, and then to Miss Rebecca Jane Bryson. To the first union was born two children, J. E. Jones and Mrs. Anna (Jones) Cox. There were five of the second family of children, viz: R. D. Jones, Mrs. Lillie (Jones) Moore, Mrs. Lula (Jones) Thackston, Mrs. Zee (Jones) Green and W. P. Jones. His second wife departed this life February 11, 1920.

R. DAVID JONES

Among the leaders in the business life of Greenville today is R. DAVID JONES, President of the Jones-McAfee Company, Funeral Directors. He was born near Simpsonville in lower Greenville County on the 4th day of October, 1873, being the son of William T. and Rebecca Jane (Bryson) Jones.

As a youth and young man Mr. Jones attended the public schools of the county located at Standing Springs and Simpsonville. After finishing his education he was engaged in farming for a number of years; then he entered the cotton seed business at Simpsonville and Gaffney. Later he conducted a general mercantile business at Simpsonville, and in 1912 added undertaking. During all these years he continued to operate his farms.

In 1922 Mr. Jones established the Jones-McAfee Company at Greenville and since then has been President of that company. The undertaking parlors of this concern are located on West McBee Avenue and were, at the time of their opening, the most elaborate and modern in upper South Carolina. The equipment of the company is ample for every need and is probably not exceeded by that of any like business in South Carolina. Both Mr. Jones and his associate, Mr. Thomas F. McAfee, are widely known over the county and this has brought a degree of success to their business which is equaled by few, if any, in the State.

Although Mr. Jones resides at Simpsonville he takes a leading part in the civic life of Greenville City. He is a member of the Greenville Civitan Club, and also holds membership in the J. O. U. A. M. In both of these organizations he is active.

At Simpsonville, where Mr. Jones lives, he was formerly a member of the Board of Trustees of the Simpsonville schools, an Alderman of the Town of Simpsonville, and a Deacon in the Simpsonville Baptist Church. Since severing his business connections at Simpsonville, however, he has consistently declined to accept offices of public trust there, thinking that he might not be able to render his best services while out of business touch with the community.

On August 13, 1894, Mr. Jones was married to Miss Lillie Butler and they have four children, L. C. Jones, F. D. Jones, Anna Bell Jones and Juliet Jones.

THOMAS F. McAFEE

THOMAS F. McAFEE, member of the firm of Jones-McAfee Company, funeral directors of Greenville City, was born in Cleveland, Georgia, on April 18, 1888. His parents were Charles M. and Lucinda (Stringer) McAfee. His paternal grandparents, Mr. and Mrs. Thomas McAfee, were the parents of 15 children who lived to celebrate their 66th wedding anniversary, at which time they had 250 direct descendants, without there ever having been a death in the family. Five sons of this venerable couple were soldiers of the Confederacy during the War Between the States. Thomas Stringer, maternal grandfather of Thomas F. McAfee, rode on horseback from Georgia to California during "gold rush" days. The family on both sides were all farmers.

Mr. McAfee, subject of this sketch, secured his education in the public schools of Georgia and then entered the employ of H. M. Patterson and Son of Atlanta, Georgia. In 1913 he left this concern and moved to Greenville where he entered the undertaking business of Ramseur-McAfee Company as one of the owners. From the beginning this concern was successful, and in 1917 secured a contract with the United States government to serve Camp Sevier as its sole undertakers. While this contract was in force the influenza epidemic of 1917-'18 swept the country, bringing death to hundreds at Camp Sevier. This was something which had not been thought of by Ramseur-McAfee Company when the contract was made, and it created a situation difficult to handle, but the contract was carried out to the letter.

In 1923 Mr. McAfee withdrew from the Ramseur-McAfee Company and assisted in the formation of a new business to be known as the Jones-McAfee Company. Immediately this new concern became a leader as funeral directors for

Greenville City and a large territory surrounding. During the years which have since passed its business has steadily grown, and today it occupies a place at the very top among those of the two Carolinas in its field.

For many years Mr. McAfee has been active in the South Carolina Funeral Directors' Association and is a Past President of that organization. He is also a member of the State Board of Examiners for Embalming, which position he has held continuously for 12 years. Another position of a public nature held by him is that of Chairman of the Board of Charities and Corrections for Greenville County.

Mr. McAfee is a member of the St. Paul Methodist Church, a member of the Greenville Chamber of Commerce, a Mason, a Red Man, a member of the Lions Club, and a J. O. U. A. M.

On November 12, 1910, he was married to Miss Mary Hill and they have three children, Thomas F. McAfee, Jr., Charles H. McAfee and Mary H. McAfee.

HENRY BOARDMAN STEWART, M.D.

Within a few months after Greenville County was opened to settlers in 1784, practically all of the children of John and Peggy Peden, recent immigrants from County Ancrum, Ireland, had taken up lands in lower Greenville County. Being of Scotch-Irish stock, these early pioneers soon felt the need of a church and set themselves to the organization of one. Their efforts were successful, and in 1786 the Fairview Presbyterian Church began its long and useful life as the oldest church in the county. And today, still vigorous, despite its more than a century and a half of life, Fairview is carrying on with a congregation composed largely of descendants of its organizers. In all the long history of this church the ministry of Rev. C. B. Stewart, which extended over a period of more than 30 years from about 1850, according to the official church history, "embraces the era of the greatest church enterprise and prosperity."

The Reverend C. B. Stewart, who so long guided the destiny of Fairview, was the son of Walter Stewart, a substantial farmer of the early days. Early in life he took up his work among the sturdy, God-fearing people and remained there till the day of his death, ministering not only to their spiritual needs but to their mental and physical wants as well. He was to that community a veritable patriarch to whom all might turn for guidance and advice in the hour of need. And so dear was he to the people among whom he lived and ministered that today (45 years after his pastorate) there rests on the walls of the church a marker placed to his memory.

On July 21, 1855, a son, HENRY BOARDMAN STEWART, was born to the Reverend C. B. Stewart and his wife, Katy Carson (Hitch) Stewart, who becomes the subject of this sketch. His paternal ancestors were Scotch-Irish as were most of the people of his birthplace, while his mother's people were English. The educational advantages of that early day were poor at best, and to make the deficiency greater, about the time young Stewart should have been acquiring an education the War Between the States and its terrible aftermath virtually destroyed the few which had existed. So his early schooling was quite meager. But as always, one really desiring an education can find a way for securing it. Working on a farm in summer and at a local ginnery the young man earned sufficient funds to enable him to attend schools at Reidville and Williamston where he secured about the equivalent of a high school education. He then became a student at Atlanta Medical College from which he graduated with an M.D. degree in 1879. While here he won Dr. Logan's Chemistry prize for proficiency in that subject. Leaving Atlanta he took a postgraduate course in Emory University.

For the practice of his profession, Dr. Stewart located in his old home community of Fairview, where he soon won the high esteem of his neighbors, not alone as a physician but like his honored father before him, as advisor for all who might seek his counsel. And being located in a beautiful farm community, he was not content to confine himself to his profession alone, especially since the agricultural methods of his neighbors were so unscientific and he saw here an opportunity to render aid. So he became a farmer, using the most approved and up-to-date methods. He was the first to introduce registered cattle, horses and poultry into his community, and became the potential founder of the Fairview Stock Show, an annual one-day fair which has been held for more than 40 years, charging no gate fees and drawing thousands of visitors each season.

Dr. Stewart is a Presbyterian, being a Ruling Elder in the Fairview Presbyterian Church, and for 42 years Superintendent of its Sabbath School.

On March 4, 1880, which was the first anniversary of his graduation, Dr. Stewart was married to Miss Eugenia M. Peden, daughter of John Mac. and Elizabeth (Smith) Peden and they have three daughters and five sons, viz: Mrs. Frennie F. Coleman of Fountain Inn, S. C., Mrs. Bessie Lowry of Fountain Inn, S. C., Mrs. Rosa Cason of Greenville, S. C., Clifford C. Stewart, principal of a school in Abbeville County; Mack M. Stewart, postmaster at Winnsboro, S. C.; Hoke H. Stewart of Fountain Inn, S. C.; David D. Stewart of Fountain Inn, S. C., and Dr. C. B. Stewart of Atlanta, Ga.

Since his graduation, Dr. Stewart has actively engaged in the practice of medicine in the same community and on March 4, 1929, he therefore, passed the half-century mark in his chosen field, being now the oldest practicing physician in Greenville County.

Recently Dr. Stewart erected a memorial stone in the cemetery of the old Fairview Church on which appear the following beautiful sentiments: "Dedicated to the memory of the 'Family Physician' " — also — "In memory of those who keep the home-fires burning during the Doctor's absence on his errands of mercy."

Doctor Stewart's prayer from early manhood has been "Lord, help me to live for thy Glory—and the betterment of mankind—Amen."

The address of Doctor Stewart is Fountain Inn, South Carolina.

AUGUSTUS WARDLAW SMITH

During the last 25 years South Carolina has produced quite a number of cotton manufacturers who stand at the very top of that industry in the United States. Of these a half-dozen or more reside in Greenville; but of this number, none surpasses AUGUSTUS WARDLAW SMITH, president of the Brandon Corporation which owns and operates the Brandon Mills and Poinsett Mills of Greenville, the Woodruff Mills of Woodruff, Spartanburg County, and the Renfew Mills at Travelers Rest in Greenville County.

Mr. Smith was born in Abbeville County, South Carolina, on April 29, 1862, being the son of Colonel Aug. M. Smith and Sarah (Wardlaw) Smith. He is of an illustrious ancestry through both his father and mother. His father was a merchant and planter of Abbeville County, who volunteered for service in the Confederate army at the beginning of the War Between the States, and was commissioned a Major in the First South Carolina regiment. Later he was promoted to Lieutenant Colonel, which rank he held when mortally wounded while leading his forces at Gaines' Mill before Richmond. Joel Smith, father of Col. Aug. M. Smith, was a wealthy planter, merchant and contractor of Abbeville County. The father of Joel Smith was William Smith, who moved from Virginia to Stoney Point, Abbeville County, at a very early period and founded the family in South Carolina. As were so many of these pioneer up-country settlers, he was of Scotch-Irish stock. The grandfather of Aug. W. Smith on his mother's side was D. L. Wardlaw, a distinguished lawyer and jurist, who was the first male child born in Abbeville County. He was a member of the House of Representatives from 1826 to 1841 and in 1836 was Speaker of that body. In 1841 he became a Judge of the Circuit Court and later was Associate Justice of the Court of Appeals. A brother of D. L. Wardlaw (Francis) is said to be the author of the Ordinance of Secession. The father of D. L. Wardlaw, John W. Wardlaw, was the first Clerk of Court of Abbeville County, which position he held for 38 years. The Wardlaws also came from Virginia and were likewise Scotch-Irish.

As a boy, Aug. W. Smith attended Prof. Benet's school at Cokesbury, then Abbeville, now Greenwood County. Later he was a student in the schools of Baltimore, and then entered the University of the South at Sewanee, Tennessee, where he remained for two years. In 1876, after the carpetbaggers were ousted from South Carolina, he entered the South Carolina College as a member of the first class under the new regime. At 18, he left college.

After his school days were over, Mr. Smith worked on a farm for one year and then for a few years was a clerk in the store of his uncle. In 1883 he entered the mercantile business for himself in a small way, but in 1900 he moved to Spartanburg, where he founded Aug. W. Smith and Company, which rapidly expanded till today it is one of the largest and most successful department stores in South Carolina. Mr. Smith is still President and owner of this establishment.

In 1900 Mr. Smith became interested in the cotton manufacturing business, and organized the Woodruff Cotton Mill which he still operates with success. For four years he lived at Woodruff, and while there he organized the Bank of Woodruff of which institution he has been President from its beginning. After the four years in Woodruff, he returned to Spartanburg to live till 1916 when he accepted the presidency of the Brandon Mill and the Poinsett Mills at Greenville and moved his residence to that city where he now lives. Later the Renfew Mill was built at Travelers Rest as a branch of the Brandon Mill. In 1928 the Brandon Corporation, a consolidated company for all these mills, was organized and of it Mr. Smith became President.

182   HISTORY OF GREENVILLE COUNTY, SOUTH CAROLINA

Mr. Smith served as Colonel of the Third South Carolina Regiment of Militia during the years 1890-'91; and was Mayor of Abbeville in 1891-'92. He is a member of the Greenville Chamber of Commerce, a K. of P., and an Episcopalian.

He married Miss Mary Noble of Abbeville on January 5, 1887. She is now dead. He married a second time to Miss Belle Perrin, daughter of Lewis W. Perrin of Abbeville on June 5, 1901, and they have four children, Mrs. Floride (Smith) McBee, Mary, Augustus W., Jr., and Lewis Perrin.

The address of Mr. Smith is Greenville, S. C., his home being a beautiful country place about five miles out from the city, off the Augusta road.

ROBERT LEE MARCHANT, M.D.

For more than half a century the name of Marchant has stood out in the Greer community of Greenville County as a beacon light pointing to business success and professional integrity. Back in the days of the War Between the States Martin Luther Marchant was engaged in the manufacture of cotton for the Confederate army at the Batesville mill, located only a few miles from the present town of Greer. He and his wife, Mary (Smith) Marchant, were the parents of a family of boys who were to play a conspicuous part in the building of Greer. Of this number was ROBERT LEE MARCHANT, born at Batesville in 1866.

As a youth and young man Mr. Marchant attended the public schools, first in the Batesville community and then at Greer. Following his school days at Greer he became a student at the Kentucky School of Medicine, from which he was later graduated with the degree of M.D.

Having finished his medical education Dr. Marchant returned to the community of his birth to practice his profession at Pelham. Here he remained for five years following the hard life of a country doctor as it was before the days of good roads and modern means of conveyance. After this he moved to Greer, where he entered actively upon the general practice of medicine, which he has consistently and conscientiously followed for 29 years. When he came, Greer was no more than a country community, but it has grown with the passing years to become a thriving little city stirring with commercial activity. In the growth of the town Dr. Marchant has done his part and more, and his friends and neighbors, in recognition of his public services and broad learning in the profession, have given him through all the years a large and lucrative practice. Even the coming of younger men with the so-called "improved and modern methods" have had no effect upon him and his practice.

Dr. Marchant is a member of the Greenville County Medical Society, a Mason, and a Methodist. In all of these organizations he takes an active part.

His wife is the former Miss Emma Wham. They have four children, viz: Hortense (Mrs. W. C. Stallworth), Lucile (Mrs. Harold Sheib), John Luther, and Fitzhugh Lee.

MARTIN LUTHER MARCHANT

MARTIN LUTHER MARCHANT, son of Martin Luther Marchant, Sr., and Mary (Smith) Marchant, was born at Batesville, in Greenville County, in 1868. As a youth he attended the public schools of Batesville and then the Greer Graded Schools.

THOMAS M. MARCHANT

Leaving here he continued his education at the Wofford Fitting School, Spartanburg, South Carolina.

With his school days ended, Mr. Marchant entered the mercantile establishment of John W. Baker at Batesville, where he worked for one year as clerk. Then he went with H. P. Moore & Company, Greer, S. C., as clerk. Next he entered the cotton business at Greer with A. F. Burgess, where he remained for a number of years. Following this he moved to Athens, Georgia, still engaged in the cotton business. Returning to Greer he again worked for Mr. Burgess for a time. Later he was employed by the Victor Manufacturing Company as cotton buyer, when Lewis W. Parker was made President, and here he continued for some two years. He then went with W. A. Gilreath & Company, a cotton brokerage house in Greenville, as a partner. But about 1905 he quit his old line of business and became connected with the Victor Mills at Greer as Vice-President, where he remained till 1911. During this time he assisted in the organization of the Bank of Greer, of which he became Vice-President. In 1911 the Victor Mills became a part of the huge Parker Cotton Mills Company and Mr. Marchant was elected Second Vice-President of the company and moved to Greenville where he remained in that position till the Parker Cotton Mills Company was dissolved in 1918. He then returned to the cotton business, becoming connected with W. E. Mason & Company of Greenville, where he remained for five years and till he became agent at Greenville for George H. McFadden & Company, one of the largest firms of cotton merchants in the world. This connection he still retains.

Mr. Marchant is active in civic affairs, and in religious affiliation is a Methodist. He has been twice married, first to Miss Sally Few of Greer, now deceased, and next to Miss Kathleen Morrah of Abbeville County. By his second marriage he has four children: Luther M., Jr., John, Mary, and Francis.

THOMAS M. MARCHANT

The little community of Batesville has contributed largely to the textile industry of Greenville. Here was built one of the very earliest cotton manufacturing plants in the county, and this small mill has been the school from which many of the Piedmont's leading manufacturers have graduated into leadership among the textile executives of the nation. Of this number THOMAS M. MARCHANT is a worthy example.

The name, Marchant, has long been synonymous with the cotton mill industry of upper South Carolina. Before the War Between the States, Martin Luther Marchant was manufacturing cotton at Batesville, and during the years of that fearful struggle he operated his mill to capacity in furnishing goods for use by the Confederate army. And here at Batesville on the 8th day of July, 1880, was born Thomas M. Marchant, son of Martin Luther Marchant and his wife, Mary (Smith) Marchant.

As a boy, Thomas M. Marchant attended the public schools of his community, and later took a business course. In 1899 he began his life's work by securing a connection with the Victor Manufacturing Company of Greer, South Carolina. His first work here was as a mere office boy, but love of the mill business was in his blood, and from the beginning, he showed an aptitude for textiles. Rapidly he advanced with his company by successive stages till June 30, 1923, he was elected President and Treasurer of the Victor-Monaghan Company, a huge concern composed of his old Victor Manufacturing Company, the Monaghan Mills of Greenville, and a number of other large cotton manufacturing plants in the Piedmont section of South Carolina.

The Victor-Monaghan Company of which Mr. Marchant is still the executive head, is one of, if not the largest cotton manufacturing concern in the South. It has 185,000 spindles and 5,400 looms, employs about 3,000 people to whom it pays annually upward of $2,000,000 in wages, and has an annual output of between $8,000,000 and $9,000,000 in finished product. But regardless of the great number of people dependent upon this one concern for a living, it has never had any labor troubles. Due largely to the big-heartedness and all-inclusive love of mankind which characterizes Mr. Marchant in all his dealings, there exists an unusual friendship between employer and employees at all the Victor-Monaghan plants. And no doubt this fact has had much to do in making this large company so successful.

Mr. Marchant has twice been President of the South Carolina Cotton Manufacturers' Association. Among cotton mill men it is considered quite an honor to head this association for a single term of one year, and to be elected for a second term is a distinct recognition of uncommon ability in the recipient of that honor. But the reputation of Mr. Marchant as a successful cotton manufacturer is not confined to his native state, nor alone to the South. He is a member of the Board of Governors of the American Cotton Manufacturers' Association, an organization of the mills of the entire nation. And of the two vice-presidencies, the Southern vice-presidency of the Cotton Textile Institute is held by Mr. Marchant.

But Mr. Marchant has not confined his business activities to the Victor-Monaghan Company, for he is President of the Wallace Manufacturing Company of Jonesville, South Carolina; Vice-President of the Marion Manufacturing Company of Marion, North Carolina, and a director in both the First National Bank of Greenville and the Greer Bank & Trust Company of Greer.

Outside of business, Mr. Marchant is an active, public-spirited citizen, taking a leading part in many of the civic undertakings of his home city. He is a member of the Greenville Country Club, and he also holds membership in the Biltmore Forest Club of Biltmore, North Carolina.

Mr. Marchant was married to Miss Jessie Speed of Abbeville on October 29, 1912, and they have two sons, Thomas M., Jr., and Preston B. The family home is on North Main Street in the City of Greenville.

ROBERT E. HENRY

ROBERT E. HENRY, President of the Dunean Mills of Greenville, was born in Tazewell, Virginia, on the 9th day of July, 1880, being the son of Robert Randolph Henry and Lucy (Ashby) Henry.

Mr. Henry received his education in the public schools of Virginia and at the Hampden-Sidney College, from which institution he holds an A.B. degree. He subsequently took a course in Textile Engineering in the Philadelphia Textile School

and soon thereafter commenced his career with textile mills in Chester, Pennsylvana, where he remained for three years.

Later he held positions with the Brighton Mills at Passaic, New Jersey, and with the Maginnis Mills at New Orleans. Following this he was general superintendent of the Springs Mills, Chester, South Carolina, for about six and one-half years.

Mr. Henry came to Greenville in 1915 to become manufacturing manager of the Victor-Monaghan Mills. He held this connection until 1917, when he became general superintendent of the Utica Steam Cotton Mills. These mills were devoting their whole effort to war work. When the war ended he was made treasurer and general manager of Dunean Mills of Greenville, and became President of that corporation in 1920, which position he now holds.

In addition to his duties as President and active head of the Dunean Mills, Mr. Henry is also President and Treasurer of the Watts Mill at Laurens, South Carolina.

He takes a prominent part in various civic enterprises in Greenville, being a member of the Advisory Committee for the Community Chest Fund and a member of the Board of Trustees of the American Red Cross. He is a member of the Board of Trustees of the American Red Cross. He is a member of the Greenville Chamber of Commerce, and of the Greenville Country Club. In church affiliations he is a Presbyterian, being an Elder in the Fourth Presbyterian Church of Greenville.

Mr. Henry was married to Miss Sarah Emmie McCrary in 1914, and has one son, Carter Henry.

B. S. H. HARRIS

B. S. H. HARRIS, son of J. W. and M. F. Harris, was born in Anderson County, South Carolina, in 1868. Both his parents were native South Carolinians, his father being of English descent and his mother predominantly Irish.

Mr. Harris was reared on his father's farm, and as his services were necessary in helping support a large family, the education which he was able to secure came principally through his own efforts, unassisted by schools. In fact he may be truly termed "self-educated."

After reaching maturity Mr. Harris worked as a carpenter and builder for fifteen years, and then at the age of 35 years entered the Baptist ministry. From 1905 to 1923 he was pastor of the Riverside Baptist Church in the City of Greenville. Although successful as a Minister of the Gospel, Mr. Harris, being of an inventive and mechanical turn of mind, saw great possibilities in a pump which would furnish fresh water directly from a well or stream to the home, without the old style storage tank. To manufacture such a pump he established a small factory in 1910. This was moved to Greer from Greenville in 1918, and in 1928 the old Batesville cotton mill property was purchased and the plant moved to it in April, 1929. The Batesville village is now known as Harrisdale.

Since its organization in 1910 the Harris Pump Manufacturing Company has gradually expanded its business till today it sells its output in very nearly every state in the Union. The pump manufactured by this company is distinctive in its field. It may be installed in a well, lake or cistern. A gas engine or electric motor drives an air compressor which stores compressed air in a tank; when the spigot in the home is turned the water pump automatically operates under pressure from the air tank, thus furnishing fresh running water to any point where it may be piped. This invention affords to country homes a water supply equal to that of the cities. No other plant of the kind is located in South Carolina.

Mr. Harris resides in the city of Greenville and takes a prominent part in the religious and civic affairs of the city and county. He is a member of the Riverside Baptist Church, belongs to the J. O. U. A. M.; is a Mason and Shriner.

In 1893 Mr. Harris was married to Miss Bettie Hughes of Abbeville County, and they are the parents of seven children: Mrs. Ann Deane, Mrs. Eunice Corea, Mrs. Ruth Harrison, Mrs. Frances Rodgers, J. C. Harris, Miss Kathryn Harris and B. S. H. Harris, Jr.

CAPTAIN LEONARD WILLIAMS

Among the leading citizens of Greenville during the War Between the States, the reconstruction period, and the quarter century of progress just preceding the advent of the twentieth century, was CAPTAIN LEONARD WILLIAMS. He came of patriotic stock and bore a name which is associated with some of the most heroic incidents in the history of our country.

In 1700 John Williams and his wife (ancestors of Captain Leonard Williams), emigrated from Shangallon, Wales, and settled in Hanover County, Virginia. Their descendants moved from there to Granville County, North Carolina, and later (just prior to the Revolution) to Ninety-Six District, South Carolina. Daniel Williams, one of the sons of John, married Ursula Henderson, sister of those famous North Carolinians, Judge Joseph and Colonel Richard Henderson. Daniel and Ursula Williams contributed four sons to the cause of American Independence: Henry and those three gallant colonels, John, James and Joseph Williams. John and Joseph had previously been members of the Continental Congress. Henry, the eldest son, enlisted in the Continental army, but his advanced age kept him from continuing in active service; however, with his means he largely aided the cause of liberty and shared the suffering and losses which fell upon the loyal patriots of that time.

Davis Williams, son of Henry, was the father of Leonard Williams; his wife (mother of Leonard) was Anne Andrews, daughter of Ephraim Andrews, a captain in the Revolutionary war, and granddaughter of Captain Laughlin Leonard, who, in 1781, fell a victim to Tory hate and violence at the "Massacre of Hay's Station."

Leonard Williams was born on his father's plantation, "Sycamore Grove", Newberry District, in 1828. As a boy he was instructed by private tutors and at Dr. Herbert's school at Newberry. At the age of 17 he entered the South Carolina College, from which institution he was graduated *magna cum laude.*

In 1855 he moved to Greenville and entered business as a merchant and planter. Here he took an active part in the social and civic activities of the town and county.

In June, 1861, at the first call to arms, he enlisted in that famous cavalry company, "The Brooks Troop", Hampton Legion, subsequently Company K, Second South Carolina Cavalry. In 1862 he became captain of his company and later senior captain of his regiment, commanding a squadron. He led his men gallantly in many battles, notably, Williamsburg, Seven Pines, Sharpsburg, Chancellorsville and Gettysburg. In the hand to hand fight at Upperville he was severely wounded. After the engagement at "Jack's Shop" Captain Williams was called for by General J. E. B. Stuart and publicly commended for "efficiency and conspicuous bravery."

At the close of the war Captain Williams returned to his Greenville home and immediately entered upon the work of assisting in the rehabilitation of his county and state. As a merchant and farmer "he conducted his business on those high principles which ruled his life" and his influence was soon felt over the entire upper part of the state. He was deeply interested in the various problems of the farmer and was one of the pioneers in practicing and encouraging intensive farming in Greenville County. With pen and by public speech he advocated the return, for taxation, "of all moneys, stocks, bonds and such elusive property, so that the farmer might be relieved from the burden of unequal taxation."

Captain Williams did not restrict his activities to matters of business, but was always concerned in public affairs. During the Sessions of 1871-'72 he was a member of the House of Representatives from Greenville County, being one of the few Democrats to hold membership in that body during those troublous times. In 1876 he bore a conspicuous part in the Hampton campaign. For four years he was auditor of Greenville county and for several terms was an alderman of the city of Greenville.

His part was large in the successful effort to bring the "Air Line", now the Southern Railway, through the upper Piedmont; and throughout the days of his activity he took a leading part in all enterprises which he felt would be for the uplift of his fellow citizens.

Captain Williams was twice married, first, just prior to the war, to Annie O. Laval and next to her sister, Julia H. Laval, both daughters of Colonel William Laval of Charleston, who served his state for nearly 40 years in the capacities of State Treasurer and Comptroller General, and who was Assistant Secretary of the Treasury during President Polk's administration. Captain Williams died May 23, 1908, being survived by five children: Mrs. W. J. Langston of Greenville, Mrs. I. M. Mercer of Richmond, Va. (now deceased), Davis H. Williams of Malvern, Pa., Miss Julia G. Williams of Greenville, and Mrs. T. M. Douglas of Chester, S. C. His grandchildren are Mrs. J. M. Kesler of Winston-Salem, N. C., Misses Carolyn and Suzanne Mercer of Raleigh, N. C., and Thomas Williams Douglas of Chester, S. C.

WHITNER K. LIVINGSTON

WHITNER K. LIVINGSTON, wholesale merchant and public-spirited citizen of Greenville City, was born in Seneca, Oconee County, South Carolina, in 1878, being a son of Colonel J. W. Livingston and Clara (Kilpatrick) Livingston. His father was born at Abbeville, South Carolina, and served with distinction as an officer of the Confederate army during the War Between the States, being wounded in the Battle of Gettysburg. After the war he settled on a large plantation in Oconee County, and later moved to Seneca. He was prominent in the public affairs of his county, being at times a member of the general assembly of South Carolina in both the House of Representatives and the Senate. His mother was from Pendleton, South Carolina, and a sister of Colonel Whitner Kilpatrick.

The education of Mr. Livingston was had in the public schools of Seneca and at Clemson College. Having finished his education he became manager of the Lockhart Mill store at Lockhart, South Carolina, where he remained for some time. Then he returned to Seneca and entered the wholesale and jobbing business. His business rapidly expanded, and in August, 1917, he moved to Greenville and founded Livingston & Company of which he became President and active head, with his brother, J. K. Livingston, a cotton merchant of Savannah, Georgia, as an associate in business.

Livingston & Company, from the beginning, has enjoyed a profitable and ever-expanding business, being exclusively wholesalers and jobbers. Greenville claims the distinction of being the distributing center for the grocery trade of the South Carolina Piedmont. This is primarily due to the fact that a number of large and financially strong wholesale and jobbing merchants are located there. Of these none is of more importance than Livingston & Company, which does a large business in Greenville, Anderson, Pickens, Oconee, Laurens, Spartanburg and Greenwood Counties.

Mr. Livingston takes an active interest in the civic affairs of his home city, being a member of the Greenville Chamber of Commerce and a director of the Kiwanis Club. He is a member of the U. C. T. and of the T. P. A., and is active in both these organizations. He is a Mason, a Shriner, a member of the Knights of Pythias, and a Deacon in the First Presbyterian Church of Greenville.

Mr. Livingston was married to Miss Willie C. Cherry of Seneca, and they have three children: Whitner K., Jr., Mary Eliza, and William Cherry. The family home is on Washington Road in the City of Greenville.

HARVEY CLEVELAND BEATTIE

HARVEY CLEVELAND BEATTIE, son of Harvey Cleveland and Margaret (Haynsworth) Beattie, was born in Greenville on the 23rd day of December, 1892. He is a member of the Greenville family of Beatties who have been so prominently connected with the major business activities of the county for more than three-quarters of a century.

Mr. Beattie secured his education in the public schools of Greenville, at the University of South Carolina, and in Cornell University. Leaving college, he became connected with the Victor-Monaghan Mills and here he remained until the outbreak of the World War. Then he volunteered for service and was commissioned a First Lieutenant in the Field Artillery branch. For a time he was stationed at Camp Jackson, Columbia, South Carolina, and then at Camp Sill, Oklahoma, until the close of the war.

Following the war he was associated with W. E. Mason and Company of Greenville in the cotton business for nine years. After this he organized his own company which he still conducts. It is engaged in the cotton business as merchants and brokers and operates over a wide expanse of territory, handling a large volume of business each season.

In the public affairs of his home city, Mr. Beattie is deeply interested. For six years he has served Greenville as a member of the Police Commission and for one term he has held the office of Alderman. He is an Elk and takes an active part in the various charitable activities of that order.

Mr. Beattie was married to Miss Pariolie Goldsmith, a native of Atlanta, Georgia, but then living in Greenville, and they have two children, viz: Sarah Cleveland, and Harvey Cleveland, Jr. The family home is at 301 East North Street in the City of Greenville.

DR. H. LeROY BROCKMAN

Dr. H. LeRoy Brockman, prominent physician of Greer, was born in the Reidville section of Spartanburg County on February 16, 1886, being the son of James H. and Frances E. (Hoy) Brockman. His father was a member of a prominent Virginia family which came to South Carolina during the early days of the last century, and his mother was of the Dean family of Spartanburg County.

Dr. Brockman secured his early education in the public schools of Reidville and then was a student at Furman University for two years. From here he went to the Medical College of South Carolina at Charleston, where he remained for one year. Following this he went to Oklahoma and was for four years a student at the University of Oklahoma, from which institution he received the degrees of B.S. and M.D.

In 1920 he returned to South Carolina and entered upon the practice of his profession at Greer, in partnership with his brother, Dr. Thomas Brockman. Although he conducts a general practice of medicine he gives special attention to diseases of children and to obstetrics. The partnership with his brother was dissolved in 1928 and he now practices alone.

During the World War Dr. Brockman was a member of the Medical Officers' Training Corps. He is deeply interested in the various organizations of his profession, being a member of the American Medical Association, the Southern Medical Association, the South Carolina Medical Association, and the Greenville County Medical Association. He is a charter member of the Civitan Club of Greer and is active in its many civic undertakings.

Dr. Brockman was married to Miss Grace Witt of Oklahoma, and they are the parents of three children, viz: Harold LeRoy, Owen Dean, and Betty Lou, deceased. The family resides at Greer, South Carolina.

B. B. SMITH

Pickens County has furnished Greenville with many of her leading citizens. Among these is B. B. Smith, former grand jury foreman and now President of the Oregon Lumber Company.

Mr. Smith was born in Pickens County on the 23rd day of May, 1889, being the son of T. H. Smith and Malinda (Boggs) Smith. His parents were farmers, both natives of Pickens and members of old and prominent families of upper South Carolina. He received his education in the public schools of Pickens County supplemented by a business course at Massey's Business College, Columbus, Georgia.

Having completed his education Mr. Smith went to Columbus, Georgia, where he secured a position with Julius Friedlander & Company as shipping clerk. Here he remained for four years and then became superintendent of delivery for the Atlantic Ice & Coal Company of the same city. This position he held for one year, after which he returned to South Carolina to engage in farming for three years, two of which were spent in Pickens County and one in Greenville.

In 1919 Mr. Smith moved to Greenville City and became connected with the Oregon Lumber Company as shipping clerk. But with this company he remained for only one year, resigning in 1920 to become a partner in the Blue Ridge Lumber Company, also of Greenville. This connection was held till 1925 when he sold his interest in the company and with two others bought the Oregon Lumber Company. After three years Mr. Smith purchased the interests of his associates and became President and sole owner of the company. There followed a period of general expansion which continues. The concern does a large business in dressed and rough lumber, laths and general builders' supplies.

Mr. Smith takes an active interest in public affairs, having for the years 1927 and 1928 been a member of the Greenville County Grand Jury, during one year of which time he was foreman. During his tenure in office, the grand jury requested and secured an independent audit of all county offices. This revealed startling irregularities in a number of offices and led to changes in the county government which have already proved their necessity. He has also served as a member of the Greenville County Purchasing Agency.

In his religious affiliations Mr. Smith is a Presbyterian, being an Elder in the Third Presbyterian Church of Greenville. He is also a Mason.

In 1912 he was married to Miss Essie Williams of Greenville and they had four children: Ethel Ruth, B. B. Smith, Jr., Sarah Evelyn and Ralph Edward.

In 1920, his first wife having died, he married Miss Addie Anthony of Greenville and by this union there are three children, Dorothy, Laura and Kenneth.

DR. MARK SHARPTON ELLIS

During Colonial days DeWitt's or Devit's Corner was the location of a flourishing trading post. Following the Cherokee war of 1776 the treaty which gave the new State of South Carolina present Greenville, Anderson, Pickens and Oconee Counties was signed there. After the Revolution its name was changed to Due West, and here for many years past has been located Erskine College and the Due West Woman's College, institutions of higher learning for the Associate Reform Presbyterian Church (A.R.P.). The town and community of Due West are widely known for the pious and sturdy character of the people living there. Here DR. MARK SHARPTON ELLIS was born on the 16th day of June, 1885.

Doctor Ellis is the son of John W. and Agnes (Sharpton) Ellis. His father was a soldier of the Confederacy, and following the war was engaged in the mercantile business at Due West for many years. Both parents were members of old and prominent families of the Piedmont. As a youth Doctor Ellis attended the public schools of Due West and then became a student at Erskine College. Later he entered Vanderbilt University from which he secured the degree of D.D.S. in 1914.

Immediately after finishing his college work Doctor Ellis began the practice of dentistry at Simpsonville in lower Greenville County where he remained until 1918 when he moved to Greenville and associated himself with Dr. H. T. Sterling. After this connection had continued for a few years he opened offices in the Professional Building where he continues to practice his profession.

In the various organizations of his profession he takes a leading part, being a member of the Greenville County Dental Association, President of the Bosworth Dental Club of South Carolina, President of the Piedmont Dental Association, and a member of the American Dental Association.

Dr. Ellis is prominent in the religious and civic life of the city. He is a Deacon of the First Baptist Church and Assistant Superintendent of the Sunday School; he is a Mason and a member of the Greenville Kiwanis Club.

He was married to Miss Florine Jackson of Atlanta, Georgia, in 1915 and they have one child, Florine Agnes.

Mrs. Ellis is an active worker in the various ladies' organizations of the First Baptist Church and is also prominent in the club life of the city. Her chief civic interest is child welfare. She and her husband are lovers of flowers and grow them in profusion at their home on Memminger Street.

BENJAMIN F. NEVES

BENJAMIN F. NEVES of the Tigerville community is a member of one of the oldest families of upper Greenville County. He was born in 1852, being the youngest child of A. A. and Ann (Poole) Neves, who were the parents of eleven children. Because of the demoralized condition and poverty-stricken state of the whole South following the War Between the States, he had very meager school advantages, but during all the years of his long and useful life he has continued to be a student and in this manner he has overcome many of the educational deficiencies which he had as a young man. After his marriage he studied surveying and has devoted much of his time to that profession.

During the greater part of his life Mr. Neves has devoted himself to farming, surveying and merchandising in the Tigerville community. He now owns 800 acres of land which he cultivates in a modern scientific manner; for 35 years he conducted a general mercantile business at Tigerville; and until advancing years caused him to retire from that line of work, he did practically all surveying in his home community, being generally recognized as one of the best in that field.

But the personal business affairs of Mr. Neves have not taken the whole of his time by any means. He has always been a leader in the public affairs of his community, and because of this has held many positions of honor and trust. Among these may be mentioned the Chairmanship of Draft Board No. 1 in Greenville County during the World War, membership on the building committee of the new seven-story Greenville County Court House Building, and membership on the Greenville County Charities and Corrections Commission.

Mr. Neves is a Mason and a Democrat who has voted a straight party ticket at every election since he was 21 years of age.

In 1874 he was married to Miss Lou E. McKinney of Tigerville and they have five children: Emma Cora, now Mrs. Truluck, wife of the Reverend B. K. Truluck;

William D. Neves of Greenville City; Elsie O. (Mrs. E. E. Reese) of Walhalla, S. C.; Dr. Carl A. Neves of Johnson City, Tennessee, and Ralph Grady Neves of Tigerville.

WILLIAM D. NEVES

The Neves family has long been prominently identified with the public affairs of upper Greenville County, and is generally recognized as being a strong factor for good in that section. Of this family comes WILLIAM D. NEVES, engineer and road builder of Greenville City.

Mr. Neves was born in the Tigerville community on March 28, 1876, being the son of B. F. Neves and L. E. (McKinney) Neves. As a boy he attended the Tigerville schools and then became a student at the Gaffney Academy of Gaffney, South Carolina. Desiring to fit himself for civil engineering he then took two correspondence courses in that branch of study.

Having finished his education Mr. Neves devoted some years to surveying and then in 1905 went to Lumberton, North Carolina, where he became City Engineer. While there he did the surveying for two large lumber concerns in eastern North Carolina. In 1907 he came to Greenville to become City Engineer. This position he held till 1909 when he went into business for himself. In 1914 he became affiliated with the J. E. Sirrine Company, perhaps the largest mill achitects in the South, where he remained until 1918. During the time he was with this company he assisted in laying out Camp Sevier, one of the largest engineering propositions ever undertaken in the city of Greenville. In 1918 he again became City Engineer for the city of Greenville, and during the time he held this position he inaugurated a "City Block Book" system which has been of incalculable value. Under it all houses were re-numbered, property lines established and ownership ascertained. Because of this work much property formerly escaping taxation was put upon the books. Much street paving was done and many lines of sewers laid during this period of his connection with the city.

In 1925 Mr. Neves severed his connection with the city of Greenville and formed a partnership with R. E. Dalton, under the name of Dalton & Neves. This concern has done and is still doing much emergency work for both the county and city of Greenville. One of the large jobs recently completed for the county was the surface treatment of 106 miles of county highways under a county "Cross-Country" road bond issue. They are also assisting in the city water extension program and in the water and sewerage work at City View, a suburb of Greenville City.

Mr. Neves is an active member of the Baptist Church, a member of the Civitan Club of Greenville, a Knight Templar, Mason and a Shriner.

In 1899 Mr. Neves was married to Miss Bessie Williams of Wilmington, North Carolina, and they have had one child, Ida Lou, deceased.

DR. JAMES LELAND ANDERSON

Among the many illustrious families originally composing the congregation of Nazareth Church, Spartanburg County, none excels that of the Anderson. In this section resided the Hamptons, the Harrisons, the Pedens, the Andersons, and many others, all Scotch-Irish Presbyterians, originally from North Ireland. Many of these pioneers came directly from Ireland, while others emigrated from Pennsylvania, where they had resided for a few years after coming over. Colonel Clarke was the first to arrive in the community, and is thought to have been the first permanent settler in what is now Spartanburg County.

Several years before the Revolution, William Anderson emigrated from Pennsylvania to the Waxhaws in South Carolina, moving from there to Charleston and then to the Nazareth section where he arrived about 1763. At the outbreak of the Revolution, William Anderson aligned himself firmly with the Whigs and throughout the war he rendered every possible assistance to the Patriot cause, although he was much too old to fight. In 1783, during the closing days of the war, a party of Tories paid a visit to the home of Major David Anderson in the night time, disguised as Indians, and finding William Anderson there, brutally murdered him. His wife escaped and during the night waded two rivers, clothed only in a thin nightdress, to reach the home of a neighbor. Major Anderson and his wife were away from home at Prince's fort and thus escaped death. Their house, however, was burned.

One of the sons of William Anderson was Major David Anderson, at whose home he was killed by the Tories. Major Anderson, before the war, held both a civil and a military commission under the British government but upon the coming of war, he resigned his offices and engaged himself actively in the cause of the province. He was at Ninety-Six, Charles Town, Eutaw Springs, Augusta, and many other major engagements of the conflict, fighting as private, lieutenant, captain and finally as major, with great distinction to himself and tremendous assistance to his country.

Major Anderson married Mariam Mason, daughter of Major Mason, who was at Ninety-Six during the early stages of the war, when the first blood was shed in upper South Carolina. Upon returning from Fort Prince after the death of his father and the burning of his home by the Tories, Major Anderson and his family took up their abode in an out-house where they were living when their son, James M. (Tyger Jim), was born. This son became a prominent farmer and business man, who in his lifetime accumulated a large property.

On January 30, 1830, a son was born to James M. Anderson and his wife, Polly (Miller) Anderson. This was Frank L. Anderson, who became a Major in the War Between the States. Throughout that struggle, he served with distinction and upon its conclusion returned to his home near the present Reidville community, which had been in the family for four generations, and spent the balance of his life there, highly respected and unusually successful as a scientific farmer. He married first Miss Susan Norris, and upon her death, Miss Ada Eppes of Sussex County, Virginia.

By his second marriage the sixth child of Major Anderson was DR. JAMES LELAND ANDERSON, the subject of this sketch, who was born at the old family homestead on January 20, 1883. He attended the Reidville schools, and afterwards Davidson College from which institution he was graduated with the degree of A.B. in 1903. Then he became a student in the Medical department of the University of

Maryland, from which institution he was graduated with the M.D. degree, and after a year in the hospitals of Baltimore, Dr. Anderson took up the practice of his profession in the city of Greenville in 1910, where he has been eminently successful.

During the World War Dr. Anderson was Secretary and Interne for the Medical Advisory Board for the Western District of South Carolina; and is now a Major in the Medical Reserve Corps. He is a member of the Greenville Civitan Club, being an ex-Vice-President of that organization. Formerly he was President of the Greenville County Medical Association; and at one time he was President of the Fourth District Medical Association. He is also a member of the Kappa Psi fraternity, and holds memberships in the Greenville County Medical Society, the South Carolina Medical Society, the Southern Medical Association, and the American Medical Association. The Presbyterian Church holds his membership true to his ancestry.

In 1915 Dr. Anderson was married to Miss Alline Matheson of Hartwell, Georgia, and they have two children, Mary Elizabeth and James Leland, Jr. They reside on Pinkney Street in the City of Greenville.

JOHN WILKINS NORWOOD

During the last 25 years the Piedmont Carolinas has made almost unbelievable progress in the cotton manufacturing industry. But in the beginning of the movement to put the two Carolinas at the top in this line, a majority of the mills found themselves badly handicapped because of under-capitalization and a scarcity of operating funds. Northern financiers had not yet been convinced that the South could successfully compete with the old and expertly managed mills of the East, so they were slow to come to the assistance of this young and, as they thought, indifferently conducted business of the South. But as South Carolina was now producing her own manufacturers, she let it be known that she had at least one citizen with sufficient financial acumen and business foresight to assist the infant industry. And it is more largely due to this man that success came to the cotton mill business in North and South Carolina than is known to the general public; but among the cotton mill executives themselves, JOHN WILKINS NORWOOD is recognized as being the one man who has done more than any other to advance the mill interests of those two states.

John Wilkins Norwood was born in Hartsville, South Carolina, in March, 1865, being the son of George Alexander and Mary Louise (Wilkins) Norwood. He attended the schools of his home community and later was a student at the Citadel, Wake Forest College and the University of South Carolina.

Leaving college, Mr. Norwood became a clerk in the cotton firm of G. A. Norwood and Company of Charleston where he was engaged until he moved to Greenville to become Cashier of the Peoples Bank (now Peoples National Bank) in the spring of 1887. In the fall of 1887 he organized the Greenville Savings Bank and became its President, which position he held till 1892 when he organized and became President of the Atlantic National Bank of Wilmington, North Carolina. This connection he held till 1902. From 1894 till 1910 he was President of the Wilmington Savings & Trust Company and is now Vice-President of that large financial institution. In 1898 he organized the Blue Ridge National Bank of Asheville, North Carolina, and was its President till 1907. From 1903 to 1906 he was President of the City National Bank of Greenville, which bank his father had organized in 1896. In 1907 he organized the Norwood National Bank of Greenville and was its President till 1925 when it became a part of the South Carolina National Bank System. Since that time he has been a director of the consolidated institution and Chairman of the Board of the Greenville branch.

In addition to his large banking interests, Mr. Norwood is Vice-President of the Brandon Mills, the Peoples Building & Loan Association, and the Title Guarantee & Trust Company, all of Greenville. For a few months he was President of the American Spinning Company of Greenville, and in many other of the large manufacturing and financial institutions of the two Carolinas he is a director.

But with the multiplicity of his interests, Mr. Norwood has not let business absorb his life. In public-spiritedness and in untiring endeavor to advance the standard of governmental affairs he has few, if any, equals in South Carolina. When a real civic need arises he can always be found ready and willing to give of his time and money. And in politics he never stands in the middle of the road. One can always count upon Mr. Norwood to make his position clear. Often men of large business affairs take no active interest in politics for fear of hurting their business; but with Mr. Norwood the public good is considered higher than private gain.

From 1915 to 1918 Mr. Norwood was Chairman of the Greenville County Highway Commission, and in that capacity supervised the expenditure of a million-dollar bond issue in making Greenville the pioneer road-building county in South Carolina. But active as he has been in politics, he has never been a candidate for public office, membership on the Highway Commission having been by appointment. Often he has been urged to become a candidate for office or to accept an appointment on some important Board or Commission, but always he has declined, believing that he could serve best on the "side lines", except for the Highway Commission and the quasi-public positions of a trustee of the Greenville Public Library and membership on the Board of Directors of the Southern Institute of Politics, both of which places he now fills with distinction.

Mr. Norwood is a Unitarian and his life well exemplifies the teaching of that sect which hold belief in "The fatherhood of God, the brotherhood of man, the leadership of Jesus, Salvation by character and the progress of mankind onward and upward forever."

He has been married three times; first to Miss Vina Patrick of Anderson, South Carolina, who is deceased; next to Miss Lidie Goodlett of Spartanburg, South Carolina, who is also deceased; and last to Miss Fannie Conyers of Greenville. By his second marriage Mr. Norwood has two children, George Norwood, who is now Vice-President and active head of the Greenville Branch of the South Carolina National Bank, and Miss Laura Cleveland Norwood. His first wife lived only a short time and they had no children; but by his last union he has four children: John W., Benjamin, Oliver and Frances.

The Norwood home is on Belmont Avenue in the City of Greenville.

WILLIAM C. BEACHAM

Looking about for words to best describe the subject of this sketch, "caution and conservatism" immediately come to the minds of those who know him. WILLIAM C. BEACHAM is one of the foremost bankers and business men of Greenville and his success is largely attributable to the exercise of the characteristics represented by those words.

Mr. Beacham was born at Carnesville, Georgia, on October 1, 1860, being the son of Dr. James D. and Eugenia (Douthit) Beacham. His father was a member of the Medical Corps of the Confederate army during the War Between the States and died in the service. At seven years of age young Beacham came to Greenville, where he secured his education in public and private schools of the community.

Leaving school, Mr. Beacham worked as clerk in a local store till 1887 when he entered the newly organized Peoples Bank as bookkeeper. After a few years he became cashier of the institution, which position he held till 1914, when he succeeded the late Frank Hammond as President. Only 16 years have passed since Mr. Beacham assumed the leadership of this financial institution, but it has grown amazingly during that time. Deposits of the bank are now more than three times what they were in 1914. Then the institution was a State bank housed in a rented building at the corner of Main and Washington Streets, but it now has a National charter and owns a beautiful and commodious home on West Washington Street.

In addition to his banking interests Mr. Beacham has a number of other business connections, among which is the Presidency of the Carolina Loan & Trust Company. Because of his recognized business ability, Mr. Beacham and his financial institutions are named as executor or trustee for large estates. Because of this Mr. Beacham has probably settled more large estates than any other man in Greenville.

But Mr. Beacham has not confined himself to his personal affairs by any means. For many years he has been chairman of the Greenville City Water Commission. While serving in this capacity the Table Rock water shed has been acquired and Greenville's new "ten-billion-gallon-capacity reservoir" constructed, at a cost of more than $2,000,000. He is also chairman of the Greenville City Democratic Committee. In the religious life of the city Mr. Beacham is also an active participant, being a Steward of the Buncombe Street Methodist Church.

He was married to Miss Shields Isbell and they have four children: James D., Isbell (Mrs. D. F. Pearce), Emily (Mrs. P. M. Taylor) and Eugene W. The family home is on North Main Street in the City of Greenville.

FOUNTAIN FOX BEATTIE

During the last days of the War Between the States, the officials of the State Bank, located in Charleston, began to fear that its liquid assets would be confiscated by the Federal army then "marching through Georgia." Looking about for a safe place to hide these assets they thought of Mr. Hamlin Beattie, then a prominent merchant in the town of Greenville, and forwarded him $35,000 in silver, which on reaching its destination was bricked into the cellar wall of Mr. Beattie's store, then standing near the present location of the First National Bank.

Following the war it became evident to Mr. Beattie that the growing town of Greenville should have a bank, and being a man of high integrity and recognized business acumen, he had little difficulty in securing the cooperation of the leading business men of the community for launching such an undertaking. So in 1872 the National Bank of Greenville, with Mr. Hamlin Beattie as President, commenced business, as the first bank in Greenville County. The young financial institution was safely steered through the turbulent waters of Radical rule and Reconstruction by its able President and in a few years was recognized throughout the state as "safe and sound."

Upon the death of Mr. Hamlin Beattie in 1914 his brother, John E. Beattie, succeeded him as President of the bank, then very generally referred to as "Beattie's Bank." Under its new head the institution continued the old Hamlin Beattie policies and continued to grow with the city and county of Greenville till 1916, when he died, it had deposits of $600,000 which was considered large for that time. Following Mr. John E. Beattie as President of the bank came his son, F. F. BEATTIE, the subject of this sketch, who was born in Greenville on the 29th day of July, 1878. His mother, Mary Mayes Beattie, who is still living, was Miss Mary Caroline Mayes, daughter of Richard Mayes, before her marriage.

After attending school in the City of Greenville, F. F. Beattie became a student at Furman University. Afterward he attended the University of Michigan, and in 1902 was graduated with the degree of LL.B. from George Washington University. Upon leaving college he was admitted to the bar of South Carolina, and began the practice of his profession in the city of Greenville with John H. Earle, at one time Railroad Commissioner, now deceased, as a partner. Later he was in partnership with Proctor A. Bonham, who for eight years was Solicitor of the Thirteenth Judicial Circuit, followed by eight years as State Senator from Greenville County. Mr. Beattie was elected to membership in the House of Representatives from his native county in 1904 and served in that branch of the General Assembly during the 1905 and 1906 sessions, voluntarily retiring from politics upon the expiration of his term.

In 1911 Mr. Beattie became connected with the bank founded by his uncle, now having changed its name to the First National Bank, as Assistant Treasurer of the Piedmont Savings and Trust Company, the savings department of the First National. Soon he was elected Treasurer of the Trust Company, and shortly thereafter the position of Vice-President of the First National was added. In 1916 he assumed the presidency of the First National Bank, and still retains that position.

Under the guiding hand of Mr. Beattie, the First National Bank has greatly expanded. When he became its President the deposits of the institution were $600,000, while they now exceed $4,000,000. The building which now houses this institution was the first banking house to be owned by a Greenville city bank.

In the banking circles of the state, Mr. Beattie is recognized as a leader. He has nothing of the spectacular about him, but conducts himself and his business along the safe, sane, and conservative lines which have distinguished the Beattie name for so many years. He has held numerous positions of honor and trust in the state organization of banks, and in 1927-'28 was president of the South Carolina Bankers' Association.

Mr. Beattie was married to Miss Janell Cobb Arnold of Greenwood in 1912 and they have three children: Fox, Jr., Jane Arnold, and Dannitte, and live on East Washington Street in the City of Greenville.

SAMUEL MARSHALL BEATTIE

The oldest textile plant now operating in Greenville County is the Piedmont Manufacturing Company, organized in 1873 by Colonel H. P. Hammett. Colonel Hammett was a son-in-law of William Bates, who came from Pawtuckett, R. I., to Greenville County, S. C., during the first quarter of the nineteenth century, and built "Batesville." After his marriage, Colonel Hammett became a member of the firm of William Bates & Company, which operated the cotton manufacturing plant at Batesville, and here he remained till 1862 when the Batesville mill was sold. A portion of the proceeds from this sale went into the purchase of the lands where Piedmont now stands (then known as Garrison Shoals). So Piedmont is not only the oldest cotton mill now operating in the county, but through its founder, his wife and his father-in-law, it is directly connected with the very early textile industry of the up-country.

Upon the first Board of Directors of the Piedmont mills was Hamlin Beattie of Greenville, who during the previous year had organized the first bank of the county (now the First National Bank of Greenville). Later a son of Hamlin Beattie (William E. Beattie) was to become President of the mill, which position he held for many years to be succeeded by his son, SAMUEL MARSHALL BEATTIE, who yet retains that position.

Samuel Marshall Beattie was born on October 27, 1886, being the son of William E. Beattie and Kitty (Marshall) Beattie. His father is a member of the well-known Beattie family, prominent in the business affairs of Greenville County since long before the War Between the States; while his mother is a sister of the late John B. Marshall, long a leader in the business affairs of the County and for two terms Mayor of the City of Greenville.

Young Marshall Beattie attended the public schools of Greenville, and then was a student at the University of the South. Leaving this institution he entered Cornell University, from which he was graduated with an M.A. degree in 1911.

Having finished his college education, Mr. Beattie became an employee of the Piedmont Manufacturing Company. Here he filled various clerical positions till 1914 when he was elected Vice-President of the company. Upon the retirement of his father, William E. Beattie, he became President and Treasurer of the mill, and this position he still holds.

Although the Piedmont Manufacturing Company has been operating for almost sixty years, it has never been in financial difficulties. A very high percentage of the textile manufacturing companies of the county existing prior to 1918 have at various times undergone reorganizations. This was necessitated by many causes, but the one most common was lack of capable management. Piedmont, however, has been fortunate during the whole of its life in having men of unusual ability to

RICHARD F. WATSON

direct its affairs. And today it finds itself still under the guidance of an efficient head. The mill operates 69,000 spindles and 1,984 looms, and manufactures heavy sheetings and drills. The average number of employees is about 900.

Mr. Beattie resides in Greenville City, although the Piedmont Manufacturing Company is located about 12 miles away. He plays a prominent part in the civic and social affairs of his home community, and at all times labors for better living conditions among his employees and their families.

Mr. Beattie's wife was before her marriage Miss Ruth McGee of Greenville. The Beatties have two children, Samuel Marshall, Jr., and Ruth McGee.

MAJOR RICHARD F. WATSON

Among the progressive citizens of Greenville, none is more active or versatile than MAJOR RICHARD F. WATSON. He was born in Edgefield County (now Saluda), South Carolina, on the 19th day of May, 1879, being the son of Colonel Robert B. Watson and Lucy (McIver) Watson.

As a boy Major Watson attended the public schools of his native county, and later became a student at Furman University, where his father had graduated. Here he received the degree of A.B. in 1900. He then taught school for several years, after which he worked for the government at Washington and studied law. In 1905 he was graduated from Georgetown University Law School with the degree of LL.B.

Being admitted to the South Carolina bar in 1905 Major Watson took up the practice of his profession at Greenville, where he continued actively in the practice till the time of the World War. Since then he has devoted the major portion of his time to his large farming interests, practicing his profession only incidentally.

As a young man Major Watson interested himself in military affairs. He enlisted in the Butler Guards of Greenville and by successive advancements became Captain of that Company. When the trouble with Mexico arose in 1916 he went to the border as a Major in the South Carolina National Guard, where he served with distinction, resigning his commission when his regiment returned from Texas. Later, during the World War, though over draft age, he volunteered his services, and was commissioned Captain of Infantry in the National army; he was later recommended for promotion and now holds the rank of Major in the R. O. T. C.

With the close of the World War the cotton farmer found himself in dire straits. Major Watson owned considerable farming lands around Greenville, so he set himself to the task of making the best of a bad situation. He adopted the most approved farm methods, took personal control of his lands and began the cultivation of various crops. Among his "diversifications" was the starting of a large peach orchard from which he gathered 18,000 bushels of peaches in 1929.

In public affairs Major Watson has always taken an active interest. For several years he was a member of the Board of Trustees of the Greenville City Schools, to which he acted as Secretary. Later, and for a number of years, he was a member of the Board of Health of Greenville City. For eight years he held the position of Greenville City Recorder. In 1923 he became a candidate for Mayor of the city of Greenville and was elected by a large majority. This position he filled with ability, and his administration is a notable one in Greenville history. Not only is it remembered for its general efficiency in all the business of conducting a city's affairs, but it stands out as the one in which three great enterprises of tremendous importance to the permanent welfare of the city were launched and, in great measure, accomplished.

These were, first, the addition of a large system of parks and playgrounds, adequate for the future needs of a rapidly growing city; second, the creation of the Greater Greenville Sewer Commission, which lays the foundation for the complete sanitation of Greenville and the surrounding community; third, and most important of all, the building of the magnificent Table Rock reservoir and water system, by which Greenville is furnished with a bountiful supply of the purest mountain water, a water system unsurpassed in the whole United States.

Major Watson was reelected for a second term without opposition, and at the expiration of this term he voluntarily retired from the office of Mayor. He has, however, continued to take an eager and active interest in all that concerns the progress of his city and county, and is at this time serving the city officially as member of the Greater Greenville Sewer Commission.

Major Watson was married to Miss Susan Coker, daughter of Major J. L. Coker of Hartsville, in 1911, and they have four children: Margaret Armstrong, Susan Coker, Lucy McIver and Richard F., Jr. The family home is on James Street in the City of Greenville.

W. FRANK WALKER

The building of the Piedmont Manufacturing Company by Colonel H. P. Hammett and associates marked the real beginning of the textile industry on a large scale in Greenville County. From the starting of the machinery there on March 20, 1876, until 1890 the history of cotton manufacturing in the county is little more than a recital of the steady growth of that mill. Perhaps in no other textile plant of the state have so many of the leaders in that industry received their training as at Piedmont. Among this number was W. FRANK WALKER, late of Greenville City.

Mr. Walker, son of Stanhope and Mary (Smith) Walker, was born near Westminster, Oconee County, South Carolina, on March 17, 1858. His father was a school teacher and superintendent of a large plantation. The son received his early education in the public schools of his home community and through instruction from his father in night schools; but he continued to be a student all his life and may be said to have been largely self-taught.

At the age of 14 years Mr. Walker secured employment with a small cotton mill in Spartanburg County and here began a life of business activity which was to keep him in textile manufacturing for 47 years. When he entered the field the cotton mill industry in the South was a mere infant, but during those 47 years he witnessed its growth into the largest single industry of his native state.

Four years after taking his first position Mr. Walker went with the Piedmont Manufacturing Company, then just beginning its long and successful career in cotton manufacturing, and here he remained for more than 25 years. Through various subordinate positions he kept steadily climbing upward until 1896, when he was elected Superintendent. At that time the mill had just completed its No. 4 plant, making it the largest in the state.

Leaving Piedmont after his long service there Mr. Walker was connected with various cotton mills until 1912 when he came to Greenville City to be with the Brandon Mills. This position he held for five years, retiring from active business in 1917, but still retaining his residence in Greenville until his death on December 31, 1927.

He was a public-spirited citizen, active in the promotion of civic betterment, and liberal in his support of charities. In religious affiliation he was a Methodist, being a Steward in the St. Paul Methodist Church of Greenville.

Greenville County and the State of South Carolina owe a large debt of gratitude to those who pioneered in the textile manufacturing industry, and looming large among that number was W. Frank Walker.

He was twice married, first to Miss Harriet McElrath, who died in 1912, and then in 1914 to Miss Lena Wright of Anderson County. His second wife survives him and resides in Greenville.

THOMAS M. NORRIS

THOMAS M. NORRIS, cotton manufacturer, was born in Orangeburg County in 1876, being the son of G. M. and H. H. Norris. His father is a veteran of the Confederacy and still lives in Orangeburg County. Mr. Norris (subject of this sketch) secured his early education in the public schools of Orangeburg and then became a student at Furman University, from which institution he was graduated with a B.S. degree in 1895. During the summer and fall of '95, he attended the Eastman Business College at Poughkeepsie, N. Y., completing a thorough course in business and banking.

Soon after leaving college Mr. Norris became secretary of the Norris Cotton Mills, located at Cateechee, in Pickens County, South Carolina. The mill had been organized and built by his uncle, Col. D. K. Norris, in 1895. In 1905, upon the death of Col. Norris, he became President of the company and has since conducted its affairs in a highly efficient manner.

Until 1918 Mr. Norris resided at Central, S. C., but during that year he moved with his family to Greenville and immediately identified himself with the public affairs of his adopted city and county. He has been very active in the affairs of the Greenville Chamber of Commerce and for one year served as President of that body. He is a charter member and ex-President of the Civitan Club of Greenville. All worthwhile civic undertakings of the city draw his support.

In 1900 Mr. Norris was married to Miss Florine Bolt of Pickens County, and they have two children, Lucile (now Mrs. France of Spartanburg) and James M.

Mr. and Mrs. Norris reside on East North Street in the City of Greenville.

JAMES H. PRICE

Among the leaders at the Greenville bar must certainly be numbered JAMES H. PRICE. And not only is he a leader in his profession, but in the religious, civic and political affairs of the city and county he plays an unusually prominent part. He is the son of James M. and Eliza (Laud) Price and was born in the city of Greenville on November 6, 1883. His father was a native of Georgia and his mother of Anderson County, South Carolina.

Mr. Price secured his education in the public schools of Greenville City and at the George Washington University of Washington, D. C. From the latter he was graduated with the degree of LL.B. in 1906. During his school days and for a time thereafter he was engaged in newspaper work, and the love of printer's ink still clings to him. Occasionally he contributes an article to the local papers on some public question which furnishes interesting reading.

In May, 1906, Mr. Price was admitted to the South Carolina bar and immediately thereafter began the practice of his profession in Greenville. At various times he has been associated with the Honorable John J. McSwain, now Congressman from the Fourth Congressional District, Judge Joseph A. McCullough, George M. Pritchard, now Congressman from the Asheville (N. C.) District; Wilton H. Earle, Henry K. Townes, Proctor A. Bonham and J. D. Poag. At this time he is senior member of the firm of Price and Poag. This partnership enjoys an extensive practice on both the Civil and Criminal sides of the Court, which is fast expanding.

In public affairs Mr. Price takes a deep and active interest. For 17 years he was a member of the Greenville City Board of Health. Now and during the last eight years he has held the position of Chairman of the Executive Committee of the Democratic party in Greenville County and before this he was secretary to the Committee for six years. Many times he has acted as President of the County Democratic Convention. As a presiding officer he has few equals. Formerly political meetings in Greenville County often degenerated into a vocal endurance contest among "leather-lunged" participants, but nothing of this kind takes place with Mr. Price in the chair. Under his direction politics has become a "tame affair" for those who would have the old style "bally-hoo." In 1929 he became County Attorney, which position he still holds.

Mr. Price is a Baptist, being a member of the Board of Deacons of the Central Baptist Church; he is a member of the Knights of Pythias, a Mason, a Woodman of the World and a member of the Sons of the American Revolution.

He was married to Miss Alice Baker of the Simpsonville community on October 29, 1912, and they have three children: James H., Jr., William B. and Bessie M.

JOHN D. LANFORD

JOHN D. LANFORD, lawyer, planter and business man of note was born near Gowensville in upper Greenville County on November 4, 1880. His parents, W. L. and Sarah (Mitchell) Lanford, were both natives of the county, each representing distinguished families.

Mr. Lanford received his early education in the public schools of the Gowensville community. Later he attended the University of South Carolina, from which he was graduated in 1907 with the degree of A.B. After graduation he returned to the University and spent one year in the study of law.

In 1909 Mr. Lanford was admitted to the bar and soon thereafter began the practice of his profession at Greer. He remained here till 1914 when his practice demanded his removal to the county seat. After practicing alone for two years he decided a partnership would be desirable and in 1916 he became connected with James M. Richardson. This firm enjoyed an extensive practice till 1919, when it was dissolved. Since that time he has practiced alone.

Besides his large legal practice Mr. Lanford has numerous other business connections. He is President of the Peoples Trust Company of Greer; a director of the Greer Oil Mill and Feed Company; organizer of the Cotton States Land Auction Company, which has developed many farm properties throughout the state. He also owns and successfully operates large farms in the Gowensville section of the county.

Although he has maintained an office in the City of Greenville for many years, Mr. Lanford has resided at Greer since he commenced the practice of law in 1909. For one year he was Recorder, and for two years Municipal Judge of the town of Greer.

Mr. Lanford is an active member of the First Baptist church of Greer, a member of the Greenville Bar Association, a member of the South Carolina Bar Association, and is a Mason and a Shriner.

On December 27, 1910, Mr. Lanford was married to Miss Ethel Ballenger, of near Greer. They are the parents of six children: Ruth, Helen, Katherine, Hugh, Lucile and Luke. The family resides in Greer, S. C.

DOCTOR ROY J. DRUMMOND

Dr. Roy J. Drummond, prominent dentist of Greenville City, was born near Woodruff, in Spartanburg County, South Carolina, on the 17th day of May, 1889. He is a son of S. S. and Margaret Drummond, both members of old and prominent families of farmers in lower Spartanburg County. After attending the public schools of Woodruff he was a student at Furman University, Greenville, for two years. Following this he entered the University of Maryland, at Baltimore, from which he was graduated with the degree of D.D.S. in 1910.

Having finished his college work, Dr. Drummond returned to Woodruff where he engaged in the practice of his profession until 1917, when he moved to Greenville. Here he has succeeded in building up a large practice, due not only to his recognized ability in his profession, but as well to his personal popularity.

In recognition of his consistent work to raise the standard of his profession, Dr. Drummond was elected President of the Greenville County Dental Association during the fall of 1929, and this position he still holds. He is a member of the Xi Psi Phi College fraternity, a Mason and an Elder in the Third Presbyterian Church of Greenville.

In 1914 he was married to Miss Annie Switzer of Spartanburg County, and with his wife resides on Arlington Avenue in the city of Greenville.

W. D. BROWNING

The year 1861, which saw the opening battles of the War Between the States, saw also the birth of a boy who through the years of his manhood, was to leave a marked impression upon Greenville, the city of his adoption. This boy was W. D. Browning, whose early years were spent in Laurens County, but who chose Greenville to be the home of his manhood. Left an orphan when quite young, the boy was reared by an uncle. He attended school in Laurens, and later was enrolled in the Perry Business College of Greenville.

At the age of 21, he came to Greenville and was employed as bookkeeper, later entering the grocery business with a Mr. King. Shortly thereafter he organized the firm of Briggs and Company, wholesale dealers in feed, flour, and grain. The structure which he built to house this firm is now used by Ballentine Packing Co. Mr. Browning entered the furniture business in the firm of Symmes & Browning, which later became King & Browning. The loss of his health forced him to give up his work, and in 1912 he went into real estate.

It was during these years that he was engaged in bringing about some important innovations in the city. One of these was a packing house. Mr. Browning felt that such a business would not only bring financial success to its founder but would also be an asset to the town. It was an organization of this type that Mr. Ballentine and Mr. Browning effected, and its success has shown that its founders were not deceived in their visions of the future.

Varied as were Mr. Browning's business connections, his circle of friends and acquaintances was even wider. He was a good mixer, loved people in general, and young men in particular. His geniality, coupled with the sterling worth of his character, made him exceptionally popular, and his life left a marked influence upon the youth of Greenville. He was a member of the Board of Stewards and also a Trustee of the Buncombe Street Methodist Church; his interest in his church never flagged, and he was always its loyal supporter.

He was married to Miss Mamie Parkins, daughter of George W. Parkins, who was the owner of Parkins Mill, and a very prominent man of his day. They had one son, Paul Browning, who is now a citizen of Greenville. Mr. Browning died at Greenville on August 14, 1926, his wife having died about a year previous to this time.

PAUL BROWNING

Born and reared in the city of Greenville, PAUL BROWNING has remained true to the traditions of his father and is today a loyal, patriotic citizen, looking always toward the furthering of the best interests of the city.

Mr. Browning, the only son of W. D. and Mamie P. Browning, was born in the year 1894. He attended the public schools of Greenville, and received his higher education at Woodberry Forest School, and at Davidson College. He subsequently took a business course at Draughan's Business College in Greenville. While in college he was a member of the Beta Theta Pi Fraternity, and is now President of the Greenville Alumni organization of that fraternity.

Upon completing his education, Mr. Browning became connected with the American Bank of Greenville; he remained with this institution for seven years, during which time he received constant promotion, and was, at the time of his resignation, Assistant Cashier of this institution.

Upon leaving the bank, he entered the real estate and insurance business with his father, under the firm name of W. D. & Paul Browning. This firm continued in operation until the death of the elder Mr. Browning, in 1927, since which time the business has been carried on by the son, Paul Browning. Among other properties, Mr. Browning owns and supervises the Parkins Building, a structure erected by his maternal grandmother.

Civic as well as religious and fraternal activities claim Mr. Browning's attention: he is a prominent member of the Civitan Club and of the Chamber of Commerce; is Secretary of the Board of Stewards of the Buncombe Street Methodist Church; and is a member of the Masonic order. He was a member of the United States Naval Reserves during the World War.

Mr. and Mrs. Browning, nee Miss Ethel Smith of Charleston, have three children: Paul N., W. D., and Mary Elizabeth Browning.

JAMES A. CANNON

Greenville County has the distinction of having been the home of one who is thought to hold the record of the United States for continuous service as postmaster at the same office. For 49 years, beginning in 1873 and continuing till 1922, JAMES A. CANNON was postmaster at Fountain Inn; and authentic records fail to show that any other person in the nation has served a postoffice for that length of time.

Mr. Cannon was born in Rutherfordton, N. C., on June 4, 1853. In early life he moved with his parents to South Carolina where they settled in Spartanburg County. Later the family moved into the lower part of Greenville County, near the present town of Fountain Inn, where the father, Noah Cannon, bought considerable lands and engaged in farming and the mercantile business. After acquiring such education as the primary schools of that day afforded, the son entered business with his father and for many years they conducted a general mercantile store. Later Noah Cannon moved to Greer, but the subject of this sketch remained at the old home and thereafter conducted the mercantile business alone, having purchased his father's interest.

In 1873 Mr. James A. Cannon was appointed postmaster at Fountain Inn, then nothing more than a country community, with no railroad. His appointment came from President Grant, and although himself a Democrat, he continued to hold office through the administrations of both parties till 1922 when, under Civil Service regulations, he became ineligible for reappointment on account of his advanced age. With the coming of a railroad, and the establishment of a station on his property in 1886, Mr. Cannon saw the advantage of this location for a thriving town, and set himself to the task of building one. Being the owner of most of the lands about the station, he laid out a village and here was born the town of Fountain Inn. For many years the growth of the town was slow, but Mr. Cannon continued in his task of bringing in new inhabitants and assisting in the establishment of new industries till he had at last built a real, thriving little city around him.

Mr. Cannon continued in the general mercantile business for many years, till seeing the needs for an undertaking establishment in his town, he disposed of his general line of merchandise and entered that business, to which he held for the balance of his life. Always public-spirited, he invested of his time and money in all such enterprises as he thought would add to the growing town. Largely through his efforts a cotton mill was secured, which has grown till it is today a great factor in the business life of the community. But Mr. Cannon did not confine himself to the business of his home town, for in every worthwhile civic movement he was one of the moving spirits.

For many years Mr. Cannon was Mayor of the town of Fountain Inn. He was a faithful and active member of the Methodist Church and the land upon which that church at Fountain Inn stands was given by him. In his church, he was for many years a Steward and Trustee of church property. He also held membership in a number of fraternal organizations, including among others the Masons, the Knights of Pythias, Odd Fellows, Woodmen, and Redmen.

Mr. Cannon was married to Miss Elizabeth West, daughter of Dr. William West, and they have three surviving children: A. D. Cannon and Miss Maude Cannon of Fountain Inn, and Mrs. R. P. McGowan of Laurens, South Carolina.

On May 9, 1928, Mr. Cannon died, and of his passing it may be truly said, there goes one whose life has added much to the happiness and well-being of those among whom he lived.

PASCAL DACUS HUFF

One of the outstanding citizens of lower Greenville County during the last half of the nineteenth century was PASCAL DACUS HUFF of the St. Albans section. He was born near Dacus Shoals on Reedy river in Greenville County on April 8, 1838, being the son of Philemon and Louisa Amanda (Dacus) Huff, and resided in the county during the whole of his life, except for the days of the War Between the States.

Philemon Huff, father of Pascal Dacus, was a son of James and Rebecca (Mosely) Huff, who emigrated from Brunswick County, Virginia, to the Rehaboth Church section of Greenville County, South Carolina, in 1817. He was born while his parents still resided in Virginia. The family was founded in America by John Hough, who came over from England with William Penn and settled in Buck County, Pennsylvania, in 1683. The spelling of the name is not the same, nevertheless the subject of this sketch (P. D. Huff) was a direct descendant of John Hough.

Pascal Dacus Huff secured his education at the Williamston Male Academy, which was a noted institution of learning in the days before the middle of the last century. Leaving school he engaged himself in farming till the outbreak of the War Between the States, when he enlisted in Company B. (Butler Guards) Second South Carolina regiment. During the entire four years of the war he served with the same regiment, taking part in all the important battles engaged in by his company.

At the close of the war Mr. Huff returned to his old home, where he, as all other returned Confederate soldiers, found everything in a state of chaos; but undaunted, he entered upon the task of rehabilitation. First he married (to Miss Jane Adelaide Sullivan of near Tumbling Shoals, Laurens County, on June 13, 1865) and then undertook his life's work of farming in earnest. Slowly, but steadily, he enlarged his operations and expanded his holdings till he became one of the largest and most successful farmers in the county. He also devoted much of his time to surveying, in which work he was recognized as an authority.

Throughout his life Mr. Huff was always deeply interested in promoting the welfare of his community and took a prominent part in all movements having that

PASCAL DACUS HUFF

JAMES A. CANNON

as their object. He was instrumental in the establishment of the St. Albans school; for many years he was postmaster of a "Star route" post office established at his home largely through his efforts; the Fellowship Methodist Church, of which he was an active member, is the outgrowth of his work to secure a church in his community. Although Mr. Huff never sought political office he was always interested in securing the best available men for public positions. For a number of years he was a magistrate by appointment. He was a Mason, and assisted in establishing a Lodge of that order in his community.

Mr. and Mrs. Huff were the parents of eight children, viz: Annie Laura, who died June 20, 1889; Warren Rutledge, Junius Kershaw, Velona (Mrs. H. S. Garrison), Cornelia Ellen (Mrs. W. H. Bozeman), Agnes Lee (Mrs. J. T. Childers), Swan Burnett, and Virginia, who died January 4, 1887.

After a long and unusually useful life Mr. Huff died at his home near the intersection of the Fork Shoals and Georgia roads on July 11, 1910. The place of his death marks the site of the old homestead of his wife's grandparents, John Moon and Mary Adkins Dacus Cureton, who were pioneer settlers of the county.

SWAN BURNETT HUFF

SWAN BURNETT HUFF, son of Pascal D. and Jane (Sullivan) Huff, was born in the St. Albans community of Greenville County on September 30, 1882. Both parents were descended from early settlers of the Piedmont Section. He secured his early education at the Sandy Springs school and then studied at the Bliss Electrical school.

His school days finished, Mr. Huff worked at the electrical business in Spartanburg, South Carolina, for three years, but he then returned to St. Albans and engaged in farming, which occupation he has ever since followed. He now owns and resides upon the old homestead of his father, near the intersection of the Fork Shoals and Georgia roads. His farm consists of 300 acres of as fertile land as is to be found in the county. Here he applies modern scientific methods of farming and is unusually successful. He is Vice-President and a member of the Board of Directors of the Farmers Bank of Simpsonville.

In religious affiliations Mr. Huff is a Methodist, being a member of the Fellowship Methodist Church, which was established largely through the efforts of his father. He is Superintendent of the Sunday School department of the church.

In 1912 Mr. Huff was married to Miss Meda Lee Hunt and they have two children, Darrall and Roscoe.

W. W. CARTER

Among the concerns engaged in construction work upon a large scale in the South is the Fiske-Carter Construction Company, of which W. W. CARTER is Treasurer and directing head of its Greenville, South Carolina, branch.

Mr. Carter was born in Millbury, Massachusetts, on the 21st day of April, 1866, being the son of Rufus Carter. After completing his education and engaging in various lines of business for a few years, he became connected with the J. H.

Cutting Construction Company, which was the builder of the original plant of the Woodside Cotton Mills of Greenville.

Leaving the Cutting Company, Mr. Carter assisted in the organization of the Fiske-Carter Construction Company of Worcester, Massachusetts, in 1908. Two years later the business of the concern had expanded to such an extent that it was decided to open a branch in the South. Greenville was chosen for the Southern location and Mr. Carter took charge and has remained the active head of all Southern operations continuously from that time till the present.

The Fiske-Carter Construction Company, from its Greenville branch, has done much of the large construction work in North Carolina, South Carolina, Virginia, Georgia and Alabama during the twenty years of its Southern existence, including such undertakings as the Textile Hall, *The News* Building, the Piedmont and Northern warehouses, and the Dunean Mill and village of Greenville, the newly constructed Rayon plant at Covington, Virginia, the Bemis Bros. plant at Talledega, Alabama, Chicopee Manufacturing Corporation of Georgia, Gainesville, Georgia, and many other of the new cotton mills of those states. The largest construction work of the company, however, was the building of Camp Wadsworth at Spartanburg during the World War. This was the second largest National Guard camp to be constructed by the government and called for an expenditure of about four and a half million dollars. The average annual business of the Greenville branch of this company exceeds $3,000,000.

Mr. Carter is a large stockholder in the Woodside Cotton Mills Company, and has been a director of that concern for 20 years.

In 1895 he was married to Laura Grace Whitney, who died in 1928. They have three children, Lorraine W. Carter, who is connected with the Fiske-Carter Company at Greenville, W. W. Carter, Jr., of Worcester, Mass., and Mildred Carter Lawrence of Anderson, South Carolina. Mr. Carter's address is Greenville, South Carolina.

THOMAS E. CHRISTENBERRY

Any contacts that a man may make, whether with other men or with affairs, are sure to be of use to him later; and this is more particularly true in the case of a politician or any one involved in public affairs. So it has proved with T. E. CHRISTENBERRY, whose able handling of the matters under his jurisdiction as Clerk of Court reflects the experience gained in years of business administration.

Mr. Christenberry was born on September 2, 1882, at Morgan Springs, Alabama, one of the eight children of William A. and Annie O. Christenberry. His maternal grandfather, a captain in the Confederate Army, was wounded during the Civil War; after the close of the war, he was elected to the office of County Treasurer of Perry County, Alabama.

Thomas E. Christenberry attended public school in Alabama, and later received his business training at the Eastman Business College, Poughkeepsie, New York. His first employment was with the American Trust & Savings Company of Montgomery, Alabama; shortly thereafter he became connected with the Birmingham branch of Swift & Company, an association which lasted through more than a decade and carried Mr. Christenberry to various points in Georgia and Florida. He served in many different capacities in this organization—cashier and bookkeeper of the Tampa, Florida, branch, collector, city salesman, etc. During all the years of his employment with this company, Mr. Christenberry never lost a day from business.

On June 10, 1919, the Greenville branch of Swift & Company was placed under the managership of Mr. Christenberry, but after two years this connection with Swift & Company was severed. Mr. Christenberry, for a short time, was employed by the local concern of Balentine & Company, after which he took over the brokerage account of George A. Hormell & Co., meat packers, of Austin, Minnesota.

It was at about this time that Mr. Christenberry began to consider the question of a political career. The year 1928 was election year in Greenville County, and the race for the office of Clerk of Court proved to be one of the hottest, as well as one of the most interesting, in the campaign. Mr. Christenberry was elected to this office by an overwhelming majority; a result more impressive in consideration of the fact that this was his first venture in politics, whereas his opponent was one who had been for years in the public eye, and had already held several county offices. The success which has attended Mr. Christenberry's activities in his new field, proves that the people of Greenville County were not mistaken in their estimate of his ability.

Varied as have been the business and political avocations of Mr. Christenberry, he has found time and opportunity for affiliation with numerous fraternal orders, and has occupied positions of honor in more than one. He is a member and Steward of Buncombe Street Methodist Church, Past Master of Walden Lodge of Masons of Greenville; Worthy Patron of Eastern Star, Greenville Chapter No. 31; member of Knight Templars, Shriners, Junior Order United American Mechanics, U. C. T., and T. P. A.

While in Key West, Florida, Mr. Christenberry met Miss Jennie Earnhardt of Lenior, North Carolina, whom he subsequently married. They are the parents of three children: George A., Thomas E., Jr., and Robert E. Christenberry.

CHARLES TAPPEY SQUIRES

Among those who have made noteworthy contributions to the religious, moral, social and educational progress of Greenville County during the last five years should be numbered the REVEREND CHARLES TAPPEY SQUIRES, Pastor of the Fourth Presbyterian Church of Greenville City.

Mr. Squires was born in the city of St. Louis, Missouri, on November 13, 1878, being the son of Charles Winder and Emily Elizabeth (Tappey) Squires. His father was a native of New Orleans, Louisiana, and his mother of Petersburg, Virginia. His father served in the Confederate army during the entire four years of the War Between the States, having risen to the rank of Lieutenant Colonel of Artillery before its close; while his great grandfather was a soldier in the War of 1812, being killed in the defense of Washington.

The boyhood of Mr. Squires was spent in St. Louis and Petersburg, and he attended the public schools of both places, being graduated from the Petersburg

High School in 1896. Leaving high school he entered business in St. Louis where he was able to accumulate sufficient money to defray the expenses of a higher education. In 1908 he was graduated from the Union Theological Seminary of Richmond, Virginia, and entered immediately upon his life's work of a Presbyterian minister.

For almost three years following his graduation Mr. Squires held a pastorate in St. Louis. Following this he was at Lenoir, North Carolina, for seven years, and then moved to South Carolina. For seven years he was at Laurens, and since leaving there, in the latter part of 1924, has been with the Fourth Presbyterian Church of Greenville.

In all his pastorates Mr. Squires has not only taken a deep interest in the religious life of his community but has entered actively into its various civic and educational undertakings. While at Lenoir he was a member of the Board of Trustees of the city public schools, and during his residence at Laurens he was a member of the Board of Trustees of the Presbyterian College and Chairman of the Home Missions Board in South Carolina Presbytery.

Since he assumed the pastorate of the Fourth Presbyterian Church in Greenville, that church has experienced a sustained growth. Under his leadership the new Highland Presbyterian Church has been organized and he ministers to this new congregation as well as that of the Fourth Presbyterian.

Mr. Squires is a lover of sports and a baseball or football game is rarely played in Greenville without his being in attendance. This characteristic puts him in close touch with the man in the street, thus enabling him to render a peculiar service to a large class of people usually not reached by Ministers of the Gospel. He is a Knight Templar of the Masonic fraternity and an active member of the Kiwanis Club of Greenville.

In 1911 Mr. Squires was married to Miss Nona Markley Harris of Culpepper County, Virginia, who was a native of South Carolina, being the daughter of Prof. J. M. Harris, who occupied the Chair of Science in Furman University for more than 20 years. The children of this union are five, all of whom are living. They are: Charles T., Jr., Mary Elizabeth, Malcolm Hart, William Harrison and Nona.

DR. WILLIAM BUCK SPARKMAN

DR. WILLIAM BUCK SPARKMAN, son of William Irvine and Hattie (Buck) Sparkman, was born at Dirleton, Georgetown County, South Carolina, on February 15, 1883. He was a grandson of James Ritchie Sparkman and Mary (Heriot) Sparkman of the same community. His boyhood was spent at Dirleton, Statesburg and Georgetown. In the schools of these towns his early education was had. Following this he attended Clemson College for three years and then went to Poughkeepsie, New York, where he was a student at the Eastman Business College for a year. After this he accepted employment with the American Tobacco Company in New York and for a year he held this position.

From New York Dr. Sparkman went to Charleston, South Carolina, to become a student in the South Carolina Medical College. Here he was first honor graduate on April 28, 1909. Following his graduation he was an interne at the Roper Hospital, Charleston, for a few months. He then left Charleston and became an interne at the City Hospital, Blackwell's Island, where he remained until he came to Greenville in 1910.

In Greenville Dr. Sparkman was engaged in the general practice of medicine from 1910 until 1924, except for a period of nine months in 1916 when he served upon the Mexican border as Captain in the South Carolina Medical Corps. In 1924 he went to Chicago where he pursued special studies in surgery. Following this he became a student in the hospital of the celebrated Mayo Brothers at Rochester, Minn. Having completed his studies there he returned to Greenville, where he engaged in the practice of surgery until his death on March 27, 1929.

He was a member of the American College of Surgeons, the South Carolina Medical Society, the Mayflower Society, the Masons and Elks.

Dr. Sparkman was married to Miss Lucy Sloan Poe, Daughter of Francis Winslow and Harriet (Maxwell) Poe, of Greenville, South Carolina, in 1913, and to this union were born four children, viz: William Buck Sparkman, Jr., born June 13, 1914; Lucy Poe Sparkman, born January 19, 1916; Elizabeth Temple Sparkman, born August 13, 1920, and Harriet Maxwell Sparkman, born December 25, 1922.

In the death of Dr. Sparkman, which came while he was still in the prime of life and just as he was entering upon a broader field of service in his profession, Greenville suffered a distinct loss. He was an asset which the city could ill afford to lose.

FREDERICK W. SYMMES

FREDERICK W. SYMMES, textile manufacturer and public-spirited citizen of Greenville, was born in Greenville County, South Carolina, being the son of James Whitner Symmes and Nettie (Alexander) Symmes. His father was the youngest child of Dr. Frederick W. Symmes, and for many years was a prominent attorney at the Greenville bar.

Of Dr. Frederick W. Symmes, grandfather of the subject of this sketch, in his History of Old Pendleton District, R. W. Simpson writes:

"Dr. Frederick W. Symmes was for many years one of the most prominent and influential citizens of Pendleton in its best days. He was a noted physician, a man of sterling character, and a fluent writer. He was for years editor of the *Pendleton Messenger,* a newspaper and political organ that did more to shape public opinion in South Carolina than any other paper in the state. Dr. Symmes was a close relative of President Benjamin Harrison, and was possessed of many of the characteristics peculiar to that celebrated family. He married Sarah Whitner, daughter of Joseph Whitner, and sister of Judge Joseph N. Whitner."

Fred Symmes, as he is generally known, obtained his education in the public schools of Greenville, and at Furman University. His first business connection was with the Symmes-Williams Furniture Company of Greenville. Of this concern he was one of the owners.

In 1910 he organized the Nuckasee Manufacturing Company and became its President and Treasurer, which position he continues to hold. This company confines itself exclusively to the manufacture of athletic underwear. At first it employed only 30 people but so remarkable has been its growth that it today has 450 employees, and is the largest of its kind in the South. The annual output of the company is about 200,000 dozen garments.

The Piedmont Plush Mills was organized by Mr. Symmes in 1926 and of that concern he has been President and Treasurer since its beginning.

But the business activities of Mr. Symmes are not confined entirely to manufacturing. He is a director in both the First National Bank of Greenville and the South Carolina National Bank. With each institution he serves as a member of the Loan Committee. For a number of years he was Vice-President of the Greenville Building & Loan Association.

The civic affairs of Greenville have a large place in the life of Mr. Symmes. He is an active member of the Greenville Chamber of Commerce and one of its Ex-Presidents. For many years he has been a Director of the Community Chest Fund and during one year was Chairman of the Board. He is also a member of the Board of Trustees of "Green-Acre" and is active in children's welfare work. It was largely through his efforts that Greenville County secured its Juvenile Court.

Mr. Symmes is unmarried.

D. D. DAVENPORT

D. D. DAVENPORT, merchant, financier, and public-spirited citizen, was born near River Falls, in Greenville County, on the 20th day of August, 1844, and died at Greer June 30, 1918.

Mr. Davenport's boyhood was passed at a time when there were practically no schools in upper South Carolina and this is reflected in the fact that he attended school for only a few weeks during his life. But no one could say that D. D. Davenport was an uneducated man. Of knowledge acquired from books, he might have had little, but being possessed of an uncommonly keen intellect, he was a lifelong student of man in his relations with the world about him, and from this valuable source of knowledge he drank deeply. As a very young man he went to North Carolina where he lived for a few years; but his native state called him back and he located at Holly Springs, in Spartanburg County, where he engaged in the mercantile business for a time. Later he moved to Welford, where he operated a store for six years.

Leaving Welford, Mr. Davenport located at Greer, where he resided for the balance of his long and useful life. For many years he was there engaged in the mercantile business with phenominal success. He branched out and entered other fields of endeavor, notably the acquisition and improvement of real estate. Many then thought that there was "no future" to real estate ownership in Greenville. Mr. Davenport thought differently, so much of the money he was making in his mercantile business went to purchase realty in Greer, Greenville, Spartanburg, and Columbia. In Greenville, he erected the Davenport Apartments on West Washington Street, still, after many years the leading property of its kind in that city; the Davenport Building on Main Street, and many other residential and business houses; not alone in Greenville, but in the other cities where he acquired real estate. He organized and successfully operated till his death, the Greer Oil Mill Company, and invested heavily in many other manufacturing businesses, notably hydro-electric.

And in all his undertakings he was unusually successful. Living at a time when money was scarce in South Carolina and wealthy men were virtually unknown, he accumulated a large estate, probably being the wealthiest man, with one exception, in Greenville County at the time of his death.

Mr. Davenport was deeply interested in the public welfare, and gave much from his large means for the education of the youth, and the betterment of living conditions for working girls.

Mr. Davenport married Miss Martha A. West while living at Holly Springs and they had two children, May (Mrs. John D. Wood) and M. Cliff, both of whom are deceased.

M. C. DAVENPORT

Among the younger business men of Greenville County, none has a brighter future than M. C. DAVENPORT of Greer. He is the son of M. Cliff Davenport and Clara (Merchant) Davenport, and the grandson of D. D. Davenport, notable merchant and financier, and was born at Greer, South Carolina, on June 14, 1902.

Mr. Davenport acquired his early education in the public schools of Greer, and then entered the University of Southern California. Later he was a student at the University of Alabama and at Trinity College (now Duke University).

Leaving college, Mr. Davenport resided in California where he was connected with a bank. Returning to Greer in 1924 he became Assistant Cashier of the First National Bank of Greer, and two years thereafter he became President of that institution, which position he still holds with distinction.

Mr. Davenport takes an active interest in all the public activities of his home city. He is a charter member of the Civitan Club of Greer, and a Mason. In religious affiliations he is a member of the Methodist Church.

Mr. Davenport married Miss M. Guens in Springfield and they have two children: M. C., Jr., and Patricia. The family home is on Randall Street, in the town of Greer.

DR. BENJAMIN FRANKLIN FEW

Among the very early settlers of upper Greenville County was the Few family, which was founded in South Carolina by William Few, who came from Georgia. This William Few had a son, William Few, who was married to Sarah Ferguson, and among their children was DR. BENJAMIN FRANKLIN FEW, who was born on a plantation about eight miles above Greenville City on May 11, 1830.

Dr. Few secured his early education in the schools of his home community and later became a student at the Charleston Medical College, from which he graduated with the degree of M.D. Upon leaving college he took up the practice of his profession at Marietta where he remained till the outbreak of the War Between the States. Immediately upon the commencement of hostilities he volunteered as a surgeon in the Confederate army where he remained, rendering valiant service till the close of the war. Back at home he located in the Sandy Flat Community and there practiced his profession till 1882, when he moved to Greer where he remained until his death on January 22, 1923, at the age of 93. At Greer he was for many years the leading physician, but several years before his death he retired on account of advanced age.

Dr. Few was married to Rachel Kendrick in 1863, who passed away November 7, 1922, only two months before her husband. They were the parents of five children: Rev. Robert A. Few, a member of the South Carolina Conference, who died in 1897; Dr. William P. Few, now President of Duke University of Durham, N. C.; Sallie Few, who was married to M. L. Marchant, and who died in 1889; Ignatious P. Few, who resides at Greer; and Miss Ellie Few, who also lives at Greer.

All his life Dr. Few interested himself in good works, and especially those causes pertaining to the betterment of the public health, the church and the schools. He was keenly interested in all phases of education, and sent his own children to college at a time when college educations were uncommon. He was an active church worker, and had much to do with the founding of the First Methodist Church at Greer. He served the church in every layman's capacity, and was ever a staunch supporter of Methodism. Both a son and grandson entered the ministry of the Methodist Church.

William Few, the father of Dr. Few, was a soldier of the War of 1812, while James Few, great-grandfather of Dr. Few, was one of the first to lay down his life for the cause of liberty in the American Revolution. James Few was a son of Colonel William Few, who with his sons, rendered public service of a high order in the colonial period, during and, after the Revolution. The founder of the family in America was Richard Few, who came over with William Penn. One of the descendants of Richard Few was a member of the Continental Congress from the State of Georgia and a signer of the Constitution of the United States.

Richard Few, the first of the family in America, married Miss Mary Wheeler. He was a Quaker, while his wife was a member of the Roman Catholic Church. The descendants of this couple were practically all Quakers until the coming of John Wesley, when the Few families joined the Methodist movement and rendered valiant service in that cause, even down to the present day.

Dr. Benjamin Franklin Few, like his great pioneer ancestors, was a true servant of his church and state; and he was always to be found alligned squarely behind the great moral and social causes of mankind. His community, his county and his state are richer that he lived.

DAKYNS B. STOVER

DAKYNS BROCKENBROUGH STOVER, solicitor and lawyer, was born in Spartanburg, South Carolina, on May 25, 1899, the son of William Wirt and Mable Lee (Price) Stover. His grandfather, John Gilbert Stover, was professor of Ancient Languages at Staunton, Virginia. Mr. Stover is a direct descendant of Lord Lieutenant Brockenbrough, Governor of London Tower, England, during the reign of Richard III, and sixth in descent from King Carter, early settler on Virginia side of the Potomac river during the Cromwellian period.

Mr. Stover received his early education in the Greenville City Schools, and in 1915, he won the State High School Oratorical Contest. He also won the declamation medal in 1914 and 1915. He holds the Cothran Debater's Medal and the Endel Declaimer's Medal, which he won while in high school, and the Euphradian Orator's Medal (U. of S. C.). In 1919 he graduated from the University of South Carolina with the LL.B. degree. Since graduation, he has engaged in the practice of law in Greenville.

Mr. Stover was elected Greenville County Solicitor in 1922 to succeed W. E. Bowen. He was re-elected in 1926, without opposition. During the World War he volunteered and served 60 days in Camp Gordon, Georgia, Officers' Training Camp, from October 1, 1918, to December 1, 1918. He is the author of the Dakyns B. Stover Oratorical Medal, awarded by the Greenville City High School each year since 1920.

Mr. Stover is a staunch Democrat, and is a member of the Red Men, J. O. U. A. M., American Legion, Lions Club and Chamber of Commerce. He is affiliated with the Presbyterian Church.

Mr. Stover was married to Miss Edith Marie Leversedge, of Albany, Georgia, on October 28, 1925, the daughter of John Hunter and Daisy Marie Leversedge. To them have been born two children, Edith (deceased) and Dakyns B. Stover, Jr.

Mr. Stover's address is Greenville, South Carolina.

BOYD BRANDON RAY

BOYD BRANDON RAY was born in Laurens County, South Carolina, on the 22nd day of February, 1888, being the son of James Long Ray and Jane (Brandon) Ray. Through his mother he is descended from Colonel Thomas Brandon, the first owner of the property on which Greenville City is now located. His maternal grandfather, John William Brandon, was among the first to volunteer for service in the Confederate army and was seriously wounded in the Battle of First Manassas. Thomas R. Ray, his paternal grandfather, was the only child of the Reverend Thomas R. Ray, an eminent divine of the Baptist Church during the early days. The Reverend Thomas R. Ray was no ordinary man. Having large means for his day he donated the land and built Padgett's Creek Baptist Church in Union County and for more than 20 years served it as pastor without pay. It was here that the Reverend John G. Landrum, noted preacher, educator and public citizen, was ordained to the Ministry in 1830. It is highly probable that the Reverend Ray took part in this service. In 1831 Landrum, Ray and others conducted a series of religious services (preaching under the trees surrounding the court house) at Spartanburg, South Carolina, which reached their climax in the organization of three churches (Baptist, Presbyterian and Methodist), which were the first in the town. Upon his death the membership of Padgett's Creek Church hung a portrait of the church's founder upon its walls and here it remained for many years as a reminder of the great good which had been accomplished by the Reverend Thomas R. Ray.

The subject of this sketch, Boyd Brandon Ray, remained in Laurens County, attending the public schools of his neighborhood, until he was 12 years of age, when he moved with his parents to Union County. Here he continued his education, being graduated from the Union High School in 1905.

Having finished his education, Mr. Ray came to Greenville where he accepted employment with the Poe Hardware & Supply Company. For 18 years he remained with this concern, first as clerk, next as traveling saleman and then as sales manager. Resigning his position here he entered the real estate business with the firm of Henderson & Martin, where he remained for three years. Then he entered the employ of the Mountain City Steel & Foundry Company as traveling representative for the Greenville and Spartanburg plants of this concern in Georgia and the two Carolinas, and this position he now holds. The business of this concern is transacted largely with cotton mills, and Mr. Ray is peculiarly fitted for this class of work.

Mr. Ray is an Episcopalian, being a vestryman in the St. James Episcopal Church; he is a 32nd degree Mason, a Shriner, a Woodman, and a member of the J. O. U. A. M.

In 1912 he was married to Miss Rene Johnson of Greenville, who is a granddaughter of Professor W. L. Johnson, teacher of music at the Greenville Woman's College during its early days. They have one child, William Brandon Ray. The family home is on Buncombe Street in the City of Greenville.

R. D. DOBSON

Among the citizens of Greenville County who have been eminently successful in business is R. D. DOBSON, President of the R. D. Dobson Lumber Company of Greer and of the Piedmont Lumber Company, of Greenville, and Vice-President of the companies handling the Chevrolet automobile at Greer and Greenville.

Mr. Dobson was born in Spartanburg County on the 2nd day of August, 1887, the son of J. P. and Martha Dobson.

He received his education in the public schools of Spartanburg County and at Greer.

Mr. Dobson entered the lumber business at Greer in 1913 when he organized the R. D. Dobson Lumber Company which has grown to be one of the largest lumber companies in the State. The firm has a large plant which includes a mill where the rough lumber is finished. The company does business all over Greenville County and to some extent in North Carolina.

Mr. Dobson is a director of the Citizens Building & Loan Association and is a member of the Civitan Club of Greer, and fraternally he is a Mason and a Shriner.

In addition to these interests he has found time to give considerable attention to the public affairs and is a member of the City Council of Greer. His religious affiliations are with the Baptist Church.

He was married to Virginia Hutchins and has two children, Edmund D. and Virginia.

JOHN D. HARRIS

It has been said that a large percent of our prominent and successful men have come from the country. One of these, whose love for his boundaries has kept him there, is JOHN D. HARRIS. His love for farming and its other interests is perhaps an inherited tendency. His father, W. C. Harris, was a substantial farmer of Laurens, South Carolina, who married Mary Jane Ashmore and moved to Greenville County, settling on the Fork Shoals road. Here in 1861 was born the subject of this sketch. Living on his father's farm, he learned the rudiments of that occupation, in the meantime attending school near his home. The schools of this period were very poorly equipped but by application and observation, Mr. Harris ably fitted himself for the position of importance which he was later to assume.

Arriving at man's estate, he immediately launched into the operation of a large farm according to the most modern and approved methods. Mr. Harris is one of the county's largest farmers, having more than 1,100 acres under cultivation. His specialties have long been cotton and grain, though his is a farm upon which may be found almost everything which grows successfully in the Piedmont Section. Realizing that farming and stock-raising must go hand in hand, Mr. Harris maintains an 87-acre stock farm which not only supplies his own farm, but has done much to raise the standard of blooded stock in the county.

In addition to his large and varied farm interests, Mr. Harris for many years has been prominent in business circles. He is a director of the South Carolina National Bank and held stock certificate No. 1 in the Norwood National Bank. When this concern became the South Carolina National Bank, he still was holder of this certificate.

Mr. Harris is an active member of the Methodist Church and has the distinction of twice having been a member of the General Conference of that body. His membership is with the Conestee Church, where for forty years he has filled the office of Steward.

Mr. Harris was married in 1893 to Miss Lizzie Willimon and to this union have been born the following children: John D., Jr., Mrs. Marie Lyon of Anderson, S. C., Robert Earle, Mrs. Elizabeth Hair of Spartanburg, S. C., and Nellie Harris.

Mr. Harris is a member of the Lions Club of Greenville and also takes an active part in Masonic circles of the State. He is also a Shriner.

To his mother, who has reached the advanced age of 92 years, Mr. Harris attributes much of his success.

JOHN BARRATT MARSHALL

JOHN BARRATT MARSHALL was born in Abbeville County, South Carolina, on April 4, 1853, being a son of Dr. S. S. and Anne Barratt Marshall. His father was a prominent physician and surgeon in the Confederate army. Samuel Steen Marshall, his paternal grandfather, was a native of County Tyrone, Ireland, and emigrated to Abbeville County, South Carolina, as a young man. His maternal grandfather, Dr. Barratt, was of English birth and gained wide recognition during his lifetime as a scientist, student and collector. Through his mother, he was a cousin of General M. C. Butler, Confederate soldier and United States Senator.

Mr. Marshall (subject of this sketch) secured his education at the Kings Mountain Academy, Furman University and the University of Virginia. From the latter institution he was graduated in law at the age of 21 years. Following his graduation he located in Madison, Florida, where he was engaged in the practice of law for a number of years. Later he returned to Greenville where he had moved from Abbeville with his parents when only seven years of age. Here he lived until his death on February 9, 1925.

For many years, beginning with 1885, when he returned to Greenville from Madison, Florida, Mr. Marshall was engaged in the ice manufacturing business, having built four plants during his active years of business life. He was the promoter and builder of the first ice plant erected in Greenville. He sold out his large holdings to the Carolina Public Service Company, now known locally as the Greenville Ice & Fuel Company, but remained with the company as manager of its Greenville plant until 1918, when he retired from active business.

But during the years of his busy life Mr. Marshall found time to accomplish much in the public affairs of his home city. For twelve years he was an Alderman of the city of Greenville, followed by four years as Mayor. When he became a member of the City Council the city of Greenville had no paving, but, due largely to his efforts, many miles of concrete and asphalt were laid during the years of his official life. The present magnificent bridge spanning Reedy river at the Main Street crossing was constructed during his administration as Mayor.

Mr. Marshall was a charter member of the Greenville Elks Club, and was twice its Exalted Ruler. He was an Episcopalian, being a member of Christ Church.

In 1918 he purchased a magnificent estate of 103 acres on the Buncombe road about four miles above Greenville. This he named "Tyrone Terrace" for the county in Ireland of which his ancestors were natives.

Mr. Marshall married Miss Sally R. Bythewood of Madison, Florida, and to this union 11 children were born. Of this number five are now living, these being as follows: Blythewood B. Marshall; Alfred Marshall, Frances W., wife of C. C. Withington, a former postmaster at Greenville; Sarah, wife of Albert M. Rickman; and Dan H. Marshall.

Mrs. Marshall survives her husband and resides in the city of Greenville.

FRANK HAMMOND

One who contributed much to the advancement of Greenville was FRANK HAMMOND, who began his long and active business career there in 1872 and continued it till his death in 1914. He was born on July 22, 1852, in Tipton, Iowa, being the son of Willard and Susan (Gower) Hammond. His parents were of English descent, the first of the line in America being William Hammond who emigrated from Suffolk County, England, and settled in New Hampshire at an early colonial date.

Mr. Hammond secured his education in the schools of his boyhood home community, but suffering the handicap of poor health, his school days were cut short and he entered life meagerly equipped in this particular; but having a naturally keen mind, he did much in later years to remove this deficiency.

At the age of 12, Mr. Hammond entered a printing office where he worked for one year. Then till 17 he worked on a farm, when he moved to Greenville to remain for the balance of his life. Four years after coming to Greenville he entered the mercantile business which he followed for many years. Leaving the mercantile field he entered the banking business which he followed with unusual success till his death. For many years he was President of the Peoples Bank (now Peoples National Bank) where he became widely known for his sound and conservative business judgment.

A. C. MANN

Due to his recognized financial ability, Mr. Hammond was much in demand as an advisor to large business interests, and as a consequence he held many positions of trust with Greenville enterprises. Among these were Vice-President of the Greenville Savings Bank, Director of the Piedmont Savings & Investment Company, Vice-President of the Paris Mountain Land Company, Vice-President of the Greenville Fertilizer Company, Director in the Blacksburg Land Company, Director in the Gower Supply Company, President of the Westervelt Mills (now Judson), President of the Guaranty Trust Company, President of the Piedmont Warehouse & Compress Company, a Director in the Greenville & Knoxville Railway Company, and a Director in many of Greenville's cotton mills.

Mr. Hammond was a member of the Presbyterian Church and took an active interest in religious matters.

In 1877 he was married to Miss Mary B. Caine and they had eight children: Frank, Jr., deceased; Susan, deceased; Mary, deceased; Eugenia, deceased; Eliza (Mrs. J. D. McGee), Maud (Mrs. A. L. Lewis), and Eugene Willard. Mr. Hammond died on January 27, 1914; his widow is still living in Greenville.

HONORABLE A. C. MANN

Many notable men have held the office of Mayor in the city of Greenville, and this together with the heavy responsibilities of the place, clothe that position with unusual distinction. So for one to be elected Mayor of Greenville without opposition shows that he is held in high regard by his fellow citizens. And in all the history of the city only two men have attained that office unopposed, one of whom is the present Mayor—the HONORABLE A. C. MANN.

Pickens County furnishes Greenville her present chief executive, he having been born there on September 27, 1889. His parents are A. D. Mann and Mrs. Laura Elizabeth (Tompkins) Mann, both of whom are still living. Mr. Mann, Sr., is a farmer and resides near Six Mile, of which town he was one of the first Mayors. Young Mann attended the public schools of Pickens County and later became a student at the Pickens High School, from which he was graduated as valedictorian of his class. Later he entered the University of South Carolina, from which he was graduated with an A.B. degree in 1913, again as valedictorian. One year later he received from the University of South Carolina his LL.B. degree, having done in a single year work which it usually required two or more years to accomplish.

Upon leaving college, Mr. Mann took up the practice of his profession (law) at Union, where he remained till 1917, when he moved to Greenville and became connected with the widely known firm of Haynsworth & Haynsworth. In 1925 he became associated with John L. Plyler, now Dean of the Furman University Law School, under the firm name of Mann & Plyler, and still holds this connection. His firm enjoys an extensive practice.

Mr. Mann's first venture into politics was as a Magistrate in the city of Union, to which position he was appointed. Upon the expiration of his term he became a candidate to succeed himself, but in this race he was opposed by two widely known men of the city. He, however, was successful in defeating both opponents. In 1920, just three years after taking up his residence in Greenville, Mr. Mann was a candidate for Solicitor of his Judicial circuit. There were six aspirants, all of whom had lived in the county much longer than Mr. Mann, but he ran third. In 1925 he was elected Alderman from Ward 1 of the city of Greenville without opposition; two years later he was re-elected without opposition; and in 1929 he was again re-elected, still without opposition. Soon after his third election as Alderman, Mayor Alvin H. Dean died, and Mr. Mann became Mayor for a short unexpired term by virtue of his position as Mayor pro tem., to which he had been elected by City Council. Immediately he resigned the office of Alderman to which he had just been re-elected and offered for the Mayoralty. There was no opposition. While Alderman, and still as Mayor, Mr. Mann has worked unceasingly for extension of the city limits of Greenville.

Mr. Mann is Chairman of the Board of Deacons of the Earle Street Baptist Church and takes an active interest in all church work. He is a Trustee of the Greenville Woman's College; holds membership in the American, the South Carolina, and the Greenville Bar Association; is a Mason, and Woodman.

In 1917 Mr. Mann was married to Miss Nina Griffin of Pickens County and they have five children, four boys and one girl: A. C., Jr., James R., Joe Griffin, Betty Lanelle, and John Plyler. The family resides on Earle Street in the city of Greenville.

DR. C. C. JONES

For a city to bestow its highest governmental office upon the representatives of two successive generations of the same family is rather unusual, but Greenville has done this in at least one instance—that of the family of Dr. William R. Jones. It was largely through the instrumentality of this gentleman that the town of Greenville was incorporated under its present charter, and it was he who became the first Mayor of the "City of Greenville."

CLINTON C. JONES, son of Dr. William R., was born in Greenville on October 17, 1859, and grew up with the town, receiving his college education at Furman University. He later attended Bellevue University, now the Medical Department of Columbia University, New York City, from which institution he was graduated with the degree of M.D. He returned to Greenville and continued in the practice of his chosen profession until shortly before his death, which occurred on January 6, 1918.

The civic patriotism which he had imbibed from his father soon manifested itself, and Dr. C. C. Jones took his place as a leader in the furthering of Greenville progress along lines religious, political, and social. His popularity and success as a physician gave him a wide range of loyal and enthusiastic friends, who were later to prove ardent political supporters. So great, indeed, was the public confidence in his ability, that when he announced his candidacy for the office of Mayor, he met with no opposition, and so was unanimously elected to this position. Nor did he fall short of that which was expected of him, as is evidenced by the fact that twice thereafter he was returned to the Mayor's chair.

Busy as he was, however, with civic and professional duties, he had also time for business activities, being largely interested in real estate in and around Greenville. As a member of the Presbyterian Church he identified himself with the religious advancement of the town and rounded out an exceptionally well-balanced life.

He was married to Miss Virginia Doyle and was the father of two sons—W. R. Jones, planter of Fountain Inn, South Carolina, and Clinton C. Jones, Jr., of Greenville.

COLONEL WILLIAM HENRY KEITH

Many of those who have been prominent in the affairs of Greenville County during the last quarter of a century were born without the boundaries of the county. These "Builders of Greenville" have come from practically every county of South Carolina as well as from many other states. And of all those who have adopted Greenville as their home during that time none has entered more wholeheartedly into her activities than COLONEL WILLIAM HENRY KEITH.

Colonel Keith was born at Timmonsville, in Florence County, South Carolina, on February 7, 1873, his parents being Jesse E. and Kate (Sykes) Keith. He attended the public schools of the community and the Citadel and later Central University, Richmond, Kentucky. Soon after leaving college he entered the employ of his step-father, John McSween (his father having died and his mother becoming the wife of Mr. McSween) who was engaged in the general mercantile business at Timmonsville. The McSween business was unusually successful and in 1899 it was incorporated and Colonel Keith become Vice-President of the new concern under the name of McSween Mercantile Company. The company also conducted a store at Lamar. Upon the retirement of Mr. McSween in 1917, Colonel Keith assumed the presidency of both stores. The business continued unusually prosperous under the guiding hand of its new president till he disposed of his interests in 1920.

In his native town of Timmonsville, Colonel Keith has held the offices of Alderman and of Mayor, both of which he filled with distinction. And during the World War he was Chairman of the Exemption Board of Florence County. Governor Richard I. Manning appointed him to a colonelcy upon his staff; and later in the administration of Governor Thos. G. McLeod, he also held the title of colonel on the staff of the governor.

After disposing of his Timmonsville business, Colonel Keith moved to Greenville in 1920, buying a block of property on North Main Street known as the "Endel home." This he developed, building thereon the Craig-Rush Building and the Rivoli theatre. For some years he was engaged in the real estate and insurance business, but in 1925 he became the owner of "Keiths, Incorporated", a ladies' ready-to-wear and dry goods department store, which has enjoyed more than the usual amount of success.

Upon the urgent solicitation of friends Colonel Keith became a candidate for the House of Representatives in 1924 and was elected. Twice since then he has been re-elected and a distinctive feature in this is the fact that all of his colleagues from Greenville County who have offered for re-election have been defeated. In the General Assembly, Colonel Keith has played a conspicuous and enviable part. He has never resorted to the playing of petty politics, has been frank and open in every position he has taken. This has lost for him many positions of distinction in the

Assembly, but has caused him to gain and hold the respect and gratitude of the people of the State. They feel that Keith can always be counted upon to take a positive stand on every question and stick to his position till the end. There is none of the "fence-straddling" or "policy advocacy", so common among public officials of today, in Colonel Keith.

During his term of office, Greenville County has paved all her principal highways; and the whole state of South Carolina has moved rapidly forward along many progressive lines. Legislation of a progressive nature has ever had his support, but any radical or retrogressive movement has met his bitter opposition. In the House of Representatives Colonel Keith was for the past two years a member of the Ways and Means Committee. Since then he has held the Chairmanship of the Committee on Military Affairs which made him a member of the Board of Visitors of the Citadel. In 1929 he became Chairman of the Educational Committee, which made him a member of the Board of Trustees of Winthrop College and the University of South Carolina. He is also Chairman of the Penitentiary Committee and in addition serves on the Committees on Banking and Finance, and State Hospital. During the 1929 session of the General Assembly he led the fight against a huge State bond issue for road-building, taking the position that the road-building law under which the State was then operating was sufficient and should not be amended without a vote of the people. In this position he was very generally supported by the business men of the whole state and by the combined suffrage of the Piedmont section. But he had the opposition of almost all the active politicians. The fearless manner in which he fought for what he considered right in the face of so great odds attracted the attention of the leading newspapers of the state. He is now (July, 1930,) a candidate for Governor with bright prospects of being elected.

Colonel Keith is an Elder in the First Presbyterian Church of Greenville, a member of the Kiwanis Club, a Mason, a Shriner, and a member of the Knights of Pythias.

He was married to Miss Cora Byrd in 1897 and they have two daughters—Mrs. Dorothy (Keith) Hunter and Miss Margaret Louise. The family home is on East Washington Street in the city of Greenville.

MARSHALL B. PREVOST

MARSHALL B. PREVOST was born in Anderson, South Carolina, on January 16, 1877, being the son of John Blair Prevost and Mary (Orr) Prevost. His father was a member of the medical corps of the Confederate army during the War Between the States, and was a planter and merchant. His mother was a daughter of Colonel James L. Orr, Speaker of the United States House of Representatives, Confederate States Senator, Colonel of the First South Carolina Regiment during the War Between the States, first Governor of South Carolina to be elected after the war, and Minister to Russia at the time of his death. Indeed a noble ancestry.

Mr. Prevost's education was secured in preparatory schools of Washington, D. C., at the Freehold Institute (preparatory), at Furman University of Greenville, and in Princeton. At Furman he coached the first football team to be put out by that institution.

For a time after finishing his education Mr. Prevost acted as private secretary for his uncle, James L. Orr of Greenville. Then he went to Mexico City where he was connected with the Mitchell Mining Company. In 1902 he and W. L. Vail started publication of the *Mexico Daily Record,* which they continued until 1909. With the paper they also published the *Mexican Journal of Commerce.* Later in 1909 he left Mexico, but still retains a number of investments there. From Mexico he returned to Greenville where he entered the real estate, stock and bond business. Since 1915, however, he has been inactive in business.

Mr. Prevost devotes much of his time to the finer arts. He is a director of the Greenville Art Museum, and does practically all of the work for exhibitions. He is a widely recognized authority on fine prints (etchings and engravings), and bears the distinction of having coached Lawrence Adams, John Sitton, James E. Birnie, Carol Mittell and Helen Bozeman, all of Greenville, in black and white drawing. All of these except Miss Bozeman have finished courses in the Yale School of Fine Arts. Of these Mr. Adams is now a portrait painter in New York City; Mr. Sitton is winner of the highly coveted Prix of Rome, 1929, and is now in Rome continuing his studies; Miss Bozeman is on the staff of *The Vogue,* and the other two are still pursuing their studies with bright prospects of unusual success in their field.

During 1920 and 1921 Mr. Prevost was a member of the Greenville City Council; he is an Elk, a member of the Greenville Country Club, and a 32nd degree Mason in Mexico.

On May 16, 1903, Mr. Prevost was married to Miss Gerda Luyties of St. Louis, Missouri, and they are the parents of five children: Marshall Lawrence, deceased; Gerry, Tournay, Christie and Gerda II. The eldest son, Marshall Lawrence, died on March 21, 1926, while a student of Engineering at the University of South Carolina.

The Prevost home is on East McBee Avenue in the City of Greenville.

W. FRANK HIPP

Within recent years the industrial insurance business has grown into large proportions in South Carolina. Leading the field is the Liberty Life Insurance Company of Greenville, which has as its president and directing head W. FRANK HIPP.

Mr. Hipp was born in the county of Greenwood, South Carolina, on August 24, 1889, being the son of John C. and Alice P. (Wheeler) Hipp. His maternal grandfather was killed while serving with the Confederate forces during the War Between the States.

While still quite young Mr. Hipp moved with his parents to Newberry County, where his father had acquired large farming interests. As a youth he attended the public schools of Newberry County, and then became a student at Newberry College, from which he was graduated with an A.B. degree in 1907. Leaving college, he entered the insurance business in the City of Newberry, where he remained for five years. Then for the next six years he lived in Spartanburg as General Agent for Southeastern Life Insurance Company. In 1918 he became a resident of the city of Greenville, where for two years he was engaged in the stock and bond business. In

1919 he organized the Liberty Life Insurance Company with its home office at Greenville, and became its President.

Although the Liberty Life Insurance Company is just ten years old, it ranks ninth among the industrial insurance companies of the entire United States in volume of business written annually. In 1928 (1929 records not available) of all the companies writing industrial insurance in South Carolina the Liberty Life had the greatest gain. Its nearest competitor is the largest industrial company in the United States, and it surpassed this large company by more than $3,000,000. Of the ten South Carolina companies writing this class of business, the net gain of the Liberty for that year was almost four times the combined gain of the nine other companies. But the company does not confine itself to the industrial field. After becoming firmly established it began to write all classes of "old line" policies and is now doing a large volume of business in that field. The company employs 225 full time agents who cover every section of South Carolina. It owns its home office building at the corner of Main and East Court Streets and is known as the Blue Building. The rapid growth of the Liberty Life is largely due to the efficient management of Mr. Hipp, who has continued as its president up to the present time.

Mr. Hipp is a member of the Trinity Lutheran Church, and an active worker in all the activities of his denomination in the state, being at this time Vice-Chairman of the Executive Board of the Synod of South Carolina, and a trustee of Newberry College.

In 1909 he was married to Miss Eunice Jane Halfacre of Newberry, and they are the parents of five children: Francis, Herman, Dorothy, Calhoun, and Hayne, deceased. The family home is on Bennett Street in the City of Greenville.

JAMES A. DAVENPORT

JAMES A. DAVENPORT was born in lower Greenville County in 1852, being one of a family of 15 children, all of whom grew to maturity. His parents were Francis M. and Winnie (Chapman) Davenport, both of whom were members of families which have resided in the county since the early days of its history. Francis M. Davenport was a man of power and influence in his home community, and was a member of the General Assembly from Greenville County at one time during his long and useful life.

Mr. Davenport (subject of this sketch) secured his education in various private schools of his home community, and then became engaged in farming. For many years he successfully operated extensive plantations in Dunklin Township, where he resided. Later he sold a portion of his farm lands and moved to Greenville City, where for a time he was engaged in the cotton business; but until his death in May, 1922, he continued to be interested in large farm properties. In addition to his farm and cotton business interests he was an investor in numerous enterprises, among which was the Norwood National Bank, of which he was long a director.

For many years, and until his death, Mr. Davenport was a member of the Methodist Church. In politics he was a consistent Democrat who held decided opinions as to "high character and honorable dealings in private life," being a primary qualification for public office.

Mr. Davenport was married to Miss Frances McDaniel, member of another old and prominent family of the county, and they were the parents of five children: John T. Davenport of Greenville, James F. Davenport of Greenville, Hattie Davenport (Hardy) of Greenville, Rosa Davenport, deceased, and Henry Allen Davenport, deceased. Mrs. Davenport survives her husband and resides with her son, James F., in the McDavid Apartments on East North Street in the City of Greenville.

JAMES F. DAVENPORT

Among the younger men of Greenville City who are conducting their affairs in such a manner as to win the respect and esteem of the business interests of the city, is JAMES F. DAVENPORT. He is the son of James A. and Frances (McDaniel) Davenport and was born in Greenville County.

Mr. Davenport secured his early education in the public schools of Greenville County and then became a student at Furman University. From there he studied at Draughon's Business College.

After completing his education, Mr. Davenport entered the Norwood National Bank of Greenville (1911) as "runner" and gradually worked his way up through the various subordinate positions to become Assistant Cashier of that institution. Staying with the bank after it was merged with the Bank of Charleston and the Carolina National Bank of Columbia to become a part of the strong South Carolina National Bank, he was elected Cashier of the Greenville branch of this powerful financial institution. This position he now holds.

During the World War Mr. Davenport was a sergeant of senior grade in the Quartermaster Corps, stationed at Camp Sevier.

Mr. Davenport is a member of the Greenville Country Club, the Cotillion Club and the Revelers. He is unmarried and resides with his mother on East North Street in the City of Greenville.

C. D. SPEEGLE

Although not a native of Greenville, Mr. Speegle arrived in this city at such an early age that Greenville can surely claim him as one of her own sons. C. D. SPEEGLE, son of Dudley Speegle, was born in Lexington, South Carolina, on October 20, 1877, and there spent the first six years of his life. His father then moved to Greenville where he conducted a butcher shop. The boy attended the Greenville City Schools, but very early turned his thoughts to business; and business to C. D. Speegle has always been synonymous with lumber. Starting at the very bottom with the Greenville Manufacturing Company, he mastered every detail of the business and worked his way steadily up through his own efforts, to a position of trust and confidence.

Following this, Mr. Speegle was for two years employed by J. W. Cagle, another lumber man. Then came five years with the Gates Desk Factory, after which Mr. Speegle removed with his family to Spartanburg, where he became connected with the Rigby Company, remaining there five years.

Upon his return to Greenville, Mr. Speegle took over the Greenville Lumber Company, then a very small concern. During the 18 years that have elapsed since that time, this company has grown to be one of the largest and most successful in the city. The company not only handles lumber of all kinds, but a manufacturing plant is also operated, turning out quantities of doors, sash, mantles, and mill work of every description. In the rather extensive building program which Greenville—both publicly and privately—has been engaged in recently, the Greenville Lumber Company has played a most important part. Mr. Speegle, as President and principal owner of the business, should have most of the credit for its success.

Among the other business enterprises that claim Mr. Speegle's attention are the South Carolina Savings Bank, and the American Building & Loan Association; he holds the position of director in both of these organizations. He also belongs to the "Hoo-Hoo" Lumberman's Association and to the fraternal orders of Elks and Masons.

Mr. Speegle was married to Miss Ida Roberts; they have seven children, two boys and five girls. The eldest son, C. D. Speegle, Jr., is engaged in business with his father; the others are: Lillie (Mrs. Richard Osborne), Lou Ellen, Doris, Tempie, Ralph, and Linnie.

JOHN E. SMITH

The mountain region of our State has always loved men famed for daring and quick action; men who love freedom and delight in fighting for it. From stock of this sort comes JOHN E. SMITH, Chief of the Greenville City Police, who has unflinchingly followed the ideals of his fathers, and has never stepped aside from the path of duty, no matter how dangerous that path might be.

Born in Pickens County, August 20, 1879, he grew up on a farm and attended a rural school in the neighborhood. He was the son of N. K. Smith and Elizabeth Mary Singleton. His maternal grandfather, W. B. Singleton, was a well-known Baptist minister. W. L. Smith, his paternal grandfather, served in the 10th South Carolina Regiment throughout the entire duration of the War Between the States.

In 1898 there came another war, and 19-year-old John Smith promptly enlisted. He saw service in Cuba for over three years, after which he returned to Pickens. In 1902 he enlisted again. During the next two years he was stationed in the Philippine Islands, where skirmishes and engagements with the Insurgents were constantly taking place. During one of these, on a Christmas Eve, Smith was badly wounded by a shot in the chin.

Returning to Greenville, Mr. Smith served for a time as Deputy Sheriff at Brandon Mills and later, on October 6, 1911, joined the City Police Department. He remained a private in this force until April, 1918, when he was made Sergeant. It was while serving in this capacity that Sergeant Smith met and bested a gang of four yeggs who had blown up and robbed the safe of a wholesale grocery store in the city. In the face of a rain of bullets, the Sergeant pursued the fleeing culprits and returned their fire with such prompt certainty that they soon dropped their booty. Although the criminals escaped. tne loot was recovered and was found to amount to some $10,000 in cash, besides numerous valuable papers. The coolness and heroism displayed on this occasion have never failed Mr. Smith in the more responsible duties that have been his as Chief of Police, a position which he has occupied since October, 1921.

Mr. Smith is an active member of the Baptist Church and of the fraternal orders of Odd Fellows and Masons. In 1907 he was married to Miss Ida Henton; they have one son, John Hugh Smith.

C. D. SPEEGLE

JOHN E. SMITH

WILLIAM C. CLEVELAND

In the Golden Grove Section of Greenville County lived the family of Jeremiah and Florence (McKenzie) Cleveland. The forebears of this couple were all farmers and fighters. Jeremiah Cleveland fought for four years during the War Between the States, and two of his brothers, Vannoy and W. C. Cleveland, also took part in this war. It was for the latter of these that WILLIAM CHOICE CLEVELAND, born March 5, 1883, was named. The boy grew up in his father's home at Golden Grove, attending the public school in that community. Further education was obtained at Cokesbury School and at Wofford College, in the latter he was enrolled as a member of the class of 1905. He left this institution, however, in 1904, before receiving his degree.

Upon leaving, Mr. Cleveland went to Spartanburg County and accepted the position of paymaster with the Enoree Manufacturing Company. Leaving this company in 1905, he came to Greenville where he became associated with the Carolina Supply Company, remaining with them until February, 1908.

Mr. Cleveland at about this time interested himself in the banking affairs of Greenville, and was made President of the Fourth National Bank of the city. He held this position until this bank sold out to the First National Bank. He then entered the First National Bank as Vice-President, which office he continued to fill until 1923, at which time he retired from active business.

Throughout a business career filled with so many and such various activities, Mr. Cleveland has always found time to serve his city in any capacity in which he was needed. During the years 1908-'10, he was Councilman from Ward 4, and by this body was appointed Paving Commissioner for the City of Greenville. His services in this capacity were so markedly successful that a short time later he was made Commissioner of Public Works, a position which he has held for the past 15 years. Mr. Cleveland has been generous, not only with his time, but also with his material possessions. One of the most outstanding of the benefits conferred upon the city by this public-spirited gentleman is the park which bears his name. Realizing the need of Greenville for more park space, Mr. Cleveland donated to the city a tract of more than 100 acres of beautiful, wooded land, lying along the banks of Richland Creek and Reedy river. The development of this tract has given Greenville one of her very loveliest sylvan retreats.

Among other activities in which Mr. Cleveland's name occupies a prominent place are the Chamber of Commerce, of which he was at one time President, the Rotary Club, Masons, Shriners, and Knights of Pythias. He is a member of the Baptist Church, having affiliated himself with the Golden Grove Church during his early years.

In 1910, Mr. Cleveland was united in marriage to Miss Alice Burnett of Spartanburg. They have four children, Gertrude, Alice, Harriet, and William Choice, Jr.

A. A. BRISTOW

Among the many outstanding citizens of Greenville City, few, if any, have contributed more to its upbuilding during the last 35 years than A. A. BRISTOW. He was born in Bennettsville, South Carolina, on April 22, 1854, being the son of

Abner Nash Bristow and Ann Elizabeth Bristow. His parents and their ancestors had long lived in that section of South Carolina.

Mr. Bristow received his education in the schools of his home community, and as a young man entered the mercantile business as a clerk in an establishment of his home county of Marlborough, where he remained for a number of years, learning the business in all its details. Resigning this connection he accepted a position as traveling salesman for a large New York clothing house. For many years he covered the two Carolinas for this concern, but in 1891 gave up the position, moved to Greenville and with Jesse R. Smith organized the Smith & Bristow Clothing Company. For nearly 30 years this concern, located at the corner of Main and Washington Streets in the Beattie Building, represented the "last word" in men's clothing. In 1920 Mr. Bristow sold his interest in the business to his partner, Mr. Smith, and shortly thereafter retired from active business.

During the years of his business activity Mr. Bristow was interested in a number of business enterprises other than that to which he devoted the major portion of his time. From 1890 to 1910 Greenville was growing from a country town into a commercial city and in that growth Mr. Bristow was a prominent figure. At different times he was a director in the City National Bank, the Fourth National Bank and the Norwood National Bank, all financial institutions of note in the life of Greenville.

But Mr. Bristow did not confine his activities to business. He was deeply interested in all civic matters and took a leader's part in promoting them. He was one of the organizers of the old Greenville Board of Trade, out of which the present Greenville Chamber of Commerce grew, and its first president. He was instrumental in the organization of the company which built the Ottaray Hotel in 1908, and gave to Greenville her first modern commercial hotel. With William Goldsmith he secured the opening of a street connecting Pettigru Street with East North Street, thus giving the city Broadus Avenue, one of its most beautiful residential streets of today. He and Mr. Goldsmith were the first to build on Broadus Avenue and after 33 years Mr. Bristow still lives there. Mr. Goldsmith moved to another part of the city in 1929.

For 25 years Mr. Bristow served as a Deacon in the First Baptist Church of Greenville, and is still an active member of that organization despite his advancing years.

In 1885 he was married to Miss Annie Hudson, daughter of the late Judge Joshua Hudson, and they have three children: Joshua Hudson Bristow, Eunice Elizabeth (Mrs. W. C. Hearin) and Annie Hudson (Mrs. Richard E. Carey).

LAWRENCE PETER HOLLIS

LAWRENCE PETER HOLLIS, widely known welfare worker and educator, was born in Chester County, South Carolina, on the 29th day of November, 1883, being the son of Peter and Juliet (Gaston) Hollis. Both parents were members of prominent families, who had lived in Chester and Fairfield Counties since the days of the Revolution. His father was a farmer.

Mr. Hollis secured his early education in such schools as Chester County afforded, and then became a student at the South Carolina College, now University of South Carolina, from which he was graduated with an A.B. degree in 1905. Leaving college, he located in Greenville, where for 18 years he was engaged in welfare work for the Victor-Monaghan Company and other cotton mills about Greenville. Being one of the pioneers in this field of endeavor, he contributed largely toward making it the tremendous force for good which it occupies today among the textile employees of practically all Greenville County cotton mills.

In 1923 the Parker School District, embracing 11 cotton mill communities and a number of other residential sections about Greenville, was organized. Mr. Hollis was elected superintendent of all the schools within the district and this position he still holds. When the district was organized it contained ten grammar schools, but since then a modern high school building and five other grammar schools have been built, giving to the school system 16 schools. The Parker district is the wealthiest school district in the state of South Carolina and the enrollment of white children in it is the greatest of any school district in the State. The teachers employed number 218, and the pupils enrolled for the 1929-'30 session exceed 6,700. The organization of the district and its rapid progress have been largely due to the efforts of Mr. Hollis. Of him and his work the *Greenville News,* in its issue of September 29, 1929, said:

"Parker High School, established in the suburbs of Greenville in 1923, has just entered upon what promises to be the most successful session ever conducted from the standpoint of both enrollment and activities. Although total enrollment figures for the present term have not been formulated, they are expected to exceed those of last year, which were 840, which in turn showed almost 350 per cent over the enrollment of the first year of the school's existence.

"Mr. Hollis, who has been in charge of educational work in the Parker District since the opening of the high school and standardization of grammar schools, is prominent in state school activities, having been President of the State Teachers' Association in 1927-'28. Under his supervision at the local high school such practical features as manual training, home economics, mechanical drawing, carpentry, and textile courses have been added to the regular academic branch.

"Many clubs allowing students to participate in activities most interesting to the individual have been organized. Among them are, the High Y., Boy Scouts, Girl Reserves, press club, literary societies, dramatic club, expression club, declamation and debating societies, and music clubs. The Parker chorus and orchestra occupy a prominent place in the state musical work, a feature of which is the annual Parker thousand-voice chorus conducted by George Nilson."

Mr. Hollis is an active member of the Monaghan Methodist Church, being Superintendent of its Sunday School; he is a member of the Greenville Rotary Club and a Mason.

He was married to Miss Emma Clyde of Greenville, and they are the parents of four children: Mary Elizabeth, Louise, Juliet, and L. Peter, Jr.

CAPTAIN OSCAR KERN MAULDIN

Among the families who have played an important part in the business, social and economic life of Greenville, none is more generally respected than the Mauldins. Inseparably linked with the Piedmont Section of South Carolina, they have served long and ably in many capacities.

CAPT. OSCAR KERN MAULDIN, truly "a noble son of a noble race", was born in Greenville in 1875. He is the son of Governor W. L. Mauldin and Eliza Kern Mauldin. Capt. Mauldin's early education was obtained in the public schools of Greenville, after which he entered the Citadel and later attended Furman University. Believing that a practical training in legal practice was most valuable, he studied law in the office of Earle & Mooney, one of the most brilliant legal firms in the State at that time. After a few years' study, he was admitted to the bar in 1896. He immediately built up a large and influential clientele and has long been recognized as one of the leading attorneys of the Greenville bar.

In addition to his extensive legal business, Capt. Mauldin has always had a strong penchant for military activities. When very young he joined the Butler Guards and was one of its most enthusiastic supporters. At the outbreak of the Spanish-American War he was made captain of his company. The Guards were mustered into service May 4, 1898, and remained under the command of Capt. Mauldin until November 10, 1898. Shortly thereafter, they were mustered out and Capt. Mauldin returned to his legal practice. After several years he turned his attention to things political. Carrying out the precepts of his illustrious father, one of South Carolina's most able Lieutenant Governors, he was elected on his maiden venture, as a member of the General Assembly. With the same acumen and tenacity of purpose which had characterized his previous endeavors, he worked untiringly for Greenville County, until 1917, when he resigned his seat to do his bit for his country, then in the throes of the terrible World War. He joined the Officers' Training Corps and was sent to Fort Oglethorpe for training. His former experience stood him in good stead, and he was very soon commissioned as Captain and assigned to duty in the regular Army as Captain of Company H, 57th United States Infantry.

He sailed for France on August 3, 1918. On arriving there, he was immediately sent to the front, where he remained with his command for 50 consecutive days in the bloody San Mihiel or Toul section. While on duty there, he was badly gassed and invalided home, reaching Greenville on February 12, 1919. Shortly after, he was given his honorable discharge. Since that time he has practiced law, as the senior partner of the firm of Mauldin & Love.

Capt. Mauldin has been twice married, first to Miss Elizabeth Heidt of Charleston, now deceased, and second to Miss Grace McHardy Jones of Asheville, North Carolina. The second Mrs. Mauldin comes from a prominent North Carolina family of jurists and lawyers, being the daughter of Benson M. and Lily (Woodfin) Jones. Her maternal grandfather, Col. Nicholas W. Woodfin, was one of North Carolina's most prominent lawyers. Mrs. Mauldin is very active in Club work. Before her marriage she was regent of the Asheville Chapter, D. A. R., and since has been State Regent of South Carolina. Also she has served most capably as President of the

Woman's Bureau of the Greenville Chamber of Commerce and in many other positions of civic importance. She is a direct descendant of General Charles, and Major Joseph McDowell of Kings Mountain fame.

CHARLES OTIS ALLEN

Among those who have contributed greatly toward the building of Greenville is CHARLES OTIS ALLEN. He was born in Hendersonville, North Carolina, during the year 1855, being the son of J. H. and Harriett (Leach) Allen. His father was a native of Polk County, North Carolina, while his mother was born in Bridgewater, Massachusetts. In 1866 his parents moved from Hendersonville to Columbus, North Carolina, where his mother died in 1868. His father then moved to Spartanburg, South Carolina.

Mr. Allen secured his education in the schools of the various communities in which he lived as a boy, and having finished his education engaged in various lines of business until 1899, when he moved to Greenville and organized the firm of Pates & Allen. Business was commenced in a building located on East Washington Street, near the present Allen Building, which property was then owned by the firm. From its beginning till 1917, when it was dissolved, the firm of Pates & Allen was a large factor in the life of Greenville County. It dealt extensively in live stock, buggies, wagons and general farm supplies and operated feed and sales stables. Perhaps no other concern of like kind in upper South Carolina did so extensive a business for 30 years or more. Mr. Pates was a non-resident of Greenville and the business was conducted under the direct management of Mr. Allen. In 1917, Mr. Allen purchased the interest of Mr. Pates and organized the C. O. Allen Company, which deals in buggies, wagons, harness, automobile tires and general farm supplies on Brown Street in a building owned by Mr. Allen.

Being generally recognized as a man of unusual business ability, Mr. Allen has been much in demand in other than his own special line of endeavor. At one time he accepted the presidency of the American Bank of Greenville, which position he held for six years. For a number of years he was a Director of the Norwood National Bank and is now a Director of the South Carolina National Bank and Director of Dunean Mill.

Although his business demands have been great, Mr. Allen has found time to perform many public services. Among these may be mentioned active participation in the affairs of the Greenville Chamber of Commerce, of which he was one of the organizers, and is an ex-director, and a member of the Greenville City Council and a member of the State Highway Commission of South Carolina. In the last mentioned position he was extremely active, working untiringly for a state system of highways at the lowest possible cost.

His interest in good roads for this section has always been keen, standing among those first to agitate building good roads in upper South Carolina. He was an active supporter of the delegation which secured the passage of the Act allowing the sale of $1,000,000 bonds for road-building in Greenville County and thus secured the first top soil roads in South Carolina.

He has always been much interested in the development of youth and has been generous in his help to those striving for an education. The agitation which he started through the Chamber of Commerce for Greenville township to be organized into a school district with the High School situated in the city, finally resulted in the organization of the Parker District.

In 1928 Mr. Allen took charge of the Greenville Nursery Company with which he has been identified since its organization, 18 years ago, and which is now considered the largest nursery in South Carolina.

Always he has been one of the farmers' best friends, encouraging improved methods of farming and varied crop production; and now being no longer in active business he spends much of his time managing his farming interest.

The residence of Mr. Allen, located at the corner of Broadus Avenue and Pettigru Street, occupies the site of the old home of General Waddy Thompson, one of Greenville County's most illustrious sons.

In 1890, Mr. Allen was married to Miss Nannie Jefferies of Union County, and they are the parents of five children, viz: Charles Allen, deceased; Ramath Jefferies (Mrs. W. C. Humphreys), Virginia (Mrs. W. T. Potter), Elizabeth (Mrs. Allen Askins), and Walter H. Allen, whose wife is Effie Lloyd (Pegues) Allen.

CLIFF R. BRAMLETT

In Greenville County political interest centers around the office of Sheriff. To hold that office with any degree of satisfaction to the citizenship of the county one must exercise a high degree of diplomacy as well as efficiently exercise the duties of the office in an efficient manner. CLIFF R. BRAMLETT, Sheriff since 1928, is showing himself to be a man possessed of the necessary qualifications for that office.

Mr. Bramlett was born in the Walkers Cross Roads section of Greenville County on October 8, 1880, being a son of Captain George W. and Sarah Bramlett. His father, descended from an old and prominent Greenville County family, was captain of a cavalry troop during the War Between the States and after returning from that struggle became a prominent planter.

The public schools of his home community afforded the only educational advantages which Mr. Bramlett had, nevertheless he has always been a keen observer of men, and is possessed of a high degree of learning in the realm of human nature. Leaving school, he engaged in farming, at which he was successful; but in addition to his agricultural interests he was soon devoting much of his time to road-building. During the last 10 or 15 years he has built roads in almost every section of the State. An example of his ability in this work is seen in the North Main Street extension, which leads through the North-Gate Heights subdivision. During the World War he held the position of Superintendent of Road Construction at Camp Sevier, where much work of this nature was done by the Government.

In 1912 Mr. Bramlett was appointed Supervisor of Greenville County to fill out the unexpired term of the late J. P. Goodwin. His road-building experience stood him in good stead here, and he was able to fill that office with satisfaction to the people. He entered the law enforcement ranks of the county by becoming a Deputy Sheriff under Sheriff Sam D. Willis in 1925. Upon the death of Sheriff

Willis he was highly recommended for appointment for the unexpired term, but another was appointed. Upon the expiration of the appointee's term Mr. Bramlett became a candidate for the office against him and four others. The contest was relentlessly waged by all candidates, but Mr. Bramlett secured the election, since as a Deputy Sheriff he had convinced the people of his high qualifications. The Sheriff's office employs nine deputies to assist in law enforcement and Sheriff Bramlett shows himself well able to direct their activities. He still lives in his old home community and engages in cultivating a 200-acre farm, as well as fill the office of Sheriff.

Mr. Bramlett takes an active interest in the civic activities of the county. He is a member of the J. O. U. A. M., a Woodman of the World, and a Red Man.

He has been twice married, first to Ida May Bramlett, who died in 1906. Next he married Sunie A. Cox. To the first union were born three children, viz: Thelma, Jess and George, and to the second two, Evelyn and Marguerite.

BENJAMIN AUGUSTUS AND IDA (BATES) GREEN

Before that portion of the Cherokee lands now embraced within Greenville County was officially opened to settlers, a number of pioneers had established themselves there. Many of these later received grants to the land which they occupied. Among this latter number of early settlers was Isaac Green, who received original grants to 1700 acres of land in what is now Greenville County. Tradition credits him with being the owner of a mill near the present site of Greenville City before 1786, when Greenville County was given its name by legislative act.

Mr. A. S. Salley, secretary of the South Carolina Historical Commission, and one who is deeply versed in South Carolina history and tradition, gives it as his opinion that Greenville County was named for Isaac Green. There are those who do not agree with Mr. Salley, but they seem unable to establish any other source for the name. But whether or not Isaac Green passed his name on to his adopted county, he certainly was a prominent citizen of the early days. The public records substantiate this.

Isaac Green was a descendant of John Green, surgeon, who in 1635 emigrated from Salisburg, County Wilts, England, and settled in Warwick, Rhode Island. In 1741 Nathanael Green, Sr., and five brothers, descendants of John Green, bought a large tract of land in Coventry, Rhode Island. By 1768 more than a hundred families had settled in that vicinity and the community bore the name of "Greenville." Isaac, son of one of these six brothers, born in 1762, settled in Greenville County, South Carolina, and fought for the Patriot cause during the Revolution, although a very young man. In 1790 he married Phebe West, descendant of a brother of Lord De La Warr. To this union was born five sons. All these sons except Abraham left South Carolina when young, going to Texas, North Carolina and Georgia.

Abraham Green, son of Isaac, was born in Greenville County on May 10, 1802. He married Jane Bradley, who was born on October 10, 1843. Abraham Green died on June 11, 1884, but his widow, Jane (Bradley) Green, lived until September 19, 1913.

One of the sons of Abraham and Jane (Bradley) Green was BENJAMIN AUGUSTUS GREEN. He was born in Greenville County on October 7, 1866. After securing a common school education, and finishing at Dr. Patrick's Military Academy, he moved to Pickens County, South Carolina, and settled a few miles north of Easley in the Maynard School section. Here on December 25, 1888, he was married to Miss Ida Bates, daughter of Esley H. Bates, a member of the famous "Wallace House", and a leader of his day. The Green and Bates plantations adjoined, and upon the death of Mr. Bates were joined in the ownership of Mr. and Mrs. Green.

Although Benjamin Augustus Green died on March 15, 1902, when only 35 years of age, he was a striking example of the intelligent and successful farmer. He owned and cultivated a large plantation, and besides this owned and operated a large mercantile establishment, a cotton gin, a sawmill and a grist mill. He was much interested in the upbuilding of his community, and worked consistently toward that goal. The land upon which the Maynard school stands was donated by him.

Children born to Benjamin Augustus and Ida (Bates) Green were: Bates, Jennie, Kathleen, Mary, Nada and Christine. Bates moved to Canton, Georgia, where he died in 1919, being at that time the owner of one of the largest wholesale marble plants in that State. He married Miss Estelle Ellis and they were the parents of three children, viz: Ida, Bates and William. Jennie married W. Harry Cary, and they now reside in Columbia, South Carolina. Kathleen is now Mrs. Charles S. Glover of Charleston, South Carolina, and has one daughter, Beverley Glover. Nada is the wife of John C. Carey, and she and her husband and two children, John and Pete Carey, reside at Pickens, South Carolina. Mary and Christine are unmarried and reside with their mother at 302 Pettigru Street, Greenville City.

Mrs. Ida Bates Green is a woman of striking personality, as well as business ability. Left a widow at 31 years of age with six small children, five of whom were girls, she successfully operated the farm and other interests of her late husband and provided a college education for all of her children. In 1910 she moved to Greenville where she erected the beautiful home at 302 Pettigru Street, from which she still operates her plantation.

Although there is a large number of the Green name residing in Greenville County, and many of these are descended from early settlers of the county, none of them trace their ancestry to Isaac Green except the children of Abraham.

Originally the name was spelled "Greene", but of late years the final "e" has been dropped.

T. OREGON LAWTON

It is quite an accomplishment for a life insurance company to lead all competitors in net gain of insurance in force during the fourth year of its existence. Yet this is what the Pioneer Life Insurance Company of Greenville did in 1928 as to all business written in the State of South Carolina of the class it writes. And of this company T. OREGON LAWTON, subject of this sketch, is President.

Mr. Lawton is a member of an old and prominent family (one of the most distinguished members being General Alexander R. Lawton, a celebrated soldier, lawyer and statesman of the State of Georgia). He is the son of Thomas O. Lawton, a veteran of the War Between the States, and Mary Willingham Lawton, and was born in what is now Allendale County on September 9, 1876. Soon after his birth, the Lawton family moved to a large plantation in Hampton County, where young

Lawton grew to manhood, doing the usual work of a country boy and attending the neighborhood schools, which were poor indeed at that time. Later he became a student at Furman University, and afterward entered Erskine College, from which he was graduated with the degree of A.B. in 1897.

Upon leaving college, Mr. Lawton taught school for two years, and then entered the lumber business with his brother, F. A. Lawton. In 1910, however, he retired from the lumber business to become active head of the Southeastern Life Insurance Company of Greenville, in which he had acquired a substantial interest. Till 1924 he directed the affairs of this company, which had by then become one of the leading life insurance companies of the whole South. But believing that the South should have a strong mutual life company, Mr. Lawton sold his interest in the Southeastern and organized the Pioneer Life Insurance Company with the understanding that so soon as its business would justify, all stock should be retired and the company conducted on a mutual basis. He became President of this new company and now after five years it is well on its way to becoming the mutual it was intended for.

Mr. Lawton believes firmly in the future of his city, county and state; and is one who thinks that the agricultural development of the State does not depend upon the culture of cotton, corn, and the usual truck crops. For years he has owned a large pecan grove, the largest in the state. This is in Hampton County.

In the religious and civic affairs of his home city, Mr. Lawton has always taken a leading part. He is a Deacon in the Pendleton Street Baptist Church, and for many years has been one of the most outstanding members of his denomination.

As a writer, Mr. Lawton has gained an enviable reputation for the simplicity and clarity of his work, which is intended primarily for children. One of his books, "Jockey and Other Stories", has gone into three editions of over 10,000 copies.

In 1899 Mr. Lawton married Miss Bessie Miller of Elkton, Virginia, and they have four children, viz: Samuel Miller Lawton, Mrs. Mary (Lawton) Poteat, Miss Frances Elizabeth Lawton, and Thomas Maxwell Lawton. The family home is on Pendleton Street in the City of Greenville.

LEWIS WARDLAW PARKER

The changing times in the cotton mill industry of the South are well illustrated in the uplift work accomplished by the late LEWIS WARDLAW PARKER, lawyer and manufacturer of Greenville. As late as 25 years ago many mills were paying starvation wages to employees whom they worked long hours, penned together like so many cattle in shacks which passed for living quarters. But in an age of reform it was inevitable that this barbaric system should be outlawed, and one of the first men to face the situation with voluntary humanitarian measures was Mr. Parker, and it is to a considerable extent due to him and his efforts that Southern textile workers of today are well fed, well clothed, well housed, and happy.

Mr. Parker was born July 11, 1865, at Abbeville, S. C., of distinguished ancestry. His father, William H. Parker, was a lawyer, banker and soldier of the Confederacy; his mother was a daughter of David L. Wardlaw, a Justice of the Supreme Court. His paternal grandfather, Thomas Parker, a native of Charleston and a lawyer, married Ellen Legare Frost, and moved to Abbeville about 1825.

His great-grandfather, Thomas Parker, United States District Attorney of Charleston, married Mary Drayton, daughter of William Henry Drayton, famous in the Colonial and Revoluntionay history of South Carolina.

As one of a large family, and born during Reconstruction days, Mr. Parker experienced difficulty in obtaining an education. Until he was 15 he attended the public schools of Abbeville and then entered a mercantile establishment as clerk, where he remained for two years. Then he became a student at the South Carolina College from which he was graduated with an A.B. degree in 1885. Later he completed a law course at the same institution and after two years of teaching entered upon the practice of his profession at Greenville.

Soon after beginning the practice of law it became evident that Mr. Parker would become successful in his chosen field. Early he developed a clientele among the cotton manufacturing corporations which were then just beginning to enter the Southern field on an extensive scale. At different times he was in partnership with Joseph A. McCullough and H. J. Haynsworth. During this time, as the opportunity presented itself, he invested in the cotton mills of the section. In 1897 one of the cotton mills in which he had invested, and for which he was counsel, became financially involved, and he was requested by Northern stockholders to take charge and straighten out the tangle. And so well did he acquit himself in this duty that he soon decided to give up his law practice and devote himself entirely to the cotton mill business.

The first mill to be taken in charge by Mr. Parker was the Victor Manufacturing Company of Greer. He next became one of the organizers of the Monaghan Mill of Greenville. Later the "Whaley group" of mills was reorganized and Mr. Parker became President and Treasurer of the consolidated company, which included the Olympia Cotton Mills, the Richland Cotton Mills, the Granby Cotton Mills, and the Capital City Mills, all of Columbia, and the Appalache Mills of Greer, a combination representing a capital of $5,000,000 and 340,000 spindles. Later these mills, together with the Victor Manufacturing Company, the Monaghan Mills, and others, were included in the gigantic merger composing the Parker Cotton Mills Company, of which Mr. Parker became President and Treasurer. The new concern was backed by millions of dollars and operated more than a million spindles. Mr. Parker now stood in the forefront of South Carolina manufacturers, controlling more spindles than any individual in the business.

Mr. Parker, as early as 1898, employed two workers of the Young Men's Christian Association to take charge of the welfare work among the mill workers. And he was one of the first mill executives to maintain parks and playgrounds on the mill properties, and to introduce the community center with its gymnasium, swimming pool, shower bath, library, reading and rest rooms and other club features. His gifts to civic and charitable movements were large, as matters pertaining to the public good were dear to him. In religious affairs he was a vestryman in Christ Episcopal Church. He held membership in many clubs, trade organizations and legal societies.

But on April 11, 1916, at the early age of fifty, Mr. Parker died, leaving the

tremendous enterprises which he had built up to be continued by those whom he had trained in the work.

On June 6, 1893, Mr. Parker married Miss Margaret Smith, daughter of A. Austin and Betty (Harrison) Smith of Richmond, Virginia, and their children number four: Mrs. Lucia Parker Patterson, Austin Smith Parker, Mrs. Margaret Norvell and Lewis Wardlaw Parker II.

GEORGE W. SIRRINE

Loving all children and being generally loved by them marks a man as possessed of a kindly heart and a tender, sympathetic soul. Such a person was GEORGE W. SIRRINE, who died on December 26, 1927, while Chairman of the Board of Trustees of the Greenville City Schools.

Mr. Sirrine was born in Danbury, Connecticut, on the 20th day of December, 1847, being the son of William Sirrine and Emma Roberts. When a child he moved to Americus, Georgia, where he went to school. Later he engaged in the manufacture of buggies and wagons with his father till 1874, except for the years spent in the War Between the States.

Mr. Sirrine entered the Confederate Army at the age of 16 and served during the last year of the war as a member of Harvey's Scouts, which was a mounted unit attached to Jackson's Cavalry Division, Army of Tennessee. In the Georgia campaign it operated chiefly in the rear and on the flanks of Sherman's army. General Sherman compared it to a "nest of yellow jackets continually buzzing about my train and stinging severely when I attempted to drive them away." General Stephen D. Lee said of this company of daring horsemen: "They were everywhere conspicuous for activity, enterprise, persistence and intrepidity." They did a great deal of scouting service; they were armed with repeating rifles and each man carried two six-shot revolvers. The captain of this organization, and for whom it was named, was Addison Harvey of Canton, Mississippi, where the company was organized.

In 1875 he went to Charlotte, North Carolina, where he was in the carriage and wagon business for little more than a year; and then in January of 1876 he moved to Greenville, where he resided for the remainder of his long and useful life. For 35 years after coming to Greenville, he was engaged in the carriage and wagon business, being connected with the old and widely known firm of Gower and Cox, later Gower, Cox & Markley, and within comparatively recent years, the Markley Manufacturing Company. About 1910 he retired from this business and spent the remaining days of his life in various private activities, but mainly in rendering public services to his city.

In 1914 Mr. Sirrine became a Trustee of the Greenville City Schools and upon the death of P. T. Hayne, succeeded to the Chairmanship of the Board, which position he held as long as he lived. He possessed the happy faculty of being able to endear himself in the hearts of all who knew him and especially so as to the youth. Mr. Sirrine lived to be 80 years of age, yet he never grew old; and in his passing the children of Greenville felt more keenly than is seldom seen that they had lost a real friend.

Aside from his connections with the schools, Mr. Sirrine was always deeply interested in the public good and took an active part in all undertakings looking to the betterment of his community.

He was the founder of the first public free library in Greenville. About 1895 he and Mrs. Sirrine established a library at their residence on West McBee Avenue, and Mrs. Sirrine gave her services as librarian. All the books were kept there until the death of Mrs. A. Viola Neblet, when they were transferred to her residence, which is now the High School Library.

Mr. Sirrine was married to Miss Sarah Rylander of Americus, Georgia, in 1867, and she died in 1925. They had two sons, both of whom are still living, being among the most prominent citizens of Greenville today. William G. Sirrine, the elder, is an attorney of more than usual ability, while J. E. Sirrine is head of one of the largest mill architectural concerns in the South.

THOMAS H. POPE

THOMAS H. POPE, son of the Reverend Thomas H. Pope and Mary Charles (Gary) Pope, was born in Greenwood, South Carolina, on March 25, 1872. The Popes came to South Carolina from Virginia and settled in Newberry County. Judge Thomas H. Pope, grandfather of the subject of this sketch, was an eminent lawyer and jurist, and a brother-in-law of Judge John Belton O'Neall. He was associated with Judge O'Neall both in the practice of law and the building of the Greenville and Columbia railroad. The Reverend Thomas H. Pope, son of Judge Pope, was a Baptist minister of considerable prominence. Mary C. Gary, wife of Reverend Pope and mother of Thomas H. Pope, of whom this is being written, was a daughter of the late Doctor Charles H. Gary of Newberry, and a relative of the late Chief Justice Eugene B. Gary.

The subject of this sketch came to Greenville with his parents at the age of seven years and here received his education in the public schools, at the Patrick Military Academy and in Furman University. Following his school days he secured employment with Ferguson & Miller, who conducted a large mercantile business in Greenville. Here he remained for a number of years, and then became a traveling salesman. While pursuing this line of work he formed attachments which have followed him through life. He has always been deeply interested in the problems of the traveling man and is widely known because of his activities in their organizations. For many years he was State Secretary of the T. P. A., and is now a member of the State Council for the U. C. T. Both of these organizations have large memberships in Greenville.

In 1917 Mr. Pope was appointed postmaster at Greenville, and this position he held to the entire satisfaction of the patrons of the office until 1922. During this period Camp Sevier was maintained in the suburbs of Greenville and the efficient service rendered by the Greenville post office won high praise for Mr. Pope from the soldiers stationed there.

Following his term as postmaster, Mr. Pope was connected with the Carolina Baking Company as local manager for a time, and then in 1925 purchased a controlling interest in the Greenville Baking Company and became President and Treasurer of the company. This connection he still holds.

Mr. Pope is very active in civic affairs; he is a Baptist, a Mason and a charter member of the Kiwanis Club of Greenville.

He was married to Miss Kate Miller of Greenville, and they have six children, viz: Louise (Mrs. W. D. Reece), Thomas H., Jr., Mary C. (Mrs. Raymond Maxwell), Dorothy, J. Miller, and Harriett. The family home is in Alta Vista, Greenville, S. C.

FRANK G. HAMBLEN

FRANK G. HAMBLEN, business man of recognized ability and President of the Greenville Chamber of Commerce, was born in Polk County, Missouri, on March 4, 1886. He is the son of Nathan Henry and Mary Alice (Munson) Hamblen. His father was a native of Kentucky, but moved to Missouri in 1870, being a pioneer settler of Polk County.

Mr. Hamblen received his education in the public schools of his native state, and in 1907 entered the employ of the Frisco railway at Springfield, Missouri. His first work was "pushing a truck", but he advanced rapidly, and in 1909, when he severed his connection with that company, he held a responsible position. He went to Rogers, Arkansas, as agent for the Kansas City & Memphis Railroad. Here he rose to the position of Traffic Manager and Assistant General Manager of that system, with headquarters in Rogers and Fayetteville, Arkansas. In this capacity he served until 1917 when he became associated with the American Red Cross, in charge of traffic for the Central Division, composed of the States of Illinois, Iowa, Nebraska, Wisconsin and Michigan. His headquarters for this work were Chicago.

In 1920 Mr. Hamblen, having completed his work with the American Red Cross, came to Greenville associated with the Saluda Land & Lumber Company. This concern has large holdings of timber in the upper section of South Carolina and owns the Greenville & Northern Railway. Mr. Hamblen is now General Manager of the Saluda Land & Lumber Company and Vice President, Secretary and General Manager of the railroad. Under his leadership the railroad has been much improved and converted into a commercial, industrial line. And with the improved transportation facilities thus afforded, upper Greenville County (somewhat backward in this respect) is fast taking a commanding position as an industrial section. Within the last three years large textile plants have begun operation at both Slater and Travelers Rest.

Mr. Hamblen is very active in the civic affairs of Greenville. He is now President of the Greenville Chamber of Commerce, a Past President of the Civitan Club. Both of these organizations have made much progress under his leadership. He is also a Mason and a Deacon in the First Baptist Church.

He was married to Miss Adabelle Crow, of Missouri, in 1909, and they have one child, Frances. The family home is at No. 13 Belmont Avenue in the City of Greenville.

COLUMBUS BENJAMIN MARTIN

Adjoining counties have contributed many of the men and women who are today making the history of Greenville County. But of these none have surpassed Laurens, either in the number or character of those whom she has sent. For in all the leading professions and businesses may be found one or more of those at, or near, the top who was born in Laurens County. And among these is COLUMBUS BENJAMIN MARTIN.

Mr. Martin was born in Youngs Township, Laurens County, S. C., on November 14, 1876. His father was F. B. Martin who volunteered for service in the Confederate army at 16 years of age and served until the close of the war in the 27th South Carolina Volunteers, Hagood's Brigade; and his mother was Martha (Wallace) Martin. Both parents were lifelong residents of Laurens County. As a boy, Mr. Martin attended the public schools located in the community of his father's plantation, and later became a student at Furman University from which he was graduated in 1899 with an A.B. degree. Then after an interval of four years spent in teaching, he entered Cornell University, from which he was graduated with the degree of M.A. in 1905.

After graduating from Furman, Mr. Martin taught in the Hendersonville, N. C., public schools, and then for three years he was with the Furman University Fitting Schools, the last two years of which as Headmaster. Then after a session in Cornell he returned to Furman University, this time as professor of Latin in the college proper, where he remained till 1917, when he resigned to enter business. Since then he has been engaged in the real estate and insurance business with the addition of mortgage loans, since 1927.

But Mr. Martin has not devoted his entire attention by any means, to his personal affairs, extensive though they have been, for in his busy life he has found time to perform many acts of public service, and, too, almost entirely in positions which carry no remuneration except the satisfaction derived from a task well done. In 1914, while still a professor in Furman University, he was elected an Alderman for the City of Greenville, which office he held for four years, being at the same time Mayor pro tem. Later he was appointed to membership on the Greenville County Cross-Country Road Commission, and became Chairman of that body. When the work for which this Commission had been created was completed, he became, again by appointment, a member of the Greenville County Road Surfacing Commission, which position he now holds. His appointment upon the second commission came from the same source as did the first and was due entirely to the efficient manner in which he did his work on the first.

For many years Mr. Martin has been deeply interested in the work of the Greenville Chamber of Commerce, of which organization he has been Vice-President and many times a Director. He is a charter member and past President of the Civitan Club, a member of the J. O. U. A. M., belongs to the Quaternion Club (representing scholarship in Furman University), and is a member of the Kappa Alpha College fraternity. In church affiliation, Mr. Martin is a Baptist, having been for many years a member of the First Baptist Church.

In 1908, Mr. Martin was married to Miss Willie Gray Harris of Laurens County and they have four children: Willie Gray, Louisa Harris, Columbus Benjamin, Jr., and Martha Wallace. The family home is on Crescent Avenue, in the City of Greenville.

Mrs. Martin is not unlike her husband in her keen interest in public affairs. She is now serving her second term as President of the Woman's Bureau of the Greenville Chamber of Commerce, and it was principally through her efforts that the Piedmont Historical Society (largely a Greenville organization) was formed.

W. FRANK GRESHAM

W. FRANK GRESHAM, prominent merchant of Simpsonville, was born at Walkersville, Greenville County, on September 19, 1873, being the son of W. P. and Carrie Gresham. Both his parents were natives of Greenville County, and moved to Simpsonville from Walkersville while that town was still nothing more than a country community. W. P. Gresham was long a merchant at Simpsonville where he won distinction, not only as a business man, but as a progressive and outstanding citizen as well.

The education of Mr. Gresham (subject of this sketch) was had in the public schools of Simpsonville, with a business course in Augusta, Georgia, later. Having finished his education, he became assistant Postmaster at Simpsonville, which position he resigned to become assistant agent of the Charleston & Western Carolina Railway. Leaving the railroad to better his position, he became bookkeeper for the Simpsonville Oil Mill, where he remained till offered a better position, by the oil mill at Woodruff. He remained with the Woodruff concern till 1901 when he accepted a position as bookkeeper for the Mahon-Arnold Company (now Meyers-Arnold Company) of Greenville City where he remained for five years.

In 1906 Mr. Gresham resigned his position with the Mahon-Arnold Company and assisted in the organization of a new business, to be known as Buchanan, Lindsay and Gresham, of which he was one of the partners. For four years he remained with this firm and then, selling his interest, returned to his old home at Simpsonville, where he entered the general mercantile business. Since that time he has continuously devoted himself to merchandising and farming at Simpsonville, where he resides.

Mr. Gresham enters actively into the life of his home town and community, always striving to better civic conditions. For eight years he served as magistrate for Austin township, and is now a member of the Board of Trustees of the Simpsonville schools. He is a director of the Farmers Bank of Simpsonville, a Deacon in the First Baptist Church of Simpsonville and a member of the Woodmen of the World.

Mr. Gresham's wife is the former Miss Bright Lanford of Woodruff, S. C. They have four children: Metz, Sarah, Bright and Helen. Metz has won distinction in college athletics, being center on the Clemson College football team of 1928-1929.

A. D. FRYE

The coming of the Piedmont & Northern Railway (electric) brought to Greenville a number of her most prominent and progressive citizens. Among these is A. D. FRYE, Superintendent of motive power for the entire system of that railroad.

Mr. Frye was born in Lincoln County, Ohio, in 1880. His early education was obtained in the public schools of his home community. Later he entered the Ohio

State University, where he specialized in electrical engineering, and was graduated with a B.S. degree. Leaving college, he accepted employment with the Westinghouse Electric Company, where he remained doing construction work in various parts of the country and test work at the factory till 1912, when he was sent to South Carolina to electrify the Piedmont & Northern lines.

Having finished the work for which he came to South Carolina, Mr. Frye left the employ of the Westinghouse company to accept the superintendency of motive power for the new railroad company, with headquarters in Greenville. That position he still holds. The Piedmont & Northern owns and operates 125 miles of electric railway through the highly industrial Piedmont sections of North Carolina and South Carolina and at this time (March, 1930) is constructing additional trackage of about the same number of miles. When this new construction is completed the railroad will form part of a great "trunk line" system extending from eastern Ohio coal fields to Florida. The principal "shops" of the company are now, as they have always been, located in Greenville with Mr. Frye in authority. Here, about 125 workmen are employed.

Mr. Frye takes an active part in the civic life of Greenville. He is a member of the Civitan Club, and was at one time its Vice-President. He is also a Mason and Shriner, being a member of the Shrine Patrol.

His wife is the former Miss Bessie Eurech. They have one child, Sarah Jane, who is now a third year pupil in the Greenville High School.

DECATUR LEE BRAMLETT

DECATUR LEE BRAMLETT was born near Simpsonville, in Greenville County, South Carolina, on December 16, 1872, being the son of Allen Turner Bramlett and Elizabeth (Mayfield) Bramlett. His father was a farmer and wagon maker, and during the early days of the War Between the States was engaged in building wagons for the Confederate Army. However, when his oldest son went away to the war among the 16-year-old recruits, he followed, to remain in the service till the close of the war.

The subject of this sketch attended the Simpsonville public schools till he was 18 years of age, when he was able to secure a teachers' second grade certificate. For the next five years he alternately taught in the rural schools about his home community and attended the Simpsonville School. At 23 he entered Furman University at Greenville from which he was graduated with an A.B. degree in 1900.

The mother of Mr. Bramlett died when he was but seven, and at 13 he was left an orphan through the death of his father. His parents left him with no money, and although his half brother, John L. Smith of Simpsonville, furnished him a home, it was necessary for him to earn his own education. This he did by teaching, securing a one-year scholarship at Furman, and giving instructions in Algebra during his Senior year at college.

Following his graduation from college, Mr. Bramlett became a teacher and followed that vocation for 14 years—four years as principal of the Simpsonville High School, two years as Superintendent of the Kershaw High School, one year as principal of the Healing Spring High School (Barnwell County), five years as principal of the Greenville City High School (then Central High School), and two years as Superintendent of the Seneca High School. Leaving Seneca in 1914, he returned to his old home at Simpsonville and became one of the organizers of the Farmers Bank, of which institution he became Cashier and executive head. In 1920 he was elected President of the bank and still holds that position.

Mr. Bramlett is a Baptist and has always taken a prominent part in the various activities of that denomination. Because of his interest in, and untiring work for the advancement of his church he has been chosen to lead in many of its undertakings. For two years (1910-'12) he was Superintendent of the Sunday School at the Pendleton Street Baptist Church of Greenville; from 1922 to 1928 he was Superintendent of the Sunday School of the First Baptist Church of Simpsonville; during four successive years (1923-'27) he was Moderator of the Greenville Baptist Association; he is now a member of the General Board of the South Carolina State Baptist Convention, and was recently selected for membership on the Executive Committee of that body, but asked to be relieved of that honor. At present he is Clerk of the Greenville Baptist Association, having succeeded the late D. Townsend Smith in 1929.

Among other positions of honor and trust held by Mr. Bramlett are: membership on the Greenville County Board of Education from 1901 to 1904; a trustee of the Simpsonville High School for ten years (1915 to '25); a member of the Board of Trustees of the Greenville County Tubercular Hospital.

In 1905 Mr. Bramlett was married to Miss Carrie Irene Gresham, daughter of the late Capt. W. P. Gresham of Simpsonville, and they have four children: Carolyn Elizabeth, graduated from the Greenville Woman's College in 1929; Frances Cornelia, now a Junior at G. W. C.; D. L., Jr., a pupil in the ninth grade of the Simpsonville High School, and Martha Alberta, a fourth grade pupil in the Simpsonville School.

Mr. Bramlett is a member of the Advisory Board of the History of Greenville County.

FRANK HARRISON CUNNINGHAM

From the neighboring county of Anderson, Greenville has acquired many of her prominent and substantial citizens. Of this number none has held a higher place in the esteem and affection of his fellow townsmen than has FRANK HARRISON CUNNINGHAM, the subject of this sketch.

Mr. Cunningham was born in Anderson, South Carolina, on the 13th day of March, 1880, being the son of Joseph Gilbert and Sarah Harrison Cunningham, and the grandson of Colonel Francis Eugene Harrison. The father was for many years one of the substantial merchants of Anderson, and the sturdy characteristics of his Scotch-Irish ancestry he passed on to his son.

Frank H. Cunningham received his early education in the city schools of Anderson. After finishing there he attended Clemson College where he was graduated in 1903.

Immediately following the completion of his college course he went to New England and worked for a period of two years, returning to Anderson where he practiced his chosen profession—Architecture—with marked success till 1908, when he came to Greenville and formed a partnership with his brother, J. G. Cunningham. The firm has held an enviable position, both among members of the architectural fraternity and the business men of the city since its formation. Many important public buildings are numbered among the achievements of these builders. The beautiful Trinity Lutheran Church located on North Main Street and the Science Hall of Converse College, Spartanburg, South Carolina, are striking examples of their beauty and dignity of construction, both of these being designed by the late F. H. Cunningham, the senior member of the firm.

School buildings have held a large place in the field of labor of these brothers. In addition to the local schools they have planned and supervised the construction of numerous others throughout the State. Private dwellings by the score have been built by them. The Imperial Hotel Building, the largest hotel in the city of Greenville, is a product of F. H. and J. G. Cunningham, which they not only designed, but assisted financially at a time when the continued progress of the city demanded a modern hotel.

In 1910 Mr. Cunningham married Miss Eoline Ligon, daughter of the late H. A. Ligon, prominent textile executive of Spartanburg. To this union were born three children: Frank H., Jr., Eoline, and Sarah.

In the death of Frank Cunningham on November 26, 1928, Greenville has sustained a distinct loss. He was a man of sterling character and artistic temperament; generous, unselfish, and ever loyal to his friends. Throughout his life Mr. Cunningham was a loyal and consistent church member, being, at the time of his death, a member of Christ Episcopal Church.

WILLIAM NOLLEY CRUIKSHANK

When WILLIAM NOLLEY CRUIKSHANK died on December 31, 1929, Greenville County lost one of the most faithful and efficient public servants she has had the good fortune to number among her office-holders during recent years.

Mr. Cruikshank was born in Atlanta, Georgia, on the 29th day of April, 1882, being the son of William Montgomery and Annie (Gouldsmith) Cruikshank. At the age of one year he moved with his parents to Greenville, where he spent the balance of his life. His education was secured in the public schools of Greenville and at the Presbyterian College of South Carolina.

Having finished his education, Mr. Cruikshank entered the grocery business as a clerk. From this he became the owner of a grocery store. Later he was engaged in the wholesale and retail drygoods business. Leaving the mercantile business, he became a public accountant, and for a number of years he followed this line of work. In 1915 he became Supervising Auditor of Greenville County, and so well did he perform the varied and difficult duties of this office that he was reappointed each four years, till at the time of his death he was serving his fourth term.

In 1915 a law was enacted changing the entire system of government in Greenville County. One of its provisions was the creation of the office of Supervising Auditor. The duties of this official were to audit the books and accounts of all other county officials, furnish expert advice as to the systems of accounting in each office, see that all claims presented were in accord with the law, and approve warrants

WILLIAM NOLLEY CRUIKSHANK

FRANK HARRISON CUNNINGHAM

drawn for their payment when found correct and proper, generally exercise supervision over all the financial affairs of the county, and report quarterly to the Grand Jury and annually to the County Delegation. A difficult task without doubt! But a man thoroughly competent to do all this and more was found in W. N. Cruikshank, and he secured the appointment for a term of four years.

When Mr. Cruiskshank assumed office, the county was torn asunder by bitter political factionalism. Strife and discord held sway among the public officials. Cooperation among the differing factions was unthinkable. The business of the county was as nothing compared to that of "standing by our friends." But the office of Supervising Auditor could know no factions. It must deal with each branch of the county's affairs, and come into direct contact with every official. Few men could have performed the duties of such an office with any degree of satisfaction. But 14 years of continuous service speak more clearly than words as to how Mr. Cruikshank handled this difficult situation.

Under the directing hand of Mr. Cruikshank the financial affairs were put into excellent shape and kept there. Year after year he was highly commended by Greenville County Grand Juries for the excellent manner in which he performed the duties of his office. And in 1929, only a few months before his death, an auditing firm which had just completed a thorough audit of the financial affairs of the county said of him: "Your Supervising Auditor is, in our opinion, a gentleman of character and integrity, placed in a position with specified duties well-nigh impossible of performance. The supervision of officers elected by popular vote, who, as a consequence, feel that they are responsible to the voters only, is a difficult task."

With the passing of Mr. Cruikshank the office of Supervising Auditor has been abolished and another with less trying duties created. No doubt it was generally conceded by the Legislators of the county that no other could be found to fill the shoes of this unusual man. So it comes about that William Nolley Cruikshank will for all time bear the distinction of being the only person to fill the office of Supervising Auditor of Greenville County.

Mr. Cruikshank was a member of the First Presbyterian Church, the Greenville Country Club, the Cotillion Club, and a Mason.

He was married to Miss Genevieve Raynor of North Carolina, and they have one son, William Nolley, Jr. His widow and son survive him.

JOHN M. CHARLOTTE

One of Greenville's premier sportsmen who occupies a prominent place in the social and civic life of his community is JOHN M. CHARLOTTE. Born in Beaufort, North Carolina, on September 25, 1872, he is the son of Captain Geo. W. and Margaret W. (Manson) Charlotte. Captain Manson, his maternal grandfather, held a commission during the War of 1812, signed by President James Madison. His father, Captain Charlotte, served throughout the War Between the States in the Army of Northern Virginia.

Mr. Charlotte received his education in the public schools of Newbern, North Carolina, and the Newbern Academy. Leaving school, he took up newspaper work with his father, who owned and published three papers in and near Newbern. In

1900 he left Newbern and came to Greenville, where he started *The Daily Herald,* an afternoon paper. This paper was later sold and became *The Daily Piedmont.* Mr. Charlotte was Managing Editor and Editorial writer for the *Greenville News* and *Daily Piedmont* until 1914 when he severed this connection to become Greenville representative for the *Atlanta Journal,* the *Columbia State,* and the *Washington Post.* During the years 1908 and 1909 he conducted a campaign for stock-raising and dairying through the columns of his Greenville papers, and much was accomplished. Since then there has been an insistent cry for diversification among the farmers of the county, and although there is still much to be done in that field, there are today many successful dairymen about the county.

In addition to his newspaper work, Mr. Charlotte has always been much interested in sports, particularly golf, and is a regular contributor for various golf periodicals over the country.

For several years he has devoted his entire time to the duties of secretary and treasurer of the Greenville Country Club. The club has made rapid strides under his management and is the most popular recreational place about the city. Greenville's golf course ranks high in the esteem of golfers, both local and visiting, and has been the scene of many animated tournaments and professional matches.

Mr. Charlotte is a member of the Methodist Church, the Chamber of Commerce, and the Rotary Club, and takes an active interest in the civic and social life of the city.

He was married in 1905 to Miss Fredericka Cushman, the daughter of Captain F. B. Cushman. The Cushman family originally lived in Georgetown, but moved to Greenville many years ago. Mr. and Mrs. Charlotte are the parents of an attractive and interesting family of five children: Katherine (Mrs. Rustin), John M., Jr., Fred B., Mary B., and David.

J. C. CUNNINGHAM

J. C. CUNNINGHAM was born near Greer, in Spartanburg County, on October 4, 1876, son of A. C. and Mellisa Gibson Cunningham. His parents were both natives of the state and his father was a pioneer merchant of Greer. His mother was the daughter of Samuel Gibson, an old-time Baptist preacher, who emigrated from England many years ago to Greenville County, where he organized a number of the Baptist Churches in the county.

Mr. Cunningham was raised on his father's farm and received a limited education in the country schools near Greer. From the time he was 18 years old he has engaged in the building and contracting business and has built during the last 25 years over half of all the buildings erected during this period in Greer, and in addition has done a considerable amount of business outside of that city.

Mr. Cunningham has always taken an interest in public affairs and is now and has been for the past eight years Chairman of the Commission of Public Works of the city of Greer. He is a Director of the Greer Bank and Trust Company and belongs to the Civitan Club and is a member of the Baptist Church and a Mason and Shriner.

He was married at Greer to Lillie Burnett, who is also a native of that town. Three children have been born to this union: Lee Cunningham, an architect in Birmingham, Alabama; Ruth (Mrs. J. S. Pagett), and Nelle Cunningham.

DR. THOMAS BROCKMAN

DOCTOR THOMAS BROCKMAN

A benefactor to suffering mankind, and as such holding a large place in the hearts of his ever-growing number of patients, is DR. THOMAS BROCKMAN of Greer, South Carolina. His parents, James Hiram and Frances (Hoy) Brockman, were prominent citizens of the Reidville section of Spartanburg County. His father's people came originally from Virginia, while his mother belonged to the Dean family of Spartanburg County. She was the daughter of Major William Hoy of Reidville, South Carolina, who was for many years correspondent for *The Carolina Spartan,* weekly newspaper of that day. For many years his father has owned and operated a farm in the Reidville section, and there on October 11, 1881, Thomas Brockman was born.

Doctor Brockman's education was started in the village of Reidville. After finishing the work there, he entered Furman University at Greenville where he remained one session. Deciding that medicine should be his vocation in life, in the year of 1905 he entered the Atlanta School of Medicine, now Emory University, where he remained one year. Having received a scholarship by appointment of Governor Heyward, the following year found him enrolled as a student in the South Carolina Medical College at Charleston, South Carolina. From this famous old school he was graduated as one of the honor men with the degree of M.D. in 1909. Feeling, however, that he wished more study, he went to New York to do postgraduate work, preparatory to the field of general medicine. Following this he practiced in Greer for a period of 14 years.

Seeing the great need and demand for more knowledge regarding colon and rectal diseases, Dr. Brockman decided to specialize in work of this nature. He therefore pursued special courses dealing with that branch of medicine in New York City and Louisville, Kentucky. In the year 1923 he opened a Proctologic Clinic, the only one of its kind in South Carolina. From the beginning he enjoyed a lucrative practice, drawing his patients not only from his own community, but from the entire State of South Carolina and portions of North Carolina and Georgia. His clinic, with its laboratories, is one of the best equipped and most modern in the South for this special line of work. Doctor Brockman's surgical success in his chosen field has won recognition for him, among members of his profession, as well as the general public. His practice is confined entirely to his special field, and in addition to his work at his own clinic, he does the operative work of that nature at the Chick Springs Sanatorium.

Doctor Brockman is a member of the American Proctologic Society, one of the most important exclusive organizations among the medical fraternity. He also holds membership in the American, Southern, Tri-State, State and Greenville County Medical Associations. He is also a member of the Phi Chi Medical fraternity. He is a member of the Memorial Methodist Church of Greer, a member and ex-President of the Civitan Club, being largely responsible for the organization of that club.

On October 27, 1914, he was married to Miss Bernice Wood, daughter of the late J. Terry Wood and Mrs. Lulie Leonard Wood of Greer, South Carolina, most prominent and influential citizens. They are the parents of four children: Thomas, Jr., Elinor, Joe Ben and Nancy McGee. The family resides at Greer.

W. T. POTTER

Greenville is the home of a number of the largest and most successful contracting and building concerns doing business in the two Carolinas. Among these is Potter & Shackelford, Inc., of which W. T. POTTER is President.

Mr. Potter was born in Greenport, New York, on November 23, 1889, being the son of Edmund A. and Florence L. Potter. His education was had in the public schools of his home community and at the Worcester Polytechnic Institute of Worcester, Massachusetts. In 1912 he was awarded a B.S. degree by the latter school.

Upon the completion of his education, Mr. Potter accepted employment with the Fisk-Carter Construction Company of Worcester, which connection he held for a number of years. In 1913 he moved to Greenville, still with the Fiske-Carter Company. This concern does a large business in the South, principally as builders of cotton mill plants, and maintains a large office in Greenville as well as that in Worcester. Here Mr. Potter secured the training which so ably fits him for the business in which he is now engaged.

In 1920 he left the Fiske-Carter Company and organized Potter & Shackelford, Inc., which met with success from the first. The concern operates over a wide territory and does a large annual business. Among some of its recent construction work in the Piedmont may be mentioned: the hotel and store buildings at Lake Lure, North Carolina; the Carolina Theatre, Shriners' Hospital for Cripple Children, the Greenville County Tuberculosis Hospital, additions to the Union Bleachery, the Piedmont Print Works, the Piedmont Plush Mills, the Buncombe Street Methodist Sunday School Building and the Thompson (Ford) Building, all in or near Greenville City.

Mr. Potter is active in the civic affairs of the city, being a member of the Greenville Chamber of Commerce and also holding membership in the Kiwanis Club of Greenville. He is a Methodist, a member of the Greenville Country Club, and belongs to the S. A. E. college fraternity and is a Director in the Peoples State Bank of South Carolina.

In 1921 he was married to Miss Virginia Allen, daughter of C. O. Allen of Greenville, and they have two children, viz: Edmund L. and Virginia Allen. The family home is located at 702 East Washington Street.

CHARLOTTE TEMPLETON

CHARLOTTE TEMPLETON, member of the Advisory Board of the History of Greenville County, was born in Brinkley, Arkansas, in 1877, being the daughter of Robert and Jane (Coleman) Templeton. Her father's family comes from Ayrshire, Scotland, while her mother's people are from Nantucket Island, off the Massachusetts coast. She attended the public schools of her home community, and then entered the University of Nebraska, from which she was graduated with an A.B. degree in 1902. Following her graduation, she was a student at the Library School of Pratt Institute, Brooklyn, New York.

Upon the completion of her education Miss Templeton became Director of the State Library Commission of Nebraska, which position she held for 14 years. While there she interested herself in organizing library service for prisons, state hospitals, and reformatories. At that time little attention had been given to systematic library service in such institutions. Leaving Nebraska she went to Georgia to organize the work of a newly established State Library Commission. Here she remained three years. From Georgia she came to Greenville to accept the position of chief librarian with the Greenville Public Library. That was in 1923, soon after the organization of the Greenville library.

Under the capable direction of Miss Templeton, the Greenville library, in the seven years since she became its chief librarian, has taken an enviable position among public libraries of the country. It developed the first complete county library system, not only in South Carolina, but in the entire South. Because of this it attracts visitors from many states, being looked upon as a demonstration library in this particular field of work.

Miss Templeton is active in the American Library Association, serving on the Council and on various committees. In the National League of State Library Commissions she is likewise active, having served as its Secretary for a number of years. She has served as President of the South Carolina Library Association, and is now President of the Southeastern Library Association.

She is a member of the Thursday Club, and of the Greenville Branch of the American Association of University Women; she is also a member of the Phi Beta Kappa college sorority.

CHARLES O. MILFORD

Formerly very nearly all the life insurance carried by South Carolinians was written by out-of-state companies. This was because the State had no companies of its own with sufficient resources to handle the business. But within the last few years this condition has changed; South Carolina now boasts a number of companies amply able to care for the needs of her people, and these are getting a large proportion of the insurance of the state as well as much from without. In this matter of Life Insurance companies, Greenville leads the way with four, of which number the Southeastern is by far the largest, having $44,000,000 of business in force in 1929. CHARLES O. MILFORD is President of this company.

Mr. Milford was born in Anderson County, South Carolina, on the 13th day of October, 1886, being the son of Charles J. Milford (now deceased) and Lou (Saylors) Milford. He is descended from the early Scotch-Irish settlers of Virginia, who later came to South Carolina as pioneers of the up-country. The elder Milford was a farmer and true to farm traditions, the son spent much of his early life assisting in farm work. As a boy he attended the public schools of his community, and was later a student at Dayton College of Music in Virginia, where he took courses in vocal and instrumental music. From here he went to Furman University, Greenville, S. C., from which institution he was graduated with the degree of A.B. in 1914. While at Furman he was a member of the College Glee Club, and directed the Church Choir at the Pendleton Street Baptist Church.

From college, Mr. Milford went to Simpsonville, Greenville County, S. C., where he became principal of the Simpsonville schools. Here he remained for four years, till, when in 1918 he entered the insurance business with the Southeastern Life and was assigned to Anderson, S. C., as General Agent. After one year he was promoted to the General Agency of his company in Greenville, which position he held for four or five years. Then he was elected Vice-President of the company and remained such till 1924 when he became its President. Since that time the Southeastern Life has grown by leaps and bounds, having almost doubled the amount of insurance which it had in force. The company is now 25 years old, and although ably managed for its first 20 years, at the expiration of that time (1924 when Mr. Milford became President) it had only $24,000,000 of insurance in force as compared to the $44,000,000 which it had five years later. During the summer of 1929, Mr. Milford assisted in the organization of a $22,000,000 life insurance holding company to operate in the South. The Southeastern has entered this company. With it Mr. Milford holds a Directorate. He is also a director in the Peoples National Bank of Greenville, and has many other business connections.

Although Mr. Milford has great business responsibilities, he finds time to take a prominent part in the social, civic, and religious life of his home city and county. He is a member of the Kiwanis Club, having at one time been its President, and at another time its Treasurer; a Mason, and a member of the Chamber of Commerce. His religious affiliations are Baptist, he being a member of the First Baptist Church of Greenville.

Mr. Milford married Miss Clara Todd of Simpsonville, who was a graduate of Cox College, and they have three children: Charles O., Jr., Morgan, T., and Sarah E. The family home is on Bennett Street in the city of Greenville.

CARL F. LAGERHOLM

Citizens of the South Carolina Piedmont often boast that the residents of that section are more nearly 100 per cent pure American than those of any other industrial area of the United States. Listening to this, one might think that none but the native born could find a place in the life of Greenville. But any such thought would be entirely without foundation, as evidenced by the high regard in which CARL F. LAGERHOLM is held by the people of his adopted home city.

Mr. Lagerholm was born on December 31, 1867, in Norrkoping, Sweden, being the son of Carl G. and Amelia Charlotte (Olson) Lagerholm. His education was obtained in the public schools of his native land, after the completion of which he entered the tailoring trade, which was the business of his father before him.

While still a young man, Mr. Lagerholm came to America where he took up his residence in New York City. Here he remained for 17 years, first as inspector for a "ready made" factory for five years, then for seven years as head tailor with Wannamaker, and afterwards in business for himself. In 1905 he came to Greenville, where he soon acquired an enviable reputation not only as a high class, dependable business man, but as a public-spirited citizen. Just a year after locating in Greenville, Mr. Lagerholm suffered the loss of his business by fire. But undaunted, he set himself to the task of "getting back upon his feet", and within a remarkably short time he had again built up a business of note. Today and for many years past, he has been proprietor of the G. F. Lagerholm Tailoring Company, which does a large business throughout the Piedmont section.

Mr. Lagerholm is a member of the Lutheran Church. For 17 years he has been an Elk and many times has held responsible offices in that organization. He is a member of 15 years' standing in the Knights of Pythias, and is a member of the Greenville Chamber of Commerce.

He was married to Miss Emma Maria Osterberg of Brooklyn in 1890, and they have five children: Fred Emanuel, Arthur Elsworth, Edward Theodore, Clarence Victor, and Eric Gustav. Two of these children live in Charlotte, North Carolina, two in Greenville, and one in Buffalo, New York. The family home is on Park Avenue in the city of Greenville.

JAMES A. WINN

JAMES A. WINN, son of the Reverend Paul P. Winn and Sue (Anderson) Winn, was born at Lenoir, North Carolina, on the 13th day of July, 1878. His father is a Presbyterian minister and for many years played a prominent part in the various activities of that denomination, but he is now retired.

Mr. Winn received his education in the public schools of his home community and at Davidson College, Davidson, North Carolina. From the latter institution he was graduated as an A.B. in 1900. Leaving college, he taught for a time at the Bingham School, near Asheville, North Carolina, and then became principal of the University School for Boys at Jacksonville, Florida. Following this he went with the Audit Company of the South, of Atlanta, Georgia, as Vice-President, and here he remained until 1921, when he moved to Greenville.

In Greenville he organized James A. Winn & Company, a firm of certified public accountants, and since then has been actively in charge of its affairs. The business of the concern is large, being of both a public and private nature. An office is maintained in Spartanburg as well as Greenville.

The public activities of Mr. Winn are many. He is deeply interested in the civic affairs of his home city and devotes much of his time in their promotion. He is a member of the Greenville Chamber of Commerce, a member of the Greenville Country Club, and a Mason. In the many activities of the Greenville Rotary Club he takes a leading part. He has held various offices in that club and is now its President. He is also a member of the Beta Theta Pi college fraternity, and member of the Presbyterian Church.

Mr. Winn was married to Miss Elizabeth Curry of Memphis, Tenn., in 1911, and they are the parents of three children: Elizabeth, John and Albert. The family home is on Capers Street in the City of Greenville.

ROBERT MURRAY HUGHES

ROBERT MURRAY HUGHES, President of the Planters Savings Bank of Greer, was born at Bailey's Cross Road, two miles south of Greer, on December 31, 1881, being the son of Simeon Hughes and Jane (Wood) Hughes. His father, Simeon Hughes, one of the very earliest merchants of Greer, was a native of that community and fought in the Confederate army in Company "C", 22nd Regiment of South Carolina volunteers. He was severely wounded on March 29, 1865, and spent six weeks thereafter in a hospital at City Point, Virginia. Later he was in a hospital at Washington, D. C., and then in a military prison at Elmira, N. Y. His mother was a daughter of John T. Wood and Thurza Mayfield Wood. She was born near Woods Chapel church and attended the famous Reidville Female Academy. Her father, John P. Wood, was a member of Company "C", 22nd Regiment of South Carolina volunteers in the Confederate army, and fought throughout the entire war. Her great-grandfather was the Reverend Henry Wood, who was a Revoluntionary soldier and the founder of Woods Chapel Methodist Church, one of the oldest in the upper part of the State of South Carolina.

Mr. Hughes, the subject of this sketch, attended the public schools of the town of Greer, and in 1896 began work at Greer with the Victor Mills store. Later he was manager of the Peoples Store, which succeeded the Victor Mills store. In 1907 he assisted in the organization of the Planters Savings Bank of Greer and became its cashier. This position he held until 1928, when he was elected President of that bank. The Planters Savings Bank is one of the strongest financial institutions in Greenville County, and is noted for its conservatism. Its usefulness has recently been enlarged by the acquisition of the First National Bank of Greer. In addition to his connection with the Planters Bank during the last several years, Mr. Hughes has held the position of President of the Greer Oil Mill & Feed Company, which he assisted in organizing.

Mr. Hughes is a public-spirited citizen and takes a deep interest in the civic affairs of his home community. He is also interested in the up-building of the county and at this time is a member of the Board of Trustees of Greenville County Tuberculosis Hospital. He is also a member of the Board of Trustees of a trust fund established by the late D. D. Davenport.

Mr. Hughes is a member of the First Baptist Church of Greer and in all the work of that organization he is unusually active, taking a prominent part in the North Greenville Baptist Association as well. From 1907 to 1928 he was Superintendent of the Sunday School of his church, and again in 1930 was chosen for this position and still holds it. He is also a member of the Masonic order; and is a member of the Advisory Board of the History of Greenville County.

On July 10, 1907, Mr. Hughes was married to Miss Lura Pitts Langston of Conway, South Carolina, and they have four children: Robert Simeon, James Langston, Robert Murray, and Lura Pitts.

LEE HAMILTON WELCH

During the World War the United States army maintained Camp Sevier, one of its largest training posts, on the outskirts of the city of Greenville. Here near a hundred thousand soldiers were trained in 1917 and 1918. The first to come and the longest to stay were the men of the famous "Thirtieth Division"; and being principally from North Carolina, South Carolina and Tennessee, the people of Greenville, feeling that they were "home boys", extended them an open hand of hospitality. Many of these young men were so impressed with the "Greenville spirit" that they returned to the city following the war, and now constitute a potent factor in the life of Greenville. Among these is LEE HAMILTON WELCH.

PART II — BIOGRAPHICAL

Mr. Welch was born in Chicago, Ill., on March 18, 1897, being the son of Frank Walter Welch and Marguerite (Ott) Welch. His father, now deceased, was a prominent attorney of Chicago, being associated in the practice of his profession with Judge Kennesaw Mountain Landis for a number of years. Both parents of the elder Mr. Welch came to America from Ireland, while on his mother's side, the subject of this sketch is of German descent.

Young Mr. Welch attended the public schools of Chicago and later became a student at the T. M. I. of Tennessee. From this latter institution he was graduated in 1915. While a student Mr. Welch took an active part in athletics, winning letters in football, baseball, basketball and track.

After leaving Chicago and before taking up his work in the Tennessee Institute Mr. Welch spent a year upon a ranch in Texas. Following his graduation in 1915 he became assistant cashier of the Hayne-Henson Shoe Company, and here he remained till 1917 when he enlisted as a private in the Second Tennessee Infantry.

Having entered the army in July, 1917, Mr. Welch was immediately sent to Camp Sevier at Greenville, South Carolina, for training. Here in August, just a month after his enlistment, he became a sergeant, and in September of the same year he was promoted to first sergeant. In April of 1918 he was commissioned a second lieutenant, and three months later (July, 1918) he was promoted to first lieutenant, which rank he held till the close of the war in October, 1918. Since the war he has taken an active part in the affairs of the Officers' Reserve Corps and now holds a commission as Captain in that branch of the service.

After being mustered out of the army Mr. Welch returned to Greenville and in 1919 became Agency Cashier of the Southeastern Life Insurance Company. In 1921 he was promoted to Agency Supervisor, which position he held for about a year, when he purchased an interest in the Home Office General Agency of the company. In 1929 he purchased full control of the "Home Agency", which business he now conducts.

Although Mr. Welch has been more than ordinarily successful in his business affairs since coming to Greenville, he has devoted much of his time to religious, social and civic activities of the community. He is a member of the First Baptist Church and teaches a large class of 17-year-old boys. For a number of years he has been an active member of the Junior Chamber of Commerce, having been one of its organizers, and was a Director in that organization during 1926 and 1927. He is a Mason, a member of the Alpha Chi Sigma fraternity, a charter member of the Greenville post of the American Legion, in which he has served as adjutant, and a member of the executive committee, and a charter member of the "La Societe Des 40 Hommes Et 8 Chevon." During 1928 and 1929 he was President of the local branch of the Officers' Reserve Corps. In the various Community Chest drives he has always taken a leading part, and in 1930 is an official in charge of one branch of the work.

On July 17, 1917, Mr. Welch married Miss Bess Tatum of Greenville, and they have two children: Jack Tatum Welch and Betty Lee Welch. The family home is on Lavinia Avenue in the City of Greenville.

LAWRENCE P. SLATTERY

LAWRENCE P. SLATTERY was born on March 17, 1884, and is the son of John Slattery and Mary (Grace) Slattery. His father was born in Kilrush, County Clare, Ireland.

He entered Clemson College, where he specialized in engineering and graduated with the degree of A.B. and later received the degree of C.E.

Mr. Slattery married Miss Louise Phillips of Savannah, Georgia, in 1917 and they reside at 204 Butler Avenue in the City of Greenville.

DR. BENJAMIN B. STEEDLY

Among the men who make a community, none stand higher in the estimation and real affection of the people at large than do those who devote their lives to preserving and physically improving the lives of others. From the old-fashioned family doctor with his horse and buggy and his bag of medicines, down to the most skilled surgeon of today in his shining laboratory, members of the medical profession have been esteemed worthy of a reverence, second only to that accorded the minister of God. In the annals of this profession, one finds among the more prominent names from our State that of BENJAMIN B. STEEDLY, physician and surgeon.

Dr. Steedly was born in Barnwell County, South Carolina, on December 24, 1874, the son of William B. and Georgette C. (Garris) Steedly. The elder Steedly was also a doctor, practicing for many years at Athens, Georgia. It was here that Benjamin attended school and college, graduating from the University of Georgia. Further professional training was obtained at the New York College of Physicians and Surgeons, Columbia University, New York City, from which institution he received the degree of M.D.

Returning to his native state, Dr. Steedly began the practice of medicine in Gaffney, South Carolina, in the year 1902. After seven years of general practice in that town, Dr. Steedly moved to Spartanburg, South Carolina, where he limited his field to surgery, and it is in this line that he has come to occupy a position in the very front rank of eminent surgeons. For some years Dr. Steedly owned and operated a private hospital in Spartanburg, one of the best equipped and most up-to-date in the section. In 1919, he became interested in the Chick Springs property and was largely influential in remodeling the old hotel building into a sanatorium.

It was during these years that Dr. Steedly became interested in the treatment and cure of cancer; this interest led to study, both intensive and extensive, of all phases of the subject. So successful have been his endeavors along this line that he is now recognized as one of the South's leading authorities in the field of radium and cancer treatment.

For a time, South Carolina lost the services of her eminent son, while he was in charge of a cancer research clinic in Atlanta, Georgia. But after a short service in this capacity, Dr. Steedly returned to Spartanburg and since that time has spent most of his time at Chick Springs Sanatorium. He now owns and operates this institution which occupies the unique position of being the only hotel sanatorium in the section. Its excellent location makes it admirably suited to function in both capacities. Dr. Steedly also maintains a clinic in Spartanburg in association with Dr. W. S. Zimmerman.

Among his fellow-practitioners, as well as among a host of grateful former patients, Dr. Steedly is accorded a prominent place in medical circles; among the professional organizations of which he is a member are: the State Medical Association, the County Medical Association, the Tri-State Medical Association, the Southern and the American Medical Associations. He is also a Fellow of the American College of Surgeons. He finds time likewise, to take an active part in the affairs of the Masons and Knights of Pythias, with which he is affiliated.

Dr. Steedly was married to Miss Florence Pittman, of Thomasville, Georgia; they have two children: Edith and Benjamin B., Jr. The family divides its time among Spartanburg, Chick Springs, and New York.

DOCTOR CHARLES HARDY FAIR

Reading the pages of early Greenville County history, one finds that a high percentage of those citizens who accomplished things worth while were immigrants from Virginia. And since those early days this same Virginia stock which furnished the sturdy pioneer settler of the Piedmont has continued to send some of its best representatives into upper South Carolina, and especially Greenville. As late as 1911 the son of a native Irelander came down from Warrenton, Va., and is now one of the leading surgeons of Greenville. This is DR. CHARLES HARDY FAIR, who, with his family, resides on Manley Street.

Doctor Fair is the son of Robert Fair and Elizabeth (Hardy) Fair, and was born at Warrenton, Fauquier County, Virginia, in 1881. His father was born in Ireland and emigrated to Virginia as a young man where he married a daughter of Thomas Hardy for whose family Hardy County (now West Virginia) was named. As a boy, Dr. Fair attended the primary schools of his community and was prepared for college at Bethel Academy, an excellent school near Warrenton, of which Dr. Alderman (later President of the University of Virginia) was President. Finishing here, he entered George Washington University, from which he was graduated in 1909 as an M.D. During his school years Dr. Fair worked variously in railroad offices and drug stores, but upon leaving college he engaged actively in his profession, first for two years at Warrenton and then in Greenville where he moved in 1911.

For several years after locating in Greenville Dr. Fair engaged in the general practice, but having done post-graduate work in New York and other clinical centers, he decided to devote himself exclusively to surgery in which branch he has been unusually successful since undertaking it in 1918. He is upon the staffs of both hospitals in the city of Greenville, and practices in any other hospitals where his professional duty calls him. He is a Fellow of the American College of Surgeons, and holds memberships in the American, Tri-State, South Carolina, and Greenville County Medical Associations. He is a Major in the Medical Corps of the O. R. C.

Dr. Fair takes an active part in many of the county's activities, and especially those pertaining to the public health. He is an Elk and a member of the Greenville Country Club.

In 1916 Dr. Fair was married to Miss Annie Akers of Atlanta, Ga., and they have three children: Elizabeth, Annie Rosa, and Lucy.

HAMPTON P. BURBAGE

HAMPTON P. BURBAGE, attorney-at-law of Greenville City, was born in Greenville, South Carolina, on the 20th day of January, 1883, being a son of Samuel P. and Ellen E. Burbage. His literary education was obtained in the public schools of Greenville, at Wofford College, Spartanburg, South Carolina, and Furman University, Greenville, South Carolina. His legal training was had in law office work and at Columbia University of New York.

Mr. Burbage taught in the public schools of upper Greenville County and Pickens County for two years, after which he was admitted to the South Carolina bar in 1902, being at the time under age, and immediately entered upon the practice of law at Greenville, where he has practiced alone, except for one year when he and Adam C. Welborn were in partnership as Welborn & Burbage. For more than 25 years Mr. Burbage has remained at the Greenville bar, during which time he has been quite successful in the general practice of his profession.

Mr. Burbage is a writer of some note, often contributing articles to the newspapers and magazines. For about four years he published at Greenville a monthly literary magazine, *The Libertarian,* of which he was Associate Editor and Business Manager. He is also a student of early South Carolina history and has been able to unearth much valuable information for those interested in that field. His private library is possibly unequaled by any in the city.

Mr. Burbage was married to Miss Agnes Roddey of Charleston, South Carolina, who is a musician of note. The Burbage home is on West Earle Street, in the city of Greenville.

GEORGE FINLEY

Retiring and unassuming, GEORGE FINLEY pursues the even tenor of his way, quietly doing a great deal for the good of his city and his fellow man.

The characteristics of rugged honesty and dignified simplicity possessed by him come down to this citizen from his parents, John and Jean Finley, who came from Scotland and settled in Henderson County, North Carolina, about the year 1872. Here George Finley was born.

Having received his education in the public schools of Henderson County, he, with his brother, came to Greenville. Upon his arrival here he immediately opened up a wholesale grocery business and for many years operated it with marked success. In 1910 he sold his business and since that time has devoted his entire time to his real estate interests. He is in charge of the estate of his brother, James Finley, and has offices in the Finley Building, which is a part of this estate. In addition to his interests in the city he owns and operates a large farm in Saluda Township.

Mr. Finley is unmarried.

JAMES A. BULL

JAMES A. BULL was born near O'Neall in upper Greenville County. His father, Daniel H. Bull, and his mother, Martha (Fowler) Bull, were both natives of that section of the county. William Bull, his paternal grandfather, came from England to Greenville County in 1836. An uncle and an aunt of his came to the county during the early days of the nineteenth century and acquired large properties. Upon their deaths, William Bull came over to handle the estate, was married here and remained to become the founder of the Bull family in upper South Carolina.

The subject of this sketch, James A. Bull, secured his education in the public schools of his community. At 17 years of age he left school and became a drygoods store clerk in Greenville. After a few years he entered the grocery business in a small way and year by year expanded his businss until it finally became one of the largest retail grocery businesses in South Carolina. He retired from the grocery business and since that time has devoted himself to agriculture and the development of his properties at Chick Springs, where he now resides.

Mr. Bull acquired the widely known Chick Springs property in 1905. Here flows a mineral spring, the medicinal qualities of which were known to the Indians, discussed by Mills in his Statistics of 1824, and made famous by Doctor Chick in the forties of the last century. Here in 1914 Mr. Bull and associates constructed a hundred-thousand-dollar hotel. He became President of the hotel company. However, the coming of the World War interfered with the operation of the hotel and in 1919 it was converted into a sanatorium and with 30 acres of land surrounding was sold to the Steedly Clinic and Sanatorium. Of this new institution Dr. B. B. Steedly, a widely famous surgeon of Spartanburg, became President and Mr. Bull Vice-President. The clinic and sanatorium still operates with success and increasing fame.

Of his Chick Springs property Mr. Bull retains 80 acres upon which is operated an amusement park and soft drink bottling plant. Water from the famous "Chick Spring" is bottled and shipped to all parts of the United States. Mr. Bull also engages extensively in farming.

Of Mr. Bull and his life while a citizen of Greenville City, the *Greenville Piedmont* recently said:

"When Greenville was in its infancy as a city and when housekeepers ordered their groceries at 8 a. m. to have them on the table for the mid-day meal, J. A. Bull was known as a pioneer grocer of this city. He is no longer in the grocery business but the courtesy and the desire to serve, which fairly stood out in his establishment, are still fresh in the memory of Greenville's older inhabitants. Those who visited his store in person, and those who relied upon the telephone for their grocery cares, will recall that his establishment fairly radiated the personality and the courtesy of its owner.

"Mr. Bull, now a resident of Chick Springs, has not lost interest in the city, even though he is no longer in business here. In fact, those who know him best declare that 'Jim' Bull never lost interest in any worth-while project. They make that statement, realizing that in the past he has befriended many persons, some of whom in turn did not show their appreciation.

"In the days when grocers relied more upon honesty than upon cash registers and adding machines, Mr. Bull knew hundreds of his customers by name. He also knew something of the financial situation of many of them and many times he 'sold' or gave some needy family the necessities which tided them over for a time.

"Generous and not exacting when the other fellow is in the wrong, he has often demonstrated that he is filled with brotherly love for his fellowmen. In his way, he is still doing much for others. He would not be happy if he lived for self alone."

He was married to Miss Sunie E. Stroud and they have seven children: Martha (Mrs. J. J. Hunter), Frances, Ruth (Mrs. L. B. Aull), James A., Jr., Paul, Margaret, and Dan.

CHARLES H. YATES

CHARLES H. YATES was born in Charleston, South Carolina, being the son of Charles L. and Elizabeth H. Yates. At the age of four years he moved with his parents to Greenville, South Carolina, where his education was obtained in the public schools.

Leaving school at the age of 17, he engaged in several lines of mercantile business at various times until the year 1907, when he became associated with the late Charles W. Ellis in the operation of the Greenville plant of the Coca-Cola Bottling Company. He is now Secretary and Treasurer of this company, and since the death of Mr. Ellis has been its directing head. He is also President of the Verner Springs Water Company which also does a large business in the bottling of high grade carbonated beverages. Mr. Yates has seen the business grow from an unpromising weakling up to the present time. Today it is the largest concern of its kind in the State of South Carolina. Their new plant on Buncombe Street is said to be one of the finest in the United States.

In addition to his holdings in the Coca-Cola Bottling Company and the Verner Springs Water Company, Mr. Yates is interested in a number of other business enterprises in Greenville. He is a director of the South Carolina Savings Bank, and also a director of the American Building & Loan Association.

He is a member of the United States Chamber of Commerce, the Greenville Chamber of Commerce, the South Carolina Bottlers' Association and Greenville lodge 858, B. P. O. E. In the public affairs of Greenville he is greatly interested and is active in many civic undertakings.

JAMES T. WILLIAMS

South Carolina owes much to the Old Dominion, for that state has furnished many of our most prominent and substantial citizens. Not the least of these was Dr. T. B. Williams, who came to Greenville in the early days of her history. Bringing with him the sturdy characteristics of his forebears, he founded here one of the most influential families of this section. His son, James T. Williams, married Miss Anna D'Oyley and they became the parents of JAMES T. WILLIAMS, the subject of this sketch, who was born in 1845.

Mr. Williams' boyhood came at the time of the fearful War Between the States. Though very young, having not yet passed his sixteenth birthday, he enlisted in Co. A, 16th South Carolina Infantry. His military career was long and varied and he saw active service in South Carolina, Alabama, Georgia, Mississippi, and Tennessee, being wounded at the Battle of Franklin.

Following the close of the war, Mr. Williams, along with other men of the South, was confronted with the stupendous task of rehabilitation. Arduous years followed during which Mr. Williams spent his time farming and doing any other honorable work possible. He was not satisfied with his success, however, and in 1875 entered the hardware business as a member of the firm of Williams & Williams, purchasing the interest of his partner in 1882. For 35 years he was recognized as one of Greenville's leading merchants. During this busy period of business activity, he found time to serve his city long and well in the capacity of Chief Executive, holding this office from 1893 to 1901.

Mr. Williams was twice married, first to Miss Eliza Cleveland, who lived but a short while. Some years later he married Miss Sally McBee at Lincolnton, North Carolina. She was the daughter of Vardry McBee who did much for Greenville during the early days of her history. To this union were born six children: James T., Jr., Mayor Vardry McBee, Major Silas, Miss Mary Elizabeth, and Miss Sarah McBee. Each has taken an enviable position in his or her chosen field.

Mr. Williams has far outlived his three-score-and-ten years, and is one of Greenville's most dearly beloved. His residence is at 611 Pendleton Street, Greenville, South Carolina.

GEORGE G. WELLS

For many, many years the name "Wells" has stood for prominent, substantial citizenship in Greenville County. This was one of the early families of the county and its members have done much toward the making of Greenville. O. H. Wells was the owner and publisher of *The Mountaineer,* the first newspaper to be published in the county. His son, G. G. Wells, Sr., was a leading member of the Greenville bar for many years, being a member of the firm of Cothran, Wells, Cothran & Ansel.

GEORGE G. WELLS, subject of this sketch, was born on January 23, 1879, being the son of G. G. Wells and Mary J. (Hill) Wells. His early education was obtained in the public schools of Greenville City. Later he was a student at Furman University for two years.

Leaving College, Mr. Wells entered the employ of the Southern Railway where he remained in various capacities for 20 years. He sold the first ticket from the present Southern railway station at Greenville. In 1918 he was elected City Clerk and Treasurer of Greenville City, which position he still holds. So efficient and popular is he that for the last eight years he has had no opposition for the office; and he has the further distinction of having held the position of City Clerk and Treasurer longer than any other person. Annually he handles more than a million and a half of money passing through the city treasury.

Mr. Wells is a member of the First Baptist Church of Greenville. He is a Mason, a Shriner, a member of the J. O. U. A. M., and of the Red Men, and is an Elk and a Civitan. He is active in all these organizations, having at various times held offices of responsibility in many of them. In the Masonic order he is a Past Master.

Mr. Wells was married to Miss Bessie Gary of Greenville, S. C., and they have five chilren: G. G. Wells, Jr., Frances (now Mrs. J. B. Terry), Caroline Wells, Archie Wells, and Betty Wells. The family home is on Pinkney Street in the city of Greenville.

Editorial Note: The above sketch was written and delivered to the printer December 1st, 1929. Since then Mr. Wells has resigned as City Clerk and Treasurer.

W. HENRY WILLIMON

Among the progressive farmers who have put Greenville County at the very top in the State's agricultural industry, none ranks higher than does W. HENRY WILLIMON.

Mr. Willimon is the son of R. C. Willimon and Martha C. (Ashmore) Willimon, and was born on his father's large plantation October 27, 1867. His boyhood was passed assisting about his father's farm and in attending the public schools of his community. As a young man he took a business course in Lexington, Kentucky, and returned to accept a position with the American Bank of Greenville, where he remained for only a short time, however.

Leaving the American Bank, Mr. Willimon engaged in farming, to which he has adhered with eminent success up to the present time. In a county where small farms are the rule, he bears the distinction of owning near a thousand acres of the best farming lands to be found in the Piedmont section. Years ago much of this land was not considered of much value because the farm methods then employed in the county had depleted it of all its fertility; but with progressive, up-to-date methods, Mr. Willimon has proved that "value is in the man and not in the land", for today his plantation is pointed out as a "model farm" where one may easily learn the value of scientific soil cultivation. And during these last years when farming has reached such a low ebb throughout the entire nation, and especially so in the South, the Willimon plantation stands as a striking refutation of the much-prated statement that "farming can no longer be engaged in with profit."

Being always interested in good government and holding to the theory that this can be had only when the best men can be induced to accept public office, Mr. Willimon gave of his time for five years (1915 to 1921) to serve Greenville County as Supervisor. First he was appointed to the office at a time when conditions were such as to need the services of a "big man", and then upon the expiration of his term he became a candidate to succeed himself and was elected by a large majority.

In religious affiliation Mr. Willimon is a Methodist.

On October 18, 1905, he was married to Miss Maude Pack, daughter of Dr. C. H. Pack of Greenville City, and they have six children: Robert C., Henry P., Eugene P., Alice, Ann, and Charles P. The Willimon country home is on the Fork Shoals road about eight miles south of the City of Greenville.

Editorial Note: Since the above was written Mr. Willimon has been appointed County Comptroller, which office he now holds.

JAMES H. MORGAN

Before the Revolutionary War, Colonel Hite resided upon a 1,300-acre plantation in what is now the eastern part of Greenville County, but then a part of the Cherokee Nation. Here in 1776 Colonel Hite, his wife and a number of his children were murdered by the Indians. Those of the family who survived this bloody massacre returned to their old home in Virginia, abandoning the plantation. Following the Revolution, a portion of the Hite land was granted to Isaac Morgan, whose descendants lived there till well past the middle of the last century. One of

these descendants to be born on the ancestral estate was JAMES H. MORGAN, son of Benjamin and Elmira Morgan.

James H. Morgan was born on May 9, 1848. His education was received in the schools of Greenville and Pickens Counties, the War Between the States depriving him of a college career. He remained on his father's farm until he was 19 years of age, coming to Greenville at that time to accept a position with the pioneer mercantile firm of T. W. Davis. After three years' association with Mr. Davis as an employee, he was accepted into partnership with his employer, and the firm was known and continued for many years as Davis and Morgan. The business met with unusual success, and after a few years became one of the most important in the town. Later Mr. Davis sold his interest and the firm became James H. Morgan & Bros. The new concern continued with even greater success than the old till 1898, when, following a disastrous fire, it was discontinued.

In 1896 Mr. Morgan became interested in the textile business, organizing the Sampson Mill. Later the name of the concern was changed to the American Spinning Company. Upon its organization Mr. Morgan became President of the Sampson Mill and continued as such with it and its successor for 30 years, when he retired on account of his advanced years. Under his guidance the mill became one of the outstanding and most successful textile plants in the Piedmont. Besides his major activity as a cotton manufacturer, Mr. Morgan was long identified with many of Greenville's enterprises, including banking institutions and varied mercantile establishments.

Upon his death, which occurred on January 9, 1928, the *Greenville News*, writing editorially of Mr. Morgan, said:

"James H. Morgan was nearly 50 years old when he organized the Sampson Mill, the parent of the present American Spinning Company. He was at the age when many men think of retiring, and when only a few consent to launch into an entirely new enterprise, particularly one as uncertain as the textile industry was in South Carolina in the year 1896.

"But life had always been a matter of perseverance to Mr. Morgan. He had known the hardships of the Civil War and the Period of Reconstruction. For 19 years he had lived on a farm, where he became accustomed to the practice of helping to earn a living from the soil. As a young man he came to Greenville and entered the mercantile business. For nearly 30 years he followed that occupation earnestly and intelligently. When fire put him out of business he did not stop. He saw the possibilities of textile manufacturing which was just then showing signs of flourishing in this region. And he went into that business with the same dominant zealousness that he tackled another business as a young man.

"The career of Mr. Morgan shows to what extent the personal background and integrity of the founders entered into the successful establishment of the textile industry in South Carolina. The necessity of Mr. Morgan's early life inculcated in him the corner stone of business management—thrift. He knew the value of a dollar. He demonstrated his ability to handle it well. It was a rigorous and trying apprenticeship, but it was the kind of training that enabled him and others like him to make a success of running a cotton mill in the days when that was not easy."

Mr. Morgan was a member of the First Baptist Church of Greenville and for many years one of its Deacons. He was by nature and training very religious, and was a liberal contributor to many benevolent, educational and religious institutions.

Mr. Morgan was twice married, his first wife having been Miss Lidie Jones, daughter of Dr. William R. Jones of Greenville. She died in 1912. From this union there survived two sons—Clinton J. Morgan and James H. Morgan, Jr. His second wife, who survives him, was Miss Virginia Waddell, daughter of Dr. George H. Waddell, a physician of Greenwood.

ROBERT POWELL SWEENY

ROBERT POWELL SWEENY, inventor and mill executive, was born in Charleston, South Carolina, February 7, 1883, son of Colonel Robert Hayne and Catherine Friendly Sweeny. His father served in the Confederate army, and was a Colonel on the staff of Governor W. H. Ellerbe of South Carolina in 1897.

He is the great-grandson of Captain Robert Hatch, who was a soldier in the Revolutionary War, and later lost his life in a naval engagement with the British in Stono River, near Charleston, South Carolina, during the War of 1812.

He received his academic education in the public schools of Charleston, South Carolina, attended Wofford College at Spartanburg, South Carolina, and graduated in Textile Engineering at Clemson College, Clemson, South Carolina.

From 1903 to 1908 he was Secretary and Resident Manager of Ware Shoals Manufacturing Company at Ware Shoals, South Carolina. Soon after, he became Superintendent of the Fairmont Manufacturing Company at Fairmont, South Carolina, where he remained for two years and then became Superintendent of the Wylie Mills at Chester, South Carolina, which mills were built under his supervision for the Parker Cotton Mills Company.

His next connection was with the New York Cotton Mills at Utica, New York, as Superintendent, where he remained for four and a half years; after which he returned South to become Manager of the Social Circle Cotton Mills Company at Social Circle, Georgia, which is a part of the Cannon Group of Mills. At the end of five years with these mills he became Manager of the Buffalo Mills at Union, South Carolina.

He gave up mill work in 1921 and came to Greenville, South Carolina, and organized the R. P. Sweeny Company, of which he is President and Treasurer. This company handles machinery of all kinds, but one of the most important articles which the company handles is the Sweeny "Pneu-Way" Vacuum Cleaner, a machine which Mr. Sweeny invented himself, and on which he owns a number of valuable patents. This machine is used in cotton mills and in other large industrial plants, and has had a very large sale in the United States, and even abroad. Through the advertising of the Vacuum Cleaner in national magazines the city of Greenville has received very valuable publicity.

Mr. Sweeny is a 32nd degree Mason and a Shriner, and a member of the Methodist Episcopal Church, South.

In 1905 Mr. Sweeny was married to Miss Jennie Eloise Hellams of Gray Court, South Carolina, and they have one son, Dial F., and two daughters, Jennie Catherine and Dorothy.

JOSEPH ALLEN McCULLOUGH

Of all those who have had a hand in the building of Greenville during the last 50 years none have played a more prominent role than Joseph Allen McCullough. He was born in Dunklin township of Greenville County, being a son of the Reverend A. C. Stepp and Ann Rebecca Stepp. Early in life he was adopted by his maternal uncle, Colonel James McCullough, and by special legislative act his name was changed from that of Stepp to McCullough. His father, A. C. Stepp, was a prominent Baptist minister, who at one time was a member of the General Assembly from Greenville County. Colonel James McCullough, his adopted father, was colonel of the 16th South Carolina Regiment of Volunteers during the War Between the States. The McCullough family was early in the county, being founded in South Carolina by Joseph McCullough, grandfather of Joseph Allen, who emigrated from County Antrim, Ireland, and settled in lower Greenville County, where he built the famous "Old McCullough Home" (still standing) about 25 miles below Greenville City on the Augusta road. Of this old home Harriett Kershaw Leiding writes in her book, "Historic Homes of South Carolina."

After attending public and private schools of his home community, Mr. McCullough entered Wofford College where he remained for one session (1882-'83). Then he was a student at the South Carolina College till 1887, being graduated from that institution with the degrees of A.B. and LL.B. While in college he was extremely active in student affairs, holding, during the time, the offices of President of the Clariosophic Society (literary), President of Y. M. C. A., editor-in-chief of the *South Carolina Collegian,* and assistant editor of the S. A. E. (college fraternity) official publication. In 1905 he returned to his alma mater to deliver the alumni address on the occasion of the college Centennial celebration, at which time the honorary degree of LL.D. was conferred upon him.

Having finished his college education, Mr. McCullough entered upon the practice of law at Greenville. Business came rapidly and he was soon one of the leaders of the Greenville bar, and while still a very young man was recognized as being among the first of his profession in the state. Year by year his practice grew until it was exceeded by few, if any, in South Carolina, when in 1918 he gave it up to accept the position of Chief Counsel for the United States Fidelity and Guaranty Company of Baltimore, Maryland. This new work necessitated his leaving Greenville, but he continues to hold business and professional connections here, and is still considered by his old friends and associates as a citizen of Greenville. In October, 1928, after serving with the Guaranty Company for ten years, he resigned and resumed the private practice of law.

In the public affairs of South Carolina and also of Maryland, Mr. McCullough has had a large share. He served the City of Greenville as attorney for a number of years, was a member of the South Carolina General Assembly for several terms, and on numerous occasions acted as Special Judge in the courts of South Carolina. He was a member of the Greenville legislative delegation which passed the "Million-Dollar Road Bond Act" of 1915, being an active supporter of the measure. He was author of the first child labor bill to be enacted into law by South Carolina, was Chairman of the South Carolina Child Labor Commission and a member of the

Executive Board of the National Child Labor Commission. He held membership on the South Carolina Historical Commission for a number of years; was one of the organizers of the State Board of Charities and Corrections (South Carolina); one of the organizers and first Chairman of the Board of Trustees of the Bruner Home (Greenville); at one time a Trustee of the Salvation Army Rescue Home (Greenville); was one of the organizers and first President of the "Thirty-Nine" Club of Greenville, and President of the first Y. M. C. A. organization in Greenville. For many years, and till he moved away from South Carolina, he was a Trustee of Wofford College. At one time he was a Trustee of the South Carolina College (now University of South Carolina) and is now a Trustee of Emory University, Atlanta, Georgia. In Baltimore, Maryland, his present home, he is a member of the Board of Governors of the Maryland General Hospital and Chairman of its Executive Committee, and is also a member of the Board of Governors and Executive Committee of the Franklin Square Hospital.

Mr. McCullough is a Methodist, a member of the "Thirty-Nine" Club, a Mason, an Elk, a member of the Maryland Club, of S. A. E. (college fraternity), a W. O. W., and a member of the Country Club of Baltimore.

During the World War Mr. McCullough volunteered for overseas work with the Y. M. C. A., but was rejected on account of his physical condition at the time. However, he took an active part in all phases of war work "overhere."

Numerous publications have carried sketches of Mr. McCullough's life and accounts of his work. Among these are Who's Who in America, Who's Who in Jurisprudence, the Tercentennial History of Maryland, Who's Who in the East, Snowden's History of South Carolina and South Carolina and her Builders.

Mr. McCullough has been twice married, first to Miss Maud d'Alvigny of Atlanta, Georgia, and after her death to Mrs. Emma Lumpkin Clark of Baltimore, Maryland, also deceased. By his first marriage he has two sons: James D. McCullough of Rocky Ridge, Maryland, and C. Fred McCullough of Greenville, S. C.

C. G. WYCHE

Among the younger members of the Greenville bar none enjoys a more enviable reputation in his profession than does C. G. WYCHE. He is the son of Dr. C. T. and Carrie (Sease) Wyche, and was born at Prosperity, South Carolina, on September 3, 1890. His father is a native of North Carolina, while his mother is a South Carolinian.

Mr. Wyche as a boy attended the public schools of Prosperity, and later became a student at the University of South Carolina, from which institution he was graduated with the degree of A.B. His legal education was obtained at Georgetown University where he was awarded a LL.B. degree.

In 1916 Mr. Wyche became a resident of Greenville upon being appointed Assistant United States District Attorney. Until 1921 he held the position of Assistant to the District Attorney, located at Greenville, when he resigned to enter the private practice of law. For several years he was a member of the widely known firm of Dean, Cothran & Wyche, and after Mr. Cothran withdrew from the firm in

1928, he continued as junior partner with Colonel Alvin H. Dean. Since the death of Colonel Dean in 1929, Mr. Wyche has practiced alone.

In all undertakings of a civic nature which contribute to the public good, Mr. Wyche is deeply interested and in these he is often found taking the part of a leader. He is a member of the American, South Carolina and Greenville Bar Associations. He is a Mason and a member of the Phi Alpha Delta College (legal) fraternity. He is an active member of the Earle Street Baptist Church in the city of Greenville.

Mr. Wyche married Miss Mary Wheeler of Newberry in June, 1914, and they have five children: Mary, Caro, Sarah, Martha, and Cyril Thomas. The family home is on West Earle Street in the city of Greenville.

ROBERT LEE GRAY, JR.

Greenville has a number of young lawyers, many of them able, but among them none is held in higher esteem than ROBERT LEE GRAY, JR. Born at Gray Court, South Carolina, October 1, 1902, he is the son of Robert Lee and Emma Dial Gray. His youth was spent in the little town of Gray Court, where his parents are among the town's and county's most prominent and influential citizens.

A long line of distinguished business and professional men and charming women form the ancestry of the subject of this sketch. His uncle, Nathanial B. Dial, has long been a most prominent citizen of Laurens. As a member of the Laurens bar and an ex-United States Senator, he has served his county and state well in numerous capacities. Robert Lee Gray, Sr., is a man of large interests and his genial personality as well as his keen business acumen have made him universally popular. He is President of the Bank of Gray Court, also a large planter and merchant, conducting one of the most popular mercantile establishments in his home town.

Mr. Gray, Jr., received his early education in the public schools of Gray Court and the Gray Court-Owings High School. Completing his work there he entered Duke University, and in 1923 was graduated from that institution with the degree of A.B.

Following the penchant of many members of his family, he took up the study of law and spent the years of 1924 and 1925 at Harvard Law School. In the fall of 1925 he came to Greenville and entered the Furman Law School, from which he was graduated in 1926 with the degree of LL.B. He immediately began the practice of his profession, specializing in Civil Law. His offices are located in the Chamber of Commerce Building.

Mr. Gray is a member of the Buncombe Street Methodist Church, an active member of the Junior Chamber of Commerce and the Elks Club. He is a member of the Sigma Chi fraternity.

Editorial Note: Since the above was written Mr. Gray has accepted a position with the legal department of the Standard Oil Company and is now located in Charleston, S. C.

HARRY A. DARGAN

One of the most popular and efficient public officials Greenville County has ever had was HARRY A. DARGAN, who died on July 9, 1928, while serving his fourth term as Clerk of Court.

Mr. Dargan was the son of Dr. William James Dargan and Hannah Elizabeth (Coggeshall) Dargan, and was born in Greenville County, South Carolina, on the 22nd day of March, 1870. His father was a practicing physician for many years in Sumter County, but his health failing, he gave up his profession, moved to Greenville and established the book store of Dargan & Felton. He was the son of James Harvey and Louise James Dargan of Sumter County, South Carolina. The mother of Harry A. Dargan was a daughter of Peter Collins Coggeshall and Ann Pawley Coggeshall of Darlington County, South Carolina. The Dargans are of French descent, having come to South Carolina early in its history along with other Huguenots who left their native country on account of religious persecution; while the Coggeshall family is English, being the founders of the village of "Coggeshall" in England.

The early education of Harry A. Dargan was meager but he took advantage of every opportunity offered him and in later years did much to overcome this handicap. At the early age of 13 years he began work in the office of Perry, Perry & Heyward, attorneys-at-law of Greenville. Later he was with the law firm of Irvine & Mooney. At various times he held positions in the office of Register of Mesne Conveyance under Colonel Woodside; with A. J. Mosely, J. A. McDaniel, and John M. Cureton, while each of these served as Clerk of Court; with Felton's Book Store; with Earle & Wilson, drygoods merchants; with the clothing firm of Smith & Bristow; as Clerk for the Greenville Fire Department; and as Assistant Clerk of the city of Greenville. For several years he was also engaged in the real estate and insurance business.

Upon the death of John M. Cureton in 1915, Mr. Dargan was appointed to fill his unexpired term as Clerk of Court. In 1916 he was a candidate for the office and was successful against four opponents; and so well did he fill the office that in 1920 he was re-elected without opposition. Again in 1924 he was a candidate to succeed himself, and was elected for another four years, but before the expiration of his term he died. During all these years in public office, Mr. Dargan's effort was "efficiency", and he succeeded to a marked degree. Many times, as the official records show, he was highly commended by presiding Judges and Grand Juries for the manner in which he kept his records and expedited the proceedings of the Courts.

Mr. Dargan was an active member of many fraternal orders and civic organizations through which he accomplished much good for Greenville. Among these were the Knights of Pythias, Elks, Woodmen of the World, Red Men, J. O. U. A. M., Loyal Order of Moose, D. O. K. K., Lions Club, Greenville Chamber of Commerce, and Spanish-American War Veterans. In religious affiliations he was a Baptist, being a member of the First Baptist Church of Greenville.

In 1915 Mr. Dargan was married to Miss Lucile Smith, daughter of the Honorable Chas. D. Smith of Dunklin Township. Upon the death of her husband Mrs. Dargan offered for election to the office which had so long been held by her husband; but between the first and second primaries, while leading a field of four candidates, she was forced to withdraw from the race on account of her health. Later having recovered her health she accepted the position of Deputy Clerk of Court, which office she now holds.

ELMER G. McCOIN

HARRY A. DARGAN

ELMER G. McCOIN

North Carolina has contributed much to the commercial growth of the great Carolina Piedmont, in both men and material; and in so doing she has furnished Greenville many of her most substantial citizens, who coming here imbued with the old Tar Heel spirit of progress, have greatly assisted in the building of their adopted city. Of those coming within comparatively recent years was ELMER G. McCOIN, who moved from Winston-Salem, North Carolina, to Greenville in 1912.

Mr. McCoin, who died in Greenville on June 11, 1928, still in the full vigor of young manhood, was born in Winston-Salem, North Carolina, on December 6, 1879, being the son of J. W. McKaughan and Martha (Pitts) McKaughan. The difference in spelling of the names is accounted for by the fact that the son, when entering business as a young man, found that his name was almost invariably misspelled by those hearing it, so he adopted the simplified form and used it throughout the remainder of his life. The family is of Scotch-Irish descent and characteristic of that stock, is well known and highly respected for the sturdy manhood and pious womanhood of its members.

After attending the public schools of Winston-Salem, Mr. McCoin entered the employ of the R. J. Reynolds Tobacco Co., with which concern he was connected in various capacities until his death. First he traveled out of Knoxville, Tennessee, then returned to Winston-Salem to live for a number of years, still with the Reynolds Company. In 1912 he became Division Manager for his company in South Carolina and parts of North Carolina and Georgia, with headquarters at Greenville, South Carolina. Here he moved his family to reside for the remainder of his life.

During the latter years of his life Mr. McCoin was an exceptionally active Churchman, being a member of the First Baptist Church of Greenville. He was a member of the Civitan Club, a Mason, a Shriner and a Knight Templar; and in all of these organizations he was deeply interested, taking part in many phases of their activities.

On June 18, 1907, he was married to Miss Margaret Ellen Leonard of Winston-Salem and they have three children: Elmer G., Jr., Kathleen Doris, and Anna Louise. The family resides on East Park Avenue in the city of Greenville.

Elmer G. McCoin cared nothing for the publicity which comes with spectacular undertakings, nor did he seek the public acclaim of his fellow-men; but his life was spent in radiating sunshine and cheer among those so fortunate as to know him as a friend. Truly in him there lived a *man,* of whom it may be said, "They also serve who only stand and wait."

A. C. WALKER

Much of Greenville's growth and development in the past few decades has been due directly or indirectly to the cotton industry. Likewise, many of her most prominent citizens have found in this business a field for the exercise of their financial acumen. Prominent among these ranks was the late A. C. WALKER. Mr. Walker was born in Columbia, Alabama, on December 21, 1881. The early years of his life were spent in this town and it was here that he received his education.

After finishing school, Mr. Walker entered the cotton business in Atlanta, Georgia. Later he became connected with the McFadden Company and was transferred to Charlotte, North Carolina, as their agent. It was in the employ of this same company that he first came to Greenville. After one year with McFadden in Greenville, Mr. Walker decided to go into business for himself as a cotton merchant and this proved a very wise and advantageous move on his part. He continued to enjoy marked success in this work until his death, which occurred November 6, 1927.

Among organizations listing Mr. Walker as a member, were the Elks Club, and the Greenville Country Club. As a director of the Peoples National Bank he identified himself with the financial interests of the city. At the time of his death, Mr. Walker was the owner of the Walker Building on West Washington Street, and other properties of great value and business importance.

Mr. Walker was married to Miss Emma Howard, who survives him, as do four children, Curtis, Elmore, Jean, and Betty. The Walker home is in Sans Souci, Greenville.

MAJOR EDGEWORTH M. BLYTHE

Before the close of the 18th century, William Blythe and his wife emigrated to South Carolina from North Carolina, where they had lived for a few years after coming down from their original home in Virginia, and settled in upper Greenville County, near Lima. They were the grandparents of Absalom Blythe, who practiced law in the city of Greenville for many years, and was City Recorder at the time of his death in 1925. The younger son of Absalom Blythe and his wife, Emily Earle Blythe, was born in the city of Greenville on July 31, 1872, and is EDGEWORTH M. BLYTHE, subject of this sketch.

After attending the public schools of Greenville, Mr. Blythe studied at Furman University and then became a student at The Citadel, the Military College of South Carolina, from which he was graduated with the degree of B.S. in 1891. For two years after leaving the Citadel he taught in the schools of Greenville County and then became an Instructor and assistant to the Commandant, with the rank of Major in Clemson College, where he remained for two years. While at Clemson, Mr. Blythe was engaged in the study of law, and in 1896 was admitted to the South Carolina bar. But not content with the preparation which he had, he entered the Law Department of the University of Michigan, from which he was graduated with the LL.B. degree in 1901, completing the three years' course in one year.

Returning after graduation to Greenville, Mr. Blythe began the practice of law in partnership with his father under the firm name of Blythe & Blythe. Later he formed a partnership with H. J. Haynsworth and L. O. Patterson, which continued for a few years. Then he became junior partner in the firm of McCullough, Martin & Blythe, which practiced extensively over several counties till the senior partner, Hon. Joseph A. McCullough, moved to Baltimore to become General Counsel for the United States Fidelity & Guaranty Company. The firm's practice was continued in Greenville by Martin & Blythe until 1925, when there was a dissolution, after which Mr. Blythe practiced alone until the firm of Blythe & Bonham, consisting of E. M. Blythe and P. A. Bonham, was organized in May of 1927. Of this firm Mr. Blythe is now senior partner.

Being a Citadel graduate, Mr. Blythe has always taken a deep interest in military affairs. In 1899 he organized and became Captain of Company "A" of the First South Carolina Infantry, which rank he held till 1905, when he was promoted to Major. Trouble with Mexico arose in 1916, and he went to the Mexican border as Colonel of his regiment. After several months of duty here, his regiment returned to South Carolina and was mustered out. Then feeling that his private affairs demanded his entire attention, Colonel Blythe resigned his commission and for the first time in 18 years was out of military service. However, the United States soon entered the World War and it was not many months until Colonel Blythe volunteered, and was commissioned Major of Infantry in the National Army. He was assigned to Camp Lee, Virginia, where he remained until the close of the war.

From 1903 to 1917 Major Blythe was United States Commissioner at Greenville, which position he resigned to enter the World War. For several months in 1917 and 1918 he was secretary and a member of the Greenville County Exemption Board, serving without pay. In 1921 he was appointed Referee in Bankruptcy at Greenville, which position he still holds. Major Blythe has held the position of Attorney for Greenville County and also that of Greenville City and at this time is attorney for the Greater Greenville Sewer District. He is also a member of the Board of Trustees of the Greenville City Schools, being Chairman of that body. From 1899 to 1917 he was a member of the Board of Visitors of the Citadel.

Major Blythe is an active member of Christ (Episcopal) Church. He is also a Past Master of Recovery Lodge No. 31 of Ancient Free & Accepted Order of Masons. Formerly he was President of the Rotary Club of Greenville, and is still active in that organization.

In 1906 Major Blythe was married to Miss Anna H. Hardin, daughter of Colonel M. B. Hardin, formerly Professor of Chemistry at Clemson College, and they have three sons, namely, Edgeworth M., Jr., Bernard H. and Lauriston. The family resides on East North Street in the city of Greenville.

PROCTOR ALDRICH BONHAM

Few families have been so prominent in the political and judicial history of South Carolina during the last three-quarters of a century as the Bonham and Aldrich families. During the War Between the States, General M. L. Bonham, highly efficient as a commanding officer, at the urgent call of his state, assumed the office of Governor of South Carolina, succeeding Francis W. Pickens. Later he was Railroad Commissioner, being the first to hold that position in South Carolina. His son, M. L. Bonham, was for many years an eminent lawyer at the South Carolina bar and is now Judge of the Tenth Judicial Circuit. A. P. Aldrich was a Judge of note in this State after the War Between the States. The Reconstruction regime removed him from office, but with the regaining of power by the Democrats in 1876, he was restored to office. Upon his death, his nephew, James Aldrich, succeeded him in office, who in turn was followed by Robert Aldrich, the son of A. P. Aldrich.

Judge M. L. Bonham was married to Miss Daisy Aldrich in Barnwell, South Carolina, and thus were these two prominent South Carolina families united. To them was born on August 28, 1883, PROCTOR ALDRICH BONHAM, the subject of this sketch. After attending the public schools of Columbia and Anderson, to which latter place his parents moved when he was 11 years of age, Proctor A. Bonham was a student at Georgetown University, Washington, D. C., for two years, at the College of Charleston for one year, and then the University of North Carolina Summer Law School in 1905. He studied law in the office of his father and was admitted to the bar of South Carolina in December, 1905.

Soon after becoming a member of the bar, Mr. Bonham moved to Greenville and entered upon the practice of his profession. In 1908 he was elected Solicitor of the Thirteenth Judicial Circuit, which position he filled in an able manner for eight years, retiring voluntarily in 1916. Politics called him again, however, and he became a candidate for State Senate, to which office he was elected in November, 1916, by the largest majority ever given a candidate for that office in Greenville County up to that time. After spending two terms of four years each as Senator from Greenville County, he declined to become a candidate again and has since then devoted himself exclusively to the practice of his profession.

While Solicitor, Mr. Bonham made an enviable reputation as a prosecuting officer; regardless of the fact that he put forth every effort in his prosecution, he was nevertheless known as a fair fighter. When he assumed the duties of that office, the Greenville bar was composed of as able lawyers as were to be found in the State; however, Mr. Bonham, despite his inexperience, was able to hold his own against all who appeared against him. During his term in office many important cases were tried, among them being the famous T. U. Vaughan criminal assault prosecution which perhaps excited more public interest than any case tried in Greenville County during the last quarter of a century. As Senator, Mr. Bonham was always found on the side of progress, and at the time of his retirement was urged to become a candidate for Governor, but this he declined to do, stating "I cannot afford to give further time to politics for the present."

At this time Mr. Bonham is a partner in the practice of law with Major E. M. Blythe. This firm (Blythe & Bonham) devotes itself principally to the Civil law. Formerly, however, Mr. Bonham practiced Criminal law very widely, proving himself the equal of any advocate in the State. As an orator he is equaled by few. He is Assistant Division Counsel for the Southern Railway and numbers many other large corporations among his clients. During his practice of the law, Mr. Bonham has been in partnership with B. A. Morgan, now Greenville City Attorney; F. F. Beattie, at this time President of the First National Bank of Greenville, and Jas. H. Price, who is County Attorney, besides his present partner and others.

Mr. Bonham is a member of the A. T. O. College fraternity, First Vice-President of the Little Theatre, and a member of Christ Church (Episcopal).

In 1913 he was married to Miss Margaret Rion of Columbia, granddaughter of Colonel James H. Rion of Winnsboro, and great-granddaughter of Preston S. Brooks of Edgefield. They have five children: Milledge L., Lucelle A., Margaret R., William R., and Daisy. They reside on Prestiss Avenue in the city of Greenville.

JOHN W. ARRINGTON

Among the leaders in the textile industry of the South is JOHN W. ARRINGTON of Greenville City. He was born in Warren County, North Carolina, in 1866, and is the son of Samuel P. and Hannah (White) Arrington. His parents moved to Petersburg, Virginia, while he was still quite young, and there he spent his boyhood and secured his education. With his school days finished he entered the cotton manufacturing business in Richmond, Virginia. After a few years spent here he moved to Reidville, North Carolina, where he remained, still engaged in the textile business, until 1904, when he moved to Greenville to become President of the Union Bleachery.

The difficulties encountered by Mr. Arrington and the manner in which he overcame them were recounted in a Greenville newspaper during the summer of 1929 when the plant of the Union Bleachery was being enlarged. In part it reads:

"Twenty-five years ago J. W. Arrington came to Greenville from Richmond, Virginia, to take over the management of the Union Bleachery, just built and equipped.

"His career as executive head of the new industry was launched at a time when sheer nerve and faith in the South as an advantageous place for the development of the textile finishing business were required.

"Two other bleacheries in the South had just failed, and the future of the bleaching industry in this section rested upon the fate of the Union Bleachery. Mr. Arrington succeeded.

"Within a few years, the bleachery's business had so increased that it became necessary to double the physical plant and the capacity of the bleachery.

"Now another large building program has been started. An addition is being erected that will materially add to the floor space, so keenly needed for new machinery and equipment demanded by changing requirements in high grade finishing of textile materials. The bleachery is spending about $300,000 to enlarge its plant.

"The Union Bleachery is the largest in the South. It has a capacity of 2,000,000 yards per week, and now employs 300 men and women.

"The success of the Union Bleachery turned attention to the South as a new field for textile finishing, and that phase of the textile industry has developed rapidly in recent years.

"Mr. Arrington, in addition to being President of the bleachery, is a very active public citizen, assisting in all civic enterprises of merit.

"His sons hold responsible positions in the bleachery, and like their father are interested and active in all movements for the betterment of Greater Greenville. J. W. Arrington, Jr., is Treasurer of the bleachery and R. W. Arrington is Superintendent."

Mr. Arrington has been President of the Greenville Chamber of Commerce, the Poinsett Club and the Kiwanis Club, and holds membership in the Greenville Country Club, the New York Club and the Arkwright Club of New York. He is a Vestryman in Christ Church (Episcopal) and active in the affairs of his church.

Mr. Arrington was married to Miss Mary Carter Sublett of Virginia, and they are the parents of four children: John W. Arrington, Jr., Richard W. Arrington, Octavia Page, and Nelson Battle Arrington.

DOCTOR J. WARREN WHITE

DR. J. WARREN WHITE, Chief Surgeon of the Shriner's Hospital for Crippled Children, was born in Boston, Massachusetts, on March 7, 1892, being the son of H. Warren White, a physician of Boston, and Elizabeth (Dudley) White. He secured his education in the public schools of Boston and at Harvard University. By the latter he was awarded both A.B. and M.D. degrees.

Having completed his college education, Dr. White practiced his profession for a time in Boston and then enlisted in the Medical Corps of the United States Navy, where he remained for six years, four of which were devoted to Orthopedic work. In 1924 he became Chief Surgeon of the Shrine Hospital in Honolulu, Hawaii, where he remained until 1927, when he moved to Greenville to assume the same position with the Shriners' Hospital for Crippled Children, then just being opened. This institution, which is one of 15 of its kind under the control of the Shrine, confines its activities exclusively to work among crippled children in the Southeast. It accepts charity patients only, but does not confine itself to the families of Masons. It was constructed at a cost of $365,000, furnished almost entirely by W. W. Burgess of Greenville. The Board of Trustees governing the hospital is appointed by the Imperial Council A. A. O. N. M. S.

Of the Shriners' Hospital for Crippled Children and its work, the *Greenville News* said in November, 1929:

"Filled to capacity with 65 children from seven Southern States, the Greenville unit of the Shriners' Hospitals for Crippled Children is firmly established as one of the most worthy, one of the most appealing institutions of the South. A total of 559 children have been received into the institution since it opened in September, 1927, and of this number a total of 459 children have been dismissed. In practically every instance, what seems a miracle has taken place and the child who was apparently destined to exist, helplessly chained to a useless, crippled body, or perhaps doomed to pass a life bitterly handicapped by a deformity, has been brought to a normal physical condition, or a condition so nearly normal that life has been utterly changed.

"A perfect setting for such miracles is found in the hospital building—of almost absolute fire-proof construction and maintained in the most immaculate manner in the world. The wards seem to be the happiest places on earth. Everything has been designed for cheer and comfort. And then there is school. For the fact that children are in a hospital in no way interferes with the fact that it is necessary to learn. Since only children who are mentally bright are accepted at the hospital it is always possible to have lessons.

"There are seven graduate nurses with 16 attendants to look after the children. Dr. James Warren White is the Chief Surgeon and he is assisted by Dr. T. B. Clegg. At the present Miss Byrd Boehringer is Superintendent of Nurses, but upon her resignation becoming affective December 1st, Miss Luella Schleoman will assume the position."

In addition to his work at the hospital, Dr. White maintains an office in the city of Greenville, where he devotes much of his time to a private practice in Orthopedic work. His patients are drawn from a wide territory and are rapidly growing in numbers.

Although Dr. White has lived in Greenville less than three years, he has become closely identified with the civic and professional life of the city. He is a member of the Rotary Club, and a member of the Club of 39, a Mason and a Shriner. He also holds membership in the American, the South Carolina and the Greenville County Medical Associations. He is a member of the Pi Eta college, and Rhi Rho Sigma medical fraternities, and a Major in the O. R. C.

In 1917 he was married to Helen Angell of Boston, and they are the parents of two children: J. Warren, Jr., and Gilbert A.

DOCTOR J. P. CARLISLE

The oldest practicing dentist in the city of Greenville is DR. J. P. CARLISLE. He was born on Buncombe Street in the house where he has always resided. His father, James H. Carlisle, a native of Lancaster County, was one of the early students of Furman University. Leaving there he became a teacher, which honorable calling he followed for 62 years. Many of these years of teaching he spent in Greenville, where he was instrumental in securing the establishment of a free school system. The mother of Dr. Carlisle was Mary (Vance) Parker of Charleston, who was related to the Parker and Moultrie families of that city.

Dr. Carlisle secured his early education in the schools conducted by his father and the public schools of Greenville. Later he was a student at Furman University, from which institution he entered the Dental School of the University of Maryland. From the latter he was graduated with the degree of DD.S. in 1885.

Leaving college, Dr. Carlisle returned to Greenville and established dental offices in the Mauldin Building at the corner of South Main and West Washington Streets, where he has remained through all the years since. He has always worked for the advancement of his profession, and is recognized as a leader in modern methods of dental surgery. He is a member of both the National and South Carolina Dental Associations, being an ex-President of the State body, and is at present Editor-in-Chief of the Journal of proceedings of the Dental Association of South Carolina.

In numerous fraternal orders Dr. Carlisle takes a prominent and leading part, and in this field he is as well known as that of his profession. He is ex-Grand Master of the State organization of Odd Fellows and was Chairman of the Board of Directors of the Odd Fellows Orphanage, formerly located in Greenville; at one time he was Great Sachem in South Carolina for the Improved Order of Red Men, and has several times been a delegate from the State to the National Convention of that order; he is an active member of the Knights of Pythias and an ex-Chancellor Commander of the local organization. Dr. Carlisle also holds membership in the J. O. U. A. M., the Masons, and Elks.

In 1905 he was married to Miss Amanda Louise Boatright, daughter of Dr. Boatright of Aiken, South Carolina.

DR. LEWELLY CALHOUN JOHNSON

That "virtue hath her own regard" is fitly demonstrated in the general recognition that has come to DR. LEWELLY CALHOUN JOHNSON.

Born in Brushy Creek Township, Anderson County, South Carolina, the daughter of Pinckney Louis and Betty (Holcombe) Johnson, Lewelly C. Johnson spent the early years of her life on her parents' farm. At the age of 13 she moved with her family to the town of Easley, and later to Pelzer, where the family resided for several years. During the time the family resided at Pelzer she worked in the mill. Returning to Easley in 1900, Miss Johnson began work in the Easley mills. She was able to save $150 from her salary, and in 1901 went to Macon, Georgia, where she took a business course, later accepting a position at Tipton, Georgia. After being employed for a short while she returned to Easley and became stenographer and private secretary to Mr. J. M. Geer, President of the mill where she worked, from 1903 to 1913. And just here it might be said that Miss Johnson attributes whatever success she may have attained to the kind consideration and helpful advice given her by Mr. Geer during this period of her life.

Though marked success had attended her work, this ambitious young woman turned her thoughts to wider fields of endeavor, and on September 15, 1913, she entered the American School of Osteopathy at Kirksville, Mo. Here her resourcefulness was again called into play, and many and varied were the tasks performed to secure the money necessary for the completion of the course. But in May, 1916, having overcome the many obstacles encountered, Dr. Johnson was graduated with honor; and after taking the State Medical Examination, she came to Greenville and opened an office for the general practice of Osteopathy.

The success which had marked her endeavors through life followed her into her chosen profession, where with firm, sure hands she has continuously ministered to the sick and suffering of the community. Since beginning her work, in order to keep abreast of the times, Dr. Johnson spent a year at the Middlesex College of Medicine & Surgery, Boston, Mass., from which school she was graduated in June, 1919.

Universally beloved and admired, Dr. Johnson holds a large place in the hearts of the people of Greenville.

DOCTOR GEORGE W. QUICK

From its earliest history Greenville County has been largely Baptist in sentiment, and some of the oldest churches in it were of that denomination. Among these is Brushy Creek Church, organized in 1794, which became the "mother" of the Greenville Baptist Church, now the First Baptist Church.

In 1824 Vardry McBee gave a lot to the Baptist denomination, and under the leadership of Dr. W. B. Johnson a house of worship was erected on it in 1826. However, it was not until November 2, 1831, that the Greenville Baptist Church was organized. The lot given by Mr. McBee was on what is now East McBee Avenue, about opposite the C. & W. C. railway station. Here the first building stood. It was of brick construction and served as a house of worship for the church congregation until 1857, when the present First Baptist Church Building was occupied. The old church property was deeded to the Southern Baptist Theological Seminary in 1869 and was used by that institution as a lecture hall till the removal of the Seminary to Louisville.

The First Baptist Church is the largest church organization in Greenville County. During its century of life it has exerted a tremendous influence upon the religious and educational life of the county, and especially the city of Greenville. Many church organizations have grown out of it, and by it a large number of prominent Baptist ministers have been ordained. Furman University and the Greenville Woman's College have always been closely associated with the church.

Since its organization the First Baptist Church (formerly Greenville Baptist Church) has had 18 pastors. Many of these have stood at the very top of their denomination in the South. Those ministering to the church, named in the order of their pastorates, are: S. Vandiver, S. Gibson, A. M. Spalding, T. W. Haynes, J. G. Landrum, M. C. Breaker, T. T. Hopkins, J. C. Furman, Richard Furman, W. D. Thomas, J. C. Furman, J. C. Hiden, Charles Manley, W. H. Strickland, J. A. Mundy, C. S. Cardner, Z. T. Cody and GEORGE W. QUICK.

George W. Quick, D.D., pastor of the First Baptist Church since 1912, was born in Flemington, New Jersey, in 1861, being the son of Jaques Voorhees and Sarah O. (Biggs) Quick. His early education was obtained in the public schools of New Jersey and Virginia. Later he was a student at Richmond College, Richmond, Virginia, from which institution he was graduated in 1885. From here he entered the Crozer Theological Seminary, graduating there in 1888.

Following his graduation from the Seminary, Dr. Quick accepted a pastorate in Springfield, Mass. Here he remained for 16 years, and then went to the Second Baptist Church of Newport, Rhode Island. This pastorate he held for six years, leaving it in 1912 to come to Greenville as pastor of the First Baptist Church.

Immediately after Dr. Quick became pastor of the First Baptist Church a movement to enlarge the church plant was undertaken. Year by year its membership had been growing till by this time it was seen that the usefulness of the church would be greatly hindered if more adequate quarters were not provided. Committees were appointed and the "Forward Movement" was under way. In less than two years, means had been provided, and "the most complete church plant in the Southern Baptist Convention" completed. Of Dr. Quick's work in connection with this undertaking the Manual of the church, published in 1920, says:

"Thus in less than two years had been accomplished a great work, by which were laid the foundations of greater service and enlarged usefulness by the church in years to come. While this great undertaking was grandly met and brought to its happy fruition by the hearty cooperation of the united membership, too much credit cannot be awarded our pastor, who by his personal interest, untiring energy, and zealous attention to its many details contributed in no small degree to the success of the enterprise."

Under the ministrations of Dr. Quick the First Baptist Church has made great progress. Its membership has been increased and its place in the religious life of the city has been much enlarged.

Dr. Quick is not only a leader in the church life of Greenville, but in civic affairs he is unusually active.

In 1896 Dr. Quick was married to Miss Katrina Cobleigh of Gardner, Massachusetts, and they are the parents of two children: Miss Virginia Monroe, a teacher in the Greenville City High School, and Richard B., who was accidentally drowned in 1920. Mrs. Quick, like her husband, takes a leading part in the religious and civic life of the city of Greenville. For many years she has taught a class of young ladies in the First Baptist Church Sunday School, in which work she is very popular. In all phases of the ladies' work of the church she is a prominent figure.

(MISS) JAMES MARGRAVE PERRY

JAMES MARGRAVE PERRY, prominent attorney at the Greenville bar, and the first woman admitted to the practice of law in South Carolina, was born in Greenville, South Carolina, the daughter of James Margrave and Jean V. (LeGal) Perry.

Miss Perry attended the public schools of Greenville and then became a student at the Greenville Woman's College, from which she was graduated with an A.B. degree in 1913. Following her graduation here she entered the University of California, where she was awarded an A.B. degree in 1915. Continuing her studies at this institution she was graduated from its legal department with the degree of J.D. in 1917, and was thereupon admitted to the bar of California. She did not, however, engage in practice in that State, but returned to Greenville, S. C.

In January, 1918, the South Carolina legislature passed an act providing for the admission of women to the practice of law, and in May, 1918, Miss Perry took the State Bar examination and was admitted to the bar of South Carolina. At this time women were new to the legal profession in South Carolina, and for them to gain recognition more than the usual amount of application was necessary. But Miss Perry faced this condition undismayed, and in a very short time had won the professional respect and personal admiration of the entire Greenville bar. From the beginning of her career, she has been associated with the strong legal firm of Haynsworth & Haynsworth.

In the civic affairs of Greenville, and especially those pertaining to the business and professional woman, Miss Perry takes an active part, for several years being President of the Business and Professional Woman's Club. From its beginning she has worked consistently for the expansion and improvement of the Greenville Public Library, and for many years was a member of its Board of Trustees. She is a Democrat and has been a delegate to both the Greenville County Democratic Convention and the State Convention of that party. During war days she was a member of the Legal Advisory Council for Greenville County. She is a member of the Kappa Beta Pi College sorority, and is an Episcopalian.

GUY BUTLER FOSTER

GUY BUTLER FOSTER, through his mother a member of the celebrated Butler family of South Carolina, was born in Pickens County, South Carolina, on January 22, 1885. He is the son of R. M. and Elise (Butler) Foster, both of whom were natives of South Carolina.

Mr. Foster received his education in the public schools of Pickens County and at the Greenville, South Carolina, High School. After this he was engaged in various lines of work for a time and then became associated with W. N. Miller in the drayage and outdoor advertising business. Following this (1909) he entered the drayage and storage business on his own account. This occupation he followed until the outbreak of the World War, when he entered the American army as a captain. During the period of his military services he was stationed at Fort Moultrie and at Fort Monroe.

After being mustered out of the service, Captain Foster returned to Greenville and again entered the drayage and storage business; this time as an official of the Manufacturers Warehouse Company. After a few years he entered the builders supply business in his own name, and has since then been so engaged with marked success.

In all the civic and educational affairs of the city Mr. Foster is deeply interested, and many such undertakings receive his active support. Being a natural "mixer", and possessing the happy faculty of being able to make strangers "feel at home", he is often called upon to head local reception and entertainment committees when conventions and delegations visit the city. He is a member of the Greenville Chamber of Commerce, captain of the Shrine Patrol, a Rotarian, a Mason and an Elk. He is also an ex-member of the Board of Trustees of the Greenville City Schools.

Mr. Foster was married to Miss Katherine Clarke of Franklin, Tennessee, and they are the parents of three children, viz: Floyd Clarke, Elizabeth and Katherine Butler. The family home is on Lavinia Avenue in the city of Greenville.

J. ROBERT MARTIN

J. ROBERT MARTIN, prominent attorney at the Greenville bar, was born in Abbeville County, South Carolina, in 1876. He is the son of A.B. and Sarah (McDill) Martin, and is of Scotch-Irish descent. After attending the country schools of his home community for a few winter terms he was a student in the Donalds High School for one year and then entered Erskine College at Due West, from which historic institution he was graduated with an A.B. degree.

Following the completion of his college education, Mr. Martin taught for five years. First he was at Lickville and then at Old Hundred, both of which are in Greenville County, for one year each. Then he returned to Erskine to become an instructor in its Preparatory Department for a year. After this he was principal of the Piedmont Graded Schools for two years. At Piedmont he also taught a private class of boys at night. And during these years he was studying law. In June, 1902, he entered the office of former Governor Martin F. Ansel of Greenville, where he continued his legal studies, until the December following, when he was admitted to the bar of South Carolina.

After being admitted to the bar Mr. Martin remained with Governor Ansel as clerk and stenographer for four years, perfecting himself in the technique of the law and building a practice for himself. Gradually his business grew and he launched out for himself. Clients then began to come more rapidly and soon he had built up a substantial practice, which has continued to grow with the passing of years. Although he does not confine himself to that branch of the law, his practice is primarily of the personal injury branch, where he is always found for the individual and against the corporations. In 1916 he was elected Solicitor of the Thirteenth Judicial Circuit, composed of Greenville and Pickens Counties, and this position he held till 1920, when he voluntarily retired. Before and since his term as Solicitor he has often appeared as special prosecutor in criminal cases.

Starting without financial aid, Mr. Martin has been able to acquire a substantial practice, for the most part among friends of his early life, and to accumulate large real estate holdings in and near Greenville City. Among these are the Martin Building at the corner of South Main and Broad Streets; the Nokassa Hotel Building on South Main Street, and a large farm in the Tanglewood section.

Mr. Martin is a Presbyterian, a Mason, a Shriner, and an Elk. He is also a member of the State Bar Association.

He was married to Miss Lydia Rankin of Liberty, South Carolina, and they have two children, viz: Margaret, who is a graduate of Erskine College and now teacher in the Whitmire High School, and J. Robert, Jr., now a student at Washington and Lee University. The Martin family home is on Pendleton Street in the city of Greenville.

GOVERNOR MARTIN F. ANSEL

From Germany John Jacob Ansel and his wife, Frederika (Bowers) Ansel, came as immigrants to Philadelphia and subsequently moved to Charleston, South Carolina, prior to 1845. In 1850 their son, Martin F., was born, and in a few years they moved to Walhalla in the present county of Oconee, then Pickens District, where many of their fellow countrymen had recently gathered. Here MARTIN F. ANSEL, subject of this sketch, attended such schools as the community afforded. Later he entered the office of Major James H. Whitner, who was an eminent lawyer, and a gentleman of elegance and refinement, where he studied law; and at the age of 20 years was admitted to the bar of South Carolina.

For a few years after admission to the bar Governor Ansel practiced in Franklin, North Carolina. But in 1876 he moved to Greenville and embarked upon a practice which soon became quite extensive. Politics called him, and in 1882 he was elected a member of the House of Representatives from Greenville County; in 1884 he was re-elected, and again in 1886 he was returned. In 1888 he was elected Solicitor for the Eighth Judicial Circuit, and this position he held for 12 years. From 1901 to 1906 he confined himself to the practice of his profession (except that he was an unsuccessful candidate for Governor in 1902) which had become large.

The year 1906 found Governor Ansel again in the race for Governor and this time he was successful. Upon the expiration of his term he was re-elected in opposition to Cole L. Blease, since then Governor and United States Senator. While Governor, Mr. Ansel advocated a repeal of the State Dispensary law, in force since 1895 and the substitution of a County Dispensary system, which was at that time a long step toward prohibition. The recommendation of Governor Ansel was adopted by the General Assembly, and in a few years very nearly all the counties of the state had become "dry". Governor Ansel was a member of the Executive Committee of the first Governors' Conference held at the White House in 1908; and at the session of the Conference in 1910 Governor Ansel was requested to present a paper which he did well in his "A Brief Review of the Law of Extradition." A noteworthy innovation of the Ansel administration was the voluntary visit of all public schools of the State by the Governor. Of Governor Ansel's position on the Dispensary question Dr. S. C. Mitchell, then President of the University of South Carolina, said: "An achievement of which any Executive might well be proud."

After retiring from the Governor's office, Mr. Ansel returned to Greenville and took up the practice of law. In 1912 and again in 1916 Governor Ansel was requested by the Chairman of the Speaker's Committee of the Democratic party to speak for the party candidates. This he did each year, devoting several weeks to the cause. Upon the establishment of the Greenville County Court in 1920, Governor Ansel was elected Judge, which position he has held in a most able manner up to the present time.

Governor Ansel was first married to Miss Ophelia A. Speight in 1878. His wife died in 1895, and in 1898 he was married to Mrs. Addie R. Harris (nee Hollingsworth) who is still living. By his first marriage Governor Ansel has two daughters, Mrs. Gertrude Ansel Worley, now County Court Stenographer, and Mrs. Fredarika Ansel Bunch. Captain Henry H. Harris of the Greenville bar is a stepson, being the son of his second wife by a former marriage.

The high esteem in which Governor Ansel is held by the people of Greenville County is well attested by the great number of young men who bear his name. It has been said that no other man who ever lived in Greenville County can find so many namesakes.

J. BEN WATKINS

J. BEN WATKINS, County Auditor of Greenville County, was born in Hot Springs, Arkansas, on May 26, 1874, being the son of Z. B. Watkins and Frances Ann (Farr) Watkins. Both of his parents were native South Carolinians, and when their son, Ben, was only a year and a half old they returned to their native state and settled in Greenville County.

Mr. Watkins secured his early education in the public schools of Greenville, and before completing his high school course he was able to gain admission to Clemson College. At Clemson he remained three and a half years, when he decided to enter business. At once he was able to secure a position with the Southern Railway at Greenville, and here he remained, always in the Passenger Department, for 15 years.

In 1917 Mr. Watkins entered public life with his appointment to the office of Assistant City Clerk and Treasurer of the city of Greenville. This position he held with satisfaction till 1926 when he was elected to the office of County Auditor of Greenville County. Recently when an independent audit of all Greenville County offices was made and wholesale irregularities found in many offices the auditors said of Mr. Watkins and his office:

"The records of the Auditor (Mr. J. Ben Watkins), for the two years reviewed (July 1, 1926, to June 30, 1928) were found in splendid condition. In our opinion the records are satisfactory and the personnel capable."

While holding the office of County Auditor that of Register of Mesne Conveyance was declared vacant and Mr. Watkins assumed the duties of that office, discharging them as well as those of his own office for a time (till a new Register of Mesne Conveyance could be appointed) in a highly satisfactory manner.

Mr. Watkins is a member of the Earle Street Baptist Church of Greenville, a Mason, an honorary member of the Junior Order of United American Mechanics, and a member of the order of Red Men.

In 1907 Mr. Watkins was married to Miss Lula W. Hawkins and they have one child, Mary Frances.

JUSTICE THOMAS PERRIN COTHRAN

January, 1915, found Greenville County wallowing in mud. Already automobiles had become quite numerous, but as a means of transportation they were practically worthless during the winter months on account of the fearful condition of the roads. Many forward-looking citizens of the county were discussing means for improving conditions, but there was no unanimity of opinion. Some, however, went so far as to suggest submitting to the voters the matter of a half-million-dollar county bond issue. But this proposal was not received with any enthusiasm even by those favoring such a plan, for they knew the people of the county were not yet ready for so radical a step and would certainly defeat any such movement. Luckily, though, THOMAS PERRIN COTHRAN, Joseph A. McCullough and Wilton H. Earle were members of the General Assembly from Greenville, and being lawyers of more than usual learning in the profession, they brought to the attention of their colleagues a provision of the law which permitted the General Assembly to issue bonds of a county without the question being submitted to the voters. They agreed. "Then let's accomplish something worthwhile by bonding Greenville County for a million dollars to be used in road-building." The novelty of the idea was appealing. The Greenville Legislative Delegation agreed and the law was enacted. A bitter fight arose, but the law was declared constitutional. Then came the elections for Assemblymen. Strong tickets were put out against the "Million-Dollar-Bond Boys"; and the entire delegation, with the exception of Mr. Cothran himself, was defeated. Personal popularity alone saved him.

Judge Thomas Cothran, subject of this sketch, and one of the pioneer advocates of road-building by bond issues in South Carolina, was born at Abbeville, South Carolina, on October 24, 1857, being the son of Judge James S. Cothran and Emma Chiles (Perrin) Cothran. His grandfather, Wade S. Cothran of Rome, Georgia, was a banker and railroad president, while his father was a distinguished member of the bar of South Carolina, and served successively as Circuit Solicitor, Circuit Judge, member of Congress and Division Counsel for the Southern Railway. Thomas C. Perrin, his maternal grandfather, was a citizen of Abbeville, a lawyer of note, State Senator, and a railroad president. The Cothrans are of Scotch descent while the Perrins came originally from France.

After attending the schools of Abbeville, Judge Cothran went to the University of Virginia. Leaving college, he was admitted to the bar in 1878 and immediately entered upon the practice of his profession at Abbeville, where he remained till 1891, when he moved to Greenville and there continued the practice till 1921 when he was elected Associate Justice of the Supreme Court of South Carolina.

JUSTICE THOMAS PERRIN COTHRAN

J. BEN WATKINS

In the public affairs of Greenville County, Judge Cothran has played an unusually prominent part, being a member of the House of Representatives from that county for seven terms. He is author of the Greenville County Government law, under which, with only minor amendment, the county still operates. At the time it was enacted, students of governmental affairs pronounced it the ideal in county government. And the Road Bond law to which reference has already been made was, at the time of its enactment, highly progressive. Under it Greenville became the "pace-maker" among South Carolina counties in road-building, and has maintained her lead in that respect through all the years since. And Judge Cothran has not confined himself to the affairs of his adopted county, but has been the author of much legislation of State-wide importance—notable among which is the Carey-Cothran law, which repealed the State Dispensary Act. In 1918 Judge Cothran was elected Speaker of the South Carolina House of Representatives which high position he ably filled till 1921, when he was elected Associate Justice of the Supreme Court, where he is now the ranking member.

For many years before his elevation to the Supreme Court bench, Judge Cothran was Assistant Division Counsel for the Southern Railway. When, during the World War, the railroads were placed under government control, an order was issued requiring all railroad employees to resign any political position they might hold or be dismissed from railroad service, although Judge Cothran had long been attorney for the railroad, having succeeded his father, he promptly refused to resign his seat in the General Assembly, stating that since the people of his county had seen fit to honor him with that office, he considered it his duty to serve them even though in doing so he was forced to give up a lucrative legal connection. However, by some special dispensation, he was retained by the railroad.

Judge Cothran is a Presbyterian, a Democrat, a Mason, an Odd Fellow, and a member of the J. O. U. A. M. He was formerly President of the Greenville Bar Association; for many years was Chairman of the Greenville County Executive Committee of the Democratic party, as well as Chairman of the State Executive Committee for his party. He is also a member of the Kiwanis Club of Greenville.

On January 6, 1886, Judge Cothran was married to Miss Ione Smith, daughter of W. Joel and Ione (Allen) Smith, who died soon thereafter.

Judge Cothran resides in the city of Greenville at the Poinsett Hotel.

WILLIAM COULTER COTHRAN

WILLIAM COULTER COTHRAN, lawyer of the old school, public-spirited citizen, and generally acknowledged prince of good fellows, was born at Abbeville, South Carolina, on the 28th day of August, 1872. He comes of an ancestry long prominent in legal, financial, commercial and political history of the State, and is a worthy scion of an illustrious name. Wade S. Cothran, his grandfather, was a banker and railroad president of Rome, Georgia, while his father, James S. Cothran, served successively as a Circuit Solicitor, Circuit Judge, member of Congress and Division Counsel of the Southern Railway. Emma Chiles (Perrin) Cothran, mother of William Coulter Cothran, was the daughter of Thomas C. Perrin, a noted lawyer,

State Senator, railroad President and distinguished citizen of Abbeville, South Carolina.

As a boy, Mr. Cothran attended the public schools of Abbeville and then became a student at the University of South Carolina where he remained for two and a half years. Leaving college, he entered the office of his father where he studied law till his admission to the South Carolina bar in 1897.

Upon being admitted to the bar, he began the practice of his profession in the office of Cothran, Wells, Ansel & Cothran of Greenville, a legal firm of outstanding prominence in that day, composed of Judge James S. Cothran, his father; G. G. Wells, an outstanding lawyer of the Piedmont section for many years; Martin F. Ansel, ex-Governor of the State of South Carolina, and now Judge of the Greenville County Court, and his brother, Judge Thomas P. Cothran, ex-Speaker of the South Carolina House of Representatives, and now Justice of the Supreme Court. Upon the deaths of Judge James S. Cothran and Mr. Wells, he entered the firm which now became Ansel, Cothran & Cothran. Next Mr. Ansel withdrew and Colonel Alvin H. Dean, ex-State Senator and ex-Mayor of Greenville, entered the firm which was now Cothran, Dean & Cothran. For many years (till 1921) this partnership enjoyed a large practice, when Thomas P. Cothran, upon his election to a Justiceship upon the Supreme bench, retired and C. G. Wyche, then United States Assistant District Attorney, became a partner and the name was changed to Dean, Cothran & Wyche. In 1928 Mr. Cothran withdrew from the firm and entered into partnership with B. A. Morgan, now City Attorney for Greenville, where he is now engaged in the practice of his profession in the firm of Morgan & Cothran.

In recognition of his ability as a lawyer, Mr. Cothran has several times been appointed to serve as an Acting Associate Justice of the Supreme Court and as a Special Judge of the Court of Common Pleas. By his friends Mr. Cothran is known as "Judge", which title fits him admirably in view of his grasp of the law.

Mr. Cothran is a member of the First Presbyterian Church, an Elk and a member of the Phi Delta Theta Fraternity. He also belongs to the Greenville and South Carolina Bar Associations.

Mr. Cothran has never been married, and now resides at the Poinsett Hotel, Greenville, South Carolina.

DOCTOR LAWRENCE L. RICHARDSON

DR. LAWRENCE L. RICHARDSON was born near the present town of Simpsonville in lower Greenville County on July 23, 1868, being the eldest son of George W. and Lou C. (Cox) Richardson. His parents were both members of old and prominent families of that section. George W. Richardson, his father, served in the Confederate army for the entire period of the War Between the States, being among the first from Greenville County to volunteer. At the close of the war he returned to his old home community where he engaged in farming for the remainder of a long and useful life. For eight years he served as a County Commissioner (now Supervisor) and was a member of the House of Representatives from Greenville County for six years.

Dr. Richardson secured his early education in the public schools of his home community and those of Simpsonville. Later he entered the Atlanta Medical College of Atlanta, Georgia, now Emory University, from which he was graduated with the degree of M.D. in 1894. From medical college he returned to his home community and entered upon the practice of his profession as a "country doctor." Here he remained until December, 1909, ministering to an extensive practice, when he moved to the town of Simpsonville. In this new location his already large practice expanded greatly and in the years which have passed it has continued to grow. Today he is the oldest practicing physician, in years of service, in the Simpsonville community.

He is a member of the South Carolina Medical Association, and of the Greenville County Medical Association, being an ex-President of the latter. He is a Mason and a Deacon of the First Baptist Church of Simpsonville.

But regardless of the great value he has been to his community in his professional life, Dr. Richardson has perhaps rendered a greater service by his many public activities. For 15 years he has been chairman of the Board of Trustees of the Simpsonville Public Schools. Under his guidance education has been given a great impetus at Simpsonville, and the schools there have grown with well-nigh unbelievable rapidity. When he became Chairman of the Board of Trustees the Simpsonville school consisted of one building in which six teachers were employed in teaching 160 pupils. The school plant was worth no more than $5,000. Today the school plant is valued at $125,000, and consists of four buildings. Twenty-six teachers are employed, and the annual enrollment of students is 1,000. During the last 14 years he has been mayor of the town of Simpsonville for 11 years, which establishes a record in that municipality. His administrations have brought many public improvements to the town, including electric lights and a water system, both owned by the town.

Dr. Richardson has been twice married, first to Miss Burgiss Rollins of Florence, South Carolina, who died July 28, 1907, and next in 1912 to Miss Bessie Harrison of Simpsonville. To the first union were born four children: R. L. Richardson, Superintendent of schools at Calhoun Falls, South Carolina; J. R. Richardson, engaged in the life insurance busines at Greenville, South Carolina; C. R. Richardson, engaged in the mercantile business at Simpsonville; and Evelyn Richardson, a teacher in the Blackville, South Carolina schools. By the second marriage there are two children, viz: Bruce and Orrin.

JEFFERSON F. RICHARDSON

Many of those who have been instrumental in the growth of Greenville throughout the whole of her life, and especially during the last half century, have come to her from Charleston. Of this number is JEFFERSON F. RICHARDSON, who moved to Greenville in 1880 to become connected with the *Greenville News,* then just four years old and one of the three daily newspapers in the State of South Carolina.

Jefferson F. Richardson, son of Jefferson C. E. Richardson and Priscilla (Calder) Richardson, was born in Charleston, South Carolina, on the 12th day of January, 1861. As a boy he attended the St. Phillips Street graded school and the

Charleston High School. But at the age of 18 years he left school and moved to Greenville, where he took charge of the *Greenville News,* then just a small six-column, four-page daily, owned by his brother, William H. Richardson of Summerville, South Carolina. A short time thereafter, A. B. Williams, widely known as an editorial writer, became editor of the paper, and in 1887, Mr. Richardson acquired a majority of the stock. Immediately the *Greenville News* took an enviable position among the newspapers of the state. In 1886 it contracted for the Associated Press news, which was a service rarely furnished by a paper with so small a circulation. But under his able management and the progressive policy of its editor, the circulation rapidly grew till within a few years it had become quite a factor in the progress of Greenville.

In 1900 Mr. Richardson was appointed postmaster of the city of Greenville, which position he held during the administrations of Presidents Roosevelt and Taft, and till 1916 under President Wilson, his combined terms covering almost twice as many years as those served by any other postmaster at the Greenville office. During his administration $157,000 was spent in building additions to the post office property.

For seven terms Mr. Richardson has been an Alderman of the city of Greenville. During his service as Alderman, for ten years he was Chairman of the Finance Committee, and four years he served as Chairman of the Street Committee. For several years he also served as Chairman of the Police Commission, and during that time assisted in the re-organization of the Police Department upon a basis which is still in force.

Always Mr. Richardson has taken a leading part in the various civic and economic activities of Greenville. By many he is still referred to as the "Daddy" of the Greenville street railway system, since he was so active in the movement which finally terminated in bringing the Southern Public Utilities Company into Greenville; and in 1898 he probably did more than any other person to secure the Spanish-American war encampment of soldiers for his city. He was a leading spirit in the organization of the Greenville Board of Trade in 1881, and became its first Secretary and Treasurer.

In 1907 Mr. Richardson sold his interest in the *Greenville News,* and upon completing his 16 years of service as postmaster in 1916, he became Treasurer and Manager of the Acme Loom & Harness Company in which company he had acquired an interest in 1914. Since then the company has merged with another and is now a large and important addition to the textile supply manufacturing concerns of Greenville.

Mr. Richardson is a member of the Knights of Pythias, the Elks, and the Woodmen of the World.

He was married to Miss Athena Tindal of Clarendon, S. C., a graduate of the Greenville Woman's College (then G. F. C.), and they have five living children: Henrietta Athena, J. F., Jr., Mary, Eleanor and William H. The family home is on Hampton Avenue in the city of Greenville.

J. HARVEY CLEVELAND

J. HARVEY CLEVELAND, the largest landowner in Greenville County, was born at Marietta, South Carolina, on February 14, 1878, being the son of Jesse F. and Emma Cleveland. His grandfather, J. Harvey Cleveland, settled in the Marietta and Cleveland sections during the early days of the last century and his descendants have done much to develop that part of the county. Jeremiah Cleveland, early merchant and prominent business man of the town of Greenville in its infant days, was the founder of the family in the county, and the great-grandfather of the subject of this sketch.

Mr. Cleveland (J. Harvey of this sketch) received his early education in the schools of his home community and then at Furman University, Greenville, S. C. Finishing his education, he was engaged in textile work in Greenville and Spartanburg counties for a number of years. However, upon the death of his father he returned to the ancestral home and since has engaged in farming.

Greenville County is the home of small farm owners, but Mr. Cleveland has more than 4,000 acres, and is easily the largest individual land-owner in the county. But he believes in diversified farming and not the usual "all cotton" system. Upon his broad acres grow extensive peach and apple orchards and great fields of corn and oats. Some cotton is grown, but this takes a secondary place on the Cleveland plantation.

For 12 years Mr. Cleveland held the office of Magistrate in Cleveland township; eight years he was Game Warden for Greenville County; and during the World War he was a member of the Exemption Board for upper Greenville County. In 1928 Mr. Cleveland was elected a member of the South Carolina House of Representatives from Greenville County and this position of honor and trust he still holds.

Mr. Cleveland is a member of the Chi Psi college fraternity, a Royal Arch Mason, and a Woodman of the World. He is deeply interested in the problems of the farmer and spends much of his time in assisting those of his community.

Mr. Cleveland's wife is the former Miss Hazel Baker. They have three children: J. Harvey, Jr., John Baker, and Elizabeth Maxwell.

B. F. FLYNN

Between Greenville and Greer, on the "Main Street of South Carolina" (State Highway No. 8 from Greenville to Spartanburg), is the town of Taylors. For many years Taylors was nothing more than a thickly settled community, but during the last ten years two large textile plants located there have given a tinge of commercialism to the town, and it is now growing rapidly. But regardless of the fact that Taylors has commenced to expand only within the last few years, the community in which it is situated was one of the first in the county to be settled. The lands thereabout are well adapted to agriculture, and for many years some of the most influential and successful farmers of the county have lived at and near Taylors. Among these may be mentioned the Flynns.

B. F. FLYNN, the subject of this sketch, was born near Taylors in 1869, being the son of John F. and Jeannie (McAlester) Flynn. He secured his education in the schools afforded by his home community, and then entered upon his life's work of merchandising and farming. Before the end of the last century he and his brother, J. W. Flynn, established "Flynn Bros." of Greenville and for 32 years they have conducted a successful mercantile business in the city of Greenville. In 1914 he and his brother, Claud, established "B. F. Flynn & Bros." of Taylors and for 16 years this concern has done a large part of the mercantile business of Taylors, and its environs. The Greenville business is conducted under the direct supervision of J. W. Flynn, while that at Taylors is in charge of B. F. Flynn. And in addition to his large mercantile interests, Mr. Flynn operates a farm near Taylors.

Mr. Flynn is a Baptist and a Mason; he is deeply interested in the well-being of his home community and the county, and takes an active part in promoting worthwhile civic undertakings.

Mr. Flynn was married to Miss Daisy E. Crowder and they are the parents of three children: Jeannie Loede, now Mrs. Dr. Drew S. Harper; J. Royce, whose wife is the former Nelle Giles, and Lillian Virginia, now Mrs. Jake L. Woods. The family home is at Taylors, South Carolina.

NELSON C. POE, SR.

NELSON C. POE, SR., President of the F. W. Poe Manufacturing Company, is the son of William Poe and Ellen C. (Taylor) Poe. He was born in Montgomery, Alabama, on November 7, 1851. His grandfather was a brother of the grandfather of Edgar Allen Poe, the famous author. Of the mother of Mr. Poe, Colonel R. W. Simpson, in his History of Old Pendleton, writes:

"Ellen C. Taylor, a daughter of Colonel Joseph and Nancy (Sloan) Taylor, married Mr. William Poe, and removed from Pendleton. After Mr. Poe's death Mrs. Poe returned to Pendleton. Mrs. Poe was an uncommon woman. Left a widow with a family of eight children, she portrayed her excellent motherly qualities by rearing and educating a family of children honored and esteemed for many admirable qualities."

Mr. Poe, Sr., secured his education in the schools of Pendleton, South Carolina, to which place he moved with his mother when four years of age. At 17 years he accepted employment with the old Blue Ridge Railway and remained there for a year and a half. Leaving the railroad, he went to Columbia, South Carolina, where he was first employed by a grocery store and then became connected with a hardware concern. In 1875 he came to Greenville and associated himself with Wilkins, Williams & Company, in the hardware business. About 1882 he organized what is now the Poe Hardware & Supply Company, and became its President and active head. He was President of that company until 1925.

In 1895 Mr. Poe, with his brother, F. W. Poe, organized the F. W. Poe Manufacturing Company. This was at a time when textile manufacturing was in its infancy in the South. He became Vice-President of the company when organized and this position he held until the death of his brother, when he was elected President. N. C. Poe, Jr., son of N. C. Poe, Sr., is now Vice-President and Assistant Treasurer of the company and assists his father in its operation.

In addition to his connections with the F. W. Poe Manufacturing Company, Mr. Poe is a director of the First National Bank of Greenville, and a director in the Glenwood Cotton Mills of Easley, South Carolina; and is interested in a number of other cotton mills.

He married Miss Nannie Crawford, daughter of James W. Crawford of Pendleton, South Carolina, and they have three children, viz: N. C. Poe, Jr., President of the Poe Hardware & Supply Company and Vice-President of the F. W. Poe Manufacturing Company; Ellen Poe, and William Wilkins Poe, Secretary and Treasurer of the Poe Hardware & Supply Company.

FRANCIS WINSLOW POE

FRANCIS WINSLOW POE was born on October 12, 1853, in Montgomery, Alabama, where his family had removed a few years previously from Baltimore, Maryland. He was the son of William Poe and Ellen Cannon Taylor, daughter of Joseph and Nancy Sloan Taylor.

Upon the death of his father in 1855 Mr. Poe's mother returned with her children to her father's plantation near Pendleton, South Carolina. Here he spent his childhood, youth, and early manhood, attending the village school until he was 12 years of age. At that time, forced by the hardships immediately following the Civil War, he secured work in a dry goods and general merchandising store, where he worked by day and studied by night, alone, save with the occasional assistance of his mother.

When he was 25 years old Mr. Poe opened a clothing and shoe business in Greenville, South Carolina, establishing his residence there at that time. A year later he was married to Miss Harriet Augustus Maxwell, daughter of Dr. Robert Duff and Inez Sloan Maxwell. Of this marriage there were five children, Eugenia Maxwell, Harriet Augusta, Zaidee, Lucy Sloan, and Francis Winslow Poe, Jr.

While continuing his residence in Greenville and operating his business there with marked success, Mr. Poe became affiliated with the firm of Browning, King & Company of New York City, and for 18 years was actively engaged in mercantile business in both places.

In his early forties, he severed all of his mercantile relations, assembling and consolidating his entire resources in order to build the F. W. Poe Manufacturing Company, one of the oldest of the cotton goods mills of Greenville, of which Mr. Poe was President and Treasurer from its organization until the day of his death, during all of which time the mill was recognized as one of the most successful of the pioneer manufacturing industries of South Carolina.

In connection with his manufacturing interests, Mr. Poe was for many years a member of the Manufacturers' Association of South Carolina. He was a director in the Glenwood Mills of Easley and the Pickens Cotton Mills of Pickens, South Carolina, and of the Peoples National Bank of Greenville.

Mr. Poe was actively interested in the organization of the Greenville Country Club, being one of its charter members. He was also a member of the Poinsett Club, as well as a member and one time President of the Cotillion Club, the oldest social club of the city.

Following closely upon the organization of the Fourth Presbyterian Church of Greenville, Mr. Poe was made chairman of the Board of Trustees of the church property, which office he continued to fill until his death, which occurred at his home on July 18, 1926.

HENRY KEITH TOWNES

Distinguished by his quiet and gentlemanly manner and his scrupulously careful observance of the ethics of his profession, HENRY KEITH TOWNES occupies an enviable position, not only in the eyes of the legal fraternity but also that of the entire community.

The name Townes has for over a century been associated with all that is progressive and forward-looking in the city of Greenville. Prior to 1800 Samuel Townes settled in Greenville County, coming here from Virginia. He was a large planter and reared a family, each of whom performed well his allotted duties in life. His son, George F., married Mary Keith and they became the parents of the subject of this sketch. George F. Townes was educated for the bar and for many years was prominent and active in the legal and political annals of the county. He served one term as State Senator.

Henry K. Townes was born in Greenville, South Carolina, on October 16, 1876. His early education was received in the public schools of Greenville, after which he attended Furman University, being graduated in 1897 with the degree of A.B. In 1900 he was admitted to the South Carolina bar, and begun the practice of his profession in Greenville. He has had several partners over a period of years, his present connection being with J. Mac Wells, under the firm name of Townes & Wells. They specialize in the practice of civil law with particular attention to the real estate branch of the profession.

Mr. Townes is of English ancestry on his father's side and pure Scotch on that of his mother. He is a member of the Sons of the American Revolution, his ancestors having fought for the freedom of the colonies from English rule during the Revolutionary War. He is a member of the Greenville Bar Association, as well as a member of the South Carolina Bar Association, and has served as President of the first mentioned. And while he has not sought public office, he nevertheless takes a great interest in public affairs of his county and State and is at this time serving as Chairman of the Executive Committee of the Democratic party of Greenville County. In religious affiliation he is a member of the Baptist Church.

On June 6, 1907, Mr. Townes was married to Miss Ellen Hard, and they are the parents of six children: Mary, Ellen, Henry K., Jr., Charles H., Aurelia and George F.

W. E. FREEMAN

In the early days of Greenville the firm of Gower, Cox & Gower was building vehicles which found their way into many states. Under successive ownerships the firm gradually drifted into the general hardware business, but the identity of the concern has never been lost, and through almost a century, under different names, it has been a large factor in the business life of Greenville. At the beginning of the present century the concern had become the Markley Hardware & Manufacturing Company, to be succeeded later by the Sullivan-Markley Hardware Company, and in 1928 it became the Sullivan-Freeman Company, with W. E. Freeman as managing head.

W. E. FREEMAN, subject of this sketch, was born in Pickens, South Carolina, on July 13, 1885, being the son of J. B. R. and Amanda E. (Harris) Freeman. He secured his early education in the public schools of Pickens and then became a student at Clemson College, where he studied for two years.

Leaving college, Mr. Freeman went to Charleston, South Carolina, where he entered the employ of a wholesale and retail hardware concern. After his Charleston connection he became a member of the Givens Hardware Company of Savannah, Georgia, where he remained for several years. In 1913 he moved to Greenville and became connected with the Sullivan-Markley Hardware Company as Assistant Manager. This position he held until 1928 when the concern was reorganized and its name changed to Sullivan-Freeman Company. Of the new concern Mr. Freeman became General Manager and Treasurer. The Company is engaged in the hardware business upon an extensive scale, being the largest of its kind in the State. Its activities cover both wholesale and retail fields.

In addition to his mercantile interests, Mr. Freeman owns and manages the Amanda Apartments, located on East Earle Street.

Mr. Freeman is a Director of the Greenville Chamber of Commerce, a member and ex-Director of the Civitan Club, and a Deacon of Central Baptist Church. In 1929 he was elected an Alderman of the City of Greenville, which position he still holds.

Mr. Freeman was married to Miss Julia Griffin, daughter of E. S. Griffin of Greenville, and they are the parents of one child, Jack Freeman.

WILLIAM HAMPTON BALENTINE

During the last decade the civic leaders of Greenville, through the Chamber of Commerce, have put forth much effort to secure "diversified industries" for the county, and their work has not been in vain, as statistics on manufactories will show. But while outside capital was being sought by the organized forces, a citizen of Greenville came forward, and unaided, established a large manufacturing business which now promises to grow into tremendous proportions. This was no other than WILLIAM HAMPTON BALENTINE, the founder of the Balentine Packing Company.

Mr. Balentine was born in Laurens County, South Carolina, on the 24th day of June, 1878, being the son of Irby Taylor Balentine and Othella (Murff) Balentine. His education was obtained in the public schools of his home community. At 20 years of age he moved to Greenville, where by slow processes, he identified himself with the business life of the city. First he entered the meat market business with his brother-in-law, Thomas L. Gilreath. This firm was located in the "west end" section of the city for a number of years. Withdrawing from this business, Mr. Balentine purchased "Shreevers Market" on Main Street, which he operated for a number of years. Later he conducted a large market on West Coffee Street.

In 1917 Mr. Balentine disposed of the business which he had conducted with unusual success over a period of years and staked all in the meat packing industry, which he had long thought could be successfully conducted in Greenville, by organizing the Balentine Packing Company. Today the "Palmetto Brand" products, put out by this concern, are known throughout the southeast. The plant, located on East

Court Street, has a capacity of 125 hogs per hour and when running to capacity employs 175 men. It is a complete packing plant, manufacturing lard, bacon, hams and sausage, and is the only one in South Carolina. The success of this business has done much to encourage the raising of hogs in the county, as it furnishes a ready market for the farmer desiring to engage in that business. Although Mr. Balentine died on May 27, 1927, he had so thoroughly established his business that it goes on under the supervision of his sons and former employees.

But the multiplicity of his business interests did not consume the whole of Mr. Balentine's time by any means. He was a public-spirited citizen and did much for the good of his community. For one term he was an Alderman of the city of Greenville; many years he was a Steward in the Buncombe Street Methodist Church; he was a Shriner, an Elk, a Knights Templar, a member of the W. O. W. and a K. of P. For many years he was a member of the Rotary Club and at one time was a director in that civic organization. He was a member of Lodge No. 274, A. F. M., a Scottish Rite and York Rite Mason, and a charter member of Hejaz Temple.

The Shrine Magazine of August, 1927, said of Mr. Balentine: "It is with regret that we note the sudden death of Noble W. H. Balentine of Hejaz, Greenville, S. C., which occurred on May 27th, the day following the ceremonial at which his three sons became Shriners. . . . He was active in the organization work, and had always been a loyal member of the Temple's Patrol. Beattie, Carl and Louis were associated in business with their father, who owned and operated one of the largest meat packing houses in the Southern States. In addition to the Balentine boys, J. C. Rainey and W. E. Wickliffe, salesmen of the firm of W. H. Balentine, were also candidates at the Columbia Ceremonial."

On November 20, 1898, Mr. Balentine was married to Miss Lillie May Gilreath of Greenville, and they are the parents of 11 children: W. Louis, Carl E., Beattie B., Othella, Sophie, Lenora, William H., Jr., J. Marshall, Mary, Sarah, and C. David. Mrs. Balentine survives her husband and resides on Rutherford Street in the city of Greenville.

ROGER S. HUNTINGTON

ROGER S. HUNTINGTON, President of Huntington & Guerry, was born in White Plains, New York, on May 1, 1884, the son of B. W. and Helen (Seavey) Huntington. His faher was a lawyer and judge.

Mr. Huntington graduated from Pratt Institute, Brooklyn, and Cooper Union, New York. By the latter school he was awarded a B.S. degree in General Science. Following graduation, he entered the employ of the New York Telephone Company, where he remained for eight years and then became connected with the General Electric Company at Schenectady, New York. This company later transferred him to their engineering and construction departments in Atlanta, Ga.

After two years' employment in the Atlanta office, he left the General Electric Company and entered business for himself as an electrical contractor. He moved to Greenville, S. C., in 1913 and two years later became associated with DuPont Guerry, Jr., under the firm name of Huntington & Guerry. This company is among the largest of its kind in the South and does business in every Southern State.

It maintains an office also in Spartanburg, S. C. Its advent into the field came at a time when Southern industry was passing from steam to electric power on a large scale and it has played a prominent part in that transition period.

Mr. Huntington is also Vice-President of the H. & G. Refrigeration Company, with headquarters in Greenville, which distributes electrical refrigerators throughout the State of South Carolina.

He has taken an active part in the civic affairs of Greenville, through the Chamber of Commerce, the Community Chest and other organizations. He is a member of the Greenville Rotary Club, and of Hejaz Shrine Temple. He was married to Miss Jane W. Gower, daughter of Arthur G. Gower, in 1924.

DUPONT GUERRY, JR.

DuPont Guerry, Jr., Vice-President and Treasurer of Huntington & Guerry and President of the H. & G. Refrigerator Company, was born in Americus, Georgia, on April 21, 1883. He is a son of DuPont Guerry and Fannie (Davenport) Guerry. His parents are both descended from prominent South Carolina and Virginia families.

DuPont Guerry, father of DuPont, Jr., and son of William Barnett and Sarah Amanda (Dixon) Guerry, volunteered for service in the Confederate army at the age of 14 years, and two years later, when only 16, was commissioned a lieutenant. In 1868 he was admitted to the bar and soon became a very prominent attorney of Georgia. He has been a member of the Senate of Georgia and a United States Attorney. In 1902 he was a candidate for Governor of the State of Georgia on a prohibition platform. Then prohibition had not become popular and he was defeated. Following this, from 1903 to 1909, he was President of the Wesleyan College of Mason, Georgia. After this he resumed the practice of law and has since held the position of judge of the City Court of Macon, Georgia.

After attending the public schools of Macon, Georgia, DuPont Guerry, Jr., entered the University of Georgia for the study of law. However, during the gubernatorial campaign of his father he left college for a time and upon resuming his educational work had decided upon electrical engineering instead of law. He then entered the Alabama Polytechnic Institute of Auburn, from which he was graduated in 1906. His work while here accredited him for post-graduate work in the school of the General Electric Company of Schenectady, New York. This is quite an honor and affords an opportunity highly coveted by electrical engineers.

Having finished his studies with the General Electric Company, Mr. Guerry came to Greenville and became associated with J. E. Sirrine & Company in electrical engineering. Here he remained until 1916 when he and R. S. Huntington organized Huntington & Guerry. Of this concern he became Vice-President and Treasurer. From the beginning Huntington & Guerry enjoyed a large and profitable business in the electrical engineering and contracting field, and soon became one of the largest of its kind in the South. Year by year the concern has expanded its operations, devoting its efforts principally to the electrification of textile plants. In 1929 the firm organized the H. & G. Refrigerator Company and Mr. Guerry became its President. This company holds a contract for the distribution of the General

Electric refrigerator for the whole of the State of South Carolina and is doing a large business.

Mr. Guerry holds membership in a number of technical associations, is a member of the Rotary Club, the Greenville Country Club, the Kappa Alpha college fraternity, the Board of Commissioners of the Greater Greenville Sewer District, and the Methodist Church. In all fields of the civic life of Greenville he is active.

In 1910 he was married to Miss Ola Gregory of Lancaster, South Carolina, and they have two children, viz: DuPont III and Mary. The family home is in the Sans Souci section of the city of Greenville.

JAMES MADISON RICHARDSON

JAMES MADISON RICHARDSON was born in Fairview Township, near the present town of Simpsonville, on November 28, 1846, being a son of Jonathan and Nancy (Cox) Richardson, both of whom were members of old and prominent families of Greenville County.

The education of James Madison Richardson was principally of the self-taught kind, since the schools of his boyhood community were poor; but regardless of this, he developed into a man who bore a wide reputation for a deep knowledge of people. When only 16 years of age he entered the service of the Southern Confederacy and for several months of the War Between the States was a soldier.

Upon the conclusion of the war Mr. Richardson returned to his old home community and became engaged in farming, which was the occupation of his parents. From that time until his death on December 31, 1916, he lived in the Simpsonville community, spending his years cultivating his plantation, which during the last 20 or 25 years of his life was large. He was a firm exponent of the theory that a farmer should live at home, and it was very seldom during his long life that he ever purchased anything which can be produced from the South Carolina soil. Not only did he advocate the "live at home" principle, but he was noted for his thrift, being able to accumulate large properties for that time, and being at the time of his death probably the largest individual money lender in Greenville County, residing south of the city of Greenville.

He was always optimistic as to the ultimate value of good farm lands, and the principal portion of his money was loaned upon farm property. Many of the present-day farmers of lower Greenville County owe their start in life as farm owners to his assistance.

Although Mr. Richardson devoted himself principally to agriculture, he was also interested in other businesses of his community. Among these was the Bank of Simpsonville, which he assisted in organizing, and was until his death one of its directors. He also assisted in the organization of the Simpsonville Cotton Mill, and was one of its directors from its organization until his death. Upon the opening of the Bank of Simpsonville he was its first depositor, and the first cotton purchased by the Simpsonville Cotton Mill was from him.

From his boyhood days Mr. Richardson was a Baptist, being for many years a member of the Standing Springs Baptist Church, but during the latter part of his life a member of the Simpsonville Baptist Church. He assisted materially in the building of the present magnificent plant of the Simpsonville Baptist Church, and lies buried in its cemetery.

In December, 1876 he was married to Miss Mary Jane McDowell, a member on her mother's side of the well-known Peden family of the Fairview community, and they had four children, to-wit: Thomas Richardson; Pearle (now the wife of John M. Daniel, Attorney General of State of South Carolina) ; J. Furman Richardson, and Carrie Richardson. After his death his widow resided at the family homestead, a mile south of Simpsonville, until her death on December 23, 1924.

JOHN MOBLEY DANIEL

JOHN MOBLEY DANIEL, Attorney General of the State of South Carolina, was born in Edgefield County, now Saluda County, South Carolina, on July 22, 1883, being a son of Dr. John Furman Daniel and Susan (Adams) Daniel. His parents were both members of prominent families of that section and his father was long a practicing physician in Edgefield and Saluda Counties.

Mr. Daniel attended the country schools of his home community and then became a student at the Furman Fitting School of Greenville. From the Furman Fitting School he entered Furman University, proper, and from this institution was graduated with an A.B. degree in 1904. While still in college he studied law in the offices of Cothran, Dean & Cothran and soon after his graduation from Furman was admitted to the bar of the State of South Carolina.

After his admittance to the bar, Mr. Daniel returned to his old home community and practiced law in Saluda until 1907. He then moved to Greenville and entered into partnership with E. Inman, now Master of Greenville County. This partnership continued for a number of years, after which Mr. Daniel formed a partnership with Oscar Hodges of the Greenville bar. This connection he held until he was elected Magistrate of Greenville Township. He held the position of Magistrate until 1920, when he became Assistant Attorney General of the State of South Carolina under Samuel M. Wolf. Upon the retirement of General Wolf in 1924 Mr. Daniel was elected to succeed him, being successful in a race against three opponents. After two years he was again a candidate, without opposition this time, and was elected for four years, the constitution in the meantime having been amended so as to make the term of office of the Attorney General four years instead of two, as had previously been the case. Since that time he has remained in this high office.

During the time Mr. Daniel has been Attorney General his department has been called upon to handle a large amount of unusually important business. Among the litigated cases is that of the State against Columbia Railway, Gas & Electric Company and Broad River Power Company, which was for the purpose of requiring these companies to re-establish an adequate street-car service in the city of Columbia and surrounding territory. This case was bitterly contested by the railway and power companies and finally was decided by the Supreme Court of the United States, Mr. Daniel being successful in all of his contentions and the railway and electric companies being required to re-establish service. Another important matter passing through the office of the Attorney General during his administration was litigation relative to a State bond issue of $65,000,000 for the purpose of building roads. Although Mr. Daniel personally opposed the legislation, which provided for the sale of bonds without submitting the matter to a vote of the people, after the law was enacted and it became his official duty to sustain it, he entered heartily into the matter and sustained every contention of the state. This case, too, went to the Supreme Court of the United States. Another matter of more than passing importance is the litigation with the Southern Railway Company by the South Carolina Tax Commission with reference to the payment of about $400,000 in taxes. The Railway Company refused to make this payment and suit was brought for the recovery thereof. Although the case is still pending a favorable decision for the State has been rendered by a special referee to which the matter was referred. The entire road laws, school laws, and tax laws of the state have been revised and rewritten since Mr. Daniel went into office. He has been called upon for advice at every stage of these changes and the General Assembly and State officials following that advice have been almost uniformly successful in establishing these new laws without coming into conflict with either the State or Federal constitutions.

Mr. Daniel is a member of the First Baptist Church of Columbia, formerly being a Deacon therein. He also holds membership with the Knights of Pythias, W. O. W., Red Men, J. O. U. A. M. and the Lions Club. He is very active in the affairs of the W. O. W., having at one time been Head Consul for that order in the State of South Carolina, and now being one of the Sovereign Representatives of the State.

On June 26, 1918, he was married to Miss Pearle Richardson of lower Greenville County and they have one child, Janie Sue.

Although the family home is now in Columbia, because of the fact that Mr. Daniel's official duties call him there, a residence in Greenville is still maintained and here both Mr. and Mrs. Daniel pay their taxes and vote.

BONY HAMPTON PEACE

BONY HAMPTON PEACE, prominent business man, public-spirited citizen, and publisher of the two Greenville daily newspapers, was born at Tigerville, in upper Greenville County, being a son of Captain Jackson Patrick and Judith Ballenger (Tinsley) Peace. Through his father he is of Scotch-Irish descent, while his mother's ancestors were English. Both families were among the early settlers of upper South Carolina.

Mr. Peace obtained his education in public and private schools of Greenville and Spartanburg Counties, and early in life became connected with the *Greenville News*. In 1916, when it was a moribund property, with a circulation of less than 5,000 daily, he became its business manager and immediately the paper began to make itself felt in the newspaper field. Three years later he acquired control of the publication and became its editor and publisher. Within ten years the paper has become the leading newspaper in South Carolina, both in circulation and advertising patronage. In 1930 it attained a circulation of more than 31,000 net paid daily.

In 1927 Mr. Peace acquired the *Greenville Piedmont*, Greenville's afternoon daily, which he merged with the *Greenville News*. Since then the two papers have

been published in conjunction, but with separate editorial organizations. This paper, like the *Greenville News,* has made tremendous progress under the Peace management, and now has the largest circulation of any afternoon paper in the state.

Roger C. Peace is editor of the *Greenville News,* while Judson W. Chapman holds a like position with the *Greenville Piedmont.* B. H. Peace, subject of this sketch, directs the policies of the two papers and occupies the position of publisher of both.

Regarding Mr. Peace and his newspapers, a contemporary recently wrote editorially as follows:

"Perhaps few cities of similar size in the country can boast of two newspapers that are equal to Greenville's morning and afternoon papers. It is generally conceded by all who know of the progress that Greenville has made during the last score of years that the *Greenville News* and the afternoon *Piedmont* have proved great factors in the upbuilding of the splendid city in which these papers are published.

"Possessed of a desire to furnish the people of Greenville and the Greenville section a newspaper that contained clean, wholesome reading, B. H. Peace, the present publisher of the morning *Greenville News* and the afternoon *Piedmont* started out with a pace some 20 years ago, when he first acquired *The News,* that has since been kept up. Mr. Peace has built his newspapers on merit, his publications have continued clean and dignified and the papers have continued to grow in popularity as the years have passed by.

"Determined to furnish the readers of the two papers details of all of the major happenings of the world, Mr. Peace has arranged for the full lease wire services of the United Press to be coupled with the service of the Associated Press. This gives Greenville's morning and afternoon papers all that is furnished by the world's two largest and most important news gathering agencies."

Few, if any, civic undertakings of merit are entered upon by Greenville without receiving the active support of Mr. Peace and his newspapers.

Mr. Peace is a member of the Kiwanis Club and of the Sigma Delta Chi college fraternity. He is also a member of the First Baptist Church of Greenville.

On November 28, 1894, he was married to Miss Laura Estelle Chandler and they are the parents of five children: Mrs. George G. Leake, Roger Craft Peace, Mrs. Clarence T. Echols, Charlie Peace, Bony Hampton Peace, Jr., and Frances Lucille Peace.

HENRY J. HAYNSWORTH

There is probably no legal firm in the State of South Carolina having a more extensive practice than that of Haynsworth & Haynsworth. Of this partnership, HENRY J. HAYNSWORTH is the senior member.

Mr. Haynsworth, who was born in Clarendon County on August 10, 1859, is descended from a long line of illustrious ancestors. His paternal grandfather, William Haynsworth, was a noted lawyer of Sumter County, while his maternal grandfather, Peter Oliver, was an extensive planter of Williamsburg County. John R. Haynsworth, father of Henry J. Haynsworth, subject of this sketch, was a lawyer, noted for his pious living and social popularity. He was killed while fighting for the cause of his native state at the Battle of First Manassas. The mother of Mr. Haynsworth, Mary Oliver Haynsworth, was a cultured woman, who truly represented the ante bellum refinement so peculiar to the ladies of the Pee Dee and coastal sections of South Carolina in the old days.

As a boy, Mr. Haynsworth attended private schools of the community of his home and then became a student at Furman University, from which institution he was graduated with an A.B. degree in 1882. He studied law under private instructors.

Immediately after his admission to the bar he began the practice of his profession in Greenville, and at various times has been in partnership with Lewis W. Parker, afterward President of the Parker Cotton Mills Company, the largest textile organization in the state; L. O. Patterson of the Greenville bar, and Colonel E. M. Blythe, also of the Greenville bar. But for a number of years he has been in partnership with his son, C. F. Haynsworth, as senior member of the firm of Haynsworth & Haynsworth. This firm confines itself principally to corporate practice, being attorneys for many cotton mills in and near Greenville, as well as other large interests throughout the Piedmont section.

Mr. Haynsworth holds membership in the American, South Carolina, and Greenville Bar Associations; and was twice President of the South Carolina Bar Association. He is a trustee of Furman University and in 1905 and 1906 was treasurer of the institution. In church affiliation he is a Baptist, being a Deacon in the First Baptist church. He is a Rotarian and a member of the Greenville Country Club.

Only once has Mr. Haynsworth entered the political field, and then only for a brief period. In 1895 he was a member of the Constitutional Convention which framed the State Constitution under which South Carolina still operates.

In 1884 Mr. Haynsworth was married to Miss Anna Furman, daughter of Dr. J. C. Furman, for many years President of Furman University. To this union one child, Clement F., was born. Upon the death of his first wife, Mr. Haynsworth married again in 1897, this time to Miss Rhoda Livingston, daughter of Colonel Knox Livingston, and they have three children: Knox L. Haynsworth, Alice, and Henry J., Jr.

The Haynsworth family lives on North Main Street in the city of Greenville.

CLEMENT FURMAN HAYNSWORTH

CLEMENT FURMAN HAYNSWORTH, son of Henry J. Haynsworth and Annie (Furman) Haynsworth, was born in the city of Greenville on the 16th day of April, 1886. His father is a prominent citizen and eminent lawyer of Greenville, while his mother, now deceased, was a daughter of Doctor James C. Furman, first President of Furman University, and son of Richard Furman, founder of that institution.

Mr. Haynsworth secured his early education in the public schools of Greenville City and then became a student at Furman University, from which he was graduated with an A.B. degree in 1904. From Furman he went to Harvard University, where he received an A.B. degree in 1906 and that of LL.B. in 1909.

Upon leaving college, Mr. Haynsworth entered the legal firm of Haynsworth, Patterson & Blythe at Greenville which shortly thereafter became the firm of Haynsworth, Blythe & Haynsworth. This connection lasted for two years when the partnership of Haynsworth & Haynsworth, composed of Henry J. Haynsworth as senior partner and Clement F. Haynsworth as junior member was formed. This firm has continued in active practice since that time. Many of the most prominent attorneys now practicing at the Greenville bar have been connected with it from time to time. Some of these and many others received their early training with Haynsworth & Haynsworth. At this time there are nine lawyers connected with the firm as members and associates, making it probably the largest legal firm in the two Carolinas.

Mr. Haynsworth was a member of the House of Representatives from Greenville County, for one term—1913-'14—but has not since been a candidate for any public office. During the World War he was Legal Advisor and Government Appeal Agent for the Greenville County Selective Draft Board.

In all public affairs looking toward the advancement of his community, Mr. Haynsworth takes a leading part. He is a member of the Kiwanis Club, a director of the Greenville Chamber of Commerce, and belongs to the Kappa Sigma college fraternity. He is also a trustee of the Greenville Woman's College. His religious affiliations are Baptist, and he is a member of the First Baptist Church of Greenville.

On November 7, 1911, Mr. Haynsworth married Miss Elsie Hall of Washington, D. C., and they have four children: Clement Furman, Jr., Custis Hall, Elizabeth Blair, and Henry J. III. The family home is on Crescent Avenue in the city of Greenville.

WALTER S. GRIFFIN

WALTER S. GRIFFIN, cotton merchant and prominent business man of Greenville City, was born in Greenville, but when only one year of age his family moved to Edgefield County and here he was reared.

After completing his education Mr. Griffin entered the cotton business in Rome, Georgia, in 1891, with the Howell Cotton Company. This connection he held for 11 years and then went with the American Cotton Company of Atlanta, Georgia, where he remained for three years. In 1904 he returned to Greenville and established Cooper & Griffin, Inc. This company soon became one of the largest cotton concerns in the United States, with branches and offices located in all of the principal cities of the South. Until its dissolution in 1928 Cooper & Griffin, Inc., was one of the largest business enterprises with headquarters in the city of Greenville. Mr. Griffin, during the entire life of the company, was its President and directing head.

In addition to his cotton interests, Mr. Griffin has been active in various other lines of industry, being a cotton mill President and a Director in numerous other textile manufacturing plants in the South.

Mr. Griffin has always been active in the civic affairs of the city of Greenville, contributing heavily to the support of charity and education. He is a member of the Greenville Chamber of Commerce, and during the days of the World War was its President. He is also a member of the Greenville Country Club, and a Woodman of the World.

Mr. Griffin was married to Miss Annie Curry of Rome, Georgia, and they have two children: Anne, now Mrs. Mitchell King, and Walter S., Jr., who is engaged in business with his father and who is married to the former Miss Nell Mills, a daughter of Henry T. Mills, prominent business man of Greenville.

JOHN W. POWELL

In the death of JOHN W. POWELL, which occurred on June 24, 1930, Greenville lost a citizen who had contributed much to her life during the last decade. He was born at Travelers Rest on the 19th day of August, 1881, being the son of E. S. and Mary (Fowler) Powell, both of whom were born and reared in Greenville County.

Mr. Powell's education was obtained in the public schools of Travelers Rest and Tigerville. Having completed his education, he accepted a position with the County of Greenville. Here he remained for two years, after which he resigned to become a member of the Greenville City Fire Department. After eight years' service in that position he decided to enter the laundry business, so he resigned and went to Savannah, Georgia, where he remained for one year studying every phase of his chosen work. Then returning to Greenville in 1914 he, with a brother-in-law, bought out the old Gates Steam Laundry, and changed its name to the Ideal Laundry. After some years Mr. Powell purchased the interest of his brother-in-law, and became principal owner and President of the company. In 1924 the present home of the Ideal Laundry on Echols street was constructed. It is said to be the most up-to-date laundry building in the state. At the time of his death Mr. Powell was planning to enlarge and improve his plant which was already one of the largest in the Carolinas and modern in every respect.

Regarding Mr. Powell and his work the *Greenville Piedmont*, a local newspaper, said of him, at the time of his death:

"Mr. Powell came to Greenville as a young man and entered business. About 14 years ago he began the operation of the Ideal Laundry, and from a small beginning, by diligent effort and capable management, he had brought this business up to where it was one of the outstanding plants of its kind in the Carolinas. He assisted in the organization of the trade association of his vocation, and took an active part in the furtherance of its activities, having at one time served as President of the Tri-State Laundrymen's Association. Recently, he, with other laundrymen of Greenville, served as host to the Association in Convention, and received the warmest thanks of his associates for his untiring efforts towards making that convention a success.

"Mr. Powell was a public-spirited man, and was affiliated with a large number of organizations here, always evincing a ready willingness to do his part towards contributing to the success of each. He was a member of the Chamber of Commerce, the Greenville Rotary Club, the Greenville Country Club, the Greenville Lodge of Elks, the Knights of Pythias, the Junior Order, and of Blue Ridge Chapter No. 51, Order of the Eastern Star.

"He was a Steward of Buncombe Street Methodist Church, and a regular attendant at the meetings of the Men's Bible Class of his church. He was Past Master of Walden Lodge No. 274, A.F.M. As a member of Hejaz Temple, Nobles

JOHN W. POWELL

of the Mystic Shrine, he was Captain of the Potentate's Guard. When the Shriners' Hospital began operations here, he gave unstintingly of his time and efforts in assisting the hospital authorities with the installation and operation of the hospital's laundry plant.

"In the death of Mr. Powell, Greenville has lost a valuable citizen, one who could at all times be relied upon to assume his share of any responsibility toward furthering the city's interest and welfare.

"Mr. Powell is survived by his wife, Mrs. Bessie May Haynie Powell; by one daughter, Miss Emma Rebecca Powell, and by one little son, John W. Powell, Jr."

DAVIS C. DURHAM

DAVIS C. DURHAM, Clerk of the United States Court for the Western District of South Carolina, with headquarters in Greenville, was born at Shelby, Cleveland County, North Carolina, in 1867, being the son of David Noah and Esther Ruth (Coleman) Durham. His paternal ancestors are English, having emigrated to Virginia during the early part of the eighteenth century. Later members of the family moved to North Carolina. Many prominent lawyers, ministers, educators and business men have been among those to bear the name, and the City of Durham, North Carolina, was named in honor of the family. Davis Noah, father of Davis C., entered the Confederate army at 16 and upon the conclusion of the war became a merchant of Shelby, North Carolina. His business prospered and he became prominent in his field. In 1897 he moved to Greenville.

Mr. Durham, subject of this sketch, received his early education in the public schools of Shelby and then became a student at Captain Patrick's Military School at Greenville. He is a contemporary of Thomas Dickson and the Webb brothers, celebrated North Carolina jurists.

Leaving school at 16, Mr. Durham became traveling salesman for a Greenville concern. Because of his youth he was often referred to as "the boy drummer" during those days. Since that time he has been deeply interested in the problems of the traveling man. He is a Past President of the local T.P.A., as well as an ex-President of the state organization. After a few years as traveling salesman he entered business in Greenville, where he remained for 40 years in the same stand. Gilreath & Durham, Jewelers, the name under which he operated, became known throughout the entire Piedmont section for the integrity and high character of its owners, and its business became large. In July. 1920, he was appointed Clerk of the United States District Court for the Western District of South Carolina, and this position he continues to hold.

Dr. Charles L. Durham, Professor of Latin in Cornell University and widely known educator, is a brother of Davis C. Durham. He attended Furman University at Greenville, was awarded an M.A. degree by that institution, and later taught there.

During the days of the World War, Mr. Durham was a member of the Council of Defense for Greenville County. He was a prime mover in building the Masonic Temple at Greenville, and for many years was President and Treasurer of the Masonic Temple Company. For a number of years he was President of the Greenville Merchants Association. He assisted in the formation of the Greenville Chamber of Commerce and served as Chairman of its Traffic Bureau and as Director. He was also one of the organizers of the Greenville Country Club. He is a Mason and a Lion, being an ex-President of the local organization of the latter, and now District Governor for the State of South Carolina. In religious affiliation he is Baptist, being a member of the First Baptist Church of Greenville. For 15 or more years he served as Superintendent of the Sunday School of his church, and is much interested in all phases of Sunday School work. He has served as Vice-President of the Board of Trustees and Chairman of the Executive Committee of the Greenville Woman's College, and is a member of the Board of Education of the Baptist State Convention of South Carolina.

His wife is the former Miss Stella Louise Ferris of Spencer, Tioga County, New York. She is a graduate of the New England Conservatory of Music and came to Greenville as head of the Voice Department of the Greenville Woman's College. They have one child: Richard F. Durham, Jr. He is a graduate of Furman University and was one of the first Americans to enlist for service in the World War. As a member of the A.E.F., he saw service on many battle fields and was awarded the French Croix de Guerre for conspicuous gallantry during the Aisne attack at Soissons in June, 1918. He was married to Miss Bernice Hogin and they now live in New York, where he is managing editor of the *Bankers' Magazine*.

T. S. INGLESBY AND F. J. P. COGSWELL

Although Greenville County is largely dependent upon the textile industry for the leading position which she holds among the counties of South Carolina, the city of Greenville has a number of businesses closely allied to textile manufacturing which gives her a prominent place among the cities of the entire South. Of these "the mill supply business" is perhaps the leader. And in the forefront of that is found the Carolina Supply Company.

As early as 1899, when cotton manufacturing was in its infancy as a southern industry, T. S. INGLESBY, F. J. P. COGSWELL, and associates, seeing the growing need for a "mill supply" business, located among the cotton mills of this new field, organized the Carolina Supply Company, to be located at Greenville with ample capital and facilities to furnish the needs of the textile plants of its section. And as textiles grew in the southern field the Carolina Supply Company expanded, until it is today, not only the largest of its kind in South Carolina, but one of the largest in the entire South.

In 1916 F. J. Pelzer of Charleston, one of the organizers of the company, died and his interest in the company was acquired by Mr. Inglesby and Mr. Cogswell. Later these two purchased other interests and became the controlling owners, with Mr. Inglesby as President and Mr. Cogswell as Treasurer. These positions they still hold. T. H. Boyd is Sales-Manager.

The Carolina Supply Company does business over the entire South, ninety-five per cent of which is among the textile plants of that section. It employs more than 20 people and its annual sales run into large figures. In 1914 it constructed a large and modern building on West Court Street, where it has been able to care for its rapidly expanding business.

The success of this business has been due to the exceptional ability of its management.

Both Mr. Inglesby and Mr. Cogswell are progressive citizens and take an active interest in all worthwhile civic undertakings of their home city.

WILLIAM B. ELLIS

WILLIAM B. ELLIS, local manager of the Southern Public Utilities Company, was born at Winston-Salem, North Carolina, on the 10th day of October, 1892, being a son of W. B. and Clara (Nissen) Ellis. Both parents were members of old and prominent families of the South. One of the Nissen ancestors established a plant for the manufacture of wagons near 150 years ago, and from that time down to the present the "Nissen wagon" has been recognized as among the best that money could buy. During every war in which the United States has been engaged the Nissen people have made wagons for the use of the army.

After attending the public schools of Winston-Salem, Mr. Ellis entered the University of North Carolina where he was graduated with the degree of B.S. in 1911, while yet under the age of 19 years. From college he went with the General Electric Company, where he studied electrical engineering. Following this course of study he accepted a position with the steam turbine department of that company, and was located at Lynn, Massachusetts, for three years. From here he returned to Winston-Salem to accept a position with the Southern Public Utilities Company which was then just entering that city. Here he held the position of assistant to the vice-president of the company in charge of merchandise and power sales. During this period he did much work for the government, which was then engaged in prosecuting the World War.

Following the World War (1919) Mr. Ellis came to Greenville to become manager of the Southern Public Utilities Company, being at that time only 27 years of age. The "Utilities Company" has large interests in and around Greenville, and the position taken by Mr. Ellis carried great responsibilities, but for more than ten years he has discharged his exacting duties to the satisfaction of his company and its thousands of patrons.

Mr. Ellis takes a deep interest in the civic affairs of Greenville and is an active supporter of all worthwhile undertakings looking toward public betterment.

The wife of Mr. Ellis is the former Miss Caroline D. Burnett, daughter of the late W. E. Burnett of Spartanburg, South Carolina. They are the parents of two sons: William B. III and Wilbur.

DOCTOR THADDEUS B. REEVES

DR. THADDEUS B. REEVES, widely known surgeon of Greenville, was born in Laurens, South Carolina, on November 5th, 1885, being the son of F. B. and Emma (Gray) Reeves. His father was a merchant and prominent citizen of Laurens County, while his mother was a member of the well-known Gray family of the same county. Her father fought for the Confederacy during the whole of the War Between the States.

As a youth Dr. Reeves attended the public schools of Laurens County and then entered Clemson College. From this institution he was graduated with a B.S. degree in 1909. Having decided upon the medical profession as a life's work, after graduating from Clemson, he became a student at the University of Virginia, from which he was graduated as an M.D. in 1914. Desiring to specialize in surgery he then entered the University of Minnesota, and here he received the degree of Master of Science in Surgery in 1919. Following this he was a student under the world-famous Mayo Brothers at their Rochester, Minnesota, Clinic.

During the latter part of 1920 Dr. Reeves established himself in Greenville in the practice of general surgery, and during the ten years which have since passed he has gained wide recognition in his profession. At various times he has held the position of Surgeon-in-Chief at the Emma Moss Booth Hospital, consulting surgeon for United States Veterans Hospital No. 26, and orthopedic surgeon for both the Southern Railway and the Piedmont & Northern Railway.

In medical and surgical circles Dr. Reeves' opinions are highly regarded, as evidenced by the large number of papers contributed by him to the medical and surgical journals of the country. Among these may be mentioned:

"On the Presence of Interstitial Cells in the Chickens Tests"—*The Anatomical Record*, Volume 9, page 5—May, 1915.

"A Double Umbilicus"—*The Anatomical Record*, Volume 10, page 1—November, 1915.

"A Study of the Arteries Supplying the Stomach and Duodenum and Their Relations to Ulcer"—Collected Papers of Mayo Clinic, Volume 11, 1919.

"Fracture of the Skull"—*International Journal of Medicine and Surgery*, Volume 37, No. 7.

"Fracture and Dislocation of the Spine"—*International Journal of Surgeons*, Volume 35, No. 7.

"Chronic Cholecystitus"—*Journal of the South Carolina Medical Association*, April, 1922.

Dr. Reeves is a Fellow in the American College of Surgeons, a member of the Greenville City, Greenville County, and South Carolina Medical Associations; a member of the Southern Surgical Association, a Mason, a member of the Greenville Kiwanis Club, and a member of the Alpha Omega Alpha College fraternity.

In the business and civic life of Greenville, Dr. Reeves holds a prominent place. His offices are in the Jordan Building on North Main Street. He is unmarried.

JAMES F. WHATLEY

JAMES F. WHATLEY, Superintendent of Education for Greenville County, was born in the Mauldin community of Greenville County on August 29, 1891, being the son of Ransom A. and Susan (Foster) Whatley. For many years his father was employed by the Charleston & Western Carolina Railway, and was engaged in farming.

As a youth Mr. Whatley attended the public schools of Mauldin and then became a pupil in the Greenville City High School. From here he entered Furman University, and in 1911 was graduated by that institution with the degree of A.B.

Following his graduation from college Mr. Whatley taught school in various parts of Greenville, Aiken and Saluda Counties, until September 13, 1929, when he was appointed Superintendent of Education of Greenville County. This position he still holds. The public school system of Greenville County is the largest of that of any county in the state and being its head carries much distinction in the educational circles of the state. Although he has held his official position for less than a year Mr. Whatley has introduced many reforms into the school work of the county.

During the World War Mr. Whatley was a member of the Veterinary Corps, and was stationed at Camp Sevier for 20 months. He held the rank of sergeant.

He is unmarried.

MITCHEL LEE GULLICK

MITCHEL LEE GULLICK, for 18 years Auditor of Greenville County, was born in Hendersonville, North Carolina, on July 10, 1856, being the son of John C. Gullick and Emily (Kiser) Gullick. Both of his parents were descended from early settlers of Henderson County, North Carolina. John C. Gullick, father of the subject of this sketch, held the office of Clerk of Court of Henderson County, North Carolina, for 32 years.

Mitchel Lee Gullick secured his education in the public schools of Hendersonville, North Carolina, and at an early age entered business in Hendersonville, being engaged in the mercantile business and as a blacksmith. In January, 1880, he moved with his family, having then married, to Tigerville, in upper Greenville County, where he was a merchant and blacksmith for many years. During this period he served as Magistrate for Highland Township a number of terms.

In 1909 Mr. Gullick was elected to the office of Auditor for Greenville County and this high position he held for 18 years, retiring voluntarily in 1927 on account of his advanced age. As a public official he was not only courteous, but efficient to a marked degree.

For many years before moving to Greenville in 1909, upon his election to the office of Auditor, Mr. Gullick was Master of the Tiger Lodge of Masons. He also held membership with the Odd Fellows, the Red Men, and J. O. U. A. M., and was a Baptist, being a member of the First Baptist Church of Greenville.

During the whole of his life Mr. Gullick was interested in good government and the civic betterment of the various communities in which he lived, and at all times he could be counted upon to take a leading part in the promotion of any cause which was calculated to bring about these conditions.

He was twice married, first to Emily Arianna Fuller on January 14, 1879. She died on February 22, 1927, and on October 4, 1928, Mr. Gullick was married a second time, this wife being Mrs. Annie Day. By his first marriage he had nine children, only four of whom reached maturity—these being Carl Lee Gullick, now engaged in the real estate business in the city of Greenville; Guy A. Gullick, prominent attorney of Greenville; Mrs. Effie E. White, and Mrs. Nannie Fay Melchers. The five children dying when quite young were Emily Pearl, Mary Roxana, Roy Kiser and two infant sons.

Mr. Gullick died in 1930, leaving surviving him his widow and the four adult children named above.

THE MEYERS BROTHERS

Among those who have contributed largely toward the upbuilding of Greenville during the last two decades, are ALEX, MANAS, L. A. and NOLIN MEYERS. They are sons of Ben and Amelia Meyers and were born in Lovingston, Virginia.

As a young man, Alex Meyers established a business in Newport News, Virginia, and soon the three other brothers joined him. The undertaking was successful and the business grew rapidly. The brothers branched out and began to invest in other lines, including real estate. Success came to them in these new undertakings, and they were soon recognized as men of unusual business ability.

About 18 years ago two of the brothers, Manas and Alex, purchased the J. Thomas Arnold Company of Greenville, and changed its name to Meyers-Arnold Company. At that time the concern was a small dry goods establishment. In a few years this new business had grown to such an extent that the other brothers, L. A. and Nolin, joined the company, and together the four Meyers Brothers have made of the Meyers-Arnold Company the largest store in South Carolina, and probably in the two Carolinas, dealing exclusively in ladies' and children's furnishings. Although Manas and Alex, the two founders, are now dead, the remaining brothers are continuing the old policy of "the customer is always right" and Meyers-Arnold Company is yearly expanding its trade territory.

For many years prior to his death, Manas Meyers was a member of the Board of Directors of the South Carolina National Bank, and L. A. Meyers now holds the position made vacant by the death of his brother.

But the Meyers Brothers are not only business men of recognized ability, they are civic builders as well. If an undertaking is for the betterment of Greenville, these gentlemen are always found supporting it with their time and money. The interest of Greenville is considered by them as their personal affair and they work for its accomplishment just as hard as if it were a private matter. Nolin Meyers is a member of the Civitan Club of Greenville and takes an active interest in all its undertakings.

JAMES McDOWELL RICHARDSON
By BEVERLY T. (BEVO) WHITMIRE,
Reporter for *Greenville Piedmont*.

Greenville County will long remember JAMES McDOWELL RICHARDSON. This history he has written is a great service in itself, but it is only one among many. His whole life, it seems to me, has been wrapped up in the county of which he now writes. Every public act of his life has been a constructive one for the county he so dearly loves. Soon after he was elected to the South Carolina Senate he remarked to me: "I feel that no legislator should ever cast a vote while thinking of its probable effect upon his political fortunes at any future election." In that one statement, I believe, he expressed the essentials of statesmanship.

Mr. Richardson, or "Slim Jim", as we call him, did not offer for reelection to the Senate when his term expired in 1928. When he made the race in 1924 he never intended to run again. "There are just a few things I want to do", he said when offering himself as a senatorial candidate, "and if I can't do them in four years I never can." The major portion of those things he was able to accomplish.

The son of William J. and Margaret Sophronia (McDowell) Richardson, James McDowell Richardson, was born in the lower part of Greenville County, where his boyhood was spent on the farm of his parents. His ancestors on both sides were early settlers of the county. Through his mother he is descended directly from the Peden family which organized the first church in the county—the Fairview Presbyterian Church. His early education was secured in the public schools of Fountain Inn and Simpsonville, and at a business college in Augusta, Georgia. After graduating from the business college he secured employment with the Southern Cotton Oil Company of Greenville, where he remained for a year and then went with the Clinton Oil Mill of Clinton, South Carolina, for another year. With the money saved during those two years, supplemented by borrowings and summer farm work, he was able to spend three years at Furman University. While there he led the University in scholarship during his last year and was at the same time Editor-in-Chief of the Furman Echo (college literary publication). Following his college years, he was employed for a few months by Pride, Patton & Tilman (now Patton, Tilman & Bruce) of Greenville. For several years, however, he had been studying law at night, and in December, 1909, was admitted to the bar of South Carolina.

The year following his admission to the bar Mr. Richardson went to Fountain Inn where he became cashier of the Peoples Bank. While there he organized the Farmers Bank of Simpsonville and the Bank of Fork Shoals. He became Vice-President of the Simpsonville bank and was later elected President of both the Peoples Bank and the Bank of Fork Shoals. All of these connections he held for a number of years. In 1916 he came back to Greenville and entered actively upon the practice of law, building up a large practice on the civil side of the court. Crime and criminals never seemed to interest him. And in addition to his legal work he organized the Greer Oil Mill and Feed Company of Greer and for two years was its President; he organized the Peoples Agricultural Credit Corporation and Fountain Inn National Farm Loan Association of Fountain Inn, and the Simpsonville National Farm Loan Association of Simpsonville, all three of which he has continuously represented as attorney; for a number of years he was a director of the Norwood National Bank of Greenville and its successor, the South Carolina National Bank, during three years of which time he was a member of the loan committee. For a number of years he was President and principal owner of the Fountain Inn Telephone Company and the Simpsonville Telephone Company. And on top of all this he has found time for extensive farming and public work.

He served as Mayor of Fountain Inn for two terms during his residence there. In 1918 he was elected to the House of Representatives from Greenville County, leading the ticket in a field of 18 candidates. While in the House he served on the Ways and Means Committee. In 1924 he was elected to the Senate from Greenville County, securing 11,000 votes out of 18,000 cast, and carrying all but six boxes in the county. For years he has been Democratic Executive Committeeman from Ward II in the City of Greenville, has been a delegate to the Greenville County Democratic Convention a number of times, and on four occasions has been a delegate to the State Democratic Convention. For ten years or more he was attorney for the town of Fountain Inn, and with the town of Simpsonville he held a like position for several years.

But of all his public services those performed by him as Senator are to my mind the greatest. Paved roads now radiate from Greenville in every direction; the state highway cost limitation of $30,000 per mile for construction of highways—which worked such great hardship on the mountain country—has been abolished; the building of roads has become a matter of engineering and not politics, with the result that highways now run straight or curve gently, whereas they wound about all over the countryside in former days; the state has a Chief Highway Commissioner; state funds are now required to be made in interest-bearing accounts, and state officers are compelled to require security for all deposits. These things, and more, he was instrumental in securing. He consistently fought all forms of a sales tax, except that on gasoline, and worked steadily for property tax reform. Immediately upon being chosen Chairman of the Greenville County Delegation he threw all meetings of the Delegation open to the public, which was a new procedure for Greenville County, and for the whole of his term not one meeting was held at which newspapermen were not present. While in the Senate he was a member of the Judiciary, Finance, Banking and Insurance, and Roads and Bridges committees. Seldom did he speak from the floor of the Senate, but he got results.

Jim Richardson has never been of robust constitution and during war days he did not bear arms because of his health; but at home he served as best he could, being Chairman of the Legal Advisory committee for the draft men. He is a deacon and member of the Board of Trustees of the Fourth Presbyterian Church of Greenville. Among other memberships which he now holds, or has held in the past, are: South Carolina Bar Association, United States Bar Association, American Law League, Greenville Country Club, Civitan Club, Greenville Chamber of Commerce, Elks, J. O. U. A. M., Woodman of the World, Red Men, Loyal Order of Moose, and Knights of Pythias.

During the last two years it has been necessary for him to discontinue many of his activities because of the state of his health, but he is still active in the practice of law and other of his business and political connections.

On December 27, 1910, he was married to Miss Julia Prince of Landrum, South Carolina; and from that union have been born Virginia, J. McDuffie and Julia, all of whom are students of the Greenville High School.

* * * * * * * * * *

Beverly T. Whitmire, or "Bevo", as he is generally known, is a friend of mine and often I have said he was the best newspaper reporter in South Carolina. Since reading the foregoing, however, I am inclined to change my mind as to his reportorial ability. But after all he has written as a friend and not in the capacity of an unprejudiced observer. Let the reader remember this. J. M. R.

PART II — BIOGRAPHICAL 339

BIOGRAPHICAL INDEX

PAGE

Allen, Charles Otis 245
Anderson, Dr. James Leland 196
Ansel, Governor Martin F. 302
Arrington, John W. 295

Balentine, William Hampton 317
Beacham, William C. 200
Beattie, Fountain Fox 200
Beattie, Harvey Cleveland 192
Beattie, Samuel Marshall 202
Blythe, Major Edgeworth M. 292
Bonham, Proctor Aldrich 293
Bramlett, Cliff R. 246
Bramlett, Decatur Lee 258
Bristow, A. A. 241
Brockman, Dr. H. LeRoy 193
Brockman, Dr. Thomas 267
Browning, Paul 212
Browning, W. D. 211
Bull, James A. 276
Burbage, Hampton P. 276

Cannon, James A. 213
Carlisle, Dr. J. P. 297
Carter, W. W. 217
Charlotte, John M. 263
Christenberry, Thomas E. 218
Cleveland, J. Harvey 311
Cleveland, William C. 241
Cody, Dr. Zechariah Thornton 142
Cogswell, F. J. P. 332
Conyers, W. Priestly 149
Cothran, Justice Thomas Perrin 304
Cothran, William Coulter 307
Cruikshank, William Nolley 260
Cunningham, Frank Harrison 259
Cunningham, J. C. 264

Daniel, John Mobley 321
Dargan, Harry A. 287
Davenport, D. D. 222
Davenport, James A. 236
Davenport, James F. 237
Davenport, M. C. 223
Dean, Alvin Henry 139
Dobson, R. D. 226
Drummond, Dr. Roy J. 211
Durham, Davis C. 331

Ellis, Dr. Mark Sharpton 194
Ellis, William B. 333

BIOGRAPHICAL INDEX—Continued.

	PAGE
Fair, Dr. Charles Hardy	275
Few, Dr. Benjamin Franklin	223
Finley, George	276
Flynn, B. F.	311
Foster, Guy Butler	300
Freeman, W. E.	314
Frye, A. D.	257
Gower, Thomas Claghorn	153
Gray, Robert Lee, Jr.	287
Green, Benjamin Augustus and Ida (Bates)	247
Gresham, W. Frank	257
Griffin, Walter S.	327
Guerry, Dupont, Jr.	319
Gullick, Mitchel Lee	335
Hamblen, Frank G.	255
Hammond, Frank	228
Harris, B. S. H.	189
Harris, John D.	226
Hartzog, Octavus Bowen	172
Harvley, H. Clyde	168
Haynsworth, Clement Furman	326
Haynsworth, Henry J.	325
Henry, Robert E.	186
Hipp, W. Frank	235
Hollis, Lawrence Peter	242
Huff, Pascal Dacus	214
Huff, Swan Burnett	217
Hughes, Robert Murray	271
Huntington, Roger S.	318
Inglesby, T. S.	332
Johnson, Dr. Lewelly Calhoun	298
Jones, Dr. C. C.	232
Jones, R. David	177
Jones, William T.	177
Keith, Colonel William Henry	233
Lagerholm, Carl F.	270
Lanford, John D.	210
Lawton, T. Oregon	248
League, G. Frank	176
Lewis, James Overton	167
Livingston, Whitner K.	191
Mann, Honorable A. C.	231
Mann, Dr. James Lewis	165
Marchant, Martin Luther	182

PART II — BIOGRAPHICAL 341

BIOGRAPHICAL INDEX—Continued.

PAGE

Marchant, Dr. Robert Lee	182
Marchant, Thomas M.	185
Marshall, John Barratt	227
Martin, Columbus Benjamin	255
Martin, J. Robert	301
Mauldin, Captain Oscar Kern	244
Meyers Brothers	336
Milford, Charles O.	269
Mills, Arthur L.	149
Mills, Otis P., Jr.	148
Mills, Captain Otis Prentiss	147
Morgan, James H.	280
McAfee, Thomas F.	178
McCoin, Elmer G.	291
McCullough, Joseph Allen	285
McDaniel, William B.	175
McGlothlin, Dr. William J.	156
McSwain, John Jackson	140
Neves, Benjamin F.	195
Neves, William D.	196
Norris, Thomas M.	209
Norwood, John Wilkins	198
Parker, Lewis Wardlaw	249
Patton, Ernest	171
Peace, Bony Hampton	322
Perry, (Miss) James Margrave	300
Poe, Francis Winslow	313
Poe, Nelson C., Sr.	312
Poole, Joseph P.	160
Pope, Thomas H.	254
Potter, W. T.	268
Powell, John W.	328
Price, James H.	209
Prevost, Marshall B.	234
Quick, Dr. George W.	298
Quillen, Robert	143
Ramsay, Dr. David Marshall	155
Ray, Boyd Brandon	225
Reeves, Dr. Thaddeus B.	333
Richardson, James Madison	320
Richardson, James McDowell	336
Richardson, Jefferson F.	309
Richardson, Dr. Lawrence L.	308
Russell, John A.	171

BIOGRAPHICAL INDEX—Continued.

	PAGE
Sirrine, George W.	253
Slattery, Lawrence P.	274
Smith, Augustus Wardlaw	180
Smith, B. B.	193
Smith, John E.	238
Sparkman, Dr. William Buck	220
Speegle, C. D.	237
Squires, Charles Tappey	219
Steedly, Dr. Benjamin B.	274
Stewart, Dr. Henry Boardman	179
Stover, Dakyns B.	224
Sweeny, Robert Powell	284
Symmes, Frederick W.	221
Templeton, Charlotte	268
Townes, Henry Keith	314
Wakefield, J. E.	164
Walker, A. C.	291
Walker, W. Frank	206
Watkins, J. Ben	303
Watson, Major Richard F.	205
Wells, George G.	279
Welch, Lee Hamilton	272
Whatley, James F.	334
White, Dr. J. Warren	296
White, Walter P.	163
Williams, Captain Leonard	190
Williams, James T.	278
Willimon, W. Henry	280
Winn, James A.	271
Woodside, John T.	157
Woodside, Robert I.	159
Workman, William Douglas	165
Wyche, C. G.	286
Yates, Charles H.	278

ADAIR, JAMES	17	. TYGER JIM	197	BAILEY, E.C.	120	. KITTY MARSHALL	202
ADAMS, BENJAMIN C.	177	. W.H.	110	BAKER, ALICE	210	. MARGARET	-
. EDITH OGLETHORPE	177	. WILLIAM	51,56,197	. HAZEL	311	. HAYNSWORTH	192
. J.H.	144	ANDREWS, ANNE	190	. JOHN W.	185	. MARSHALL	202
. JULIA CALDWELL	177	EPHRAIM	190	BALENTINE,	219	. MARY CAROLINE	-
. LAWRENCE	235	ANGELL, HELEN	297	. BEATTIE B.	318	. MAYES	201
. SUSAN	321	ANSEL,	308	. C. DAVID	318	. MARY MAYES	201
ADKINS, IDA	168	. ADDIE	-	. CARL E.	318	. PARIOLIE GOLDSMITH	193
MARY	217	. HOLLINGSWORTH	303	. IRBY TAYLOR	317	. RUTH	205
AIKEN,	87	. ADDIE R. HARRIS	303	. J. MARSHALL	318	. RUTH MCGEE	205
AKERS, ANNIE	275	. FREDARIKA	303	. LENORA	318	. S.M.	101
ALDERMAN,	275	. FREDERIKA BOWERS	302	. LILLIE MAY	-	. SAMUEL MARSHALL	202
ALDRICH, A.P.	293	. GERTRUDE	303	. GILREATH	318	.	205
. DAISY	293	. JOHN JACOB	302	. MARY	318	. SARAH CLEVELAND	193
. JAMES	293	. MARTIN F.	127,132	. OTHELLA	318	. W.E.	101
. ROBERT	293		301-302,308	. OTHELLA MURFF	317	. WILLIAM E.	202
ALEXANDER,	35	. OPHELIA A. SPEIGHT	303	. SARAH	318	BEMIS,	218
. JAMES	58	ANTHONY, ADDIE	194	. SOPHIA	318	BENET,	181
. JOHN	58	ARCHDALE, JOHN	21	. W. LOUIS	318	BENSON, HENRY	55
. NETTIE	221	ARCHER, JOHN	61	. W.H.	102,316,318	WILLIS	74
. THOMAS	61	ARMSTRONG,	92	. WILLIAM H.	318	BENTLEY, HELEN CURRY	163
ALLEN, CATEECHEE	19	JOHN	55	. WILLIAM HAMPTON	317	BERRY, MICAJAH	64
. CHARLES ALLEN	246	ARNOLD, BENJAMIN	79	BALLENGER, ETHEL	211	BIGGS, SARAH O.	299
. CHARLES OTIS	245	. J. THOMAS	336	BALLENTINE,	212	BIRNIE, JAMES	97,167-168
. EFFIE LOYD PEGUES	246	. JANELL COBB	202	BALLOMBY, THOMAS	64	. JAMES E.	235
. ELIZABETH	246	ARRINGTON,		BARBER, BLANCHE	171	. MARY SCOTT	167
. HARRIET LEACH	245	. HANNAH WHITE	295	BARRATT, ANNE	227	BISHOP,	45
. IONE	307	. J.W.	101	BARRY,	26	BLACK, H.B.	107
. J.H.	245	. JOHN W.	295	BARTON, ELSIE	115	. HOKE B.	125
. JAMES	154	. MARY CARTER	-	BARTRAM, WILLIAM	133	. JANE	58
. NANNIE JEFFERIES	246	. SUBLETT	295	BASH, E.B.	115	. JOHN	58
. RAMATH JEFFERIES	246	. NELSON BATTLE	295	BATES,	52	BLACKMAN, JOHN B.	61
. VIRGINIA	246,268	. OCTAVIA PAGE	295	. BLOODY BILL	51	BLAKELY,	120
. WALTER H.	246	. RICHARD W.	295	. ELSEY H.	248	BLASSINGAME, JOHN	64
ALSTON,	62-63,65,68-69	. SAMUEL P.	295	. IDA	247-248	BLEASE, COLE L.	302
. ANNA	73	ASHBY, LUCY	186	. WILLIAM	97,202	BLYTHE,	327
. CHARLOTTE	73	ASHMORE, MARTHA C.	280	BEACHAM, EMILY	200	. ABSALOM	292
. JOSEPH	73	MARY JANE	226	. EUGENE W.	200	. ANNA H. HARDIN	293
. LEMUEL J.	54,60-62	ASKINS, ALLEN	246	. EUGENIA DOUTHIT	200	. BERNARD H.	293
	66-67,73	ELIZABETH ALLEN	246	. ISBELL	200	. E.M.	294,326
ALVERSON, MATILDA	122	ATKINSON, JOSEPH	56	. JAMES D.	200	. EDGEWORTH M.	292-293
ANDERSON,	26	ATTA KULLA KULLA,	23	. SHIELDS ISBELL	200	. EMILY EARLE	292
. ADA EPPES	197		25-26,29	. WILLIAM C.	200	. LAURISTON	293
. ALLINE MATHESON	198	AULL, L.B.	278	BEATTIE HAMLIN	97	. WILLIAM	292
. DAVID	197	RUTH BULL	278	BEATTIE,	63,242	BLYTHEWOOD, SALLY R.	228
. FRANK L.	197	AUSTIN,	44	. DANNITTE	202	BOATRIGHT,	
. J.L.	51	. J. THOMAS	33	. F.F.	75,201,294	AMANDA LOUISE	297
. JAMES LELAND	196-198	. MARY	175	. FOUNTAIN FOX	200	BOEHRINGER, BYRD	296
. JAMES M.	197	. MARY BIRNIE LEWIS	167	. FOX	202	BOGGS, MALINDA	193
. MARIAM MASON	197	. NATHANIEL	33-34	. HAMLIN	75,86,200-202	BOLLING, TULLY	64
. MARY ELIZABETH	198	. P.H.	167	. HARVEY CLEVELAND	192	BOLT, FLORINE	209
. POLLY MILLER	197	. T.C.	77	.	193	BOMAR,	51,120
. SUE	271	. WILLIAM	175	. JANE ARNOLD	202	BONHAM,	89
. SUSAN BELLE	143	. WILLIAM A.	121	. JANELL COBB ARNOLD	202	. DAISY	294
. SUSAN NORRIS	197	BABB, V.M.	115	. JOHN E.	201	. DAISY ALDRICH	293

BONHAM, (cont)	. JANE 225	. GEORGE W. 127	CANNON, A.D. 214
. LUCELLE A. 294	. JOHN WILLIAM 225	BRYSON, JOSEPH R. 125	. ELIZABETH WEST 214
. M.L. 293	. THOMAS 54,60,225	REBECCA JANE 177	. JAMES A. 123,213
. MARGARET R. 294	. WILLIAM 56	BUCHANAN,	. MAUDE 214
. MARGARET RION 294	BRAZEALE, MARY LOUISE 157	ALEXANDER PITT 56	. NOAH 123,213
. MILLEDGE L. 294	BREAKER, M.C. 299	BUCK, HATTIE 220	. SALLIE 120
. P.A. 292	BRECKENRIDGE, 83	BUIST, E.T. 92	CARDNER, C.S. 299
. PROCTOR A. 201,210	BRIDGES, ALICE 172	BULL, DAN 278	CAREY, 307
. PROCTOR ALDRICH 293	BRIGGS, 212	. DANIEL H. 276	. ANNIE HUDSON -
294	BRIGHTON, 189	. FRANCES 278	BRISTOW 242
. WILLIAM R. 294	BRISTOW, 75	. JAMES A. 276-278	. JOHN C. 248
BOOTH, EMMA MOSS 334	. A.A. 241	. MARGARET 278	. NADA GREEN 248
BOOZER, 83	. ABNER NASH 242	. MARTHA 278	. RICHARD E. 242
BOWEN, W.E. 225	. ANN ELIZABETH 242	. MARTHA FOWLER 276	CARLISLE,
BOWERS, FREDERIKA 302	. ANNIE HUDSON 242	. PAUL 278	. AMANDA LOUISE -
BOYCE, 75	. EUNICE ELIZ. 242	. RUTH 278	BOATRIGHT 297
W.W. 87	. JOSHUA HUDSON 242	. SUNIE E. STROUD 278	. HOWARD B. 120
BOYD, 121	BROADUS, 155	. WILLIAM 276-277	. J.P. 297
T.H. 332	BROCK, ALMA 164	BUNCH,	. JAMES H. 297
BOZEMAN,	BROCKENBROUGH, 224	FREDARIKA ANSEL 303	. MARY VANCE PARKER 297
. CORDELIA ELLEN -	BROCKMAN, BEN 267	BURBAGE, AGNES RODDEY 276	CARPENTER, 74,96
HUFF 217	. BERNICE WOOD 267	. ELLEN E. 276	. F.G. 159
. HELEN 235	. BETTY LOU 193	. HAMPTON P. 276	. LOU A. 159
. W.H. 217	. ELINOR 267	. SAMUEL P. 276	CARROLL, 133
BRADDOCK, 26,28	. FRANCES E. HOY 193	BURGESS, A.F. 185	CARRUTH, A. 64
BRADLEY, JAMES 56	. FRANCES HOY 267	W.W. 296	CARTER, 218,268
JANE 247	. GRACE WITT 193	BURGISS, W.W. 120	. KING 224
BRAMBLETT, D.L. 122	. H. LEROY 193	BURKE, 55	. LAURA GRACE -
REUBEN 121-122	. HAROLD LEROY 193	AEDANUS 54	WHITNEY 218
BRAWLETT,	. JAMES H. 193	BURNETT, ALICE 241	. LORRAINE W. 218
. ALLEN TURNER 258	. JAMES HIRAM 267	. CAROLINE D. 333	. MILDRED 218
. CAROLYN ELIZABETH 259	. JOE 267	. LILLIE 264	. RUFUS 217
. CARRIE IRENE -	. NANCY MCGEE 267	. W.E. 333	. W.W. 217-218
GRESHAM 259	. OWEN DEAN 193	BURNHAM, 75	CARY, JENNIE GREEN 248
. CLIFF 127	. THOMAS 193,266-267	BURR, AARON 55	W. HARRY 248
. CLIFF R. 246	. THOMAS P. 79	BUTLER, 89,214,244,300	CASE, ABRAHAM 56
. D.L. 123,259	BROGAN, 26	. ELISE 300	CASON, ROSA STEWART 180
. DECATUR LEE 258	BROOKS, 190	. LILLIE 178	CATEECHEE, 19
. ELIZABETH MAYFIELD 258	. BETTIE S. 154	. M.C. 85,227	CAUBLE, HENRY A. 75
. EVELYN 247	. DUNCAN 110	. WILLIAM 79	PETER 64,75
. FRANCES CORNELIA 259	. J. WESTLEY 74	BYNUM, JOHN 45	CHANDLER,
. GEORGE 247	. JAMES L. 110	BYRD, CORA 234	LAURA ESTELLE 325
. GEORGE W. 246	. PRESTON S. 294	LIDA 140	CHAPMAN, JUDSON W. 325
. IDA MAY 247	BROWN, CYNTHIA 177	BYTHEWOOD, SALLY R. 228	WINNIE 236
. IDA MAY BRAWLETT 247	. JOHN 64	CAGLE, 74	CHARLES,
. JESS 247	. THOMAS 20	J.W. 75,237	. ELLEN PAMELIA 158
. MARGUERITE 247	BROWNING, ETHEL SMITH 213	CAINE, MARY B. 231	. ELLEN PERMELIA 159
. MARTHA LABERTA 259	. MAMIE PARKINS 212	CALDER, PRISCILLA 309	CHARLOTTE, DAVID 264
. MAT 122	. MARY ELIZABETH 213	CALDWELL, JOHN 51-52	. FRED B. 264
. MATILDA ALVERSON 122	. PAUL 212-213	JULIA 177	. FREDERICKA CUSHMAN 264
. SARAH 246	. PAUL N. 213	CALHOUN, 81-82	. GEORGE W. 263
. SUNIE A. COX 247	. W.D. 211-213	. JOHN C. 14,26,52,78,80	. J.M. 95
. THELMA 247	BRUCE, 92,171,337	. PATRICK 26	. JOHN M. 263-264
BRANDON, 26,98,101	BRUNSON, A.N. 107	CAMERON, 37,44,54	. KATHERINE 264
180-181,199,209	. ALEX N. 125	ALEXANDER 34,43	. MARGARET W. MANSON 263

HISTORY OF GREENVILLE COUNTY, SOUTH CAROLINA

CHARLOTTE,(cont)		. ANN PAWLEY	288	. JOHN	75	. PEARLE RICHARSON	322
. MARY B.	264	. HANNAH ELIZ.	288	. S.S.	73	. SUSAN ADAMS	321
CHERRY,WILLIE C.	192	. PETER COLLINS	288	CROW,ADABELLE	255	DARGAN,	
CHILDERS,		COGSWELL,	333	CROWDER,DAISY E.	312	. HANNAH ELIZ. -	
. AGNES LEE HUFF	217	F.J.P.	332	CRUIKSHANK,		COGGESHALL	288
. J.T.	217	COKER,J.L.	206	. ANNIE GOULDSMITH	260	. HARRY A.	127,287-288
CHOICE,	86	SUSAN	206	. GENEVIEVE RAYNOR	263	. JAMES HARVEY	288
CHRISTENBERRY,		COLEMAN,ESTHER RUTH	331	. W.N.	129,263	. LOUISE JAMES	288
. ANNIE O.	218	. FRENNIE F. STEWART	180	. WILLIAM MONTGOMERY	260	. LUCILE SMITH	288
. GEORGE A.	219	. JANE	268	. WILLIAM NOLLEY	260,263	. LUCYLE A.	127
. JENNIE EARNHARDT	219	. JOHN T.	104	CRYNES,WILLIAM	64	. WILLIAM JAMES	288
. ROBERT E.	219	COLLINS.	26	CUMMINGS,	25	DAVENPORT,	
. T.E.	127	CONNER,JOHN	55	ALEXANDER	23	. CLARA MERCHANT	223
. THOMAS E.	218-219	URIAH	56	CUNNINGHAM,A.C.	264	. D.D.	120,222-223
. WILLIAM A.	218	CONYERS,FANNIE	199	. BLOODY BILL	51	. F. SCOTT	125
CLARK,EMMA LUMPKIN	286	. JAMES	150	. EOLINE	260	. F.S.	107
JOHN	56	. MARIE GOWER	152,154	. EOLINE LIGON	260	. FANNIE	319
CLARKE,	26,50	. MARY OLIVER	149,152	. F.H.	260	. FRANCIS M.	236
KATHERINE	301	. SAMUEL E.	149	. FRANK H.	260	. FRANCIS MCDANIEL	237
CLEGG,T.B.	296	. SARAH	152	. FRANK HARRISON	259	. HATTIE	237
CLEVELAND.	62,68,75,93	. W. PRIESTLY	149	. J.C.	264	. HENRY ALLEN	237
. ALICE	241	. W.P.	73,93,125,152,154	. J.G.	260	. JAMES A.	236-237
. ALICE BURNETT	241	COOK.	133	. JOHN	66	. JAMES F.	237
. BENJAMIN	57,68	. H.T.	41,54,111	. JOSEPH GILBERT	259	. JOHN T.	237
. ELIZA	279	. JARIOT	121	. LEE	264	. M. CLIFF	223
. ELIZABETH MAXWELL	311	COOPER,	327	. LILLIE BURNETT	264	. M. GUENS	223
. EMMA	311	COREA,EUNICE HARRIS	190	. MELLISA GIBSON	264	. M.C.	223
. FLORENCE MCKENZIE	241	CORRI,ABBI	17	. NELLE	264	. MARTHA A. WEST	223
. GERTRUDE	241	COTHRAN,	286,307-308,321	. PATRICK	39-40,51,66	. MAY	223
. HARRIET	241	. EMMA CHILES PERRIN	304	. ROBERT	39,46,50-51,66	. PATRICIA	223
. HAZEL BAKER	311		307	. RUTH	264	. ROSA	237
. J. HARVEY	125,311	. IONE SMITH	307	. SARAH	260	. WINNIE CHAPMAN	236
. JEREMIAH	62-64,68,241	. JAMES D.	304	. SARAH HARRISON	259	DAVID,	92-95
	311	. JAMES S.	307-308	. WILLIAM L.	51	. C.E.	133
. JESSE F.	311	. T.P.	106	CURETON,JOHN M.	288	. CHARLES A.	91
. JOHN BAKER	311	. THOMAS P.	106,308	. JOHN MOON	217	DAVIS,	86
. MARY	74	. THOMAS PERRIN	304	. MARY ADKINS DACUS	217	. JOHN	56
. VANNOY	241	. W.C.	139	CURRY,ANNIE	328	. T.W.	172,283
. W.C.	241	. WADE S.	307	. ELIZABETH	271	. WARREN R.	64,80
. WILLIAM C.	241	. WILLIAM COULTER	307	. HELEN	163	. WILLIAM	56
. WILLIAM CHOICE	241	COTYMORE,	30	CUSHMAN,F.B.	264	DAWSON,A.M.	122
CLINE,L.B.	75	COX,	85,152,253,314	FREDERICKA	264	DAY,ANNIE	335
CLINTON,HENRY	50	. ANNA JONES	177	CUTTING,J.H.	217-218	DEAN.	286,321
CLYDE,EMMA	243	. LOU C.	308	DACUS,JOHN MOON	217	. A.H.	139
COBLEIGH,KATRINA	300	. NANCY	320	. LOUISA AMANDA	214	. ALVIN H.	138,232,287
COCHRANE,D.W.	128	. ORGIE AGGIE	176	. MARY ADKINS	217		308
CODY,EDMUND	142-143	. SUNIE A.	247	DALTON,R.E.	196	. ALVIN HENRY	139
. JAMES	142	. T.M.	74	DALVIGNY,MAUD	286	. EUGENIA MILLER	139
. LOIS	143	. THOMAS	97	DANIEL,JANIE SUE	322	. LIDA BYRD	140
. SARAH HENDERSON	142	COXE.	75	. JOHN FURMAN	321	. SALLIE PRESTON	140
. SUSAN BELLE	-	CRAIG,	233	. JOHN M.	321	DEANE,ANN HARRIS	190
. ANDERSON	143	CRAWFORD,JAMES W.	313	. JOHN MOBLEY	321	DELAWARR,	247
. Z.T.	299	NANNIE	313	. MARY AUSTIN	-	DERIEUX,JIM	144
. ZECHARIAH THORNTON	142	CRAYTON,THOMAS	63	. MCDANIEL	176	DESOTO,FERDINAND	17
COGGESHALL,		CRITTENDEN,	74-77,133	. PEARLE RICHARSON	321	DEVIT,	49,194

HISTORY OF GREENVILLE COUNTY, SOUTH CAROLINA

DEWITT,	49,194	. B.H.	129	. ELIZABETH HARDY	275	MARY	328
DIAL,EMMA	287	. B.J.	64,79	. LUCY	275	FRANCE,LUCILE NORRIS	209
NATHANIAL B.	287	. BAYLIS	35,51,56,66-67	. ROBERT	275	FRANCIS,ALLEN	19
DILL,	34	. BAYLIS H.	90	FAISON,	166	FRANKLIN,	55,98
H.P.	128	. C.B.	67	FANNING,DAVID	49	FRAZIER,	97
DINWIDDIE.	32	. ELEANOR	167	FARR,FRANCES ANN	303	FREEMAN,	
DIXON,SARAH AMANDA	319	. ELIAS	61,66-68	FARROW,THOMAS	56	. AMANDA E. HARRIS	317
DOBSON,EDMUND D.	226	. ELIZABETH	67	FELTON,	288	. J.B.R.	317
. J.P.	226	. ELIZABETH EARLE	67	FERGUSON,SARAH	223	. JACK	317
. MARTHA	226	. EMILY	292	FERRIS,STELLA LOUISE	332	. JULIA GRIFFIN	317
. R.D.	226	. FRANCIS WILTON	-	FEW,	120	. W.E.	314,317
. VIRGINIA	226	ROBINSON	67	. B.F.	120	FRIEDLANDER,JULIUS	193
. VIRGINIA HUTCHINS	226	. G.W.	68	. BENJAMIN FRANKLIN	223	FRIENDLY,CATHERINE	284
DODD,	26	. GEORGE W.	67		224	FROST,ELLEN LEGARE	249
DONALDSON,	61	. JOHN	35,45,51,67	. ELLIE	224	FRY,JACOB	40
DOSTER.	92	. JOHN B.	167	. IGNATIOUS O.	224	FRYE,A.D.	257
DOUGLAS,	75,83	. JOHN H.	201	. JAMES	224	. BESSIE EURECH	258
. R.M.	191	. JOSEPH H.	67,90,132	. MARY WHEELER	224	. SARAH JANE	258
. ROSE	165	. MARY PRINCE	66	. RACHEL KENDRICK	224	FULLER,EMILY ARIANNA	335
. THOMAS WILLIAMS	191	. ROBERT	74	. RICHARD	224	FURMAN,	111
DOUTHIT,EUGENIA	200	. ROBINSON	67	. ROBERT A.	224	. ANNA	326
DOYLE,VIRGINIA	233	. SAMUEL	56,66-67	. SALLIE	224	. J.C.	109,299,326
DOYLEY,ANNA	278	. T.T.	67	. SARAH FERGUSON	223	. JAMES C.	110-111,326
DRAPER.	133	. WILEON H.	210	. WILLIAM	223-224	. RICHARD	109,299,326
DRAUGHON,	237	. WILTON H.	67,106,114	. WILLIAM P.	224	GAFFNEY,	196
DRAYTON,	38,42		304	FIELDING,FRANCES	167	GAINES,	155
. MARY	250	EARNHARDT,JENNIE	219	FILLMORE,	64	MARTHA	155
. W.H.	38	EASLEY,WILLIAM K.	104	FINLEY,GEORGE	276	GANTT,HENRY	92
. WILLIAM H.	37,133	ECHOLS,CLARENCE T.	325	. JAMES	276	GAPENS,	63
. WILLIAM HENRY	250	EDWARDS.	26	. JEAN	276	GARDENER,C.S.	113
DRUMMOND,		P.C.	109	. JOHN	276	GARRIS,GEORGETTE C.	274
. ANNIE SWITZER	211	ELLERBE,W.H.	284	FISHER,	34	GARRISON,H.S.	217
. J.H.	125	ELLET,	58-59	FISK,	268	. LULA	171
. MARGARET	211	ELLIOT,	89	FISKE,	218	. VELONA HUFF	217
. ROY J.	211	ELLIS,AGNES SHARPTON	194	FLETCHALL,THOMAS	38,40	GARY,BESSIE	279
. S.S.	211	. CAROLINE D.	-	FLYNN,B.F.	311-312	. CHARLES H.	254
DUDLEY,ELIZABETH	296	BURNETT	333	. DAISY E. CROWDER	312	. EUGENE B.	254
DUGAN,	26	. CHARLES W.	278	. J. ROYCE	312	. MARY CHARLES	254
DUKE,JAMES B.	112,157	. CLARA NISSEN	333	. J.W.	312	GASTON,JULIET	242
DUNCAN,	75	. ESTELLE	248	. JEANNIE LOEDE	312	WILLIAM	58
A. SLOAN	76	. FLORINE AGNES	195	. JEANNIE MCALESTER	311	GATES,	237
DUNEAN,	99,189,218,245	. FLORINE JACKSON	195	. JOHN F.	311	GAUGH,RACHEL	56
DUNHAM,B.	64,75	. JOHN W.	194	. LILLIAN VIRGINIA	312	GEER,B.E.	101,112
DURHAM,BERNICE HOGIN	332	. MARK SHARPTON	194	. NELLE GILES	312	. J.M.	157,298
. CHARLES L.	331	. W.B.	333	FORD,	45,47	. JOHN M.	101
. D.C.	127	. WILBUR	333	FOSTER,ELISE BUTLER	300	GIBBS,	42,133
. DAVID NOAH	331	. WILLIAM B.	333	. ELIZABETH	301	GIBSON,	85
. DAVIS C.	331	ENOREE,	241	. FLOYD CLARKE	301	. MELLISA	264
. ESTHER RUTH	-	EPPES,ADA	197	. GUY BUTLER	300	. S.	299
COLEMAN	331	ERWIN,	62	. J.A.	128	. SAMUEL	264
. RICHARD F.	332	EURECH,BESSIE	258	. KATHERINE BUTLER	301	GILBERT,	121
. STELLA LOUISE	-	FAIR,ANNIE AKERS	275	. KATHERINE CLARKE	301	SILAS	121
FERRIS	332	. ANNIE ROSA	275	. R.M.	300	GILDER.	34
DYER,GEORGE B.	76	. CHARLES HARDY	275	. SUSAN	334	GILES,NELLE	312
EARLE.	67,69,93,244,288	. ELIZABETH	275	FOWLER,MARTHA	276	WILLIAM	56

HISTORY OF GREENVILLE COUNTY, SOUTH CAROLINA

Name	Page
GILLILAND, ROBERT	56
GILREATH,	331
. LILLIE MAY	318
. P.D.	160
. THOMAS L.	317
. W.A.	185
GIST, NATHANIEL	32
GLEN,	25-26, 32
JAMES	17, 28
GLOVER, BEVERLY	248
. CHARLES S.	248
. KATHLEEN GREEN	248
GOLDSMITH, PARIOLIE	193
WILLIAM	242
GOODLET, WILLIAM	56
GOODLETT,	93
. JOHN H.	64
. LIDIE	199
. TOBERT	56
. ZION	64
GOODWIN, J.P.	246
. JOHN	56
. W.C.	107, 125
GOULDSMITH, ANNIE	260
GOWDY,	26
GOWEN,	34, 51
. BUCK	34, 52
. JOHN	64
GOWER,	85, 154, 253, 314
. A.G.	73
. ARTHUR G.	319
. BETTIE S. BROOKS	154
. BETTIE S. ROWLAND	154
. EBEN	74, 152
. H.A.	154
. JAMES	152
. JANE JONES	-
WILLIAMS	148
	154
. JANE W.	319
. MARIE	152, 154
. SALLY A. MARTIN	154
. SUSAN	228
. SUSAN C.	154
. SUSAN CORDELIA	148-149
. SUZANA NORTON	152
. T.C.	73, 93, 97, 150, 152
	154
. THOMAS C.	73, 93, 152
. THOMAS CLAGHORN	148
	152, 154
GOWIN, JOHN	56
GRACE, MARY	274
GRADGRIND,	20
GRAHAM, C.E.	101, 123
ELIZA CATHEY	147
GRANT,	30-32
GRAY, EMMA	333
. EMMA DIAL	287
. ROBERT LEE	287
GREEN, ABRAHAM	247-248
. BATES	248
. BENJAMIN AUGUSTUS	247
	248
. CHRISTINE	248
. ESTELLE ELLIS	248
. IDA	248
. IDA BATES	247-248
. ISAAC	13-14, 247-248
. JANE BRADLEY	247
. JENNIE	248
. JOHN	247
. KATHLEEN	248
. MARY	248
. NADA	248
. NATHANIEL	247
. PHEBE WEST	247
. WILLIAM	248
. ZEE JONES	177
GREENE.	248
NATHANIEL	13-14
GREENWAY,	75
GREER.	337
MANNING	120
GREGG,	133
J.E.	97
GREGORY, OLA	320
GRESHAM, BRIGHT	257
. BRIGHT LANFORD	257
. CARRIE	257
. CARRIE IRENE	259
. HELEN	257
. METZ	257
. SARAH	257
. W. FRANK	257
. W.F.	121
. W.P.	257, 259
GRIDLEY, M.P.	114
GRIFFIN, ANNE	328
. ANNIE CURRY	328
. E.S.	317
. JULIA	317
. NELL MILLS	328
. NINA	232
. WALTER S.	327-328
GRIFFITH, R.H.	111
GUENS, M.	223
GUERRY, DUPONT	318-320
. FANNIE DAVENPORT	319
. MARY	320
. OLA GREGORY	320
. SARAH AMANDA DIXON	319
. WILLIAM BARNETT	319
GULLICK, ANNIE DAY	335
. CARL LEE	335
. EFFIE E.	335
. EMILY ARIANNA	-
FULLER	335
. EMILY KISER	335
. EMILY PEARL	335
. GUY A.	133, 335
. JOHN C.	335
. M.L.	128
. MARY ROXANA	335
. MITCHEL LEE	335
. NANNIE FAY	335
. ROY KISER	335
HAGOOD,	89
HALFACRE, EUNICE JANE	236
HALL, ELSIE	327
HAMBLEN,	
. ADABELLE CROW	255
. FRANK G.	255
. MARY ALICE MUNSON	255
. NATHAN HENRY	255
HAMILTON, JAMES	53-54
JANE	171
HAMMETT, H.P.	97, 202
HAMMOND, C.P.	148
. ELIZA	231
. EUGENE	231
. EUGENIA	231
. FRANK	200, 228, 231
. JANE MILLS	148
. MARY	231
. MARY B. CAINE	231
. MAUD	231
. SUSAN	231
. SUSAN GOWER	228
. WILLARD	228
. WILLIAM	228
HAMPTON,	90, 152, 190-191
	196
. ANTHONY	35, 51, 55
. EDWARD	43, 51
. PRESTON	43, 45
. WADE	35, 45, 52, 55
HAMRICK, MARTHA	141
HANNON,	45
HARD, ELLEN	314
HARDIN, ANNA H.	293
N.B.	293
HARDY, ELIZABETH	275
. HATTIE DAVENPORT	237
. THOMAS	275
HARPER, DREW S.	312
JEANNIE L. FLYNN	312
HARRIS, ADDIE R.	303
. AMANDA E.	317
. ANN	190
. B.S.H.	188-190
. BETTIE HUGHES	190
. EUNICE	190
. FRANCIS	190
. H.H.	106, 114
. HENRY H.	303
. J.C.	190
. J.M.	220
. J.W.	189
. JOHN D.	226-227
. KATHRYN	190
. LIZZIE WILLIMON	227
. M.F.	189
. MARIE	227
. MARY JANE ASHMORE	226
. NELLIE	227
. NONA MARKLEY	220
. ROBERT EARLE	227
. RUTH	190
. W.C.	226
. WILLIE GRAY	256
HARRISON,	196
. BENJAMIN	221
. BESSIE	309
. BETTY	253
. FRANCIS EUGENE	259
. JAMES	41-42, 45, 54-55
. JOHN H.	64
. RICHARD	64, 74
. RUTH HARRIS	190
. S.E.	41
. SARAH	259
HARTZOG,	167, 175
. MARY OWENS	172
. OCTAVUS BOWEN	172, 175
. ROZELLE WADDELL	175
. SAMUEL J.	172
HARVEY, ADDISON	253
HARVLEY,	
. BLANCHE BARBER	171
. CLYDE	171
. H. CLYDE	168-169
. HELEN	171
. IDA ADKINS	168
. J.K.	168
. JOHN	171
HASSELL, A.M.	141
HASTIE,	75
HATCH, ROBERT	284
HAWKINS, ALLEN	106

HAWKINS,(cont)		HILL,MARY	179	. CORDELIA ELLEN	217	ISSAQUEENA,	19
LULA W.	304	. MARY J.	279	. DARRALL	217	JACKSON,	79-82,253
HAY,	190	. W.A.	120	. JAMES	214	FLORINE	195
HAYNE,P.T.	253	HIPP,		. JANE A. SULLIVAN	214	JAMES,E.C.	113
HAYNES,T.W.	299	. ALICE P. WHEELER	235	. JANE SULLIVAN	217	LOUISE	288
HAYNIE,BESSIE MAY	331	. CALHOUN	236	. JUNIUS KERSHAW	217	JAMISON,	26
HAYNSWORTH,	231	. DOROTHY	236	. LOUISA AMANDA	-	JEFFERIES,NANNIE	246
. ALICE	326	. EUNICE JANE	-	DACUS	214	RAMATH	246
. ANNA FURMAN	326	HALFACRE	236	. MEDA LEE HUNT	217	JENKINS,THOMAS	56
. CLEMENT F.	326-327	. FRANCIS	236	. PASCAL D.	217	JOHNSON,	57,87-89,133
. CLEMENT FURMAN	326-327	. HAYNE	236	. PASCAL DACUS	214	. ALEXANDER	56
. CUSTIS HALL	327	. HERMAN	236	. PHILEMON	214	. BETTY HOLCOMBE	298
. ELIZABETH BLAIR	327	. JOHN C.	235	. REBECCA MOSELY	214	. LEWELLY CALHOUN	298
. ELSIE HALL	327	. W. FRANK	235	. ROSCOE	217	. P.J.	115
. H.J.	102,111,150,250	HITCH,KATY CARSON	179	. SWAN BURNETT	217	. PINCKNEY LOUIS	298
	292	HITE,	33-34,43-45,47,55	. VELONA	217	. RENE	226
. HENRY J.	150,326-327		131,280	. VIRGINIA	217	. W.B.	298
. JOHN R.	150	. GEORGE	56	HUGER,ISAAC	30	. W.L.	226
. KNOX L.	326	. JACOB OBANNON	43,56	HUGHES,	120	JOLLY,	26
. MARGARET	192	HODGES,OSCAR	160,321	. BETTIE	190	JONES,	178
. MARY OLIVER	150,326	HOGIN,BERNICE	332	. JAMES LANGSTON	272	. ANNA	177
. RHODA LIVINGSTON	326	HOKE,DAVID	74,93	. JANE WOOD	271	. ANNA BELL	178
HAYSNWORTH,HENRY J.	325	HOLCOMBE,BETTY	298	. LURA PITTS	272	. BENSON M.	244
WILLIAM	325	HOLLINGSWORTH,	40	. LURA PITTS	-	. C.C.	232
HEARIN,		ADDIE	303	. LANGSTON	272	. CLINTON C.	232-233
. EUNICE ELIZ.	-	HOLLINGUIST,	75	. R.M.	120	. CYNTHIA BROWN	177
	BRISTOW 242	HOLLIS,EMMA CLYDE	243	. ROBERT MURRAY	271-272	. EDMUND	177
. W.C.	242	. JULIET	243	. ROBERT SIMEON	272	. F.D.	178
HEIDT,ELIZABETH	244	. JULIET GASTON	242	. SIMEON	120,271	. GRACE MCHARDY	244
HELDMAN,	76	. L. PETER	243	HUGHS,JOSEPH	56	. J.E.	177
HELLAMS,		. LAWRENCE PETER	242	HUMPHREYS,		. JULIET	178
JENNIE ELOISE	284	. LOUISE	243	. RAMATH J. ALLEN	246	. L.C.	178
HENDERSON,	68-69,226	. MARY ELIZABETH	243	. W.C.	246	. LIDIE	284
. HENRY	190	. PETER	242	HUNT,MEDA LEE	217	. LILLIE	177
. JOHN	56	HONOR,JOHN A.	73	HUNTER,	68-69,83	. LILLIE BUTLER	178
. JOSEPH	190	HOOKER,	69-70	. DOROTHY KEITH	234	. LILY WOODFIN	244
. RICHARD	190	EDWARD	61,65.68	. F.D.	121	. LULA	177
. SARAH	142	HOPKINS,FERDINAND	56	. GEORGE	20,133	. MARY RICHARDSON	177
. T.L.	121	T.T.	299	. J.J.	278	. R. DAVID	177
. URSULA	190	HORNELL,GEORGE A.	219	. W.A.	122	. R.D.	177
. W.T.	160	HORTON,BEN F.	74	. MARTHA BULL	278	. REBECCA JANE	-
HENNING,DAVID	75	HOUGH,JOHN	214	HUNTINGTON,		BRYSON	177
HENRY,	189	HOWARD,	34,45-46	JANE W. GOWER	319	. VIRGINIA DOYLE	233
. CARTER	189	EMMA	292	HUNTINGTON,B.W.	318	. W.P.	177
. LUCY ASHBY	186	HOWE,	50,133	. HELEN SEAVEY	318	. W.R.	233
. R.E.	101	HOWELL,	327	. R.S.	319	. WILLIAM R.	232,284
. ROBERT E.	186	HOY,FRANCES	267	. ROGER S.	318	. WILLIAM T.	177
. ROBERT RANDOLPH	186	. FRANCES E.	193	HUTCHINGS,THOMAS	120	. ZEE	177
. SARAH EMMIE	-	. WILLIAM	267	HUTCHINS,VIRGINIA	226	JORDAN,FLETCHER	114
MCCRARY	189	HUBBARD,WILLIAM	64	INGLESBY,	333	JORDEN,JAMES	56
HENTON,IDA	238	HUDSON,	176	T.S.	332	JOYCE,JOHN H.	64
HERBERT,	190	. ANNIE	242	INMAN,E.	127,321	JUDSON,	99-101,110-111
HERIOT,MARY	220	. JOSHUA	242	IRBY,JOHN L.M.	67		231
HEYWARD,	288	HUFF,AGNES LEE	217	IRVINE,	75,288	. CHARLES H.	109,111,113
HIDEN,J.C.	299	. ANNIE LAURIE	217	ISBELL,SHIELDS	200	. MARY C.	113

KEITH,CORA BYRD	234	LANNEAU,	98	. ELIZA MAXWELL	167	MADISON,JAMES	263
. DOROTHY	234	LAUD,ELIZA	209	. FRANCES FIELDING	167	MAGINNIS,	189
. JESSE E.	233	LAURENS,HENRY	30,40	. J. MAXWELL	168	MANLEY,CHARLES	299
. KATE SYKES	233	LAVAL,ANNIE O.	191	. J.O.	175	MANLY,CHARLES	111
. MARGARET LOUISE	234	. JULIA H.	191	. JAMES O.	168	MANN,A.C.	230-232
. MARY	314	. WILLIAM	191	. JAMES OVERTON	167	. A.D.	231
. W.H.	107,125	LAWRENCE,		. JEANETTE	168	. BETTY LANELLE	232
. WILLIAM HENRY	233	MILDRED CARTER	218	. JOHN	167	. CATHERINE F.	165
KENDRICK,RACHEL	224	LAWTON,ALEXANDER R.	248	. JOHN TALIAFERRO	167	. COKE D.	165
KENNEDY,	26	. BESSIE MILLER	249	. MARY BIRNIE	167	. ELIZA JANE MILFORD	165
KERN,ELIZA	244	. F.A.	249	. MARY LORTON	167	. JAMES LEWIS	165
KERSHAW,HARRIETT	285	. FRANCES ELIZABETH	249	. MARY SCOTT BIRNIE	167	. JAMES MOSS	165
KESLER,J.M.	191	. MARY	249	. MAUD HAMMOND	231	. JAMES R.	232
KILGORE,JOSIAH	64	. MARY WILLINGHAM	248	. RICHARD	167	. JOE GRIFFIN	232
KILPATRICK,	56	. SAMUEL MILLER	249	. ROBERT	167	. JOHN PLYLER	232
. CLARA	191	. T. OREGON	248	. SARAH MILLER	167	. LAURA E. TOMPKINS	231
. WHITNER	191	. THOMAS MAXWELL	249	. SARAH TALIAFERRO	167	. MARGARET ELIZA	165
KING GEORGE III,	33	. THOMAS O.	248	. THOMAS L.	167-168	. NINA GRIFFIN	232
KING GEORGE,	23	LEACH,	45	. WILLIAM B.	168	. SARAH AMELIA MOSS	165
KING,	212	HARRIET	245	LIGON,BLACKMAN	63,75	MANNING,RICHARD I.	233
. ANNE GRIFFIN	328	LEAGUE,		. EOLINE	260	MANSON,MARGARET W.	263
. ELIZA	156	. EDITH OGLETHORPE -		. H.A.	260	MARCHANT,EMMA WHAM	182
. MITCHELL	328	ADAMS	177	. JOHN T.	64	. FITZHUGH LEE	182
KISER,EMILY	335	. ELIZABETH MOON	176	LILLY,	68	. FRANCIS	185
KURUGA,	19	. FRANK	177	LINCOLN,	84-85	. HORTENSE	182
LAGERHOLM,		. G. FRANK	176	ABRAHAM	83	. JESSIE SPEED	186
. ARTHUR ELSWORTH	271	. GEORGE P.	176	LINDSEY,JOHN	56	. JOHN	185
. CARL F.	270	. JULIA	177	LIPSCOMB,JAMES W.	172	. JOHN LUTHER	182
. CLARENCE VICTOR	271	. WILLIAM	177	JOHN W.	172	. KATHLEEN MORRAH	185
. EDWARD THEODORE	271	LEAKE,GEORGE C.	325	LIVINGSTON,		. LUCILE	182
. EMMA M. OSTERBERG	271	LEATHERWOOD,J.G.	127	. CLARA KILPATRICK	191	. LUTHER M.	185
. ERIC GUSTAV	271	LEE,	86,152	. J.K.	192	. M.L.	224
. FRED EMANUEL	271	. HATTIE	163	. J.W.	191	. MARTIN LUTHER	182,185
. G.F.	270	. STEPHEN D.	253	. KNOX	326	. MARY	185
LANDIS,		LEGAL,JEAN V.	300	. MARY ELIZA	192	. MARY SMITH	182,185
KENNESAW MOUNTAIN	273	LEGRAND,ALICE	149	. RHODA	326	. PRESTON B.	186
LANDRUM,	17,52,133	LEIDING,		. WHITNER K.	191-192	. ROBERT LEE	182
. J.G.	299	HARRIETT KERSHAW	285	. WILLIAM CHERRY	192	. SALLIE FEW	224
. JOHN G.	225	LEONARD,LAUGHLIN	190	. WILLIE C. CHERRY	192	. THOMAS M.	101,184,186
. M.P.	14	. LULIE	267	LOCKHART,	192	MARION,	150
LANFORD,BRIGHT	257	. MARGARET E.	291	LOGAN,	21,133,180	FRANCIS	30
. ETHEL BALLENGER	211	LESTER,	69,97	LONG,DAVID	63	MARKELY,	314
. HELEN	211	PHILIP C.	64	DAVIS	75	MARKLEY,	253
. HUGH	211	LEVERSEDGE,		LORIMER,		H.C.	74
. JOHN D.	210	. DAISY MARIE	225	GEORGE HORACE	144	MARSHALL,ALFRED	228
. KATHERINE	211	. EDITH MARIE	225	LORTON,MARY	167	. ANNE BARRATT	227
. LUCILE	211	. JOHN HUNTER	225	LOVE,J.L.	107,125	. BLYTHEWOOD B.	228
. LUKE	211	LEWIS,	32	LOVELAND,ROGER	75	. DAN H.	228
. RUTH	211	. A.L.	231	LOWRY,BESSIE STEWART	180	. FRANCES W.	228
. SARAH MITCHELL	210	. ANNIE	168	LUMSDEN,L.L.	129	. JEAN	155
. W.L.	210	. BETTIE WASHINGTON	167	LUYTIES,GERDA	235	. JOHN	160
LANGSTON,DICEY	59	. CAROLINE	168	LYON,MARIE HARRIS	227	. JOHN B.	202
. JOHN	56	. DAVID	167	LYTTLETON,	28-29,31	. JOHN BARRATT	227
. LURA PITTS	272	. DAVY	45	WILLIAM HENRY	28	. KITTY	202
. W.J.	191	. ELEANOR EARLE	167	MACKEY,	75	. S.S.	227

Name	Page	Name	Page	Name	Page	Name	Page
MARSHALL,(cont)		MAYSON,	39	. ORGIE AGGIE COX	176	J. RION	133
. SALLY R.	-	MCAFEE,	177	. STELLA K.	175	MCLAUGHLEN,JOSEPH	56
. BLYTHEWOOD	228	. CHARLES H.	179	. W.A.	176	MCLEOD,F.H.	75
. SALLY R. BYTHEWOOD	228	. CHARLES M.	178	. WILLIAM A.	175	. FRANCIS H.	64
. SARAH	228	. LUCINDA STRINGER	178	. WILLIAM AUSTIN	176	. THOMAS G.	233
MARTIN,	226,257,292	. MARY H.	179	. WILLIAM B.	175	MCQUEEN,JOHN	56
. A. MCQ.	106	. MARY HILL	179	MCDANIELL,W.B.	174	MCSWAIN,	142
. A.B.	301	. THOMAS	178	MCDILL,PEGGY	58	. CHARLES	141
. COLUMBUS BENJAMIN	255	. THOMAS F.	178-179	SARAH	301	. DAVID	141
	256	MCALESTER,JEANNIE	311	MCDOWELL,CHARLES	245	. ELIZABETH RANDALL	140
. F.B.	256	MCALISTER,	121	. JOSEPH	245	. ELRIDGE T.	140
. GEORGE	56	MCBEE,	75,92,109	. MARGARET S.	337	. JANIE MCGOWAN	140
. J. ROBERT	301-302	. ALEX	73,97	. MARY JANE	321	. JOHN J.	141,210
. J.H.	97	. FLORIDE SMITH	182	MCELHENEY,ALEXANDER	56	. JOHN JACKSON	140
. JOHN C.	154	. L.M.	73	JAMES	56	. MARTHA HAMRICK	141
. LOUISA HARRIS	256	. LUTHER M.	73	MCELRATH,HARRIET	204	. SARAH MCCULLOUGH	142
. LYDIA RANKIN	302	. SALLY	279	MCFADDEN,	292	. SUSANNA WASHBURN	141
. MARGARET	302	. V.	76	GEORGE H.	185	. WILLIAM A.	140-141
. MARTHA WALLACE	256	. VARDRY	14,62-63,65,67	MCGEE,	98,123	MCSWEEN,JOHN	233
. SALLY A.	154		77,104,112,279,298	. ELIZA HAMMOND	231	MEANS,R.A.	106
. SARAH MCDILL	301	MCBETH,A.	60	. H.P.	113	MELCHERS,	
. WILLIE GRAY	256	JOHN	61	. J.D.	231	NANNIE FAY GULLICK	335
. WILLIE GRAY HARRIS	256	MCBRAYER,	147	. NANCY BROCKMAN	267	MERCER,CAROLYN	191
MASON,MARIAM	197	MCCALL,SUSAN B.	73	. RUTH	205	. I.M.	191
W.E.	112,185,192	MCCLANAHAN,JOHN	64	MCGLOTHLIN,	111,133,157	. SUZANNE	191
MASSEY,	193	MCCLUNEY,WILLIAM JOHN	75	. BESSIE MAY	157	MERCHANT,CLARA	223
MATHESON,ALLINE	198	MCCOIN,ANNA LOUISE	291	. ELIZA KING	156	METCHER,HENRY	56
MAULDIN,	92	. ELMER G.	291	. JAMES HARRISON	157	MEYERS,ALEX	336
. ELIZA KERN	244	. J.W.	291	. KATHRYN	157	. AMELIA	336
. ELIZABETH HEIDT	244	. KATHLEEN DORIS	291	. MARY LOUISE	157	. BEN	336
. GRACE MCHARDY	-	. MARGARET E.	-	. MARY LOUISE	-	. L.A.	336
. JONES	244	LEONARD	291	BRAZEALE	157	. MANAS	336
. J.	64	. MARTHA PITTS	291	. MAY BELLE WILLIAMS	157	. NOLIN	336
. J. MCH.	107	MCCRADY,	41	. W.J.	112	MIDDLETON,	30,65
. JOHN MCH.	125	MCCRARY,SARAH EMMIE	189	. W.J.A.	156	HENRY	79
. O.K.	129	MCCULLOUGH,C. FRED	286	. WILLIAM J.	156-157	MILFORD,CHARLES J.	269
. OSCAR KERN	244	. EMMA LUMPKIN CLARK	286	MCGOWAN,JANIE	140	. CHARLES O.	269-270
. SAMUEL	75	. JAMES	285	. JOHN	141	. CLARA TODD	270
. THOMAS J.	127	. JAMES D.	286	. JOHN JACKSON	141	. ELIZA JANE	165
. W.L.	75,132,244	. JANIE SULLIVAN	142	. MARY THOMPSON	141	. LOU SAYLORS	269
MAXWELL,ELIZA	167	. JOHN W.	142	. PATRICK	141	. MORGAN T.	270
. HARRIET	221	. JOSEPH A.	106,210,250	. R.P.	214	. SARAH E.	270
. HARRIET AUGUSTUS	313		292,304	. WILLIAM	141	MILLER,	147
. INEZ SLOAN	313	. JOSEPH ALLEN	285	MCILWAINE,JAMES	26	. BESSIE	249
. JOHN	167	. MAUD DALVIGNY	286	MCIVER,LUCY	205	. EUGENIA	139
. MARY C. POPE	255	. SARAH	142	MCJUNKIN,	26	. JAMES	167
. RAYMOND	255	MCDANIEL,ANNIE LOU	176	JOSEPH	56,133	. JOHN	45
. ROBERT A.	64	. FRANCIS	237	MCKAUGHAN,ELMER G.	291	. KATE	255
. ROBERT DUFF	313	. FRANCIS L. PERRETT	175	. J.W.	291	. POLLY	197
MAYES,MARY	201	. J.A.	288	. MARTHA PITTS	291	. SARAH	167
. MARY CAROLINE	201	. JAMES	64,175	MCKAY,	93	. W.N.	301
. RICHARD	201	. JAMES A.	175	MCKENZIE,FLORENCE	241	. WALTER L.	128
MAYFIELD,ELIZABETH	258	. JOHN T.	175	MCKINNEY,L.E.	196	MILLING,DAVID	56
THURZA	272	. MARY AUSTIN	175-176	LOU E.	195	JOHN	56
MAYO,	334	. MARY ELLA SMITH	176	MCKISSICK,A.F.	107,125	MILLS,	14,98,148

HISTORY OF GREENVILLE COUNTY, SOUTH CAROLINA

MILLS,(cont)		. JAMES H.	280,283-284	. FRANCES	199	PARKINS,A.R.	64
. ALICE LEGRAND	149	. LIDIE JONES	284	. G.A.	198	. GEORGE W.	212
. ANNIE	148	. VIRGINIA WADDELL	284	. GEORGE	199	. MAMIE	212
. ARTHUR	148	MORRAH,KATHLEEN	185	. GEORGE ALEXANDER	198	PARKS,JOHN W.	128
. ARTHUR L.	149	MORROW,	35,58	. J.W.	102,106,112	PATES,	245
. CORDELIA	148	MORTON,	35,58	.	114-115	PATRICK,	248,254
. ELIZA CATHEY	-	DAVID	58	. JOHN W.	199	VINA	199
.	GRAHAM 147	MOSELY,A.J.	288	. JOHN WILKINS	198	PATTERSON,H.M.	178
. HENRY T.	328	REBECCA	214	. LAURA CLEVELAND	199	. L.O.	326
. JANE	148	MOSS,SARAH AMELIA	165	. LIDIE GOODLETT	199	. LUCIA PARKER	253
. JANE GOWER	149	MOTLEY,	52	. MARY LOUISE	-	PATTON,	62,147,337
. JOHN	147	MOULTRIE,	297	.	WILKINS 198	. AVERY	171
. MARTHA LEGRAND	149	WILLIAM	30	. OLIVER	199	. ERNEST	171
. MARY ELLA MOORE	149	MUNDY,J.A.	299	. VINA PATRICK	199	. ERNEST GIBBES	171
. MARY MOORE	149	MUNSON,MARY ALICE	255	. W.C.	97	. LULA GARRISON	171
. NELL	328	MURFF,OTHELLA	317	OCCONOSTOTA,	29	. MARGARET MITCHELL	171
. O.P.	74,102,148	NEBLET,A. VIOLA	254	OGLETHORPE,JAMES	177	. WALTER LENOIR	171
. OTIS P.	149	NESBIT,JAMES	58	OLIVER,MARY	149-150,326	PAUL,	75
. OTIS PRENTISS	147,149	NESBITT,	35	PETER	325	PAWLEY,ANN	288
. ROBERT S.	64	NEVES,A.A.	195	ONEALL,	54,133	PEACE,B.H.	11,323,325
. ROGER MOORE	149	. ANN POOLE	195	. J.B.	104	. BONY HAMPTON	322,325
. SUSAN C. GOWER	154	. B.F.	196	. JOHN BELTON	254	. CHARLIE	325
. SUSAN CORDELIA	-	. BENJAMIN F.	195	ORR,	45	. FRANCES LUCILLE	325
.	GOWER 148	. BESSIE WILLIAMS	196	. JAMES L.	88-89,234	. JACKSON PATRICK	322
.	149	. CARL A.	196	. MARY	234	. JUDITH BALLINGER	-
MIMS,J.S.	109	. ELSIE O.	196	OSBORNE,		.	TINSLEY 322
MIRABEAU,	55	. EMMA CORA	195	. LILLIE SPEEGLE	238	. LAURA ESTELLE	-
MITCHELL,	142,235	. IDA LOU	196	. RICHARD	238	.	CHANDLER 325
. A.R.	171	. L.E. MCKINNEY	196	OSTERBERG,EMMA M.	271	. ROGER C.	325
. MARGARET	171	. LOU E. MCKINNEY	195	OTT,MARGUERITE	273	. ROGER CRAFT	325
. S.C.	303	. RALPH GRADY	196	OTTARAY,	75,93,242	PEARCE,D.F.	200
. SARAH	210	. WILLIAM D.	196	OVERLAND,	148	ISBELL BEACHAM	200
MITTELL,CAROL	235	NEWMAN,		OWENS,MARY	172	PEARIS,	34,38,53
MONAGHAN,	98-101,120,186	. ANNIE LOU MCDANIEL	176	OXNER,G.D.	125	. RICHARD	28,32-33,36
	189,192,243,250	. J.C.	111	PACK,C.H.	280	.	39-41,43-44,46-47,49
MONTAGUE,A.P.	111	. JOHN LEON	176	MAUDE	280	.	50,54,60,66,131,133
MONTGOMERY,	30	. MARY ELIZABETH	176	PAGETT,J.S.	264	PEARSON,	26
MOON,ELIZABETH	176	NICHOLS,	26	RUTH CUNNINGHAM	264	PEDEN,	35,196,321,337
. J. WALTER	128	NICOL,	75	PARIS,RICHARD	32,56	. A.S.	123
. ROBERT D.	64	NISSEN,CLARA	333	ROBERT	66	. DAVID	58
MOONEY,	244,288	NOBLE,MARY	182	PARK,ANTHONY	21	. ELIZABETH SMITH	180
MOORE,	26	NORRIS,D.K.	209	PARKER,	100,185,284	. EUGENIA M.	180
. ANNIE MILLS	148	. FLORINE BOLT	209	. AUSTIN SMITH	253	. JOHN	58,179
. CHARLES	51	. G.M.	209	. ELLEN LEGARE FROST	249	. JOHN MAC	180
. GORDON B.	111	. H.H.	209	. LEWIS W.	99,120,185	. PEGGY	179
. H.P.	185	. JAMES M.	209	.	326	. PEGGY MCDILL	58
. LILLIE JONES	177	. LUCILE	209	. LEWIS WARDLAW	249,253	. SAMUEL	58
. MARY ELLA	149	. SUSAN	197	. LUCIA	253	. THOMAS	58
. W.B.	148	. THOMAS M.	209	. MARGARET	253	. W.S.	123
MORGAN,B.A.	294,308	NORTON,SUZANA	152	. MARGARET SMITH	253	PEGUES,EFFIE LOYD	246
. BENJAMIN	283	NORVELL,		. MARY DRAYTON	250	PELZER,	101
. CLINTON J.	284	MARGARET PARKER	253	. MARY VANCE	297	F.J.	332
. ELMIRA	283	NORWOOD,	115,199	. THOMAS	249-250	PENDLETON,	155
. ISAAC	55,280	. BENJAMIN	199	. THOMAS F.	101,114-115	HENRY	34,54
. J.H.	101,281	. FANNIE CONYERS	199	. WILLIAM H.	249	PENN,WILLIAM	214

HISTORY OF GREENVILLE COUNTY, SOUTH CAROLINA

PERDUE,	. EMILY STACEY 160	. JULIA 338	. BESSIE HARRISON 309
. JEANETTE LEWIS 168	. HELEN CURRY —	. MARY 66	. BRUCE 309
. RHODES 168	. BENTLEY 163	. THOMAS 56	. BURGISS ROLLINS 309
PERRETT, FRANCIS L. 175	. J.P. 161	PRITCHARD, GEORGE M. 210	. C.T. 309
PERRIN, BELLE 182	. JOSEPH P. 160	QUICK, GEORGE W. 298-299	. CARRIE 321
. EMMA CHILES 304,307	. W.H. 160	. JAQUES VOORHEES 299	. EUDORA RAMSAY 156
. LEWIS W. 182	POPE, DOROTHY J. 255	. KATRINA COBLEIGH 300	. EVELYN 309
. THOMAS C. 304,307	. HARRIET 255	. RICHARD B. 300	. GEORGE W. 308
PERRY, 14,67,73,76,84-85	. KATE MILLER 255	. SARAH O. BIGGS 299	. HENRIETTA ATHENA 310
175,288	. LOUISE 255	. VIRGINIA MONROE 300	. J. FURMAN 321
. B.F. 45,66,78-83,86-90	. MARY C. 255	QUILLEN, 144	. J. MCDUFFIE 338
104,132-133	. MARY CHARLES GARY 254	ROBERT 124,143	. J.D. 121
. JAMES MARGRAVE 300	. THOMAS H. 254-255	QUILLIAN, 147	. J.F. 310
. JEAN V. LEGAL 300	PORTER, 115	RAINEY, J.C. 318	. JAMES M. 11,107,125
. JIM 114	. ANNIE 114	RAMSAY, 133	211
PERSAL, MICHAL 56	POTEAT, EDWIN M. 111	. ALLAN BRODIE 156	. JAMES MADISON 320
PHILLIPS, LOUISE 274	. MARY LAWTON 249	. ANDREW 155	. JAMES MCDOWELL 336-337
PICKENS, 50	POTTER, EDMUND A. 268	. DAVID M. 156	. JEFFERSON C.E. 309
. ANDREW 30,40,66,70	. EDMUND L. 268	. DAVID MARSHALL 155	. JEFFERSON F. 309
. FRANCIS W. 293	. FLORENCE L. 268	. EUDORA 156	. JONATHAN 320
PIKE, ELIJAH 64	. VIRGINIA A. 268	. JEAN MARSHALL 155	. JULIA 338
PITTMAN, FLORENCE 275	. VIRGINIA ALLEN 246,268	. MARTHA GAINES 155	. JULIA PRINCE 338
PITTS, MARTHA 291	. W.T. 246,268	. MARY ROBERTSON —	. LAWRENCE L. 308
PLYLER, JOHN L. 231	POWELL,	WOOLFOLK 156	. LOU C. COX 308
POAG, J.D. 210	. BESSIE MAY HAYNIE 331	. SAMUEL 155	. MARGARET S. —
POE, 225	. E.S. 328	RAMSEUR, 178	MCDOWELL 337
. EDGAR ALLEN 312	. EMMA REBECCA 331	RAMSEY, DAVID M. 113	. MARY 177
. ELLEN 313	. JOHN W. 328-329,331	RANDALL, ELIZABETH 140	. MARY ELEANOR 310
. ELLEN C. TAYLOR 312	. MARY 175	RANKIN, LYDIA 302	. MARY JANE MCDOWELL 321
. ELLEN CANNON —	. MARY FOWLER 328	RAY, 26	. NANCY COX 320
TAYLOR 313	POWERS, PHILLIP 75	. ALEXANDER 56	. ORRIN 309
. EUGENIA MAXWELL 313	PRESTON, 81	. **BOYD BRANDON** 225	. PEARLE 321
. F.W. 98,100-101	SALLIE 140	. **JAMES LONG** 225	. PRISCILLA CALDER 309
312-313	PREVOST, 50	. **JANE BRANDON** 225	. R.L. 309
. FRANCIS WINSLOW 221	. CHRISTIE 235	. RENE JOHNSON 226	. RICHARD 39
313	. GERDA 235	. THOMAS R. 225	. THOMAS 321
. HARRIET AUGUSTA 313	. GERDA LUYTIES 235	. **WILLIAM BRANDON** 226	. VIRGINIA J. 338
. HARRIET AUGUSTUS —	. GERRY 235	RAYNOR, GENEVIEVE 263	. WILLIAM H. 310
MAXWELL 313	. JOHN BLAIR 234	RECTOR, C.A. 127	. WILLIAM J. 337
. HARRIET MAXWELL 221	. MARSHALL B. 234	REECE, LOUISE POPE 255	. RICHARDSON, PEARLE 322
. INEZ SLOAN 313	. MARSHALL LAWRENCE 235	W.D. 255	RICKMAN, ALBERT M. 228
. LUCY SLOAN 221	. MARY ORR 234	REESE, E.E. 196	SARAH MARSHALL 228
. N.C. 313	. TOURNAY 235	ELSIE O. NEVES 196	RIGBY, 176,237
. NANNIE CRAWFORD 313	PRICE, ALICE BAKER 210	REEVES, EMMA GRAY 333	RILEY, E.P. 127
. NELSON C. 312	. BESSIE M. 210	. F.B. 333	RION, JAMES H. 294
. WILLIAM 312-313	. ELIZA LAUD 209	. THADDEUS B. 333-334	MARGARET 294
. WILLIAM WILKINS 313	. JAMES H. 129,209-210	**RENFEW,** 181	ROBERTS, EMMA 253
. ZAIDEE 313	294	**RENFREW.** 100	. IDA 238
POINSETT. 92,98,180-181	. JAMES M. 209	REYNOLDS, JOSEPH 56	. JOHN M. 75
308	. MABLE LEE 224	R.J. 291	ROBINSON,
. JOEL R. 64,80,82	. WILLIAM B. 210	RICHARD III, 224	FRANCIS WILTON 67
103-104	PRIDE, 337	RICHARDS, JOHN G. 165	ROBISON, JOHN A. 120
POLK, 40-41,191	PRIDMORE, A. FRANK 128	RICHARDSON, 40-41	RODDEY, AGNES 276
POOLE, 45	PRINCE, 51,197	. A.B. 310	RODGERS, 144
. ANN 195	. JOHN 66	. ATHENA TINDAL 310	FRANCIS HARRIS 190

Name	Page	Name	Page	Name	Page	Name	Page
ROGER,	96	SLATTERY, JOHN	274	. WILLIAM	56,181	. DAVID D.	180
ROLLINS, BURGISS	309	. LAWRENCE P.	274	SMYTHE, E.A.	101	. EUGENIA M. PEDEN	180
ROOSEVELT,	310	. LOUISE PHILLIPS	274	SPALDING, A.M.	299	. FRENNIE F.	180
ROWLAND,	75	. MARY GRACE	274	SPARKMAN,		. HENRY BOARDMAN	179
. BETTIE S.	154	SLOAN,	76,175	. ELIZABETH TEMPLE	221	. HOKE H.	180
. THOMAS	56	. A.	64	. HARRIET MAXWELL	221	. KATY CARSON HITCH	179
RUSH,	233	. C.E.	107,125	. HATTIE BUCK	220	. MACK M.	180
RUSSELL,		. INEZ	313	. JAMES RITCHIE	220	. ROSA	180
. ALICE BRIDGES	172	. NANCY	312-313	. LUCY POE	221	STOKES, E.R.	75
. JANE HAMILTON	171	. THOMAS	167	. LUCY SLOAN POE	221	JOHN	64
. JOHN	172	SMITH,	75,78,122	. MARY HERIOT	220	STONE, BANNISTER	64
. JOHN A.	114,171	. A. AUSTIN	253	. WILLIAM BUCK	220-221	JESSE	121
. RUTH	172	. ADDIE ANTHONY	194	. WILLIAM IRVINE	220	STONEMAN,	86
. THOMAS H.	171	. ALFRED E.	142	SPEED, JESSIE	186	STORY, GEORGE	26
RUSTIN,		. AUG M.	181	SPEEGLE, C.D.	237-238	STOVER, D.B.	127
. KATHERINE -		. AUG. W.	101	. DORIS	238	. DAKYNS B.	224-225
. CHARLOTTE	264	. AUGUSTUS W.	181-182	. DUDLEY	237	. DAKYNS	-
RYLANDER, SARAH	254	. AUGUSTUS WARDLAW	180	. IDA ROBERTS	238	. BROCKENBROUGH	224
SALLEY,	14	. B.B.	193-194	. LILLIE	238	. EDITH	225
A.S.	13,133,247	. BELLE PERRIN	182	. LINNIE	238	. EDITH MARIE	-
SAMS,	139	. BETTY HARRISON	253	. LOU ELLEN	238	. LEVERSEDGE	225
SAXTON, LARRY	75	. CHARLES D.	288	. RALPH	238	. JOHN GILBERT	224
SAYLE, WILLIAM	130	. DOROTHY	194	. TEMPIE	238	. MABLE LEE PRICE	224
SAYLORS, LOU	269	. ELIZABETH	180	SPEIGHT, OPHELIA A.	303	. WILLIAM WIRT	224
SCHAPER,	133	. ELIZABETH M.	-	SQUIRES, CHARLES T.	220	STRICKLAND, W.H.	299
WILLIAM A.	27	. SINGLETON	238	. CHARLES TAPPEY	219	STRINGER, LUCINDA	178
SCHLEOMAN, LUELLA	296	. ESSIE WILLIAMS	194	. CHARLES WINDEN	219	THOMAS	178
SCOTT, FANNIE C.	127	. ETHEL	213	. EMILY ELIZABETH	-	STROUD, SUNIE E.	278
WALTER M.	127	. FLORIDE	182	. TAPPEY	219	STUART, J.E.B.	191
SEABORN, GEORGE	64	. IDA HENTON	238	. MALCOLM HART	220	JOHN	33
SEASE, CARRIE	286	. IONE	307	. MARY ELIZABETH	220	SUBLETT, MARY CARTER	295
SEAVEY, HELEN	318	. IONE ALLEN	307	. MONA	220	SULLIVAN,	314,317
SHACKELFORD,	268	. JESSE T.	242	. MONA MARKLEY	-	. JANE	217
SHARPTON, AGNES	194	. JOEL	181	. HARRIS	220	. JANE A.	214
MARK	194	. JOHN	238	. WILLIAM HARRISON	220	. JANIE	142
SHEIB, HAROLD	182	. JOHN E.	238	STACEY, EMILY	160	SWEENY,	
LUCILE MARCHANT	182	. JOHN HUGH	238	STALLWORTH,		. CATHERINE FRIENDLY	284
SHERMAN,	253	. KENNETH	194	. HORTENSE MARCHANT	182	. DIAL F.	284
SHREEVERS,	317	. LAURA	194	. W.C.	182	. DOROTHY	284
SHUBURG, GEORGE	40	. LEWIS PERRIN	182	STEADMAN,	51	. JENNIE CATHERINE	284
SHUMATE, W.T.	120	. LUCILE	288	STEEDLY, B.B.	277	. JENNIE ELOISE	-
SIMPSON, MARGARET	121	. MALINDA BOGGS	193	. BENJAMIN B.	274-275	. HELLAMS	284
. PETER	121	. MARGARET	253	. EDITH	275	. R.P.	284
. R.W.	221,312	. MARY	182,185,206	. FLORENCE PITTMAN	275	. ROBERT HAYNE	284
SINGLETON,		. MARY ELLA	176	. GEORGETTE C.	-	. ROBERT POWELL	284
. ELIZABETH M.	238	. MARY NOBLE	182	. GARRIS	274	SWIFT,	218-219
. W.B.	238	. N.K.	238	. WILLIAM B.	274	SWITZER, ANNIE	211
SIRRINE, EMMA ROBERTS	253	. RALPH EDWARD	194	STEPP, A.C.	285	SYKES, KATE	233
. GEORGE W.	252-253	. SARAH EVELYN	194	. ANN REBECCA	285	SYMMES,	212,222
. J.E.	102,196,254,319	. SARAH WARDLAW	181	. JOSEPH ALLEN	285	. F.W.	114
. SARAH RYLANDER	254	. T.H.	193	STERLING, H.T.	195	. FRED W.	101
. WILLIAM	253	. W. BEN	125	STEVENS, WILLIAM SMITH	56	. FREDERICK W.	221
. WILLIAM G.	254	. W. JOEL	307	STEWART, BESSIE	180	. JAMES WHITNER	221
SITTON, JOHN	235	. W.L.	238	. C.B.	179-180	. NETTIE ALEXANDER	221
SLATER,	100	. WHITEFORD	73	. CLIFFORD	180	. SARAH WHITNER	221

TAFT,	310	. CHARLES H.	314	. JOHN W.	181	WESTERVELT,	99,231
TALIAFERRO, SARAH	167	. ELLEN	314	. S.L.	181	SARAH CONYERS	152
TAPPEY,		. ELLEN HARD	314	. SARAH	181	WESTFIELD, DAVID	64,76
EMILY ELIZABETH	219	. GEORGE F.	314	WARE, HENRY	73	WESTMORELAND, H.V.	120
TATUM, BESS	273	. HENRY K.	210,314	T. EDWIN	73	WHAM, EMMA	182
TAYLOR, ELLEN C.	312	. HENRY KEITH	314	WASHBURN, SUSANNA	141	WHATLEY, JAMES F.	129
. ELLEN CANNON	313	. MARY	314	WASHINGTON, BETTIE	167	.	334-335
. EMILY BEACHAM	200	. MARY KEITH	314	GEORGE	167	. RANSOM A.	334
. JOHN	61	. SAMUEL	64,314	WATKINS,		. SUSAN FOSTER	334
. JOSEPH	312-313	TRENHOLM,	97	. FRANCES ANN FARR	303	WHEATLY, PHYLLIS	115,118
. NANCY SLOAN	312-313	TRULUCK, B.K.	195	. H.H.	127,166	WHEELER, ALICE P.	235
. P.M.	200	EMMA CORA NEVES	195	. J. BEN	128,303	MARY	224,287
TEMPLEMAN, CHARLOTTE	114	TURNBULL, J.D.	172	. J. NEWT	166	WHITE, B.R.	163
TEMPLETON,	269	RUTH RUSSELL	172	. LULA W. HAWKINS	304	. CAROLINE	164
. CHARLOTTE	268	TURPIN, J.M.A.	75	. MARY FRANCES	304	. EFFIE E. GULLICK	335
. JANE COLEMAN	268	WILLIAM	75	. VIVIAN	166	. ELIZABETH DUDLEY	296
. ROBERT	268	VAIL, W.L.	235	. Z.B.	303	. GILBERT A.	297
TENNANT, WILLIAM	37	VANBUREN,	81	WATSON, LUCY MCIVER	205	. H. WARREN	296
TERRELL,	167	VANCE, MARY	297	.	206	. HANNAH	295
TERRY, FRANCES WELLS	279	VANDIVER,	20,133	. MARGARET ARMSTRONG	206	. HATTIE LEE	163
J.B.	279	. LOUISE A.	19	. RICHARD F.	204-206	. HELEN ANGELL	297
THACKSTON, LULA JONES	177	. S.	299	. ROBERT B.	205	. HELEN HARVLEY	171
. MARGARET SIMPSON	121	VAUGHAN, T.U.	294	. SUSAN COKER	206	. J. WARREN	296-297
. WILLIAM	120	VERNON,	26	WEBB, C.S.	112	. JAMES RICHARD	164
THOMAS,	46-47,49	VICKERS, A.	64	CHARLES S.	157	. JAMES WARREN	296
. JANE BLACK	58	VICTOR,	98-100,120	WEBSTER,		. MABEL WEST	164
. JOHN	35,38,56,58	.	185-186,189,192,243	. CAROLINE LEWIS	168	. MARY	164
. W.D.	299	.	250	. E.A.	115	. ROBBIE	164
THOMASON, WILLIAM	37	WADDELL, EDMUND	63	. WILLIAM	168	. WALTER P.	163-164
THOMPSON,	26,75	. GEORGE H.	284	WEEMS, PARSON	20	. WILLIAM P.	164
. ABNER	52	. ROZELLE	175	WELBORN, ADAM C.	59,276	WHITMIRE, BEVERLY T.	336
. CHANCELLOR	62,70	. VIRGINIA	284	WELCH, BESS TATUM	273	.	338
. ELISHA	55	WAKEFIELD, ALMA BROCK	164	. BETTY LEE	273	. BEVO	336,338
. GADDY	246	. ELVIRA C.	164	. FRANK WALTER	273	. NATHAN	74
. HENRY T.	81-82,133	. J.E.	164	. JACK TATUM	273	WHITNER,	81
. MARY	141	. JAMES E.	164	. LEE HAMILTON	272	. JAMES H.	302
. WADDY	74,79-82,133,176	. KATHLEEN	164	. MARGUERITE OTT	273	. JOSEPH	56,221
THOMSON,	41-42	WALKER, A.C.	291	WELLS,	308	. SARAH	221
. CHANCELLOR	62	. BETTY	292	. ARCHIE	279	WHITNEY, LAURA GRACE	218
. WILLIAM	40	. CURTIS	292	. BESSIE GARY	279	WHITTEN, SILAS R.	79
THURSTON, ANNIE P.	74	. ELMORE	292	. BETTY	279	WICKLIFF, FRANCIS	61
. RICHARD	64	. EMMA HOWARD	292	. CAROLINE	279	. ISAAC	61
. STREET	64	. GARLAND	64	. FRANCES	279	. W.E.	318
. WILLIAM	79	. HARRIET MCELRATH	209	. G.G.	279,308	WILKINS,	312
TILMAN,	171,337	. JEAN	292	. GEORGE G.	279	MARY LOUISE	198
TIMMONS, JOHN	56	. LENA WRIGHT	209	. HENRY	56	WILLIAM, ANNIE LEWIS	168
TINDAL, ATHENA	310	. MARY SMITH	206	. J. MAC	314	W.A.	168
TINDALL,		. STANHOPE	206	. MARY J. HILL	279	WILLIAMS,	44,191,312
STELLA K. MCDANIEL	175	. TANDY	64,74	. O.H.	279	. ANNA DOYLEY	278
TINSLEY,		. THOMAS G.	64	WEST, ELIZABETH	214	. ANNE ANDREWS	190
JUDITH BALLINGER	322	. W. FRANK	206,209	. JAMES I.	123	. ANNIE O. LAVAL	191
TODD, CLARA	270	. W.F.	207	. MABEL	164	. BESSIE	196
TOMPKINS, LAURA E.	231	WALLACE, MARTHA	256	. MARTHA A.	223	. DANIEL	190
TONEY, WILLIAM	63	WARDLAW, DAVID L.	249	. PHEBE	247	. DAVIS H.	191
TOWNES, AURELIA	314	. FRANCIS	181	. WILLIAM	214	. ELIZA CLEVELAND	279

WILLIAMS, (cont)		WOOD,	34	. MARY WHEELER	287
. ESSIE	194	. BERNICE	267	. SARAH	287
. HENRY	190	. HENRY	272	WYLIE,	284
. JAMES T.	278-279	. J. TERRY	267	WYLLIS,	148
. JANE JONES	148,154	. JAMES	51-52	YANCY,WILLIAM L.	67,83
. JOHN	190	. JANE	271	YATES,CHARLES H.	278
. JULIA G.	191	. JOHN	51-52	. CHARLES L.	278
. JULIA H. LAVAL	191	. JOHN D.	223	. ELIZABETH H.	278
. LEONARD	190	. JOHN P.	272	YOUNG,JOHN	52
. MAJOR SILAS	279	. JOHN T.	272	WILLIAM	64
. MARY ELIZABETH	279	. JOHN W.	61		
. MAY BELLE	157	. L.E.	107,125		
. MAYOR VARDRY MCBEE	279	. LULIE LEONARD	267		
. RICHARD	64	. MAY DAVENPORT	223		
. SALLY MCBEE	279	. THURZA MAYFIELD	272		
. SAMUEL	152	. WILLIAM	54		
. SARAH MCBEE	279	WOODFIN,LILY	244		
. T.B.	278	NICHOLAS W.	244		
. THOMAS B.	64	WOODRUFF,	180-181		
. URSULA HENDERSON	190	WOODS,JAKE L.	312		
. WEST ALLEN	154	LILLIAN V. FLYNN	312		
WILLIAMSON,	39-40,47	WOODSIDE,	160,218,288		
ANDREW	39,46	. E.F.	101,122		
WILLIMON,ABE	74	. ELLEN PAMELIA	-		
. ALICE ANN	280	. CHARLES	158		
. CHARLES P.	280	. ELLEN PERMELIA	-		
. EUGENE P.	280	. CHARLES	158		
. HENRY P.	280	. J.B.	101		
. LIZZIE	227	. JOHN LAURENS	158-159		
. MARTHA C. ASHMORE	280	. JOHN T.	101,157-158		
. MAUDE PACK	280	. LOU A. CARPENTER	159		
. R.C.	280	. LULA B.	159		
. ROBERT C.	280	. LULA B. WOODSIDE	159		
. W. HENRY	280	. ROBERT I.	150		
. W.H.	129	WOOLF,HENRY	56		
WILLINGHAM,MARY	248	WOOLFOLK,			
WILLIS,SAM D.	127	MARY ROBERTSON	156		
	246-247	WOOTEN,JOE	129		
WILSON,	288,310	WORKMAN,	166		
S.J.	122	. CHARLES E.	165		
WINN,	55	. ROSE DOUGLAS	165		
. ALBERT	271	. VIVIAN VIRGINIA	166		
. ELIZABETH	271	. VIVIAN WATKINS	166		
. ELIZABETH CURRY	271	. WILLIAM DOUGLAS	165		
. JAMES	56	.	166		
. JAMES A.	271	WORLEY,			
. JOHN	56,271	GERTRUDE ANSEL	303		
. PAUL P.	271	WRIGHT,LENA	209		
. RICHARD	41,54	WYCHE,C.G.	286,308		
. SUE ANDERSON	271	. C.T.	286		
WITHINGTON,C.C.	228	. CARO	287		
. FRANCES W.	-	. CARRIE SEASE	286		
. MARSHALL	228	. CYRIL THOMAS	287		
WITT,GRACE	193	. MARTHA	287		
WOLF,SAMUEL M.	321	. MARY	287		

www.ingramcontent.com/pod-product-compliance
Lightning Source LLC
Chambersburg PA
CBHW020638300426
44112CB00007B/158